Dostoevsky as Suicidologist

Crosscurrents: Russia's Literature in Context

Series Editor: Marcia Morris, Georgetown University

Embodying what is specific to a single culture as well as what is common to all humankind, literature has always been a privileged mode of discourse in Russia. *Crosscurrents* takes cognizance of Russian literature's simultaneous particularity and universality by exploring the aesthetic, cultural, political, temporal, and geographical contexts in which it has been written. Monographs and edited collections in the series focus on literature written across cultural periods, geographical divides, and intellectual disciplines. We welcome proposals and manuscripts focused on the intersections between literature and law, religion, philosophy, science, film, the arts, and other disciplines as well as on Russian émigré literature, literature written in Russian by non-Russians, and comparisons of different cultural periods.

Titles in the Series

Dostoevsky as Suicidologist: Self-Destruction and the Creative Process, by Amy D. Ronner
Wingless Desire in Modernist Russia: Envy and Authorship in the 1920s, by Yelena Zotova
Babel in Russian and Other Literatures and Topographies: The Tower, the State, and the Chaos of Language, by Martin Meisel
Russian Symbolism in Search of Transcendental Liquescence: Iconizing Emotion by Blending Time, Media, and the Senses, by Anastasia Kostetskaya
Chekhov's Letters: Biography, Context, Poetics, edited by Carol Apollonio and Radislav Lapushin
Physical Pain and Justice: Greek Tragedy and the Russian Novel, by Gary Rosenshield

Dostoevsky as Suicidologist

Self-Destruction and the Creative Process

Amy D. Ronner

LEXINGTON BOOKS
Lanham • Boulder • New York • London

Published by Lexington Books
An imprint of The Rowman & Littlefield Publishing Group, Inc.
4501 Forbes Boulevard, Suite 200, Lanham, Maryland 20706
www.rowman.com

6 Tinworth Street, London SE11 5AL, United Kingdom

British Library Cataloguing in Publication Information Available

Library of Congress Cataloging-in-Publication Data

Names: Ronner, Amy D., author.
Title: Dostoevsky as suicidologist : self-destruction and the creative process / Amy D. Ronner.
Description: Lanham : Lexington Books, [2020] | Series: Crosscurrents: Russia's literature in context | Includes bibliographical references and index. | Summary: "Through an analysis of suicide in Fyodor Dostoevsky's writings, Amy D. Ronner illustrates how his implicit awareness of self-homicide pre-figured theories of prominent suicidologists, shaped both his philosophy and craft as a writer, and forged a ligature between artistry and the pluripresent impulse to self-annihilate"—Provided by publisher.
Identifiers: LCCN 2020039670 (print) | LCCN 2020039671 (ebook) | ISBN 9781793607812 (cloth) | ISBN 9781793607829 (epub) Subjects: LCSH:
Dostoyevsky, Fyodor, 1821-1881—Criticism and interpretation. | Suicide in literature.
Classification: LCC PG3328.Z7 S8865 2020 (print) | LCC PG3328.Z7 (ebook) | DDC 891.73/3—dc23
LC record available at https://lccn.loc.gov/2020039670
LC ebook record available at https://lccn.loc.gov/2020039671

Dedicated to the love of my life, my husband,
Michael P. Pacin, MD, who embodies what Fyodor Dostoevsky's
Zosima commends—the "experience of active love."

Contents

Acknowledgments

While some pursuits "take a village," completing a book requires a thriving metropolis populated with embodiments of active love. The overlapping categories—family, friends, colleagues, administrators, and scholars—inhabit my metropolis. Although it is impossible to send gratitude to everyone who helped bring this book to fruition, what follows is a humble and albeit incomplete attempt.

First and foremost, I thank my loving husband and best friend, Michael P. Pacin, MD, who does everything conceivable (and more) to empower me to write and self-actualize. Beyond that, he never complains about the many hours I spend cloistered cranking out articles, books, and presentations. I am also lucky to have my stepson, Marc Pacin, his wife, Allison, along with their adorable children, Cora and Landon, who continue to amaze me with their warmth and inclusiveness.

There is no thank you big enough for my dear friend, Deborah A. Martinsen, who is essentially the godparent of this book and has given me more than I could ever repay. She has generously granted me access to her universe of Dostoevsky studies and taken time out of her busy life to painstakingly edit my work. Incidentally, Deborah has convinced me that editing is not just a talent, but a genius all its own. Also, nothing worthwhile could happen without the support of the amazing Marcia Morris and Robin Feuer Miller, who are my role models, as well as loyal, nurturing, treasured friends. The brilliant William Mills Todd III is another person I cannot thank enough. From day one, he welcomed a lawyer into the fold and facilitated her return to her true love and first career—literature. The deific translator, Carol Apollonio, deserves a standing ovation. Without hesitation, she shared her language proficiency by patiently guiding me through Russian pronunciations and happily repeating them as many times as needed.

There are other precious friends, who cared deeply about this project and cheered me on: Brett Barfield, Art Furia, Lex Israel, Judge Mily Rodriguez-Powell, James Robertson, and Judge Linda Singer Stein have sprinkled magic into my life and helped fortify my resolve to try to make this world a better place. There are also friends, colleagues, administrators, research assistants, and alumni from the law school where I am presently a law professor emeritus. I thank past-President Monsignor Franklyn Casale, Maria Catala, Anna Chan, Lourdes Fernandez, Al Garcia, John Hernandez John Kang, Gary Kravitz, Agnieszka (Nicole) Kwapisz, Lenora Ledwon, Evelina Libhen, Beatriz A. Llorente, Ricky Patel, Roza Pati, Siegfried Weissner, and Daniel Zarnowski for being such loyal allies. Also, very dear to my heart are Mitchell Kaplan and Cristina Nosti of Books & Books, the very souls who make Miami life worthwhile.

There are also beneficent forces from the past, like my father, the late Walter Valentine Ronner, who was born in Mogilev (in what is today Belarus) and introduced me to Russian literature at an early age. There are friends dating back to early childhood, like Susan Weiner, who has endured my quirks for more decades than I care to divulge. And since this is a book about suicide, I will not hide the fact that Susan once talked me out of taking my own life. I thank another childhood friend, Andrea Robin King, who brought so much love and joy to my early years. With that backward glance, I extend an overdue thank you to Alan D. Perlis, my favorite undergraduate literature professor: by launching my PhD studies and my first career as a literature professor, he helped forge the foundation for the teaching and interdisciplinary scholarship that I so enjoy today. In addition, I thank my dissertation chair, the late Robert H. Super, who galvanized my graduate studies and assisted me with the manuscript that became my first published book. There is also the late law professor, Bruce J. Winick, who helped me refine my legal scholarship over the years and incorporated my work into his valuable courses on therapeutic jurisprudence. To this list, I add the late Robert Lamont Belknap, who attended my presentation at the International Dostoevsky Conference in Naples, Italy, and enthusiastically urged me to proceed.

In addition to those already named, there is also a coterie of superb Slavic scholars, who were open to letting a law professor present papers on their panels at various conferences and those who provided insightful critiques of my work when they served as discussants. I can say that while writing this book, I often heard in my head the voices of multiple brilliant scholars, like Stefano Aloe, Anna Berman, Katherine Bowers, Ellen Chances, Evgenia Cherkasova, Julian Connolly, Paul Contino, Yuri Corrigan, Erica Stone Drennan, Thomas Dyne, Irina Erman, Milla (Lioudmila) Fedorova, Melissa Frazier, Benami Barros Garcia, Elizabeth Frances Geballe, Greta Matzner-Gore, Katya Hokanson, Kate Holland, Victoria Juharyan, Inna Kapilevich,

Brian Kim, Chloe Kitzinger, Liza Knapp, Kornelije Kvas, Eric Naiman, Susan McReynolds Oddo, Irina Paperno, Sophie Pinkham, Irina Reyfman, Gary Rosenshield, Anna Schur, Vadim Shneyder, Maya Stepenberg, Nicole Svobodny, Tatyana Smoliarova, Alex Spektor, Ilya Vinitsky, Val Vinokur, Igor Volgin, Nancy Workman, and Vladmir Zakharov. In this context, I extend a standing ovation to Irina Paperno, author of *Suicide as a Cultural Institution in Dostoevsky's Russia*, and Susan Morrissey, author of *Suicide and the Body Politic in Imperial Russia*. These superb, beautifully written books fed me background information and sources that otherwise would be inaccessible to me. An extra thanks goes out to Irina Paperno, Caryl Emerson, and Nicole Svobodny, who gave me their thumbs up when I told them about this book in process. When scholars of such stature bless a project, it feels like *mana* from heaven.

Finally, but no less important, are the empathic faces of Lexington Books, like Kasey Beduhn, Eric Kuntzman, and Alexandra Rallo, along with Caje Brennan Knight, Jayanthi Chander, and Doreen Anderson of Arc Indexing, Inc. who went well beyond the call of duty: they not only worked diligently to make sure this book was born, but they also helped keep the author relatively sane during the process.

Chapter 1

Introduction

Suicide as a Social Fact

In *A Writer's Diary*, Fyodor Dostoevsky puzzles over the Russian suicide epidemic:

> They . . . kill themselves mysteriously, for no apparent reason. We do indeed see many (and their large number is again a mystery of a kind) suicides, strange and puzzling ones committed not by reason of poverty, nor of some insult; they occur with no evident reason, and certainly not from material want, unrequited love, jealousy, illness, hypochondria, or insanity; they just happen—God knows why.[1]

Dostoevsky's lifelong polemic on suicide surfaces in his fiction as well. Safeguarding a loaded revolver, the isolated, solipsistic "ridiculous man" contemplates his last muster.[2] In Omsk prison where almost any manifestation of free will is deemed a crime, inmates have convulsive outbursts, which can and do result in lethal floggings. In *Demons*, a young man entrusted with a large sum of money, squanders it, returns to his hotel, calmly treats himself to food and wine, scribbles a note, and then shoots himself through the heart. Nastasya Filippovna claims her eternal slumber at the murderous hands of Rogozhin. Dallying with death, Ippolit Terentyev puts a pistol to his brow. Taking the next step, Svidrigailov, Kirillov, and Kraft blow their own brains out. Matryosha, Stavrogin, Smerdyakov, and Olya hang themselves.[3] In *The Adolescent*, Lydia is rumored to have "poisoned herself with phosphorus matches" and after "press[ing] his little fists to his breast," the young boy in Makar Ivanovich's tale drowns himself.[4] Hugging an ikon, the "meek one" flings herself out of the window. Dostoevsky's inquiry in the *Diary*, along with his fictive self-offenders, prefigures the etiology set forth in Emile Durkheim's groundbreaking monograph, *Suicide*.

SELF-MURDER: IS IT? HOW? WHY?

In the portrayal of a nagging enigma—the mortal lust for self-destruction—Dostoevsky is not alone. Twentieth-century psychiatrist Karl A. Menninger, who has been called "the grandfather of American suicidology," states that "the extraordinary propensity of the human being to join hands with external forces in an attack upon his own existence is one of the most remarkable of biological phenomena."[5] The word "suicide" comes from the Latin *sui*, which is "self" and *caedere*, which means "to kill." Although "self-kill" appears straightforward, a plethora of writers, poets, artists, psychiatrists, psychologists, theologians, thanatologists, philosophers, sociologists, and medical specialists have futilely tried to explain what is an ineffable, incomprehensible, timeless, and ubiquitous phenomenon: namely that drive to wipe out one's own existence.

According to George Howe Colt, the first record of a suicide appears in *The Dispute Between a Man and His Ba*, which was written over 4,000 years ago "in the first intermediate period of the Middle Kingdom in Egypt."[6] Its narrator, reminiscent of Dostoevsky's "ridiculous man," feels empty and yearns for death. This forlorn speaker, moreover, sounds nonjudgmental about suicide and never reveals whether he carries it through.[7]

In ancient Greece, there were mixed attitudes toward suicide. The Stoics and Epicureans advocated an individual's right to choose the time and manner of death, but others disagreed.[8] In Athens and Thebes, suicide was not technically illegal, but victims were deprived of funeral rites and had the offending hand severed from their arm.[9] The Pythagoreans, who decried suicide, believed that the human soul is trapped in the flesh where it might either be purified to return to divine origin or begin atonement anew by transmigrating into another body.[10] The Pythagoreans thus impugned the act of suicide because it wrongly interfered with nature's ordained process. Plato's student Aristotle followed Pythagorean teachings, but equated suicide not just with cowardice but also with an act lodged against the state itself.[11] Nevertheless, despite their anti-suicidal stance, there were reports that both Pythagoras and Aristotle ended up killing themselves.[12]

In Rome, the law proscribing suicide applied to soldiers or slaves, situations in which the state or a master had power over others' lives.[13] It also covered those who commit suicide to avoid trial for a crime, but as Helen Silving points out, in such an instance "the sanction was imposed upon the crime rather than upon the suicide."[14] Silving explains how Roman law exempted much from the suicide prohibition:

> where it was induced by "impatience of pain or sickness, some grief, or by another cause" (*impatientia doloris, aut morbi luctusque alicius, vel alia causa*)

> or by "weariness of life . . . lunacy, or fear of dishonor" (*taedio vitae . . . aut jurore aut pudore*), not, however, where it was committed "without cause," the reason advanced for making suicide a crime in such cases being that whoever does not spare himself would much less spare another.[15]

Silving adds that "in those rare situations in which suicide itself was punishable, the obligation of life was conceived of . . . as one of positive law."[16]

Colt disabuses us of the notion that the Bible itself condemns suicide: "[c]onsidering Christianity's nearly two thousand years of intense opposition to suicide, it is surprising that neither the Old nor the New Testament directly prohibits the act."[17] Since the objective of this study is not to exhaustively compile views of every cult or sect, it suffices to say that religions, with Catholicism, Eastern Orthodoxy, Judaism, and Islam as examples, have all anathematized self-homicide.[18]

From its earliest days, the Catholic Church censured suicide, and in the sixth and seventh centuries, decreed excommunication and deprivation of funeral rites for such deaths.[19] St. Augustine proclaimed it a sin violating the sixth commandment of God, "Thou shalt not kill," and St. Thomas deemed it a mortal sin against God.[20] Over time, however, the Church, ebbing toward a more nuanced grasp of mental illness and depression, began to accept the possibility that God might have mercy on those who end their own lives.[21]

Russia follows the Eastern Orthodox Church, which appears to have started at the place to which Catholicism appears to be evolving. Irina Paperno explains that "[u]ntil Peter the Great's reforms in the early eighteenth century, secular law in Russia did not concern itself with suicide" as it was under church jurisdiction. Paperno points out that while "the condemnation of self-murder was common to both the Western and Eastern Churches, their concrete formulations go back to different sources and show subtle differences in emphasis."[22] In Eastern Orthodoxy, suicide regulation dates back to the fourth-century dictates of Timotheos of Alexandria, embodied in the canons at the Sixth Ecumenical Council in 691.[23] Canon 14 prohibits offerings and prayers for suicides, which is evident in Dostoevsky's *Crime and Punishment*, when in Svidrigailov's nightmare, he sees the girl whose suicide he caused and notices that "no icons, no lighted candles stood by the coffin, no prayers were heard."[24] In *The Brothers Karamazov*, Zosima writes, "woe to those who have destroyed themselves on earth, woe to the suicides!"[25] With his love and forgiveness, he admits that even though "[w]e are told that it is a sin to pray to God for them, and outwardly the Church rejects them," he "in the secret of [his] soul . . . think[s] that one may pray for them as well."[26]

Canon 14 does carve out an exception for those who are temporarily insane and thus lack the requisite intent to commit the deed. It asks: "If someone who is not in his right mind lays violent hands on himself or hurls himself down from a height, should an offering be made for him or not?"[27] In response, the canon counsels clergy to "investigate" and ascertain whether the victim "was actually and truly out of his mind when he did his deed."[28] If the assessment is no, then "no offering ought to be made in his behalf, for he is a suicide."[29] In a parallel to the West, the nineteenth-century Russian church sought guidance from medical science. Paperno suggests that after the Great Reforms, which started with the emancipation of the serfs in 1861, suicide became more of a hot potato whereby the "nascent legal profession" was "willing to hand over the suicide's body and mind to the church," and the church, "not eager to take over[,] . . . was prepared to submit to the authority of medical science."[30]

Although Durkheim referred to Judaism's relatively few "formal" prohibitions of suicide,[31] it is apparent that old customs frowned on those who take their own life: there could be no mourning rites or funeral orations for people who kill themselves and their bodies had to be interred in an isolated part of the cemetery so that the wicked did not mingle with the righteous.[32] But, as Isaac Klein points out, in Judaism, most suicides are not treated as suicides due to rabbinical interpretations.[33] According to Klein, "[t]he only suicide for whom mourning is not observed is one who killed himself out of a cynical disregard for life," which does not include those who self-kill themselves because they cannot handle their problems.[34] Like Catholicism, Judaism also softened in its treatment of self-inflicted death as it became more sensitive to the realities of mental illness and depression.[35]

In Islam, suicide is regarded as a heinous crime for which the perpetrators are barred from Paradise and confined to an eternal Hell where they must redundantly reenact the very deed that snuffed out life.[36] Yet, as Eric Marcus observes, Islam aligns itself with Christianity's and Judaism's tempered attitudes:

> But as with Christianity and Judaism, official Islamic doctrine has been softened over time by the understanding that those who take their lives are often suffering from a mental illness and are therefore not in full control of their senses. From my reading, it seems clear that determination of whether a person of Islamic faith who takes his life goes to heaven or hell is a decision that is in the hands of God.[37]

Despite such religious and societal reprobation, self-induced death has always existed. Forever baffling, knowing neither limits nor bounds, suicide pullulates question after question. Most of these tend to fall into three categories: Is it suicide? How do individuals end their own lives? Why do individuals reject life?

Is It Suicide?

As depicted by Homer, the ancient Greeks saw some suicides as acts of honor, ones taken to avoid surrender to enemies or to uphold religious or philosophical convictions. To evade capture and dishonor, the Carthaginian general Hannibal consumed poison. Other ancient Greeks and Romans, including Demosthenes, Cassius, Brutus and Cato, heroically followed suit.[38] The debate, however, typically surrounds Socrates: did he take his own life or by drinking a cup of hemlock was he just performing his own execution in compliance with Athenian law?[39] What can be gleaned from Plato, the trial itself, and the *Phaedo*, reveal ambiguity, especially in segments where Socrates extols death as the beneficent, philosophical denouement.

In 399 BC, Socrates, who was seventy years old, stood before a jury of fellow Athenians charged with "impiety on the grounds that he was failing to acknowledge the city's gods, introducing new divinities and corrupting its youth."[40] Throughout the trial, which could result in Socrates's execution, there are indications that he dissipated opportunities to save his own life. As I. F. Stone has aptly pointed out, "Socrates did his best to antagonize the jury" and "might easily have won an acquittal."[41]

After jurors found Socrates guilty by a relatively narrow margin, the next task was to mandate the penalty.[42] Here too, Socrates appeared to facilitate his own doom: when Socrates was given the chance to design his own punishment, he might have escaped death by recommending exile.[43] Instead, with tongue in cheek, the philosopher initially suggested that he be rewarded for his conduct by being gifted "free dining in the Prytaneum."[44] When pressed for a serious penance, Plato, Crito, Critobulus, and Apollodorus persuaded Socrates to "propose [a fine of] three thousand drachmae on their security."[45] In lieu thereof, the jury sentenced Socrates to death. Pursuant to Athenian law, this meant that Socrates had to serve as his own executioner by imbibing poison.

According to Durkheim, Socrates's death was societally salutary because his "crime—his independence of thought—was useful not only for humanity but for his country."[46] That is, Socrates death was a sacrifice, which "served to prepare a way for a new morality and a new faith, which the Athenians then needed because the traditions by which they had hitherto lived no longer corresponded to the conditions of their existence."[47] In a similar, but in a more philosophical-spiritual vein, Socrates did not see his own death as tragic, but rather portrayed it as a recrudescent ascension to a preferable domain.

In the wake of the verdict, Socrates gave a speech in which he said that he did not "regret . . . the way in which [he] pleaded [his] case" and added, "I would much *rather die* as the result of this defence than live as the result of the other sort."[48] In his elocution, the philosopher praised "this thing that has happened to [him] as *a blessing*," proclaimed that "we are quite mistaken in supposing death to be an evil," and elaborated:

> Death is one of two things. Either it is annihilation, and the dead have no consciousness of anything; or, as we are told, it is really a change: a migration of the soul from this place to another . . . If . . . death is a removal from here to some other place, and if what we are told is true, that all the dead are there, what *greater blessing* could there be than this, gentlemen of the jury?[49]

Becoming more enthralled with inevitability, he, again taking a poke at his tribunal, relished the privilege of a post-life meeting with the "true jurors," like Minos, Rhadamanthys, Aeacus, and Triptolemus, along with "all those other demigods who were upright in their earthly life."[50] He asked: "how much would one of you give to meet Orpheus and Musaeus, Hesiod and Homer?"[51] Ostensibly welcoming death, Socrates confessed, "*I am willing to die* ten times over if this account is true" and referred to his passing as "a *wonderful* personal experience" and an "*unimaginable happiness*."[52] By exclaiming "I am quite clear that the time has come when it was *better for me to die* and be released from my own distractions," he revealed a craving for his own demise.[53]

Socrates's post-sentence oration is neither histrionic nor mere posturing: in fact, it rhymes with Plato's mature work, the *Phaedo*, particularly that segment in which the philosopher rebuts Simmias and Cebes's charge that he seems too eager to desert fine friends and masters in his world: "[t]his is the defence which I offer you, Simmias and Cebes, to show that it is natural for me to leave you and my earthly rulers *without any feeling of grief or bitterness*, since I believe that I shall find there, no less than here, good rules and good friends."[54] Socrates asserts that the "true . . . philosopher's occupation consists precisely in the freeing and separation of soul from body" and that for one who "has trained himself throughout his life to live in a state as close as possible to death" it would be "ridiculous . . . to be distressed when death comes to him."[55] Socrates, however, verbally refrains from chiseling away at that partition between the natural attainment of death and the self-effectuation of it.

Although Socrates stops short of endorsing suicide and even deems it "not legitimate," he elaborates that "sometimes and for some people *death is better than life*; and it probably seems amazing . . . that it should be unholy for any to whom *death would be an advantage* to benefit themselves."[56] For Socrates, death-seekers should "await the services of someone else."[57] Under his formulation, the philosopher awaited and received "the services" of the Athenian jurors. In Socrates's words, "it is not unreasonable to say that we must not put an end to ourselves until God sends some necessary circumstance like the one we are facing now."[58]

When the slave handed the poison cup to Socrates, he "received it quite *cheerfully*," prayed to the gods that his "removal from this world to the other may be *prosperous*," and then "*calmly and with no sign of distaste*, . . . drained the cup in one draught."[59] While the debate over whether this fatal gulp constituted a suicide or retributive justice will never be unequivocally resolved, substantial competent evidence tends to support Stone's conclusion that Socrates "chose death over a renewed chance of life" and that "the choice he made was voluntary, and therefore the equivalent of suicide."[60] It should later become evident that Durkheim's elastic definition of suicide implicitly concurs with Stone's thesis.

It is noteworthy that Socrates's outlook on death as a renascence into an upgraded sphere or as a means of convening with the dead has invariably been prevalent in suicidal people. C. G. Jung and his adherents stressed the unconscious need for spiritual rebirth and the prominent psychiatrist Gregory Zilboorg wrote that "the drive toward death, always with the flag of immortality in hand, carried with it the fantasy of joining the dead or dying or being joined in death."[61] Similarly, John T. Maltsberger and Dan H. Buie Jr., who parse "fantasies of transcendental 'nothingness,' " have discovered that "[a] lthough suicidal patients may say that they wish to end it all" and that "in death they would be 'nothing,' " clinical documentation shows a "fantasy that life, however, transformed, will continue in a better, more peaceful way, beyond the grave."[62]

Other suicide scholars believe that for unsuccessful attempters, "beyond the grave" does not mean a blissful afterlife but is equated with a metamorphic return to daily life with a new identity. Steve Taylor makes this point in discussing "how rare it is for survivors of even the most dangerous attempts to try to kill themselves again at the first opportunity," which he attributes to the attempter's "conviction that a 'death' has in fact taken place and that 'someone different' has arisen from the ashes."[63] Erwin Stengel analogously depicts the suicidal act as enantiosis:

> *Most people who commit suicidal acts do not either want to die or to live: they want to do both at the same time, usually the one more, or much more, than the other.* It is quite unpsychological to expect people in states of stress, and especially vulnerable and emotionally unstable individuals, who form the large majority of those prone to acts of self-damage, to know exactly what they want and to live up to St. James' exhortation: "Let your yea be yea and your nay, nay."[64]

There are others who simply let curiosity kill the cat. These individuals, who are not quite as confident as Socrates about the blessedness of quietus, surmise that suicide will enable them to peek behind the curtain to spy on hereafter mysteries. Describing suicide "as an experiment," Arthur Schopenhauer believes that the "question which man puts to Nature" and "tries to force her to an answer," is this: "[w]hat change will death produce in a man's existence and in his insight into the nature of things?"[65] But he points out that such an "experiment" is "clumsy" and preordained to falter, because "it involves the destruction of the very consciousness which puts the question and awaits the answer."[66] Yet, from time immemorial, many (like Socrates) have striven to migrate to an Elysium, or tried to reunite with lost loved ones, or have sought to conterminously live and die, or have coveted access to *terra incognita.*

How?

Suicide reached epidemic proportions in Russia in Dostoevsky's lifetime and with respect to the globe today, it is pandemic. Part of this can be attributed to the inexhaustible availability of overt and covert ways to self-destruct. In his book *Man against Himself,* Menninger quotes an excerpt from a 1908 magazine article marveling at the "agonizing and extraordinary" methods individuals employ in their lethal missions:

> [M]en [and] women have committed suicide by . . . throwing themselves upon swiftly revolving circular saws; by exploding dynamite in their mouths; by thrusting red-hot pokers down their throats; by hugging red-hot stoves; by stripping themselves naked and allowing themselves to freeze to death on winter snowdrifts out of doors, or on piles of ice in refrigerator cars; by lacerating their throats on barbed wire fences; by drowning themselves head downward in barrels; by suffocating themselves head downward in chimneys; by diving into white-hot coke ovens; by throwing themselves into craters of volcanoes; by shooting themselves with ingenious combinations of a rifle and a sewing machine; by strangling themselves with their hair; by swallowing poisonous spiders; by piercing their hearts with corkscrews and darning needles; by cutting their throats with handsaws and sheep shears; by hanging themselves with grape vines; by swallowing strips of underclothing and buckles of suspenders; by forcing teams of horses to tear their heads off; by drowning themselves in vats of soft soap; by plunging into retorts of molten glass; by jumping into slaughter-house tanks of blood; by decapitation with homemade guillotines; and by self-crucifixion.[67]

What bewildered the magazine article's author, but not the psychiatrist commenting on it, were not just the lengths to which people will go to overtly expunge their very being, but also how individuals will concoct the most inordinately painful and inefficient methods.

Socrates's concept of a permissible death through "the services of someone else" or submission to a "circumstance" anticipates the findings of others, like Freud, Menninger, Shneidman, Michael A. Church, Charles I. Brooks, and Durkheim, all of whom alert readers to multiple veiled substitutes for the overt act of self-murder.[68] Freud refers to "half-intentional self-destruction" and "purposive accidents" where people secure unconscious ways to unleash their death instinct.[69] Menninger, expanding that, opines that "unconsciously determined purposes of . . . self-destruction [can be] obtained (usually) by proxy, i.e., at the hands of a second party" and organizes disguised suicides into categories.[70] In "focal" suicide, self-destruction targets a body part, which manifests itself as malingering, "purposive accidents," impotence, frigidity, or self-mutilation.[71] In "organic" suicide, those bereft of the will to live induce illness and eventual death through cancer, heart disease, diabetes, or emphysema.[72] In "chronic" suicide, individuals wipe out existence gradually through alcoholism, asceticism, martyrdom, neurotic invalidism, antisocial behavior, or psychosis.[73] Menninger extracts commonalities between motives in such "chronic and attenuated forms of self-destruction" and in the "direct undisguised" modes of self-homicide:

> Namely, an externally directed aggressive component; a punitive drive, that is submission to punishment from a sense of guilt; an erotic motive (achievement of pleasure, the essentially sexual nature of which is cloaked in elaborate disguise); and finally, a self-destructive impulse whose sole aim is the extinction of an individual.[74]

Shneidman, applying his own nomenclature, speaks of "manifestations of indirect suicide" or "subintentioned deaths."[75] Although these behaviors in which individuals "play an indirect, covert, partial, or unconscious role in hastening [their] own demise," resemble Menninger's chronic, focal, and organic suicide, they are not identical.[76] According to Shneidman, Menninger's ideas "have to do with self-defeating ways of continuing to live," while his own "subintentioned death" is "a way of stopping the process of living,"[77] which he defines in the form of a distended query:

> What are we to make of people who act as though they were afraid they were going to be late to their own accidents, who foolishly disregard a lifesaving medical regimen, who use bad judgment to shorten or truncate their lives, who seem set on premature self-destruction, who imprudently put themselves in harm's way, who seem bent on covert self-destruction, whose health habits are known to jeopardize life, who appear to be their own worst enemies? What comes to mind, by way of understanding, are ideas like *in*direct suicide and *sub*intentioned death.[78]

For Shneidman, too many "shorten or truncate life, be less than he or she could have been; shun life's warmth and light; race toward withdrawal and self-abnegation."[79] Psychology professors Church and Brooks similarly point to "people who are living 'on the edge' and at the same time, [are] wasting their lives" with "risky behaviors, self-neglect, carelessness, and negative mood states," which is the phenomenon they call "subtle suicide."[80]

Durkheim's analogue to Freud, Menninger, Shneidman, Church, and Brooks is "embryonic suicide," where people imperil their own lives and perform acts loaded with mortal risk: there is the "daredevil who intentionally toys with death," the individual who "takes no care of [his] health and so imperils it by neglect," and "the scholar who dies from excessive devotion to study" (SU, Introduction, 45–46). Dostoevsky's Mr. Prokharchin is of this ilk: self-impoverished and on the brink of starvation, he perishes with a fortune stashed under his mattress.[81] The same assessment applies to the character that Dostoevsky's Arkady Dolgoruky mentions, the one who goes about "in tatters, begging for alms," and then dies with "as much as three thousand in banknotes sewn into his rags."[82] Whether we call it "half-intentional self-destruction," "suicide by proxy," "subintentioned death," "subtle suicide," or "embryonic suicide," suicidologists are cognizant of the innumerable methods or proxies people can deploy to let their wish to die vanquish their wish to live. Circumstances, like aggravating the wrath of one's jurors or abetting the imposition of capital punishment, abound.[83] Earth is packed with "second parties," like cops, surgeons, abusive spouses, homicidal lovers, drunk drivers, and so forth, who can be the conscripted coconspirators in a self-lethal campaign. While the forces underlying "embryonic" suicide are complex, it can be said that those who decline to do the deed overtly—to self-immolate, to garrote their necks with rope, to put a bullet in their brain, or to leap from a bridge or under a train—but instead opt for covert implosion, gain at least one psyche-anodyne: they can trick themselves into believing that they have dodged that hoary suicide-taboo with its blasts of theological damnation and self-deceptively acquit themselves of any and all self-murder charges.[84]

Why?

The guesses as to why people kill themselves are as plentiful as the stars. Today, scientists are dissecting the brain itself in an effort to learn how those of suicides differ from those who have perished from other causes.[85] There are researchers studying brain chemistry and neurobiologists, some of whom are convinced that childhood trauma hijacks normal brain maturation, upsets the stress response system, and increases the risks of developing psychopathology.[86] A summary of this work by such medical pioneers, however, falls outside the purview of this book, which aims to analyze Durkheim's etiology in *Suicide* as it pertains to Dostoevsky's artistry. Instead, for now the focal point will be a sampling of suicidologists, those who, like Shneidman, concede that "severe depression, melancholia, psychoses, and bipolar depressions are related to disorders of brain physiology or even brain structure," but assert that "*suicide* is an essentially mental process of the mind."[87] In fact, there are multiple scholars who concur with Shneidman's proclamation that "slicing Jeffrey Dahmer's brain will no more explain the mysteries of his gross psychological pathology than slicing Einstein's brain will yield $E=mc^2$."[88] This is also an opportune juncture to introduce some suicide theories, which will surface in this book in connection with sporadic attempts to tie Durkheimian paradigms in Dostoevsky's fiction to strands of psychoanalytic thought.

Menninger built upon Sigmund Freud's foundation. In 1910, thirteen years after the publication of Durkheim's masterpiece *Suicide*, Freud attended the Vienna Psychoanalytic Society's suicide symposium. Although the fifty-three-year-old Freud had clinical and personal experience with suicide, he, in contrast with speakers Wilhelm Steckel and Alfred Adler, remained relatively silent throughout the session. Freud, however, stepped forth to give the closing remarks which indicated that the inquiry, like Penelope's tapestry, was far from complete:

> I have an impression that in spite of all the valuable material that has been brought before us in this discussion, we have not reached a decision on the problem that interests us. We are anxious, above all to know how it becomes possible for the extraordinarily powerful life instinct to be overcome; whether this can only come about with the help of a disappointed libido or whether the ego can renounce its self-preservation for its own egoistic motives. It may be that we have failed to answer this psychological question because we have no adequate means of approaching it.[89]

Freud not only urged a suspension of judgment "until experience has solved this problem," but also advised that "melancholia" and "mourning" were points of embarkation.[90]

Abiding by his own advice, Freud said in *Totem and Taboo* (1913), "that impulses to suicide in a neurotic turn out regularly to be self-punishments for wishes for someone else's death."[91] In developing this in "Mourning and Melancholia," written five years after the symposium (published in 1917), Freud wrote: "[w]e have long known that no neurotic harbors thoughts of suicide which are not murderous impulses against others redirected upon himself, but we have never been able to explain what interplay of forces could carry such a purpose through to execution."[92] Freud suggests that in mourning and in its kindred spirit, melancholia, when a love object is lost, the ego creates an image of the loved one within the self. This way, that lost love can live on in the ego like a "shadow" that is not fully integrated into the personality.[93] This permits part of the ego to "split off" and observe. Through the splitting, part of the ego is free to judge and criticize the rest of the ego and even condemn it to death.[94] Suicide expresses this inner dynamic: it derives from the wish to kill another whom the suicide has loved and the only way to do that is to demolish that internalized "shadow" of him.[95] As Shneidman has put it, this is "murder in the 180th degree."[96]

"Mourning and Melancholia," with its often-cited link between suicide and murderous impulses, was not Freud's final word, but rather a step along a trajectory. As Robert E. Litman has pointed out, Freud's early essay is "modest and tentative" and its "more important creative concepts are those of regression, disorganization, and ego-splitting, pathologic processes which allow a portion of the ego to initiate action while disregarding the interests of the remainder."[97] Later, Freud's study of masochism and detection of a negative therapeutic response, whereby some patients would react to good news or milestones in their treatment with depression and self-injury, led him to propose the existence of an instinctual death drive.[98]

Freud conceived of two instincts, one of which is Eros, "compris[ing] not merely the uninhibited sexual instinct proper and the impulses of a sublimated or aim-inhibited nature derived from it, but also the self-preservative instinct, . . . assigned to the ego," and the other, Thanatos, the death drive, the "task of which is to lead organic matter back into the inorganic state."[99] For Freud, most aspects of behavior, including suicide, could be explained by the relentless jousting of Eros and Thanatos. While Thanatos has headquarters inside everybody, when someone is suicidal, this death drive takes over and trumps erotic, self-preservation.

Not all psychologists and psychiatrists believe in the existence of a death drive. Gregory Zilboorg, for example, once branded "this particular element of Freudian metapsychology" as "rather tautological" and felt that "[t]o say that the death instinct gains the upper hand over the life instinct is merely an elaborate way of stating that man does die or kill himself."[100] Freud's Thanatos, however, is a prime fixture in Menninger's work. Menninger claims that "the best theory" to explain self-destruction is Freud's hypothesis of a death instinct, which opposes and interacts with the life instinct.[101] He stresses that under Freud's construct, "both the destructive and constructive tendencies are originally self-directed but become increasingly extraverted in connection with birth, growth and life experiences."[102] When, however, these "external investments" are forcibly interrupted or when individuals confront obstacles that make it difficult to maintain "external investments," the destructive and constructive impulses "turn upon the self."[103] When "the self-destructive impulses too far precede or exceed the neutralizing constructive impulses" it ends with a self-imposed death.[104]

Menninger proposes a trifurcated definition of "peculiar" self-imposed death: "the element of dying, the element of killing, and the element of being killed."[105] Each module, which possesses conscious and unconscious motives, draws from two main sources: one, "impulses derived from the primary aggressiveness crystallized as a wish to kill," and two, "impulses derived from a modification of the primitive aggressiveness, the conscience, crystallized as the wish to be killed."[106] Menninger injects a third possible source into the calculus. This is where "some of the original primary self-directed aggressiveness, the wish to die, joins hands with the more sophisticated motives and adds to the total vectorial force which impels the precipitate self-destruction."[107] While Menninger is "certain" that suicide is not due to heredity, he recognizes that other factors, like societal, family, and community attitudes, can infiltrate the "distortions of reality" that warp personality development.[108] Menninger explains: "[t]he same individual whose childhood experiences so inhibited his emotional growth as to make it difficult for him to establish and maintain the proper external objectives for absorbing his loves and hates is likely to be one whose capacity for testing reality is so impaired as to make suicide only another game of 'going to Jerusalem.' "[109]

Like Menninger, social historian Howard Kushner's theory of "incomplete mourning" builds on Freud, but he also cites Durkheim and states that "[b]oth Durkheim and Freud would have agreed . . . that suicide is often accompanied by a combination of unresolved grief, an exaggerated belief in the hopelessness of one's condition, fear of conspiracies by others, and a wish for revenge."[110] Kushner finds that the death or disappearance of a parent, especially before or during puberty, frequently figure into severe depression and self-homicide."[111] Kushner delves into two case studies, those of Meriwether Lewis and of Abraham Lincoln, "both of whom experienced extreme loss," but responded differently: Lewis killed himself, Lincoln did not.[112] Kushner believes that Lewis and Lincoln "serve as compelling examples of the proposition that the success or failure of [strategies for dealing with loss] depends upon a confluence of historical possibilities and personal experience as they both connect with psychological and constitutional factors."[113]

Unlike Menninger or Kushner, Shneidman does not expend as much energy mulling over Freud's death drive. He holds that suicide is mainly "a drama of the mind" that features two villains: "elevated perturbation," which is "[a]nguish or disturbance . . . caused by pain," and "lethality," which is "the likelihood of an individual's being dead by his or her own hand in the near future."[114] When lethality coacts with a high level of perturbation, the stage is set for self-inflicted death: "[p]erturbation supplies the motivation for suicide; lethality is the fatal trigger."[115] Thanatologists are thus charged with the job of asking the right questions: Shneidman states that "[t]he most important question to a potentially suicidal person is not an inquiry about family history or laboratory tests of blood or spinal fluid, but 'Where do you hurt?' and 'How can I help you?' "[116]

In his thinking, Shneidman aligns himself with Harvard professor Henry Murray who was the "hero of [his] intellectual life," and the author of *Explorations in Personality*, a treatise underscoring the predominance of human needs.[117] Murray amply defines "need" as "a force in the brain region . . . which organizes perception, apperception, intellection, conation and action in such a way as to transform in a certain direction an existing, unsatisfying situation."[118] With his mentor's work in hand, Shneidman believes that all human activities, including dreams and fantasies, express needs that motivate our lives. He concludes that "[i]n almost every case, suicide is caused by pain, a certain kind of pain—*psychological* pain," which he names "*psychache*," and which invariably derives from "thwarted or distorted psychological *needs*."[119] For Shneidman, decoding suicide entails tapping into one source alone—namely, "human emotions described in plain English, in the words of the suicidal person."[120] In patient after patient, he has discovered that those who end their own lives are desperately "trying to blot out" agony stemming from the "thwarted psychological needs 'vital' for that person."[121]

Such "thwarted psychological needs" can engender hopelessness, despair, and desperation, which according to countless suicidologists are the veritable culprits in nearly every self-inflicted death.[122] Herbert Hendin explains that "[c]linicians often use the word 'despair' rather than 'hopelessness' to convey the emotional state distinguishing suicidal patients from patients who are depressed but not suicidal."[123] In an addendum, one reminiscent of egoistic and anomic Durkheimian paradigms, Hendin states that "[d]espair has been described as developing from aloneness, murderous hate, and self-contempt or, more generally, as resulting from any state that leads to the individual's 'inability to maintain or envision any human connections of significance.' "[124] While not all theorists put despair and hopelessness into distinct boxes, most are somewhat taciturn when confronting the burning question: Why do some hopeless people hang in there and recover while others opt for death?

In his book, Marcus maintains that the kind of depression and hopelessness that can lead to suicide visit everyone at some point or another. While "most of us who experience hopelessness recover relatively quickly," there are others, who simply "don't, and these people are the ones in significant danger of doing themselves harm."[125] Marcus, who could never figure out the "why" behind his own father's self-demise, admits that there is simply too much about suicide that confounds reason and admonishes: "if you are looking for an answer that will satisfy your desire to know why your loved one killed himself, I'm afraid you'll probably be disappointed because for most people, including me, there is no satisfying answer."[126] While resigning himself to suicide's undecipherability, Marcus offers a list of "causes," grouped into three subheadings.

Marcus's first subheading, "psychological and physiological," includes "major incapacitating depression," mental disorders (such as schizophrenia, personality disorder, bipolar disorder), prescription drug side effects, alcohol, drug abuse, illness, and physical infirmity.[127] To these, he adds revenge, anger, and punishment, which prompts death, or an attempt at or threat of suicide by someone intent on retaliating against a loved one for some rift, heartbreak, or grievance. His second, "social factors, custom, for a cause," covers "suicide bombers and suicide terrorists," people who sacrificially destroy themselves, activists seeking to make death their "political statement," or adherents to a social custom, like *suttee* whereby widows in India throw themselves on their husbands' funeral pyre to prove devotion.[128]

Marcus's third, most comprehensive subheading, "sudden loss, trauma, outside threat" sweeps in those who see death as their only escape from life's hardships.[129] These people kill themselves after losing a loved one or a job. They also end their own lives in response to "economic distress," or "outside threats and bullying."[130] In this group, he includes gay, lesbian, bisexual, and transgender people, who are battered by the kind of societal "pressure and prejudices" that not only engender "psychological conflicts, depression, alcoholism, and drug abuse," but also can heighten suicide risk.[131] Moreover, there are individuals, typically ones with a "high profile," who "feel trapped" after entanglement in scandals or "humiliating" situations and seize on death as their exit strategy.[132]

Charles William Wahl broaches some of the same questions as Marcus and similarly concedes defeat: "[i]t is unfortunately the painful truth that as yet we have no satisfying answers to any of [them]."[133] With help from Schopenhauer, Wahl nevertheless explores and portrays suicide as "a magical act":

> [S]uicide is not preeminently a rational act pursued to achieve rational ends, even when it is effected by persons who appear to be eminently rational. Rather, it is a magical act, actuated to achieve irrational, delusional, and illusory ends. Magic is used here as it is defined by Schopenhauer, namely an objectification of desire outside the causal nexus; an act of attempted control, or delusion of such control, of physical forces normally peripheral to human mastery.[134]

Wahl excavates four motives beneath the "magical" act of taking one's own life, the first of which is a desire to punish a "depriving figure," typically a parent or a sibling or the "extrapolation of them" which takes shape as "society or mankind."[135] For illustration, Wahl relies on Mark Twain:

> In this connection, one is reminded of the story in . . . *Tom Sawyer*. Tom, being painfully frustrated by his aunt, was strongly comforted by the fantasy of committing suicide by drowning himself in the Mississippi. He thought to himself of how sad and piteous a spectacle he would make when his body would be brought into his aunt's presence, with his curls all wet, and how consequently sorry and remorseful she would be.[136]

Wahl believes that such fantasies are "ubiquitous among children" who are "totally impotent physically and mentally" and prone to deny "the infinitude and irreversibility of death."[137] There is an analogue to Wahl's analysis in Dostoevsky's *A Writer's Diary*, when he comments on "Count Tolstoy's *Childhood and Youth*," in which a young boy dreams of dying, and after everyone finds his body, they stand around "pitying him."[138] Dostoevsky links this to the death of a twelve-year-old boy, who is featured in the news. It is surmised that this child's dread of "his father's terrible wrath," after his teacher "punishe[s] him by making him stay after school" leads him to abruptly hang himself.[139]

Wahl's second motive, the "most painful," is when the individual seeks to extinguish or reduce guilt through "an act of self-punishment" or attempt "to expiate the fantasied act of murder (death wishes) by operation of the talion law."[140] He reminds readers that in the unconscious mind, a thought or wish equals the deed itself: "[i[t says in effect, 'You wish the death of a person and therefore you must die.' "[141] He concludes that the need to expiate guilt and attain the "hostile wish by guilt induction are almost invariably present in every suicidal attempt or act."[142]

His third "more recondite" motive is the courtship of "suicide as an aid in coping with overpowering thanatophobia, or fear of death."[143] Here the slaying of the self "serves as a reaction formation to the morbidly feared eventuality of death by embracing it rather than running from it."[144] Paradoxically, some will exalt their own "sense of narcissistic immortality and omnipotence," which enables them to shun and shove back the dread of finality: "[t] he possibility of his own not-being is unconsciously so distant and remote that he can entertain and effect an act of self-destruction without the sense of self-preservation horror which it so commonly induces in others."[145] In addition, suicide does not just release these people from anguish, but becomes a magic carpet ride to a locus of empowerment where the nonliving thrive as "spirit[s], ghost[s], or poltergeist[s]" that can "transcend time and space" and even "wreak vengeance" on the putative nemesis.[146]

With respect to the fourth motive, "the phenomenon of infantile cosmic identification," which has "possible relevance to suicide," Wahl offers a response to Marcus's lingering question—why do *some* hopeless people choose death?[147] When perceived "insurmountable" obstacles bombard us and force us to "deal with situations and circumstances in which we feel ourselves to be manifestly impotent," we are pushed to revert to a "period of infantile omnipotence."[148] That is, "we are powerfully impelled to regress to that portion of our childhood in which we did indeed have a power and capacity which in adulthood is largely denied to the conscious mind."[149] In what is reminiscent of Dostoevsky's "The Dream of a Ridiculous Man," there is a regressive odyssey, which magically takes the individual to what Wahl depicts as a puerile locus of "hypostatization" and "dereism":

> The suicide achieves, as does the infant, a kind of cosmic identification. By equating the world with self, he affirms the same fallacy as the medieval mystic who said, as did St. Eustace, "Nothing outside my own mind is real; the world and all persons in it are, in reality, me." Therefore, to kill oneself is to kill everything that there is, the world and all other persons.[150]

The victim-perpetrator, delirious with "infantile cosmic identification," can blast the vast gestalt, which subsumes not merely the self, but also "the introjected parents" as well as the macrocosmic sires—namely, society itself, "which the aggrieved individual has found to be nonnurturant and nonsuccoring."[151] As Wahl sums it up, this individual "commits not only suicide but vicarious matricide, patricide, sororicide, fratricide, and even genocide."[152]

Trying to navigate quagmires similar to those in Marcus and Wahl's studies, Taylor begins by honing in on "situations" that induce self-destruction: "*suicide is more likely in situations of (almost) complete uncertainty where the individual feels that he knows nothing worth knowing or in situations of (almost) complete certainty where the individual feels that he knows everything worth knowing*."[153] For Taylor, "thanatation" is where individuals, uncertain about their own identities, impose ordeals on themselves so that they can get resolution. For these people, the uncertainty *must* be resolved and until that happens, everything else is completely irrelevant. Employing the metaphor of a "game," Taylor adds that "the suicidal actions *produced* by this are *necessarily* ordeals," which are " 'game-like' and may be described as 'ludenic.' "[154] Tending to crave relief from boredom and fatigue, thanatationists risk life in order to confirm life and "reinvest" it "with meaning and purpose."[155] One of Taylor's cases in point is Graham Greene, whose autobiography tells how playing Russian roulette banished his intense, suffocating oscitancy and inertia. Taylor explains that in such instances, thanatation "exorcis[es] death and, in the short run at least, give[s] the individual a feeling of having conquered it."[156]

Thanatation differs from Taylor's concept of "*submissive suicide*," characterized by a "psychological sense of complete certainty."[157] Submissively, suicidal individuals stubbornly adhere to the conviction that "life is already over" or that "the game is irretrievably lost."[158] These individuals do not dive into death to discover whether they are dead or alive, but rather seize death as a tautological capitulation to the reality that they are already dead. Here the act itself is apt to be more " 'serious' or purposive, as opposed to ludenic, and thus more likely to be fatal."[159] Stated otherwise, "[w]hile the thanatationist is asking *Who am I?*, the submissive suicide is saying *I am dead.*"[160]

Taylor discusses the English poet and critic A. Alvarez, who tried to kill himself at age thirty-one and ultimately emerged from this as "a different person" because he " 'experienced', yet survived death."[161] Taylor distinguishes Alvarez from the generic thanatationist whose "desire to 'experience' and 'come through' death, to renew one's life by risking it" is not the consequence of but instead the "conscious motive" or "precipitating cause" of the act itself.[162] After Alvarez swallowed forty-five sleeping pills, he was rescued. Reflecting ten years later, Alvarez similizes the self-biocidal condition to "the unanswerable logic of a nightmare, . . . a science-fiction fantasy of being projected suddenly into another dimension" or to a universe, where everything is "perverted, upside down."[163] Unlike Wahl, who probes "magical" motives or Taylor who formulates a dichotomy of "(almost) complete uncertainty" and "(almost) complete certainty," Alvarez foists the distortedly constricted mindset onto his readers and tries to make them *live* it:

> Once a man decides to take his own life he enters a shut-off, impregnable but wholly convincing world where every detail fits and each incident reinforces his decision. An argument in a bar, an expected letter which doesn't arrive, the wrong voice on the telephone, the wrong knock at the door, even a change in the weather—all seem charged with special meaning; they all contribute.[164]

Alvarez's "world of suicide," one that is "superstitious" and "full of omens" approximates the workings of the creative process itself, especially in literary artistry, in which the toiler strives to forcibly assemble, make resonant, and imbue with import the seemingly innocuous minutiae of humdrum noumenon.[165] The correlation between the pre-suicidal and the creative is no coincidence because Alvarez's book, dealing with "suicide *and* literature, not suicide *in* literature[,] . . .has to do not with specific literary suicides but with *the power the act has exerted over the creative imagination.*"[166]

Alvarez tracks artistic casualties and suicidal ideation over centuries: he goes from Dante and the Middle Ages to John Donne and the Renaissance to William Cowper, Thomas Chatterton and "the age of reason" to "Romantic agony" to "tomorrow's Zero," the transition to the twentieth century and to Dada, the era in which suicide actually became "an Art."[167] At the close of this temporal journey, Alvarez points to "one of the most remarkable features of the arts" in the twentieth century, namely "the sudden, sharp rise in the casualty rate among artists."[168] Although Alvarez recognizes that each death, of course, "has its own inner logic and unrepeatable despair," he finds it uncanny that the "casualty-rate among the gifted seems out of all proportion."[169] He attributes the twentieth-century soar to the very "nature of the artistic undertaking itself" and its "demands," which have been "radically altered" over time.[170]

Alvarez believes that the forces behind the rising suicide rate are numerous and that one of them is the artistic "continuous, restless urge to experiment" and the "constant need to change, to innovate, to destroy the accepted styles."[171] By way of example, the Romantic poets rejected "the straitjacket of the classical rhymed couplet" while early modernists "jettisoned traditional rhymes and metres" for free verse.[172] The "more serious" artists, however, cannot sate themselves with the mere tweaking of form, or indulgence in iconoclasm, but must press further: they are driven to dive into "the perennial question, 'What am I?' " and do this without the "benefit of moral, cultural or even technical securities."[173] Artists are thus sucked into the vortex, which is a "progressively more inward response to a progressively more intolerable sense of disaster" and emerge with a changed, chapfallen role in society: "instead of being a Romantic hero and liberator," the artist "has become a victim, a scapegoat."[174] Alvarez adds that the fact that artists are never "absolve[d] from the labour of art" exacerbates their plight.[175] They must huff and puff "at full pitch to produce not settled classical harmonies but the tentative, flowing, continually improvised balance of life."[176] The endeavor of attaining that "balance" is inevitably inherently "risky."[177] Those artists, "committed to truths of [the] inner life," often find themselves on a lethality spectrum, the "riskiest" place of all.[178]

Like almost every other theorist questing for the "why" behind suicide, Alvarez ultimately concedes that the task is insurmountable. Even Menninger, the author of that near 500-page tome on the "why" and who dedicated a lifetime to deciphering the causes of suicide, once blurted out at a 1984 conference, "It's a durn mystery, you know, in spite of all we've written about it."[179] Besides the unisonous nod at suicide's incomprehensibility, there is another thing upon which diverse suicidologists agree: almost all commend the work of Durkheim, who authored the first comprehensive social theory of suicidal behavior. In fact, there is scarcely a book or essay on suicide that does not pay homage to Durkheim's influential monograph.

DURKHEIM AND THE SOCIAL FACT—*SUICIDE*

Émile Durkheim, who lived from 1858 to 1917, has been called the architect of modern social science, a title he shares with Karl Marx and Max Weber.[180]

Durkheim's accomplishments, his intellectual hunger, productivity, and exacting work ethic are mind-boggling: he established the first French journal of sociology, published major studies, mentored a crop of sociology scholars in France, and eventually rose to the rank of professor at the prestigious university, the Sorbonne. While (as discussed later) there are repulsive facets to Durkheim, it is undeniable that he instrumentally forged a respected niche for sociology and helped legitimate it as a science.

An Outsider's Life

Born in Epinal in Lorraine, Durkheim descended from a long line of devout French Jews. From start to finish, Durkheim knew the sting of minority status, shattered others' expectations, and defied conventions. Although he came from a devout Jewish family and initially attended rabbinical school, Durkheim declined to follow in the footsteps of his father, grandfather, and great-grandfather, who were all rabbis.[181] Instead, he switched schools and chose secularism as his life's path. In his mature work, Durkheim portrayed religion as a social institution which gives humanity a sense of collective consciousness.[182] He saw, however, that over time, religion was dwindling in its sway, being eclipsed not only by science but also by an apotheosis of individualism. Durkheim was concerned that secularization would not be sufficient to give people the essentials—a sense of order and community.

Durkheim entered the École Normale Supérieure where he studied under the direction of Numa Denis Fustel de Coulange, a classicist with a social scientific outlook. There he read Auguste Comte and Herbert Spencer.[183] Durkheim also formed an intimate friendship with his classmate Victor Hommay, whose 1886 leap to his death might have fostered Durkheim's interest in suicide.[184] At about the age of twenty-eight, a heartbroken Durkheim discretely depicted his friend's death as an accident:

> He entered his room, on the second floor, took his notebook and sat on the edge of a very low window without a balcony, which easily induced vertigo. He made a sudden and foolhardy movement, characteristic of him, and lost his balance. A few moments later, he was picked up in the courtyard, his book of notes beside him.[185]

As Steven Lukes suggests, "the emotion" that Durkheim expressed in Hommay's obituary "foreshadows" Durkheim's concept of "egoistic suicide" in his *Suicide* treatise.[186]

During his later education, Durkheim receded from humanistic studies, psychology, and philosophy, and moved toward the study of ethics. He ultimately claimed sociology as his life's crusade. But his fixation with a scientific approach to society put him at odds with the French academy, which lacked a social science curriculum. This impeded his access to a major academic appointment and induced him to leave for Germany to study sociology at the universities of Marburg, Berlin, and Leipzig.[187] The decision proved fruitful because the time spent in Leipzig gave Durkheim respect for empiricism, which became his idiolect. Further, his efforts in Germany were productive and resulted in his publication of multiple articles on German social science and philosophy.[188] After French scholars began to notice his work, Durkheim returned home to a position at the University of Bordeaux where he founded the sociology department.

After marrying Louise Dreyfus and having two children, Durkheim published *The Division of Social Labor* (1893), his doctoral dissertation, which explored the nature and development of human society; *The Rules of Sociological Method* (1894), an influential manifesto, which defined sociology's scientific character; and *Suicide* (1897), his innovative case study, which not only influenced proponents of control theory but also distinguished social science from psychology and political thought. In addition, he founded L'Année Sociologique, the first French social science journal, which promoted the work of students and collaborators.[189] As a *gestalt*, Durkheim focused on societal maintenance of integrity and coherence in the modernist era when traditional religious and social ties were no longer assumed and where new institutions were on the rise.[190]

Durkheim's trajectory, however, was neither steady nor devoid of turmoil: the field of scientific sociology rattled some of the more conservative thinkers, who sporadically attacked Durkheim's theories and methods.[191] Politics, history, and current events not only fueled Durkheim's fascination with social phenomena, but effectually exacerbated his plight as the minority outsider. Events, like France's defeat in the Franco-Prussian War which led to the fall of Napoleon III and the rise of the Third Republic, precipitated a backlash against secular and republican rule.[192] Durkheim, a Jew and socialist, who endorsed the Third Republic, found himself in the political minority. On top of this, Durkheim took a courageous stance in the controversy involving Alfred Dreyfus, who incidentally was not related to his wife (whose maiden name was Dreyfus). This debacle began with an outbreak of anti-Semitism, which occurred after a Jewish officer, Dreyfus, was falsely charged with spying for the Germans.[193] An incensed Durkheim spoke out as an activist seeking to exonerate Dreyfus. In fact, this fight might have contributed to his failure to be elected to the prestigious Institut de France, which was an honor he had earned on the merits.[194]

Despite his defiant stance, Durkheim became the chair of Education at the Sorbonne in 1902 and later rose to full professor.[195] In 1913, he was named chair in Education and Sociology, a position that enabled him to shape future teachers. He also served as an advisor to the Ministry of Education and in 1912, he published his last major work, *The Elementary Forms of Religious Life*, which dealt with the Australian totemic system.

World War I brought setbacks and tragedy.[196] While Durkheim supported his country, he could not acquiesce in what he saw as simplistic nationalist propaganda. His dissent (and once again his Jewish background) created strife: Durkheim became a target of the ascendant French Right, who denounced him as the professor with German blood who was fostering a foreign discipline at the Sorbonne.[197] While these accusations scalded him, he worried incessantly about his beloved students being drafted into the army and mourned those who perished in the trenches.[198] When his only son, André, was among those killed while fighting on the Balkan front, the loss was beyond what he could endure.[199] Not long thereafter, Durkheim had a stroke and died.[200]

Suicide as a Social Fact

When it comes to Durkheim, one must strive to overlook the pachyderms in the room. Aside from incisive attacks that have been and still are aimed at his scholarship and methodology,[201] Durkheim was an unabashed sexist, chauvinist, and European elitist.[202] He adhered to a patriarchal hierarchy, under which women, whom he saw as less developed, had no need of the intellectual and social stimulation that was essential for men: he said that "[w]ith a few devotional practices and some animals to care for . . . the old unmarried woman's life is full," whereas men required more social contacts because they were the superior, "more complex social being[s]" (SU, Bk 2, ch. 3; 215–16).[203] Durkheim called those not classified as privileged white Europeans "savages" or "primitives."[204] In one text, he said that "although the savage does not know the pleasures that a very active life procures for us, his compensation is that he is not prey to boredom, that torment of the cultured mind."[205] While reproaching Durkheim for biases is easy but fruitless, we should take pains to underscore his prodigious accomplishments and at least concede that his concept of "social facts," which has transhistorical import, can even serve as a lens for literary analysis.[206]

Unlike his contemporaries, Ferdinand Tonnies and Max Weber, Durkheim eschewed methodological individualism and dealt with "social facts," which he defined as cultural beliefs and actions that are coercive of all even though they exist beyond individual control.[207] He explained: social facts "consist of manners of acting, thinking and feeling external to the individual, which are invested with a coercive power by virtue of which they exercise control of him."[208] He declared, it "is indisputable . . . that most of our ideas and tendencies are not developed by ourselves, but come to us from outside, they can penetrate us by imposing themselves upon us."[209] Yet, "all social constraints do not necessarily exclude the individual personality."[210] In short, while people themselves create social facts, the facts take on a life of their own: they become a living force, which inevitably impact everyone materially and morally. Moreover, Durkheim identified a wide range of things, like patriarchy, languages, division of labor, myths, racism, and even suicide, as social facts.[211]

According to Durkheim, a social scientist studies the qualities and characteristics of social facts through quantitative or experimental methodology, which means reliance on statistics.[212] In *Suicide*, Durkheim proceeded in an ostensibly counterintuitive direction in an effort to understand societal cohesion and enlisted the diametric opposite as his cynosure: namely, he focused on the individual's consummate act of rupture with the social structure.[213] Durkheim believed that those who self-annihilate repudiate cohesion because they deliberately and finally sever their umbilical cord with the communal corpus. For him, the cohesion-repudiators hold the key to unlocking the salutary power of cohesion itself.

Durkheim rebuts the assertions that religion by itself "has a prophylactic effect upon suicide" and seeks to derail that mindset: "[i]t is not because [religion] condemns [suicide] more unhesitatingly than secular morality, nor because the idea of God gives its precepts exceptional authority which subdues the will, nor because the prospect of a future life and the terrible punishments there awaiting the guilty give its proscriptions a greater sanction than that of human law" (SU, Bk 2, ch. 2; 169–70). If scriptural teachings are what dominate, all Christian faiths would be equal with respect to their suicide rates. Yet, Protestants have the highest suicide rate, even though they are like Catholics with respect to their belief in God and the immortality of the soul. Judaism, "the religion with least inclination to suicide," does not "formally" prohibit it and is "the one in which the idea of immortality plays the least role" (SU, Bk 2, Ch 2; 170).[214] Durkheim asserted that if religion is what dissuades humans from self-destruction, it is not due to "dogmas and rites" (SU, Bk 2, Ch 2; 170). Rather, it is because religion is a "society . . . capable of supporting a sufficiently intense collective life" (SU, Bk 2, Ch 2; 170).

In *Suicide*, Durkheim assembled suicide rates from Protestant, Catholic, and religiously diverse countries and asked why the average suicide rate is considerably higher among Protestants. He attributed the Protestant proclivity for suicide "to the spirit of free inquiry that animates this religion" and the fact that Protestantism "concedes a greater freedom to individual thought than Catholicism" (SU, Bk 2, Ch 2; 158). In contrast, the Catholic Church offers a structured hierarchy of authority, a "collective *credo*," and a sense of a shared moral and social code (SU, Bk 2, Ch2; 159). Durkheim elaborates:

> [T]he Catholic accepts his faith ready made, without scrutiny. He may not even submit to it in the historical examination since the original texts that serve as its basis are proscribed. A whole hierarchical system of authority is devised, with marvelous ingenuity of thought. The Protestant is far more the author of his faith. The Bible is put in his hands and no interpretation is imposed upon him. The very structure of the reformed cult stresses this state of religious individualism. (SU, Bk 2, Ch 2; 158)

Durkheim concluded that the stronger "the collective states of mind are, the stronger the integration of the religious community, and also the greater its preservative value" (SU, Bk 2, Ch 2; 159). Because the Protestant church has a less "intense collective life," it has a less "moderating effect" on self-homicide (SU, Bk 2, Ch 2; 170). Moreover, Durkheim's statistics led him to observe that unmarried individuals are more likely to kill themselves than those with families. As a whole, those with fewer social and familial ties or less affiliation with community are more prone to end their own lives.

Although Durkheim's findings and methodology have their critics, this social fact finder cannot be seriously charged with deleting psychology from the calculus.[215] Taylor points out that although Durkheim has been depicted as an " 'implacable foe' of psychological explanations," he was "a keen student of the psychology of his day" and "even contributed to some of its debates."[216] He adds that while "Durkheim was interested in the boundaries between sociology and psychology," it was really "a later generation of students who created the disjunction between supposedly 'internal' and 'external' factors in the explanation of suicide."[217] Taylor emphasizes that Durkheim's sociology "was not an attempt to show that social facts impinge on individuals from without and, as it were, 'propel' them like billiard balls in given directions; but rather that society, the collective experience of humanity, 'lives in' the subjective experience of individuals."[218]

In his *Suicide* treatise, Durkheim sees society as inextricable from individual consciousness and acknowledges psychological theory. But Durkheim believed that the drastic act of taking one's own life could not be understood solely through scoping the psyche.[219] He essentially debunked the notion that suicide is causally rooted in personal tragedy, like the death of a loved one, loss of a job, bankruptcy, or divorce. For him the veritable culprit was rapid economic, political, and social change which obscure or obliterate accepted social rules and thus engender raw antisocialism.

Suicide was not published until after Dostoevsky's death. Moreover, as Susan K. Morrissey points out, it was not until 1912 that it was even translated into Russian.[220] Morrissey explains that while Russian critics begged to differ, they "agreed wholeheartedly on the need for social solidarity, which was a catchphrase within Russian populism and Marxism" and "Durkheim's study helped to reinvigorate sociology, which, as one reviewer pointed out, was not even taught as a separate subject in Russia."[221] Significantly, Morrissey emphasizes that in Russia "what proved most attractive was Durkheim's organic vision of the social collective."[222] That social collective (or lack thereof) also constitutes a thematic thread wending its way through Dostoevsky's work, which predates *Suicide* by decades.

Examining the regulation of suicide in Russia from the seventeenth century to 1914, Morrissey states that "criminal regulation of suicide reached its highpoint in imperial Russia during the first half of the nineteenth century," that "statutes on suicide formulated in the 1830s and 1840s did not distinguish between the criminal and moral dimensions of the act," and that "[s] elf-murder was both a crime and a sin and its combined penalties reinforced this dualism."[223] In his treatise, Durkheim similarly points his finger at Russia and its effort to deal severely with what it condemned as criminal-immoral incidents of self-homicide:

> If the suicide seems not to have acted under the influence of mental disturbance, chronic or temporary, his will is annulled and all the material dispositions he made in anticipation of death are likewise annulled. Christian burial is refused him. The mere attempt is punished by a fine which is fixable by ecclesiastical authority. Finally, whoever incites another to kill himself or helps him carry out his resolve in any way, as by supplying him with the necessary instruments, is treated as an accomplice of premeditated homicide. (SU, Bk 3, Ch 2; 328–29)

Paperno points out that during Durkheim's lifetime, "[b]etween the 1860s and the 1880s, Russia was believed to have experienced an 'epidemic of suicides.' "[224] The epidemic coincides with the publication of Dostoevsky's semiautobiographical novel *Notes from the House of the Dead House*, which the next chapter addresses. The rampant suicides, moreover, correspond to the publication of other major works, including "Notes from Underground," *Crime and Punishment*, *The Gambler*, *The Idiot*, *Demons*, *A Writer's Diary*, *The Adolescent*, and *The Brothers Karamazov*. These decades were a period of great change in Russia. After the death of Nicholas I and Russia's defeat in the Crimean War, Tsar Alexander II (1855–1881) instituted reforms, which altered the fabric of Russian society, culture, and law. The Tsar's Great Reforms, which started with the emancipation of the serfs (1861), included Russian legal reforms (1864), which instituted trial by jury, the adversarial process, a professional bar, and justices of the peace.[225] Open court sessions, ones the public could attend and follow in daily newspapers, replaced the secret proceedings. Significantly, Durkheim found that in precisely such periods of turnabout, suicide rates tend to soar.

Morrissey explains how these Russian "judicial reforms [also] inaugurated a new era in the legal regulation of suicide" and that "after the 1860s . . . formal prosecution of suicide and attempted suicide became increasingly uncommon."[226] She adds, however, that although "[i]n contrast to the tendency in the first part of the century, judgment was apt to be lenient, and priests were often directed to accord suicides a religious burial[,]" such "developments were not accompanied by a decline of public interest."[227] Along these lines, Paperno explains that "it was only in the 1860's, during the Great Reforms, which created many new public institutions (organs of the press, open courts, statistical bureaus), that suicide became an object of vigorous discussions in science, law, fiction, and above all, the periodical press."[228] More than three decades after reforms were occurring in a seemingly remote land, Durkheim, cognizant of Russia's epidemic, issued a treatise that injected a sociological voice into that ongoing and intermittently discordant debate.

In Durkheim's etiology, there are four basic types of suicide: egoistic, altruistic, anomic, and fatalistic. He placed each of the four types on a chart with social regulation on the *x*-axis and social integration on the *y*-axis.[229] Egoistic suicide corresponds to the individuals' lack of integration into society, which can lead to isolation, emptiness, and the feeling that they have no place in the world or in anyone's life.[230] By contrast, altruistic suicide derives from excessive social integration: here group dynamics consume individuals to such an extent that they feel commanded to take their own life as in a religious sacrifice or as a fanatical pledge of allegiance to some political cult.[231]

Anomic suicide, possibly the most cryptic, occurs when there is insufficient regulation due to some radical social or economic upheaval. In these cases, the individual becomes angry, morally confused, and directionless.[232] The anomic, who are no longer able to reasonably expect predictability, can become enraged or sink into aimless, numb despair, a condition reminiscent of that of the superfluous man in Russian literature.[233]

Finally, at the other end of the spectrum is fatalistic suicide, which emerges in contexts characterized by excessive regulation and erupts in a situs populated by those forced to adhere to the same routine day after day, who feel that there is no egress and no way to improve their lives.[234] Durkheim suggests that fatalistic suicide is the most prevalent form in prisons.[235] He further acknowledges that his categories are not necessarily mutually exclusive, and that there exist a panoply of hybrids, including but not limited to fatalistic-altruistic, ego-anomic, altruistic-anomic, and ego-altruistic suicides.[236] As shown in the next chapter, the prison in Dostoevsky's *Notes from the House of the Dead* tends to breed a fatalistic or fatalistic-altruistic act of (or attempt at) self-murder.

Dostoevsky died in 1883 at about the same time that Durkheim was launching his sociological course.[237] The fact that the father of modern sociology does not discuss the great Russian novelist in his writings has led sociologist, Donald A. Nielsen, to conclude that Durkheim "evidently never read Dostoevsky."[238] In his succinct essay, Nielsen notes that the "names Emile Durkheim and Fyodor Dostoevsky are seldom mentioned in the same breath," yet he nevertheless invites scholars to examine "Dostoevsky's life and work in light of the ideas developed in Durkheim's sociology."[239] In writing this book, I have wholeheartedly accepted that invitation.

THE ROAD AHEAD

This book aims to show how self-homicide in Dostoevsky's fiction prefigures Emile Durkheim's etiology in *Suicide* as well as theories of other suicidologists. But beyond that, the book aspires to funnel out, chapter-by-chapter, to an exegesis of how Dostoevsky's implicit awareness of fatalistic, egoistic, anomic, and altruistic modes of self-destruction helped shape not only his philosophy but also his craft as a writer. More expansively, however, the book hopes to tackle the formidable task of forging a ligature between artistic creation and the pluripresent social fact of self-annihilation.

Chapter 2 establishes incarceration as the ordeal that shaped Dostoevsky's insights into the psyches of not only those who transgress against others but also those who self-offend. In *Notes from the House of the Dead*, there are lethal fatalistic forces at work, ones which Durkheim believes emerge in contexts characterized by excessive regulation where a populous is forced to adhere to the same routine day after day and feel that egress or amelioration is unattainable. After pinpointing these types in narrator Goryanchikov's account of prison life (or rather nonlife), the chapter analyzes what Durkheim commends and the convicts themselves fashion as antidotes to self-annihilative impulses: surviving inmates either build their own cohesive subculture, share hopes of reuniting with their original communities, or engorge collective nutrients through labor. The chapter ends with a discussion of how internment bestowed gifts on both Goryanchikov, and his author. Specifically, it explores how the self-destructive impulses within the prison engendered an epiphanic vision of collective unity, which would steadily evolve throughout Dostoevsky's career.

Chapter 3 delves into Durkheim's egoistic suicide as it figures in two Dostoevsky's masterpieces, *Crime and Punishment* and *The Idiot*. Both Durkheim and Dostoevsky see suicide as rooted in an excessive individualism that unplugs people from collective vitality. In *Crime and Punishment*, both Rodion Raskolnikov and Arkady Ivanovich Svidrigailov are pieces in an egoistic suicide puzzle. Raskolnikov has sentenced himself to a form of self-imposed exile, a state which predisposes him to take his own life.

Sidrigailov, who is adrift in a realm of indifference, boredom, ghosts, and eavesdropping, does kill himself. But in the course of the novel, he becomes more diffuse than one single egoistic self-homicide. Instead, he is reified into suicidal death itself.

In *The Idiot*, Dostoevsky discloses suicidogenic propensities in a postlapsarian world in which everyone is born irrevocably sentenced to death. This is the realm in which Rogozhin, Nastasya Filippovna, and Ippolit Terentyev either deliver, embrace, or fear death. Afflicted not just with egoism but also with unresolved grief and anomic rage, Nastasya Filippovna secures Rogozhin as her executioner and thus, commits suicide by proxy. Ippolit's botched suicide also has a shade all its own. What impels Ippolit to pull the trigger is solipsistic thanatophobia and a deep-seated need to effectuate the impossible—to joltingly renew life through the exorcism and conquest of death. The chapter concludes not only by discussing how *Crime and Punishment* and *The Idiot* proffer antidotes to self-destruction, but also by exploring how Dostoevsky's colligation of opposites fits into both his message and artistic process. While filling the notes for *The Idiot* with iterations of death, arson, rape, murder, self-homicide, and a menagerie of thanatotic specimens, Dostoevsky was intuiting not only that the drive to self-expunge is ubiquitous, but also that it can stimulate the emergence of the contrapositives that galvanize creativity.

Chapter 4 turns to anomy, which runs rampant in *Demons* and *The Brothers Karamazov*. Durkheim holds that anomic suicides skyrocket when society's equilibrium is jolted, when regulation is stripped away, when religion has lost its power, or when moral and institutional values morph or vanish entirely. In *Demons*, anomy collaborates with nihilism as the town plummets into chaotic ruin after Pyotr Verkhovensky orchestrates upheaval. In *The Brothers Karamazov*, anomy conspires with atheism, the devil, and perfidy, all of which haunt Skotoprigonevsk and spawn ruptured families, parricide, miscarried justice, and foreboded cannibalism. In times of collective rupture, passions go unchecked and individuals can vent their irritation, rage, disgust, or empty, boundless despair by killing others and themselves. Consequently, Nikolay Stavrogin, Aleksey Kirillov, and Pavel Smerdyakov, die either by the rope or the bullet. But as in *Notes from the House of the Dead*, *Crime and Punishment*, and *The Idiot*, Dostoevsky's later novels place the itineraries leading to self-annihilation alongside the alternatives, the lighted routes heading toward universal fellowship and faith. The chapter's conclusion delves into those antithetical trajectories in the novels to show how they cohere with Durkheim's suicide antidote—robust collectivity and shared faith.

Chapter 5, the conclusion, essentially revisits and builds upon its predecessors. Upon release from prison, what simmered was Dostoevsky's Russian messianism, along with his resolve to inculcate a unifying, empathic collective unity through artistry. Moreover, his term in Siberia propelled him toward his generation of electrifying communality in his celebrated Pushkin Memorial speech in Moscow. In this speech and throughout his works, Dostoevsky repeatedly juxtaposed combatant forces, like mind versus heart, egoism versus collectivity, atheism versus faith, indifference versus empathy, *ad infinitum*. Significantly, suicide versus life-affirmation is a predominant polemic. Through an analysis of the Pushkin speech, Stavrogin's dream of "The Golden Age" and "The Dream of a Ridiculous Man: A Fantastic Story," the last chapter assays to anatomize the creative process itself. When all is said and done, it attempts to shed light on the dynamic role the suicide epidemic played in Dostoevsky's antonymous artistry, one which, like music, fused, message, form, and process.

NOTES

1. Fyodor Dostoevsky, *A Writer's Diary*, Vol. 1 (1873–1878) (IL: Northwestern University Press, 1994), 737. There are two superb books that focus on suicide in Russia. One is Irina Paperno's *Suicide As a Cultural Institution in Dostoevsky's Russia* (NY: Cornell University Press, 1997). Paperno explains that "[i]n the nineteenth century, a study of suicide usually opened with a survey of celebrated cases, from Socrates to Goethe's Werther," which constitute "units of meaning" and such "[s]ymbolic meanings associated with the act of suicide found their focal points in such cases." Ibid., 6. The other is Susan K. Morrissey, *Suicide and the Body Politic in Imperial Russia* (UK: Cambridge University Press, 2006), which examines the forms, meanings, and regulation of suicide from the seventeenth century to 1914.

2. Fyodor Dostoevsky, "The Dream of a Ridiculous Man," in *Notes from Underground, the Double and Other Stories* (NY: Barnes & Noble Classics, 2008), 363–83.

3. In Fyodor Dostoevsky's *The Adolescent* (NY: Vintage Classics, 2003), Darya Onisimovna's name changes to Nastasya Egorovna in Part Three of the novel.

4. Dostoevsky, *The Adolescent*, Ibid., 68, 393.

5. Edwin S. Shneidman, *The Suicidal Mind* (NY: Oxford University Press, 1996), 63 (naming Menninger "the grandfather of American suicidology"); Karl A. Menninger, *Man against Himself* (NY: Harcourt, Brace & World, Inc., 1966), 4.

6. George Howe Colt, *November of the Soul: The Enigma of Suicide* (NY: Scribner, 2006), 129–30.

7. Colt explains that this man's soul, his *ba*, "urges him to enjoy life, to surrender himself to pleasure," and although "[i]n the end his *ba* agrees to stay[,] it is not clear whether the man goes on to kill himself." Colt, Ibid., 130.

8. See generally Colt, Ibid., 149 ("For the Stoics, suicide was a final resource, an ultimate weapon against the vicissitudes of life."); Kay Redfield Jamison, *Night Falls Fast: Understanding Suicide* (NY: Vintage Books, 1999), p. (discussing the Stoics and Epicureans).

9. See Jamison, Ibid., 13. Colt explains that the "taboos" surrounding the act of suicide "were the products less of moral judgment than of the ancient Greeks' abhorrence of any violent or untimely death—murder, stillbirth, abortion—and their horror of shedding kindred blood." Colt, Ibid., 144. He adds that "[s]uicides from starvation, which were bloodless and slow, were rarely denied ordinary rites" because "there was no sudden wrenching of the soul from the body, which the Greeks most feared." Ibid.

10. Colt, Ibid., p. 145. See also A. Alvarez, *The Savage God: A Study of Suicide* (NY.: W.W. Norton, & Co., 1990), 77 ("[T]he Pythagoreans rejected suicide out of hand since, for them as for the later Christians, life itself was the discipline of the gods.").

11. Alvarez, Ibid., 77 (For Aristotle, "suicide was an offence against the State because on religious grounds, it polluted the city and, economically weakened it by destroying a useful citizen.").

12. Colt, Ibid., 146 ("[W]hen Aristotle died in exile at sixty-two, there were persistent rumors that he had killed himself."); Jamison, Ibid., 13 ("[A]ccording to Heracleitus, Pythagoras starved himself to death).

13. Helen Silving, "Suicide and Law" in *Clues to Suicide*, eds. Edwin S. Shneidman and Norman L. Farberow (NY: McGraw-Hill Book Company, Inc., 1957), 79–80.

14. Ibid., 80.

15. Ibid.

16. Ibid., 80–81(quoting Justinian's *Digest*).

17. Colt, Ibid., 151. He adds that "[t]here are six suicides in the Old Testament," but [t]hey earn neither blessing nor condemnation." Ibid., 151–52 (listing Saul, who "fell on his sword to avoid capture"; Abimelech, who "killed himself to avoid dishonor" when he was "mortally wounded" by a woman; Zimri, who killed himself when he "realized that his siege of Tirzah was doomed"; Samson, who "pulled down the walls of the temple of Dagon, destroying both his enemy and himself"; Ahithophel, who deserted his master King David, "set his house in order and hanged himself"; Judas Iscariot of the New Testament, who committed suicide after betraying Jesus Christ").

18. See Gerald Heard, "Buddha and Self-Destruction," in *Essays in Self Destruction*, ed. Edwin S. Shneidman (NY: Jason Aronson, Inc. 1967), 78–79 (Contending that Buddha, who "did believe in the destruction of the false self," had an "aim . . and method . . . [t]o make it possible to shatter this mendacious mask so that the only true life-acceptor, life-controller, and life-advancer, the true self of whom the *persona* is the willing instrument, can emerge").

19. See generally Franco Ferracuti, "Suicide in a Catholic Country," in *Clues to Suicide*, Ibid., 70, 73 (explaining that the "Council of Toledo (693 A.D.) provided excommunication for attempted suicide, that suicide as a form of martyrdom was also "criticized and discouraged" and that St. Augustine and St. Thomas Aquinas are "very definite on this issue").

20. According to Ferracuti, St. Augustine predicates his denial of suicide on four points, one of which is "*Non occides* [Thou shalt not kill]," which is 'an absolute law" and "St. Thomas stated that suicide is a mortal sin against God who has given life

and against justice and charity." Ferracuti, "Suicide in a Catholic Country," in *Clues to Suicide*, Ibid., 72n.2. Alvarez states that "Christian teaching was at first a powerful incitement to suicide" because the Church instilled in believers the idea that this world was a vale of tears" and that "death released them into eternal glory." Ibid., 86. As such, "Why, then, live unredeemed when heavenly bliss is only a knife stroke away?" Ibid.

21. See Eric Marcus, *Why Suicide?* (NY: Harper One, 2010), 9. He refers to Rita Robinson's book, *Survivors of Suicide* (NJ: New Page Books, 2001), which explains how most religious communities today offer love and empathy to survivors even though they do not condone the act itself. Marcus tells the story of Joanne, "a devout Catholic whose teenage son killed himself," and how she feared that the church would condemn him and deny him a church funeral. Marcus, Ibid., 9–10. It turned out, however, that her "worst fear was never realized" and that the priest, who officiated at the funeral, told her that her son "wasn't in his right mind when he did this, and for that reason what he did was not a sin." Ibid., 10.

22. Paperno, Ibid., 49.

23. Ibid. See also Morrissey, Ibid., 21.

24. Fyodor Dostoevsky, *Crime and Punishment*, trans. Richard Pevear and Larissa Volokhonsky (NY: Vintage Books, 1993), 507.

25. Fyodor Dostoevsky, *The Brothers Karamazov*, trans. Richard Pevear and Larissa Volokhonsky (NY: Farrar, Straus and Giroux, 2002), 323.

26. Ibid. See also Ibid., 789 n. 16 ("Zosima's broad notions of love and forgiveness are traced by some commentators to the teachings of St. Tikhon of Zadonsk (1724–83).").

27. Paperno, Ibid., 49; Morrissey, Ibid., 21.

28. Paperno, Ibid., 50; Morrissey, Ibid., 21.

29. Paperno, Ibid., 50. Morrissey, explains that "[d]espite [the] specific reference to the motive and mental state of the person, however, church regulations from Muscovite Russia typically ignored such issues" and that "regulatory precepts were similar to those identified in Latin Christianity." Ibid., 22. She adds that "[i]n addressing suicide, churchmen focused upon the circumstances of death and, increasingly, the moral conduct of the person." Ibid. See also Dostoevsky, *The Adolescent*, Ibid., 383 (Makar Ivanovich explaining that " 'suicide is the greatest human sin . . . but the Lord alone is the only judge here, for He alone knows everything—every limit and every measure").

30. See Paperno, Ibid., 66.

31. Emile Durkheim, *Suicide: A Study in Sociology*, trans. John A. Spaulding and George Simpson (NY: The Free Press 1951) ("SU"), 170. All further citations to *Suicide* are from this translation. Hereafter, I will include the book and chapter number, as well as the page number from the Spaulding and Simpson translation, in parentheses in the text.

32. Marcus, Ibid., 10; Jamison, Ibid., 14.

33. Isaac Klein, *A Guide to Jewish Religious Practice* (NY: Ktav Publishing House, 1992), 282–83. "The general rule is that the public should participate in whatever is done out of respect for the living, but it should not participate in whatever is done out of respect for the dead." Ibid., 282.

34. Ibid., 283.

35. Ibid. See also Marcus, Ibid., 10.

36. Jamison, Ibid., 14; Marcus, Ibid., 10.

37. Marcus, Ibid., 10. Marcus raises the question: "If Muhammad said that Muslims who take their own lives go to hell, why do people who follow the Islamic faith who engage in suicidal terrorist acts believe they'll spend eternity in paradise?" Ibid., 11. He answers that "the simplest explanation for what is an exceedingly complex issue is that this belief is a perversion of traditional Islamic teachings." Ibid.

38. See Alvarez, Ibid., 81–82 (listing the "most distinguished men of the ancient world" who committed suicide). Colt explains that "[s]uicide to avoid capture was almost de rigueur among the ancient Greeks," and that "if the Greeks rationalized suicide, the Romans made it a fashion, even a sport." Ibid., 45, 148. Morrissey discusses "the cult surrounding Cato of Utica, who disemboweled himself rather than submit to tyranny under Caesar." Morrissey, Ibid., 53. As she states, "[b]efore his death, Cato was supposed to have read Plato's *Phaedo*, the text in which Socrates affirms the immortality of the soul before dying." Ibid. See also Fr. Robert Barry, O.P, "The Development of the Roman Catholic Teachings on Suicide in *Notre Dame Journal of Law, Ethics & Public Policy* 9 (1995): 449–501, who states that "[t]he suicides of Cato, Seneca, Marc Anthony, Brutus, and Cleopatra are the most famous of the Republican era, and suggest that suicide was widely practiced among the upper classes even during the Republic." Ibid., 463.

39. With respect to Socrates, Paperno explains that "[t]o this day philosophers debate whether Socrates death can be considered a suicide." Paperno, Ibid., 7. See also Colt, Ibid., 146 (stating that "the *Phaedo* provoked disparate reactions" and that "[w]hile the Greek orator Libanius claimed that the arguments in the *Phaedo* kept him from committing suicide. . . the young Greek philosopher Cleombrotus was so fascinated by Socrates' description of the souls' immortality that he flung himself into the sea and drowned").

40. Harold Tarrant, "Introduction," in Plato, *The Last Days of Socrates*" trans. Hugh Tredennick and Harold Tarrant (NY: Penguin Books, 2003), 33.

41. I. F. Stone, *The Trial of Socrates* (NY: Anchor Books, 1989), 181, 197. Stone believes that "[h]ad Socrates invoked freedom of speech as a basic right of all Athenians—not just the privilege of a superior and self-selected few like himself—he would have struck a deep and responsive chord." Ibid., 214.

42. Stone, points out that "the 500-man jury must have been 280 votes for conviction, 220 votes for acquittal," which would be a majority of sixty." Stone, Ibid., 181. He adds that "if thirty jurors had shifted their vote from conviction to acquittal, the jury would have been split evenly with 250 votes on each side, and in Athens a tie vote was resolved in favor of the accused." Ibid.

43. See Stone, Ibid., 187 (arguing that the defense should have "focused on the enormity—if not, indeed, downright illegality—of a death penalty" and should have given the jurors "a milder alternative—at the worst banishment from the city," which might have appeased "a hesitant and troubled jury").

44. Plato, Ibid., 65 (*Apology*).

45. Ibid., 66 (*Apology*).

46. Emile Durkheim, *The Rules of Sociological Method*, trans. W. D. Halls, ed. Steven Lukes (NY: Free Press, 2013), 64.
47. Durkheim, *The Rules of Sociological Method*, Ibid., 64.
48. Plato, Ibid., 67 (*Apology*) (emphasis added).
49. Ibid., 69 (*Apology*) (emphasis added).
50. Ibid. (*Apology*) (emphasis added).
51. Ibid. (*Apology*).
52. Ibid., 69–70 (*Apology*) (emphasis added).
53. Ibid., 70 (*Apology*) (emphasis added).
54. Ibid., 131–32 (*Phaedo*) (emphasis added).
55. Ibid., 129 (*Phaedo*).
56. Ibid., 121 (*Phaedo*) (emphasis added).
57. Ibid. (*Phaedo*).
58. Ibid., 122 (*Phaedo*).
59. Ibid., 197–98 (*Phaedo*) (emphasis added).
60. Stone, Ibid., 195.
61. Herbert Hendin, "Psychodynamics of Suicide, with Particular Reference to the Young," in *Essential Papers on Suicide*, eds. John T. Maltsberger, M. D. and Mark J. Goldblatt, M. D. (NY: New York University Press, 1996) [hereinafter referred to as *Essential Papers*], 612, 618. Hendin is referencing C. G. Jung, "The Soul and Death," in *The Meaning of Death*, ed. H. Feifel (NY: McGraw-Hill, 1959) and G. Zilboorg, "The Sense of Immortality," *Psychoanal Q* 7 (1938), 171–99.
62. John T. Maltsberger and Dan H. Buie Jr., "The Devices of Suicide: Revenge, Riddance, and Rebirth," in *Essential Papers*, Ibid., 397, 410, 407–8.
63. Steve Taylor, *Durkheim and the Study of Suicide* (UK: The MacMillan Press, Ltd. 1982), 148–50.
64. Erwin Stengel, *Suicide and Attempted Suicide* (NY: Jason Aronson, Inc. 1974), 87 (emphasis in original).
65. Arthur Schopenhauer, "On Suicide," in *Suffering, Suicide and Immortality*, trans. T. Bailey Saunders (NY: Dover Publications, Inc., 2006), 25, 31.
66. Schopenhauer, Ibid., 31.
67. Menninger, Ibid., 61 (quoting George Kennan, "Problems of Suicide" in *McClure's Magazine* 31 (1908), 227).
68. Plato, Ibid., 121.
69. Sigmund Freud, *The Psychopathology of Everyday Life*, trans. A. Brill (SC: Columbia, 1901). (Chapter 8, Erroneously Carried-Out Actions) ("[M]any apparently accidental injuries happening to such patients are really self-inflicted . . . brought about by the fact there is a constantly lurking tendency to self-punishment . . .[and] that the psychic conflict may end in suicide can never be excluded in these cases.")
70. Menninger, Ibid., 317.
71. Ibid., 229–350.
72. Ibid., 353–415.
73. Ibid., 87–226.
74. Ibid., 87.
75. Shneidman, *The Suicidal Mind*, Ibid., 62.

76. Edwin S. Shneidman, "Orientations Toward Death," in *The Psychology of Suicide: A Clinician's Guide to Evaluation and Treatment*, eds. Edwin S. Shneidman, Norman L. Farberow, and Robert E. Litman (NJ: Jason Aronson Inc. 1994), 10.

77. Shneidman, "Orientations Toward Death," in *The Psychology of Suicide*, Ibid., 10.

78. Shneidman, *The Suicidal Mind*, Ibid., 62–63.

79. Ibid., 63.

80. Michael A. Church and Charles I. Brooks, *Subtle Suicide: Our Silent Epidemic of Ambivalence about Living* (CA: Praeger, 2009), xi.

81. Fyodor Dostoyevsky, "Mr. Prokharchin," in *Poor Folk and Other Stories*, trans. David McDuff (NY: Penguin Books, 1988).

82. Dostoevsky, *The Adolescent*, Ibid., 79.

83. See Colt, Ibid., 276. He states that "[p]sychiatrists believe that some people commit murder in the hope of invoking the death penalty" and that there are "mental health professionals who oppose capital punishment partly because it may encourage violent, suicidal persons to murder." Ibid. See also Isaac Ray, *A Treatise on the Medical Jurisprudence of Insanity*, ed. Winfred Overholser (MA: The Belknap Press of Harvard University Press, 1962), 195 ("Nothing can be more absurd than to inflict the very punishment which the delusion of the monomaniac often impels him to seek—to put *him* to death who voluntarily surrenders himself and imploringly beseeches it as the only object he had at heart in perpetrating a horrid crime.").

84. Shneidman, *The Suicidal Mind*, Ibid., 151 ("An anodyne is a substance that, or a person who, relieves *pain*.").

85. See generally Colt, Ibid., 191–206 (discussing biological suicide research). See also Marie Asberg, Lil Traskman, and Peter Thoren, "5-HIAA in the Cerebrospinal Fluid: A Biochemical Suicide Predictor?" in *Essential Papers*, Ibid., 342–55.

86. See Colt, Ibid., 191–92.

87. Shneidman, *The Suicidal Mind*, Ibid., 18.

88. Ibid.

89. Robert E. Litman, "Sigmund Freud on Suicide," in *Essays in Self-Destruction*, Ibid., 324, 330 (quoting "Contributions to a Discussion on Suicide" in S. Freud, *Standard Edition of the Complete Psychological Works* 11 (UK: The Hogarth Press, Ltd., 1953–1965), 232.

90. Litman, Ibid., 330.

91. Sigmund Freud, *Totem and Taboo*, trans., ed., James Strachey (NY: W.W. Norton & Co., 1989), 191n.63.

92. Sigmund Freud, "Mourning and Melancholia," in *A General Selection from the Works of Sigmund Freud*, ed. John Rickman (NY: Anchor Books, 1989), 133.

93. Freud, Ibid., 131.

94. Ibid. ("[T]he shadow of the object fell upon the ego, so that the latter could henceforth be criticized by a special mental faculty like an object, like the forsaken object.").

95. Freud, Ibid., 133 ("[T]he ego can kill itself only when, the object-cathexis having been withdrawn upon it, it can treat itself as an object, when it is able to launch against itself the animosity relating to an object—that primordial reaction

on the part of the ego to all objects in the outer world."). It is noteworthy that in a study that has been amply criticized and refuted, Freud diagnoses Dostoevsky with an oedipal complex, opining that the epilepsy and fixation on patricide had their roots in his conflicted feelings over his father's death. Sigmund Freud, "Dostoevsky and Parricide," in *The Complete Psychological Works of Sigmund Freud*, XXI (1961), 175–94. According to Freud, Dostoevsky's desire for and relief over his father's demise triggered his initial epileptic seizure and infected him with festering guilt pangs that culminate in the Karamazov murder. Freud, Ibid. Scholars have rebutted Freud's theory on Dostoevsky and have pointed out its blatant mistakes. See generally Joseph Frank, *Dostoevsky: A Writer in His Time* (NJ: Princeton University Press, 2010), 45.

96. Shneidman, *The Suicidal Mind*, Ibid., 118.

97. Litman, "Sigmund Freud on Suicide," *Essays in Self-Destruction*, Ibid., 332. See also, Sigmund Freud, "The Ego and the Id," in *General Selection from the Works of Sigmund Freud*, Ibid., 231 ("If we turn to melancholia first, we find that the excessively strong super-ego which has obtained a hold upon consciousness rages against the ego with merciless fury . . . [such] that the destructive component had entrenched itself in the super-ego and turned against the ego.").

98. Sigmund Freud, *Beyond the Pleasure Principle* (CT: Martino Publishing, 2009).

99. Sigmund Freud, "The Ego and the Id," in *A General Selection from the Works of Sigmund Freud*, Ibid., 224. See also Sigmund Freud, *Civilization and Its Discontents*, ed. James Strachey (NY: W.W. Norton & Company, Inc., 1962), 66 ("I drew the conclusion that besides the instinct to preserve living substance[,] . . . there must exist another, contrary instinct seeking to dissolve those units and to bring them back to their primaeval, inorganic state" and "[t]he phenomena of life could be explained from the concurrent or mutually opposing action of these two instincts.")

100. Gregory Zilboorg, "Considerations on Suicide, with Particular Reference to That of the Young," in *Essential Papers*, Ibid., 65. Freud himself acknowledged that his "assumption of the existence of an instinct of death or destruction has met with resistance even in analytic circles," but adds that "in the course of time they have gained such a hold upon [him] that [he] can no longer think in any other way." Freud, *Civilization and its Discontents*, Ibid., 6.

101. Menninger, Ibid., 81.

102. Ibid.

103. Ibid.

104. Ibid., 82.

105. Ibid., 26.

106. Ibid., 26, 82.

107. Ibid., 82.

108. Ibid.

109. Ibid.

110. Howard I. Kushner, *Self-Destruction in the Promised Land: A Psychocultural Biology of American Suicide* (NJ: Rutgers University Press, 1989), 119.

111. Kushner, Ibid., 77–78 (explaining that "[l]oss of a parent or a sibling during childhood, increase the risk of incomplete mourning because children often are removed from the mourning process by those who wish to protect them from the horrors of death"). See also William Styron, *Darkness Visible: A Memoir of Madness* (NY: Vintage Brooks, 1992) (adopting Kushner's theory and applying it his own suicidal depression). Praising Kushner's ideas, Styron gives an account of his "lurch down pathways toward doom," which he attributes to "incomplete mourning" of his mother, who died when he was thirteen. Ibid., 79. According to Styron, an individual afflicted with "unresolved mourning . . . has, in effect, been unable to achieve the catharsis of grief, and so carries within himself through later years an unsufferable burden of which rage and guilt, and not only damned-up sorrow, are a part, and become the potential seeds of self-destruction." Ibid., 79–80.

112. Kushner, Ibid., 120.

113. Ibid.

114. Shneidman, *The Suicidal Mind*, Ibid., 4–7.

115. Ibid., 8.

116. Ibid., 6.

117. Ibid., 63.

118. Henry A. Murray, *Explorations in Personality* (NY: Oxford University Press, 1963), 124.

119. Shneidman, *The Suicidal Mind*, Ibid., 4.

120. Ibid., 6.

121. Ibid., 18.

122. Ibid., 132 (The "common *emotion* in suicide is *hopelessness-helplessness*—'[t]here is nothing I can do [except commit suicide], and there is no one who can help me [with the pain I am suffering.]"). See also David Aldridge, *Suicide: The Tragedy of Hopelessness* (PA: Jessica Kingsley Publishers, 1998).

123. Hendin, "Psychodynamics of Suicide, with Particular Reference to the Young," in *Essential Papers*, Ibid., 615–16.

124. Ibid.

125. Marcus, Ibid., 49.

126. Ibid., 31.

127. Ibid., 31–33.

128. Ibid., 33–35.

129. Ibid., 35–38. See also Don D. Jackson, "Theories of Suicide" in *Clues to Suicide*, Ibid., 11, 15 ("Many experts . . . point to the loss of something that precedes a suicide" like "the loss of health or faculties as in malignant cancer or old age; or the kind of loss that occurs in financial disaster, drop in social status or prestige, or the losing of a mate by death, separation, or divorce.").

130. Marcus, Ibid., 35, 36–38.

131. Ibid., 36.

132. Ibid. See Dostoevsky, *The Adolescent*, Ibid., 328 where Arkady Dolgorusky exclaims, "Life is over, it's no longer possible to live now" after he, accused of stealing, is disgraced at the roulette table.

133. Charles William Wahl, "Suicide as a Magical Act," in *Clues to Suicide*, Ibid., 22, 23.

134. Ibid., 23.

135. Ibid., 25.

136. Ibid. See also Ray, Ibid., 269 ("[A] girl but little over ten years of age, who being reproved for some trifling indiscretion, cried and sobbed bitterly, went upstairs and hung herself in a pair of cotton braces" and "a boy twelve years old, who hung himself by fastening the handkerchief to a nail in the wall and passing a loop of it around his neck for no other reason than because he had been shut up in his room and allowed only dry bread as a punishment for breaking his father's watch")

137. Wahl, Ibid., 25.

138. Fyodor Dostoevsky, *A Writer's Diary*, Vol. 2 (1877–1881) (IL: Northwestern University Press, 1994), 844–45.

139. Ibid., 845–46 (Dostoevsky is quoting portions of a letter from Katkov).

140. Wahl, Ibid., 26.

141. Ibid.

142. Ibid.

143. Ibid.

144. Ibid.

145. Ibid., 27.

146. Ibid.

147. Ibid., 28.

148. Ibid.

149. Ibid.

150. Wahl, Ibid., 29. Wahl describes a schizophrenic boy, who "frequently tried to slash himself with a knife . . . and . . . would smile gleefully as he watched his blood flow." Ibid. When "[a]sked why he did this, he replied 'All the world bleeds when I'm cut, but I have more blood than they do and I'll live when they are all bled out.' " Ibid. He added: " 'But . . . my parents and sister bleed most of all when I cut myself." Ibid.

151. Ibid.

152. Ibid., 30.

153. Taylor, Ibid., 167.

154. Ibid., 166–67.

155. Ibid., 152–53.

156. Ibid.

157. Ibid., 167.

158. Ibid., 168.

159. Ibid.

160. Ibid.

161. Ibid., 151.

162. Ibid., 152.

163. Alvarez, Ibid., 144.

164. Ibid.

165. Ibid.

166. Ibid., 166 (emphasis added).
167. Ibid., 167, 173, 193, 223, 235, 244.
168. Ibid., 258.
169. Ibid., 259.
170. Ibid.
171. Ibid.
172. Ibid., 259–60.
173. Ibid., 260.
174. Ibid.,
175. Ibid., 277.
176. Ibid., 278.
177. Ibid.
178. Ibid.
179. Colt, Ibid., 206.
180. A definitive study of Durkheim is contained in Steven Lukes, *Emile Durkheim, His Life and Work: A Historical and Critical Study* (CA: Stanford University Press 1973), which is one I applaud for its objectivity and rely on extensively for my overview of Durkheim's life and work. Lukes' "overall framework is that of an intellectual biography, enabling one to consider Durkheim's thought as a developing whole, of which some aspects changed and others deepened." Ibid., 1. Durkheim is also discussed in a brilliant, provocative book by two feminist sociologists, Diane Harriford and Becky Thompson, *When the Center Is on Fire: Passionate Theory for Our Times* (TX: University of Texas Press, 2008). They admit that "[a]s is true of many people trained in sociology, we had been force-fed Durkheim as undergraduates and graduate students" and "had been taught about how hard he struggled, how diligent he was, to have sociology recognized as its own, necessary discipline in France." Ibid., 158. In an effort to explain the 1999 murders by Dylan Klebold and Eric Harris in Littleton Colorado and others like it, Harriford and Thompson return to Durkheim and "acknowledge that his focus on the necessary ingredients for social order—for the moral and spiritual quality of life in modern society—was exactly the question we were still struggling with." Ibid., 160. See Morrissey, who explains that "the social explanation of suicide occurred within the idiom of modernity" and that Durkheim's *Le Suicidé* (1897) was itself a founding manifesto of sociology, an eloquent assertion of the primacy of society in shaping the human being." Ibid., 5. See also Paperno, who devotes a section to an astute discussion of "[t]he metaphorical structure of Durkheim's *Suicide*." Ibid., 36–41.
181. Lukes, Ibid., 39–43 (discussing Durkheim's childhood years).
182. Ibid., 450–84 (discussing Durkheim's views of religion). Durkheim "saw religion as social in at least three broad ways: as socially determined, as embodying representations (in two senses) of social realities, and as having functional social consequences." Ibid., 462. See also Charles Lemert, *Sociology after the Crisis* (CO: Paradigm, 2004), 42. He posits that Durkheim's resolve not to become a rabbi, as his father, grandfather, and great-grandfather had been, meant that "he lost the collective conscience of his childhood, for which he sought a new morality in the science of modern life." Ibid.

183. Ibid., 67–72 (Comte, Taine and Renan). Lukes states that "Comte's influence on Durkheim was very much a formative rather than a continuing one" and "[i]ts most important element was precisely the extension of the scientific attitude to the study of society." Ibid., 68. With respect to Spencer, his "contribution to Durkheim's social realism chiefly lay in the greater specificity of his explanations resulting from his application of the organic analogy to society" and Durkheim "tended to regard Spencer's theory as fruitful, chiefly because Spencer applied it to 'different social types which he classifies into groups and subgroups' and because he investigated 'special questions' and particular institutions." Ibid., 82–83 and nos. 87 and 88.

184. Ibid., 49 ("In the light of Durkheim's future interest in the subject of suicide, the intimacy of his friendship with Hommay and the sensitive account he wrote of the latter's life and death acquire special significance.").

185. Ibid., 51 (quoting Emile Durkheim, "Necrologie d'Hommay," *L'Annuaire de l'Association Des Anciens Élèves De L'École Normale Supérieure* (January 9, 1887), 54.

186. Ibid.

187. Lukes explains that "Durkheim had already decided by the time of his *aggregation* that the general area of research for his principal doctoral thesis was to be that of the relations between individualism and socialism." Lukes, Ibid., 66.

188. Ibid., 86–95 (discussing Durkheim's "visit to Germany").

189. Ibid., 289–95. He explains that "Durkheim's founding of the *Année* was a new departure on the organizational as well as the theoretical level." Ibid., 292. Also, "[i]t was the first example in France (apart from that of the Le Playists) of systematic collaborative work in social science, and here the German influence must have been strong, particularly that of Wundt, whose psychological laboratory in Leipzig had impressed him." Ibid.

190. Harriford and Thompson, Ibid., 161 (discussing Durkheim's concern about the "rapid social change from rural agricultural life to urban industrial life"). They assert that "Durkheim argued that modern society must control people's antisocial urges (what he thought of as limitless desires and an overemphasis on individualism) in order to ensure the social bonds that are necessary for social cohesion." Ibid.

191. Lukes, Ibid., 497–529. He explains that "Durkheim's ideas never ceased to be the centre of intense controversy" and "[i]t was not merely that they were new, often extreme, and pungently and dogmatically expressed." Ibid., 497. While Durkheim himself participated in the active debate, his critics challenged "his methodological principles, his critique of liberal economics, and his sociological treatment of morality, knowledge and religion." Ibid.

192. Ibid., 41–42 (discussing the effect of the Franco-Prussian war on Durkheim, who was twelve years old at the time). Lukes states that "[t]here is evidence that [Durkheim] witnessed, and was possibly subjected to, anti-Semitism at this time" and suggests that the "French defeat may have contributed to a strong (though in no way militant) patriotism, a defensive sense of national decadence and a consequent desire to contribute to the regeneration of France—sentiments that were, in different forms, prevalent among intellectuals of his generation." Ibid., 41

193. Karen Fields, "Individuality and the Intellectuals: An Imaginary Conversation between W. E. B. Du Bois and Emile Durkheim," *Theory and Society* 31 (2002), 435–62. She discusses how in 1894, Captain Alfred Dreyfus was the first Jewish general staff officer in France's army and how he was court-martialed for treason, publicly shamed in a military degradation ceremony, and shipped off to a prison in Guyana. Ibid., 439–41. Harriford and Thompson proclaim that as teachers of social theory, they "admired [Durkheim's] principled protest in the 1890s of the anti-Semitism at the root of the French military's imprisonment and deportation of a Jewish army colonel, Alfred Dreyfus, who was falsely accused of spying for Germany." Ibid., 159.

194. See generally Lukes, Ibid., 320–60 (discussing socialism, the Dreyfus affair and secular education).

195. Ibid., 363–78 (discussing Durkheim at the Sorbonne). Lukes explains how Durkheim's enemies "multiplied" during this time and that various writers, philosophers, Catholic priests, "opponents of the 'New Sorbonne' and sociology in particular," including "figures of the far right," would "write about him with an abusiveness and vehemence." Ibid., 363. Some felt that Durkheim "was responsible for the education of successive generations of schoolteachers whom he sought to imbue with the elements of a rationalist secular morality (some said a dogmatic secular religion)." Ibid., 364.

196. Ibid., 529 (explaining that once France was at war, Durkheim's "intellectual life [was] effectively at an end").

197. Ibid., 557 (explaining that "as a native of Alsace-Lorraine, and a Jew with a German name, Durkheim was the victim of . . . scurrilous attacks"). One attack was in the *Libre Parole*, which called Durkheim "a *Boche* with a false nose, representing the *Kriegsministerium* whose agents are swarming throughout France." Ibid. (citing a Letter dated January 26, 1916). Another attack came "from a senator, M. Gaudin de Vilaine, speaking at the *tribune* of the Senate, who demanded that the Commission charged with reviewing residence permits issued to foreigners should examine . . . 'Frenchmen of foreign descent, such as . . . Durkheim, a Professor at our Sorbonne and without doubt representing, or so it has been claimed, the German *Kriegsministerium.*' " Ibid. (citing Sarrailh, 1960, p. 9, and Durkheim's dossier in Archives Nationales). Apparently, these attacks erupted after Durkheim's own son was killed in the war and Paul Painleve, then at the Ministry of Public Instruction, pointed out Durkheim's tragic loss when he "protested indignantly" in rebutting the accusations. Ibid.

198. Ibid., 548 (explaining that "most of the students were called up" and that "of the 342 students at the École Normale Superieure, 293 were eventually sent to the firing line and 104 were killed outright").

199. Ibid., 554–59. Lukes describes the effect of the death of son André, who was "brilliant," had "just gained his *aggregation* when war broke out," and was training to be a linguist under Antoine Meillet." Ibid., 554–55. Durkheim was "greatly devoted" to André and wrote him letters full of "constant and anxious concern." Ibid., 555. When in 1915, André was sent to the Bulgarian front, he disappeared, and his death was later confirmed. Ibid., 556. After this, Durkheim deteriorated and "withdrew into an almost ferocious silence, forbidding his friends to mention the source of his grief." Ibid., 558 (quoting G. Davy, "E. Durkheim,' RFS, I, 12 [1960]).

200. Ibid., 559 (explaining that after apparently recovering somewhat and returning to his work, he died "at the age of fifty-nine, his work unfinished, having lost, in the course of the war, many of his closest collaborators and finest students").

201. Two sociologists confess that "in [their] own work and in the class room, [they] ultimately portrayed [Durkheim's] scholarship as deeply flawed." Harriford and Thompson, Ibid., 159. They elaborate:

> Like other calls for objectivity, his commitment to objectivity—though a method he considered crucial in order for sociology to be granted academic and moral authority—obscured the impact of his own social location (as a Jew in a Catholic country, as a European man) on his vision. Despite the value he placed on the ideals of the French Revolution and the republic, what was often celebrated as his blueprint for a well-ordered society also served as a grand apology and justification for maintaining social inequalities and legitimizing repressive authority. Although he was not a political conservative (in fact, he was a socialist all his life), the primacy he placed on social order rendered his work, and the ways it has often been interpreted, as hopelessly conservative.

Ibid., 159–60. See also, Lukes, Ibid. 30–36 (summarizing some of the overall criticisms of Durkheim's methods, *modus operandi*, and style). Durkheim has been chastised for his "rather high-handed way with evidence" which "spring[s] from confidence in his own theories." Ibid., 33. Apparently, when Durkheim was told that the "facts contradicted his theories," he used to reply: "The facts are wrong." Ibid. (quoting J. Chevalier *Entretiens avec Bergson* [Paris, 1959], 34). Ibid.

202. Harriford and Thompson, Ibid., 160.

203. In Durkheim's treatise, he is asking "why woman can endure life in isolation more easily than man" and explains that "it is because her sensibility is rudimentary rather than highly developed" and that "very social simple forms satisfy all her needs." Durkheim, *Suicide*, Ibid., 215–16. At another juncture, he discusses sacrifices "imposed by society for social ends" whereby "[s]ubjects as well as clothing and armor must follow their master wherever he goes, even beyond the tomb" and adds that "[s]uch is the relation of the woman to her husband." Ibid., 220. He also states that a "[w]oman's sexual needs have less of a mental character because, generally speaking, her mental life is less developed." Ibid., 272. He opines, "to be sure, we have no reason to suppose that woman may ever be able to fulfill the same functions in society as man; but she will be able to play a part in society which, while peculiarly her own, may yet be more active and important than that of today." Ibid., 385.

204. Harriford and Thompson, Ibid., 160 (pointing out that "Durkheim . . . used terms such as 'savage' and 'primitive' in reference to people not of European background, revealing his unquestioned hierarchical sense of modern and 'primitive societies' "). Harriford and Thompson state that "[w]hile Durkheim was certainly not alone among white European men of his era in terms of his ethnocentrism, this limit is particularly significant in Durkheim's case, since his early and late work extended beyond Europe in its gaze" and "[h]is books *The Division of Labor in Society* and *The*

Elementary Forms of the Religious Life theorized about the structures of societies in industrialized and colonized countries." Ibid.

205. Emile Durkheim, *The Division of Labor in Society*, trans. W. D. Halls (NY: Free Press, 2014), 189. See also Ibid., 308 ("Animals and savages work in a most capricious fashion, when they are compelled by necessity to satisfy some immediate need."). In response to this, the two sociologists say "[i]f only we were guilty of taking his words out of context" and add that their "feelings about his sexism, European elitism, and other problematic assumptions in his work are not benign." Harriford and Thompson, Ibid., 160. See also Randall Collins, "The Durkheimian Tradition in Conflict Sociology," in *Durkheimian Sociology: Cultural Studies*, ed. Jeffrey Alexander (NY: Cambridge University Press, 1988), 107. He explains:

Durkheim is regarded as a conservative defender of the status quo by the Left, as an arch-functionalist by the anti-functionalists, as a naïve unilinear evolutionist by the historicists. The subjectivistic sociologies tend to see in Durkheim, if not always a materialist, at least a social reductionist of a disturbingly deterministic sort. For the humanists, Durkheim is the anti-Christ: for the micro-sociologists, Durkheim is the most reified of the macro. Ibid.

206. Despite the criticism of Durkheim, all sorts of scholars keep returning to him and relying on his theories. See Lukes, Ibid., ix (noting that "[i]nterest in the Durkheimians has . . . grown apace," that "Durkheimian studies are plainly alive and well," and that "[a]ll this activity and the high level of recent scholarship," justified a reissue of his book). See also Harriford and Thompson, Ibid., 225 n. 10 ("We agree with Steven Lukes that Durkheim's work offers a wealth of ideas worth grappling with, both to refine and redefine."). They ponder the causes of the 1999 murders in Littleton, Colorado and ask "why two students, Dylan Klebold and Eric Harris, came to school with guns and wearing overcoats and then shot their classmates and a teacher, killing thirteen and injuring twenty-three more before killing themselves." Ibid., 156–57. They admit that they "return to Durkheim's work, flaws and all" for answers. Ibid., 160. Thus they "painstakingly reread his scholarship, begrudgingly acknowledging that his focus on the necessary ingredients for social order—for the moral and spiritual quality of life in modern society—was exactly the question [they] were still struggling with." Ibid.

207. With respect to Tonnies, Lukes explains that for Durkheim "such a social and political system, a form of State-regulated capitalism, which was Tonnies's version of socialism, could not endure" and was instead "the prelude to final dissolution." Lukes, Ibid., 144. He adds that Durkheim's case against Tonnies was "his theory of *Gesellschaft*, which accounted for social solidarity in terms of a temporary and artificial mechanism." Ibid., 146. In Durkheim's book, *The Division of Labor in Society*, he sought to "develop an explanation of social solidarity in industrial or organized societies that was consistent with his objections to Comte, Spencer and Tonnie. Ibid., 146–47. In contrasting Durkheim's approach to the sociology of religion with that of Max Weber, Lukes explains that Weber "explicitly ignores ethnographic data and addresses . . . the great world religions, focusing on the most complex of them, Christianity," while Durkheim believes that what was more instructive was the study of a very simple religion and chose a close study of totemism for development of

a 'hypothesis' about religion's essence, its elements, its causes, and its functions." Ibid., 457–58.

208. Emile Durkheim, *The Rules of Sociological Method*, Ibid., 21. According to Lukes, Durkheim "intended this only as a 'preliminary definition' " and "did not mean it as an intuitive existentialist definition, summing up all the features of the social fact, but simply as a sign by which to recognize sociological phenomenon." Lukes, Ibid., 11.

209. Durkheim, *The Rules of Sociological Method*, Ibid., 22.

210. Durkheim states:

> Not only are . . . types of behavior and thinking external to the individual, but they are endured with a compelling and coercive power by virtue of which, whether he wishes it or not, they impose themselves upon him. Undoubtedly when I conform to them of my own free will, the coercion is not felt or felt hardly at all, since it is unnecessary. None the less it is intrinsically a characteristic of these facts; the proof of this is that it asserts itself as soon as I try to resist. If I attempt to violate the rules of law they react against me so as to forestall my action, if there is still time. Alternatively, they annul it or make my action conform to the norm if it is already accomplished but capable of being reversed; or they cause me to pay the penalty for it if it is irreparable.

Ibid., 21.

211. Harriford and Thompson, Ibid., 159 (discussing Durkheim's concept of "social facts"). They explain how this is of great value to them in their own teaching:

> Myths, suicide, patriarchy, languages, the division of labor, and racism are all examples of social facts. The concept "social fact" had, over the years, come in handy for us when we taught about how patriarchy seeps into the veins of all people—not even feminists are immune; that racism is a force that, like smog, infects all of us, regardless of who is breathing the air. Like electricity, a social fact may seem invisible, but its consequences are as real as electricity's power. The underlying moral values of a society, and the mechanisms used to enforce these morals have real consequences. Attempts to resist these social facts are a sure sign of their power.

Ibid.

212. For a discussion and critique of relying on statistics and official suicide rates in research, see Taylor, Ibid., 43–122. See Elsa A. Whalley, "Values and Value Conflict in Self-Destruction: Implications in the Work of C.W. Morris," in *Essays in Self-Destruction*, Ibid., 91. Whalley comments on the work of Louis I. Dublin, who "examined the 1959 and 1960 international suicide rates to see if Durkheim's hypothesis regarding the effectiveness of religion as an antisuicidal agent still holds" and points out that Dublin "found that it does hold up very well." Whalley, Ibid., 99. See generally Louis I. Dublin, *Suicide: A Sociological and Statistical Study* (NY: The Ronald Press Co., 1963), 19–20, 74–79, and 211.

213. See Harriford and Thompson, Ibid., 162 (pointing out that "Durkheim reasoned that the best way to understand social cohesion in society was to study its opposite" and calling that "one of the truly ironic moves in the history of sociology"). Lukes, Ibid., 191–95 (considering why Durkheim turned to the study of suicide). He

suggests that the suicide of a close friend at the École, Victor Hommay, may have influenced this treatise. Ibid., 191. There were five other reasons: first, suicide "came to be regarded in the nineteenth century as a growing social problem requiring explanation"; second, "it was a subject which seemed concrete and specific"; third, "it offered an excellent opportunity for demonstrating the principles set out in *The Rules of Sociological Method*"; fourth, "since the essence of Durkheim's diagnosis of the ills of his own society was an analysis of the differential strength and impact of those forces," studying suicide gave him a way of examining causes and allowed him to suggest remedies"; fifth, "suicide was peculiarly well suited to the task of establishing Durkheim's claims for sociology" because "it was, on the face of it, the most private of acts" and "offered the clearest case of the dissolution of . . . bonds" which unite human beings. Lukes, Ibid., 191–94.

214. Durkheim elaborates on the Jews: "[t]he aptitude of Jews for suicide is always less than that of Protestants; in a very general way it is also, though to a lesser degree, lower than that of Catholics." Durkheim, *Suicide*, Ibid., 155. He says that Jews "very rarely exceed the rate for Catholics" and "it must be remembered that Jews live more exclusively than other confessional groups in cities and are in intellectual occupations." Ibid. He also explains that "if the Jew manages to be both well instructed and very disinclined to suicide, it is because of the special origin of his desire for knowledge" and adds, "[i]t is a general law that religious minorities, in order to protect themselves better against the hate to which they are exposed or merely through a sort of emulation, try to surpass in knowledge the populations surrounding them." Ibid., 167.

215. Summarizing the criticisms of Durkheim's *Suicide*, Lukes lists five complaints. One, with respect to Durkheim's "characterization of the adverse social conditions," he "saw them entirely in terms of the relative absence or excessive influence of social goals and rules" and "never saw the importance . . . of discriminating between different types of goals and rules." Lukes, Ibid., 217. Second, with respect to "identifying psychological or moral health," Durkheim "appears . . . to have ignored the difficulties in postulating a non-relative standard of psychological health, while failing to explore those of postulating a relative standard." Ibid., 218. Third, with respect to individuals, "Durkheim's account of why certain individuals are suicide-prone is indecisive." Ibid., 219. Fourth, with respect to Durkheim's assumption that "suicide is the ultimate most extreme response to socially-induced psychological disequilibrium," it is "questionable on the grounds that [suicide] or types of it result from other causes and are explicable in other ways—in particular that it may be an entirely rational response to certain situations." Ibid., 219–20. Fifth, with respect to Durkheim's theory of suicide as a whole, it is "incomplete" because "explaining suicide—and explaining suicide rates—must involve explaining why people commit it" and thus, "Durkheim failed to see that both particular (objective) circumstances and men's subjective perceptions, beliefs, attitudes and motives are all eminently amenable to sociological inquiry and explanation." Ibid., 220–22.

216. Taylor, Ibid., 17.

217. Ibid., 18.

218. Ibid.

219. Lukes explains that "Durkheim sought to proclaim sociology an independent science" and "thought it necessary to declare it independent of psychology." Lukes, Ibid., 16. While insisting that psychology and sociology are distinct, he "conceded that collective and individual forces" are related and that the individual can help to explain the collective. Ibid., 19. Lukes explains that "Durkheim's theory of suicide therefore amounts to this: that under adverse social conditions, when men's social context fails to provide them with the requisite sources of attachment and/or regulation at the appropriate level of intensity, then their psychological or moral health is impaired, and a certain number of vulnerable, suicide-prone individuals respond by committing suicide." Ibid., 217. In *Suicide*, Durkheim explains that "no psychopathic state bears a regular and indisputable relation to suicide" and a "society does not depend for its number of suicides on having more or fewer neuropaths or alcoholics." Durkheim, Ibid., 81. He adds, however, that "the different forms of degeneration are an eminently suitable psychological field for the action of the causes which may lead a man to suicide" and "the degenerate is more apt to commit suicide than the well man." Ibid.

220. Morrissey, Ibid., 202–3 (explaining that "when it was translated into Russian, it would enjoy great prestige" but "[i]nitially . . . doctors read Durkheim through the visor of their own concerns, simply citing his study alongside many others").

221. Ibid., 203. She adds that the critics "rejected [Durkheim's] therapeutics as wholly inadequate" and that "[h]is references to the potentially integrating function of the social division of labor must have seemed alien to many Russian readers, especially in this period of rapid industrialization, urbanization, and growing social ferment." Ibid.

222. Ibid. Morrissey states that "in the years following the revolution of 1905,. . . Durkheim's voice would merge into the broader debate about the threats of degeneration to Russia's modernity." Ibid., 204.

223. Ibid., 77, 104

224. Paperno, Ibid., 3.

225. See generally Harriet Murav, *Russia's Legal Fictions* (MI: The University of Michigan Press, 1955), 55 ("The legal reform . . . initiated by the government of Alexander II transformed the trial from a secret written proceeding based on the 'inquisitorial' principle into an open, public, oral proceeding organized to a far greater degree by the adversarial principle."); Ronner, *Dostoevsky and the Law*, Ibid., 44–55 (discussing how the legal reforms in 1864 had a profound effect on Dostoevsky's work); Gary Rosenshield, *Western Law, Russian Justice: Dostoevsky, The Jury Trial, and The Law* (WI: University of Wisconsin Press, 2005), 20 ("As a result of the 1864 reforms, jury trials were opened to the public ('*glasnost*') [and t]he judicial system attained autonomy."). Rosenshield explains that "[j]uries became most representative of all Russian institutions, with jurors recruited from all sectors of the population" and that "[a]n independent judiciary became well established . . . and more lawyers became trained and rose to distinction." Ibid. See also Louise McReynolds, *Murder Most Russian: True Crime and Punishment in Late Imperial Russia* (NY: Cornell University Press, 2013), 29–32 (discussing reforms in the Russian legal system);

Richard Wortman, "The Great Reforms and The New Courts," in *Dostoevsky in Context*, eds. Deborah A. Martinsen and Olga Maiorova (UK: Cambridge University Press, 2015), 13–21.

226. Morrissey, Ibid., 208.

227. Ibid.

228. Paperno, Ibid., 3. See also Morrissey, Ibid., 208 (explaining how after the judicial reforms, "suicide became highly controversial, as voices from the judiciary, medicine, and the church all combined into a discordant chorus of debate").

229. See generally Alvarez, Ibid., 99 (explaining that there has been a shift in "tone" with respect to suicide that has taken place in "the last eighty odd years" and attributing it to Durkheim's "classic" *Suicide*). Alvarez explains that "suicide while remaining humanly shocking, has at the same time become respectable" and as the subject of intensive scientific research" Ibid. After Durkheim, "the question was no longer the morality of the act but the social conditions which produce such despair." Ibid.

230. Durkheim explains: "[t]he more weakened the groups to which he belongs, the less he depends on them, the more he consequently depends only on himself and recognizes no other rules of conduct than what are founded on his private interests." Durkheim, *Suicide*, Ibid., 209. He adds, "[i]f we agree to call this state egoism, in which the individual ego asserts itself to excess in the face of the social ego and at its expense, we may call egoistic the special type of suicide springing from excessive individualism." Ibid. A. Alvarez, explaining "egoistic suicide," which occurs when the individual is not properly integrated into society but is, instead, thrown on to his own resources," points to Protestantism, "with its emphasis on free will," the "rise of science, which undercut the simple belief in the origin and structure of a natural world presided over by a more or less benevolent and omniscient God," and "the old pattern of family life—grandparents, parents and children all living intensely together under one roof,"—which "protected each member from his impulses to self-destruction." Alvarez, Ibid., 113. The two feminist, sociologists, applying egoistic suicide to Dylan Klebold and Eric Harris of the 1999 murders in Littleton, Colorado, state that their suicides "exemplify" egoistic suicide, the "form of suicide [that] reflects a prolonged sense of not belonging, of not being integrated into a community, an experience of not having a tether" and that they "manifested those states, both expressing a lack of connection or sense of belonging at school and at home." Herreford and Thompson, Ibid., 165. See also Lukes, Ibid., 206 (Durkheim "saw suicide as the individual antithesis of social solidarity, and a high suicide rate as an index of the inadequate effectiveness of social bonds."); Andrew Solomon, *The Noonday Demon: An Atlas of Depression* (NY: Scribner, 2001), 249 (Durkheim's [e]goistic suicide is committed by people who are inadequately integrated into the society they inhabit" and "[a]pathy and indifference motivate them to sever permanently their relationship to the world.").

231. Durkheim explains: "[h]aving given the name of *egoism* to the state of the ego living its own life and obeying itself alone, that of *altruism* adequately expresses the opposite state, where the ego is not its own property, where it is blended with something not itself, where the goal of conduct is exterior to itself, that is in one of the groups in which it participates." Durkheim, *Suicide*, Ibid., 221. He adds that this

suicide is called "*altruistic suicide*" because it is "caused by intense altruism," and "since it is also characteristically performed as a duty, "we call such a type *obligatory altruistic suicide*." Ibid. See Herreford and Thompson, Ibid., 166 (suggesting that Dylan Klebold and Eric Harris of the 1999 murders in Littleton, Colorado were examples of the altruistic suicide, which is "sometimes seen in the military—a highly regimented and hierarchical institution based on groupthink and acceptance of authority" and that the "two young men were enacting what the military teaches by carefully and methodically planning mass destruction").

232. In his discussion of "anomic suicide, Durkheim concludes that "economic distress does not have the aggravating influence often attributed to it" and that "it tends rather to produce the opposite effect" (SU, Bk 2, Ch 5; 245). He elaborates:

> If therefore industrial or financial crisis increase suicides, this is not because they cause poverty, since crises of prosperity have the same result; it is because they are crises, that is disturbances of the collective order. Every disturbance of equilibrium, even though it achieves greater comfort and a heightening of general vitality, is an impulse to voluntary death. Whenever serious readjustments take place in the social order, whether or not due to a sudden growth or to an unexpected catastrophe, men are more inclined to self-destruction.

Durkheim, *Suicide*, Ibid., 246. See Harriford and Thompson, who posit that Dylan Klebod and Eric Harris of the 1999 murders in Littleton, Colorado are classic examples of Durkheimian anomic suicide: "[i]t is hard to think of an example of a suicide that more fits Durkheim's description of anomic suicide than that of these two teenagers, [who] . . . were making up the rules as they went along in a world that that must have seemed both strangely boring and confusing." Ibid., 164. In a brilliant application of Durkheim's concept to today's world, Harriford and Thompson state:

> Both Dylan and Eric were facing uncertain futures economically at a time in US history when younger generations are less, rather than more, likely to do as well as their parents financially, when outsourcing and a postindustrial economy make economic security an unknown quantity for an increasing number of people. Chances are that both of them knew that living in the style they had been accustomed to was no longer their birthright.

Ibid., 163.

233. Speaking of the "children of the twentieth century" in Russia, Morrissey states that "[c]ritiques of the state's role in the economy were quite common in this period, but their use as an explanatory paradigm for suicide reflected as well a newly prominent Durkheimian view of the social body." Morrissey, Ibid., 318.

234. With respect to fatalistic suicides, Durkheim describes it as "a type of suicide the opposite of anomic suicide, just as egoistic and altruistic suicides are opposites" and is "a suicide deriving from excessive regulation, that of persons with futures pitilessly blocked and passions violently choked by oppressive discipline." Durkheim, *Suicide*, Ibid., 276 no. 2). With respect to Dylan Klebold and Eric Harris of the 1999 murders in Littleton, Colorado, the sociologists point out that "[t]he fourth type of suicide that Durkheim identified, fatalistic suicide, describes yet another set of

stresses that Eric and Dylan lived with." Hereford and Thompson, Ibid., 167. They elaborate:

> The military was so much a part of their lives—central to the town's economy, a key profession, at the center of sites they frequented on the Internet, a symbol of manhood—that there was no space outside of that institution. We know from the testimony of people who have left cults broken away from domestic abuse, and escaped slavery that release from what sociologist Erving Goffman identified as a 'total institution' does not mean the end of the trauma. Being outside of a force that is all-encompassing can be experienced as still being in it—and experienced for a long time after.

Ibid., 166 (quoting Erving Goffman, *Asylums: Essays on the Social Situation of Mental Patients and Other Inmates* [NY: Doubleday, 1961], 4). Hereford and Thompson suggest that "each of these suicides—anomic, egoistic, altruistic, and fatalistic,—and the stresses that relate to them (alienation, normlessness, ultraconformity, and stultifying regulation) . . . [are] synergistic in their effect" and that "the combination of stresses when experienced together help explain the enormity of the boys' rage, the extent of their violence." Ibid., 167.

235. Durkheim states that certain statistics "do indeed prove that prisoners are in general unusually disposed to suicide" and that "imprisonment by itself develops a very strong tendency to suicide," which he attributes in part to "cell life." Durkheim, *Suicide*, Ibid., 345–46 no. 44. See also David Lester and Bruce L. Danto, *Suicide Behind Bars: Prediction and Prevention* (PA: The Charles Press, 1993). They discuss Durkheim's theory of suicide and point out that "it may be that prisons constitute a deviant type of society where social regulation may be unduly high" and [t]hus, some prison suicides may be fatalistic in nature." Lester and Danto, Ibid., 14.

236. For example, Durkheim explains that "egoism and altruism themselves, contraries as they are, may combine their influence" so that these individuals "live a twofold, contradictory existence: individualists so far as the real world is concerned, they are immoderate altruists in everything that concerns this ideal objective" and that "[b]oth dispositions lead to suicide." Durkheim, *Suicide*, 289. See also Lukes, Ibid., 213 (explaining that Durkheim acknowledged the existence of " 'mixed types' of suicide, resulting from converging social causes—egoistic-anomic . . . , anomic-altruistic and (oddly enough egoistic-altruistic, with correspondingly mixed individual symptoms").

237. See Donald A. Nielsen, "Dostoevsky in the Mirror of Durkheim," in *Durkheim: The Durkheimians and the Arts*, eds. Alexander Riley, W. S. F. Pickering, and William Watts Miller (NY: Berghahn Books, 2013), 95–118.

238. Ibid., 114.

239. Ibid., 96. Nielsen asserts that "[d]espite their differing intellectual and personal trajectories, Durkheim and Dostoevsky have much in common [and that] they were each fascinated by the role of religion in the social order, and the balance between the competing demands of the individual and society." Ibid.

Chapter 2

Fatalistic Convulsions in *Notes from the House of the Dead*

INTRODUCTION

At age twenty-seven, Dostoevsky, already a known author, was sentenced to death "for [his] participation in criminal plans, for the circulation of a private letter containing rash statements against the Orthodox church and the highest authorities, and for the attempt to distribute subversive works with the aid of a lithograph."[1] Dostoevsky was in the second group and officials paraded them into a public square, but before discharging their fatal shots, the soldiers received a halt command.[2] By order of Nicholas I, the Russian novelist and fellow prisoners were spared and their death sentences were commuted to four years of hard labor and exile in Siberia.

Dostoevsky, in poor health, served his full sentence in Omsk Fortress and some commentators conjecture that while in prison, he experienced his first seizure of the epilepsy that would plague him throughout his life.[3] Imprisonment, moreover, affected him in a salutary way: it helped to foster his insights into people who offend not just against others but also against themselves. The ordeal, moreover, enriched his artistry and gave him a Durkheimian perspective that would evolve in later fiction. In prison, Dostoevsky began to intuit that when human beings are at their apex, they live collectively cohered, and that there is no veritable distinction between homicide and self-homicide.

THE SUICIDE INCUBATOR

When Dostoevsky entered prison at Omsk in Western Siberia to begin his term of penal servitude, he felt like he was being buried alive. In a letter to his brother Andrey, Dostoevsky elaborates on his impression of this time:

> And those 4 years, I consider a time during which I was buried alive and locked up in a coffin. I can't even tell you, my friend, what a horrible time that was. It was inexpressible, unending suffering, because every hour, every minute weighed on my soul like a stone.[4]

It was not just physical discomfort that vexed Dostoevsky: what compounded his agony were the rules and regulations that dictated every aspect of day and night.[5] These forbade the possession of books (except for the Bible) and imposed the most severe prohibition on the Russian novelist: he was barred from writing.[6] Despite being divested of his *raison d'etre*, Dostoevsky conceived of the *Notes from the House of the Dead* while in prison.[7] Apparently, during a hospital stay, Dr. Troitsky let Dostoevsky keep a notebook and his notes, mingled with memories, were later combined in his semiautobiographical masterpiece.[8] Possibly to dodge the censor or because Dostoevsky had difficulty processing his own traumatic past by writing the novel in the first person, he created a fictitious narrator, Aleksandr Petrovich Goryanchikov, a nobleman, who had killed his wife out of jealousy.[9] In *Dead House*, readers experience Goryanchikov's incarceration alongside excessively regulated beings locked away in what Emile Durkheim would denominate the virtual suicide incubator.[10]

Preexisting Lethality

In Dead House, the men are stripped of free will and "seem to grow more and more gloomy and melancholy" with "anguish . . . eating [them] up" (Pt 2, Ch 8; 288). The nocturnal howls speak for themselves: "[n]early all the convicts talk and rave in their sleep at night. . . 'We're beaten men,' they'd say . . . 'Our guts have been beaten out of us; that's why we scream at night' " (Pt 1, Ch 1; 17). Such "howls" and the horrors that precipitate them occur in regulated secrecy, inside an "irregular hexagon," guarded by detested, mistrusted officials, who abuse and lie to their captives (Pt 1, Ch 1; 8). As discussed later, while a few prisoners indulge their impulse to self-destruct within prison walls, Goryanchikov reveals that even prior to their sentence quite a few already had abundant lethality.

Emile Durkheim elastically defines suicide as "*all cases of death resulting directly or indirectly from a positive or negative act of the victim himself, which he knows will produce this result*" and a suicide attempt as "an act thus defined but falling short of actual death."[11] Some Durkheim disciples, like Maurice Halbwachs, have posited that the social and psychopathological explanations of suicide are not necessarily antithetical, but are actually complementary.[12] Also, Durkheim does not shun those psychoanalysts who believe that everyone has a variable suicide potential.[13]

In *Suicide*, Durkheim classifies "according to their essential characteristics" suicides committed by those whom specialists have labeled "insane" (SU, Bk 1, Ch 1; 62). One such classification is "[i]mpulsive or automatic suicide," which Durkheim describes:

> It is as unmotivated as the preceding; it has no cause either in reality or the patient's imagination. Only, instead of being produced by a fixed idea, obsessing the mind for a shorter or longer period and only gradually affecting the will, it results from an abrupt and immediately irresistible impulse. In the twinkling of an eye it appears in full force and excites the act, or at least its beginning (SU, Bk 1, Ch 1; 65)

What Durkheim calls an "abrupt and immediately irresistible impulse," resembles Karl A. Menninger's concept of criminality as a genus of "chronic" suicide, which tends to manifest as an unrestrained aggressive outburst.[14] Menninger states that some individuals whom some psychiatrists label psychopathic personalities are "out-and-out criminals" who "always fail" or "are, so to speak, always successful in failing" and elaborates: "[i]f . . . they pursue the career of crime, their crimes are stupidly executed, they seem to rush to be arrested rather than escape it, they frequently do everything possible to obstruct . . . their defense and seem in short to invite punishment."[15]

For Isaac Ray, some homicidal criminals who seek to fail are at times afflicted with "religious monomania," where "it is not uncommon for the [individuals] to believe that the joys of heaven are in store for [them] and under the excitement of this insane idea, to murder a fellow-creature in order that he may the sooner enter on their fruition."[16] What can bolster this delusional quest for heaven by proxy is the criminals' adherence to the notion that suicide is an unpardonable sin that cannot lead to "eternal happiness," but that murder, even in its most horrific form, "can be repented of" prior to the moment of execution.[17]

In Dostoevsky's novel, it is clear that before Siberia, the "abrupt and immediately irresistible impulse" that Durkheim describes, what Menninger brands as "stupidly executed" crimes, and Ray attributes to a religious monomaniacal lust for instant attainment of heaven, had already flared up for a bunch of inmates. Not infrequently, it was that sudden debouchment that became the ticket to the very prison that in turn helped them consummate self-annihilation. The *Dead House* narrator, pondering those crimes "among common people," marvels at how "a peasant, a domestic serf, a tradesman or a soldier," who has lived his life "quietly and peacefully," will out of the blue "suddenly" burst forth with a "strange" act:

> Suddenly something snaps in him; he can't take it anymore, and he sticks a knife into his enemy and oppressor. Here's where something strange begins to happen: suddenly the man runs temporarily amuck. The first man he killed was his oppressor, his enemy; that was a criminal act, but it was understandable; there was a motive. But then he starts killing people who aren't his enemies: he kills anyone who crosses his path, he kills for amusement, because of an insulting word, because of a look, for a string of beads, or simply "Get out of the way! Don't let me catch you! Here I come!" It's as if this man is drunk, it's as if he's in a state of delirium. (Pt 1, Ch 8; 111)

While the offender often purports to have a justification for this snap, he is at least unconsciously aware of the fact that he is jockeying for prison quietus. Durkheim similarly opines that "suicide sometimes coexists with homicide" or that some types of suicide "have a certain kinship with homicide" (SU, Bk 3, Ch 2; 355).[18] Goryanchikov confirms this when he sketches the self-exterminating cycle, which begins with an "understandable" motive (like eradication of an enemy) and escalates to an unleashed, irrational slaughter-rampage where the culprit "begins to revel in the fact that there's nothing sacred for him anymore. . . and to enjoy the most unbridled and unlimited freedom" (Pt 1, Ch 8; 111–12). In the throes of this rampage, the offender "knows . . . that a dreadful punishment awaits him," and it is that foreboding that Goryanchikov ties to the deeply interred suicidal urge. As he puts it, " [a]ll this perhaps resembles the sensation experienced by a man who stands on a high tower and feels the pull of the depths below his feet until, finally, he would be glad to throw himself downwards head first: oh, to do it quickly and put an end to it all!" (Pt 1, Ch 8; 112). Goryanchikov supplies flesh-and-blood corroboration: there is Luka Kuzmich, the Ukrainian house serf, who "for no other reason than his own amusement, had 'taken out' a certain major" (Pt 1, Ch 8; 113). There is another who "had been fond of slicing up little children, solely because of the pleasure it gave him: he'd lure a child to some convenient place; first he'd terrify the child, torture him, and then, after having fully enjoyed the terror and trembling of the poor little victim, he'd slice him up quietly, slowly, with enjoyment" (Pt 1, Ch 3; 50). There is also the "brigand" who precipitously "sliced up a five-year-old boy" after "he had first tricked him with a toy and then led him somewhere into an empty shed and sliced him up there" (Pt 1, Ch 1; 12).

Luka Kuzmich and those guilty of infanticide are not *sui generis*, but rather are similar to others, like Petrov, Akim Akimych, Sirotkin, Dutov, Baklushin, and Shishkov, all of whom court their own deaths through homicide. Incidentally, quite a few of these characters start with careers in the army and according to Durkheim, the barracks tend to awaken suicidal propensities and even breed such epidemics.[19]

Petrov, who is reputedly "fearless," has "sudden outbursts, when this man's nature reveal[s] itself fully all at once" (Pt 1, Ch 7; 106). Before prison, this fit flared up when his colonel had "struck him during drill" (Pt 1, Ch 7; 106). Although Petrov had probably "been hit many times before this," he, lashing out unexpectedly, "killed his colonel with a knife, and he did it openly, in broad daylight, in front of the assembled soldiers," an act which predictably puts him in Dead House and ripens him for a possible reoccurrence (Pt 1, Ch 7; 106).

Akim Akimych's pre-prison saga is not so different from Petrov's. While serving as lieutenant in the Caucasus, Akim confronted the chieftain of a neighboring tribe, who had set fire to and attacked his fortress. After Akim invited that chieftain "for a friendly visit," he shot him (Pt 1, Ch 2; 31). Akim did this, all the time cognizant of ramifications: he was "fully aware that he had acted incorrectly[,] . . . had known this even before he had the princeling shot, and . . . had known that a peaceful chieftain should be tried according to the law" (Pt 1, Ch 2; 31). In fact, he accelerated inevitability by immediately "giving a full account of the incident to his superiors" (Pt 1, Ch 2; 31). Through this killing, Akim sparked events that could have potentially buried him: in fact, he initially did face execution, but after his sentence was commuted, he was dumped into Dead House.

The "[q]uiet and meek" Sirotkin, who found army service unbearable, went from an overt suicide attempt to murder: first, he stuck "the muzzle of [his] musket against [his] chest, leaned on it, and pulled the trigger with [his] big toe" (Pt 1, Ch 3; 47–49). After the rifle misfired and he bootlessly tried it a second time, he devised a backup self-sabotage plan while thinking, "let them send me wherever they like as long as I get the hell out of this neckrootership!" (Pt 1, Ch 3; 49). Sirotkin then "leveled the musket like in the drill and stuck the bayonet into [his commanding officer] up to the muzzle," an act which he knew would secure him a place in Dead House's "special section," which in turn meant that sooner or later he would perish in captivity (Pt 1, Ch 3; 49).

Soldier Dutov was at first released from prison, but after tasting freedom for a few weeks, he too ignited a sequence that went from bad to worse. It all began when he suddenly stole something, which earned him a "severe punishment" (Pt 1, Ch 4; 56). But before punishment, with at least an unconscious resolve to enhance his own difficulties, Dutov "rushed with a knife at the officer of the guard who had entered the room where the prisoners were kept" (Pt 1, Ch 4; 56). While Dutov told himself that this was a sensible way to postpone that "terrible moment of punishment," he understood "very well that by such an act he'd immeasurably increase his sentence and the term of his penal servitude" and thus, would inch him closer to the potential consummation of his own demise (Pt 1, Ch 4; 56).

Baklushin, "the pioneer" who was "full of fire and life," has an analogously disintegrative narrative (Pt 1, Ch 9; 127–28). At the height of his career, he served in St. Petersburg, but after having "gotten into some trouble," he was demoted to "non-commissioned officer" and transported to a "garrison battalion in Riga," the situs from which he was sent to Siberia (Pt 1, Ch 9; 128). While Baklushin euphemizes his malefaction as "falling in love," it turns out that he murdered a German for conniving to steal his paramour (Pt 1, Ch 9; 128). Because of this betrayal, Baklushin "was possessed by such rage that [he] couldn't control [himself]" and marched off to his enemy's shop with a pistol in his pocket (Pt 1, Ch 9; 130). Upon arrival, his "rage overcame [him]" and after hurling insults, Baklushin threatened to shoot the "sausage-maker" (Pt 1, Ch 9; 131). The German declared that "dat is strictly forbidden you, and you be strictly punished for dat" and dared him to go ahead (Pt 1, Ch 9; 132). In a scene reminiscent of Russian roulette, the German, another death-seeker, persists in taunting his assailant—"you absolutely don't dare do dat to me" (Pt 1, Ch 9; 132). According to Baklushin, this riled him up so much that he "blasted him" and marched out (Pt 1, Ch 9; 132).

Predictably, in about two weeks, Baklushin was arrested and faced ten or possibly twelve years under civil law. But once again, Baklushin was not able to leave well enough alone and had another precipitous loss of control. He vented rage at the captain in attendance at his trial by verbally abusing him in earshot of the judge. This tantrum resulted in a new trial and Baklushin got not only 4,000 flogs but also landed himself in Dead House's lethal "special section" (Pt 1, Ch 9; 133).

There is also the pre-prison saga of Shishkov, "a shallow, mercurial fellow," who married Akulka Kudimovna, which embrangled him in a relentless hate-love obsession (Pt 2, Ch 4; 219). Shishkov persisted in habitually beating his wife, sometimes from morning to night and sometimes just to quell his boredom. One day, a frenzied Shishkov "grabbed" Akulka by her hair, "squeezed her between [his] knees from behind, and then . . . took out [his] knife, bent her head back and slid the knife across her throat" (Pt 2, Ch 4; 227). Then after embracing her and "screaming over her, screaming and wailing," he dashed home and "hid in the bathhouse" (Pt 2, Ch 4; 227–28). As was the foregone conclusion, when Akulka's corpse was discovered, they searched, found, and imprisoned Shiskov in Dead House.

Like a Matryosha doll, an additional suicide nests in the belly of Shiskov's self-eviscerating narrative and it is that of Akulka herself. Durkheim's definition of suicide as "*all cases of death resulting directly or indirectly from a positive or negative act of the victim himself, which he knows will produce this result*," applies to Akulka's own pursuit of finality by proxy (SU, Intro.; 44).[20] It ties into Durkheim's "embryonic suicide," in which people jeopardize their own lives (SU, Intro., 45–46). It likewise has affinity with Freud's concept of "half-intentional self-destruction," with what Menninger deems "covert human self-destruction," and with Edwin S. Shneidman's "subintentioned deaths" whereby individuals, "act[ing] inimically to their own best welfare" seek to "shorten or truncate life."[21]

Susan K. Morrissey points out that in Russia, "[s]cattered sources . . . indicate a relationship between suicide and domestic violence," where "women were often driven to suicide by their abusive husbands."[22] Akulka, the proverbial whipping post, knew full well of her husband's jealous and violent nature. She thus committed the consummate act of accelerating her own cessation by informing Shiskov that she loves another man "more than anything else in the world!" (Pt 2, Ch 4; 227). Like Nastasya Filippovna of *The Idiot*, whose drive to self-annihilate compels her to claim her final, "perfectly motionless slumber" at the murderous hands of Rogozhin, Akulka essentially signed her own death warrant.[23] Shishkov produced the anticipated closure by issuing the death sentence: "Akulina . . .[y]our end has come" (Pt 2, Ch 4; 227). After leading his prey into the forest for slaughter, he ordered Akulka to say her prayers. While "subintentioned" Akulka attained her objective, Shishkov is still chasing his last muster within prison walls by "pok[ing] his nose into other people's business, . . . gossiping, get[ting] worked up over trifles, and flit[ing] from one barracks to another, carrying the latest news, spreading slanderous rumors about people, and losing control of himself" (Pt 2, Ch 4; 219).[24] When other convicts beat him, Shishkov, feeling that his punishment is earned, would post-coitally "lapse into silence again" (Pt 2, Ch 4; 219).

While prisoners, like Luka Kuzmich, Petrov, Akim Akimych, Sirotkin, Dutov, Baklushin, and Shishkov had self-destructive leanings pre-incarceration, prison conditions effectually aggravate them and prod them to re-self-offend in what Dostoevsky portrays as, and what Durkheim sees as attempted "fatalistic" pre-suicidal acts.[25]

Regulation, Coercion, and Futility

In *Dead House*, inmates are systematically stripped of free will, a process that Dostoevsky anatomizes into three modules: excessive regulation, coercion, and futility. Through Goryanchikov, Dostoevsky depicts the physical plant, which serves as the objective correlative of the horror housed within:

> Imagine a large courtyard, two hundred paces long and a hundred and fifty paces wide completely enclosed by a high stockade in the form of an irregular hexagon, that is, by a fence of tall posts vertically thrust deep into the ground, wedged firmly together, reinforced by transverse planks, and sharpened at the top: this was the outer enclosure of the prison. In one side of the enclosure was a sturdy gate, which was always locked, and always guarded, day and night, by sentries; it was opened as required, to let the convicts out to work. (Pt 1, Ch 1; 8)

With its courtyards, enclosures, stockades, pales, cross-planks, gates, guards, and sentries, the prison, governed by "its own peculiar laws, its own dress, its own mores and customs," contrasts with "the radiant free world where people lived like everybody else" (Pt 1, Ch 1; 8). Dostoevsky's narrator, moreover, clarifies that it is not just the façade that makes this the "house of the living dead" (Pt 1, Ch 1; 8). Rather, internecine forces conspire to pulverize the human spirit.

Such oppressors exceed what Goryanchikov downplays as mere "discomforts," like "the filthy surroundings, the restraints, . . . the meager and disgusting food" and "cabbage soup with cockroaches floating in it" (Pt 2, Ch 7; 263).[26] There exist external restraints, like the shackles that thwart mobility. Affixed upon arrival, shackles are "regarded as something natural and unalterable" and "after a few years of wearing [them], a man's legs begin to wither away" (Pt 2, Ch 1; 182).[27] Each convict has to purchase accessory straps, which were vital, because without them, it was impossible to walk: "the iron keeps hitting the leg and rubbing against it, and without the under-shackle straps it wouldn't take more than a day for a convict to get sores on his legs" (Pt 1, Ch 9; 124). Oddly, Siberian shackles are vestigial and do nothing to prevent escape; they are secured as a "public shaming, a physical and moral burden" (Pt 2, Ch 1; 183). Even those inmates, apoplectic, with spindly legs, who lay dying in the hospital, stay shackled until officials excise the bonds from their naked corpses.[28] While these implements maul flesh, they gouge deep into the core to activate dormant suicidal propensities. There are also prisoners, treated like animals, who are "chained to the wall," who actually craved what they saw as a promotion—namely, mere shackled status (Pt 1, Ch 7; 100).

The prison is the domain of copious regulation and according to Goryanchikov, the real "enclosure" with a "sturdy gate" is the fact that "no one dared to rebel against the self-imposed rules and accepted customs of the prison: everyone submitted to them" (Pt 1, Ch 1; 8, 13). Here "[s]earches [are] frequent, unexpected and no joking matter," and "punishments [are] severe" (Pt 1, Ch 2; 35). Restrictions seemingly tame the population, including the most vicious, violent, and unruly:

> There were some exceptionally strong characters who found it extremely hard to submit. But still they submitted. There were men who had been totally reckless and overstepped all bounds when they were free, so that in the end it was as if it was not they who had committed their crimes; it was as if they had committed them not knowing why, in a state of delirium or intoxication, or often out of a vanity excited to the highest degree. But in our prison they were immediately put in their places, in spite of the fact that some of them, before they came here, had been the terror of whole villages and towns. (Pt 1, Ch 1; 12)

The narrator, however, does not equate submission with repentance or spiritual growth: the doomed "gather together . . . against their will," working under the "threat of the stick," without "the slightest trace of shame or repentance" without ever acknowledging their own lawlessness (Pt 1, Ch 1, 13–14). Goryanchikov adds that if the inmates "had not been depraved before, they [become] depraved in prison" (Pt 1, Ch 1; 14). Rules, punishments, and droning routines, including forced labor and solitary confinement, "achieve only false, deceptive, and external results" and "suck the vital sap out of a man, enervate his soul, weaken it, terrorize it and then hold up the morally desiccated mummy, half-demented, as a model of reform and repentance" (Pt 1, Ch 1; 16).

For Durkheim, that connective artery between individuals and their families and communities serves to deter suicidal impulses. But in *Dead House*, that life-affirming conduit has been ruptured and, in many cases, it can never be restored. The hospital with its chorus of "sick, broken, moaning" voices, where men talk about their past, their children, their wives, and "the way things used to be" expresses that tragic severance (Pt 2; Ch 3; 217). Goryanchikov feels that from "the mere sound of that distant whisper that none of the things [the convict is] talking about will ever return to him, and that he himself, the teller of the tale, is a chunk severed from that life, a piece of bread cut off from the loaf" (Pt 2, Ch 3; 217). His realization echoes Durkheim's findings that the extrication of individuals from community predisposes them to self-extermination.

What exacerbates Dead House misery is ersatz fraternity, a choiceless one where human beings are "forcibly herded together." Such forced community inevitably breeds hatred, enmity, and the kind of violence that can be directed not only at others, but at the self (Pt 2, Ch 8; 280). While this *forced cohabitation* ravages the men, spasms of relentless contradiction where loneliness congeals with no-aloneness exacerbates the pain (Pt 1, Ch 2; 24). Goryanchikov's "Old Believers," the old man from the Starodubye settlement, along with other distraught cohabitants exemplify the enmity:

[T]wo or three Ukranians, somber men; a young convict with a thin little face and a thin little nose, about twenty-three years old, who had already murdered eight men; a band of counterfeiters, one of whom was our barracks clown; and finally, several somber and sullen individuals, with heads shaved and faces disfigured, silent and envious, who looked with hatred and distrust at everyone around them and who intended to keep on looking that way—to keep on scowling, being silent, and hating everyone around them for many long years to come—for the entire duration of their imprisonment. (Pt 1, Ch 4; 69)

For Goryanchikov, such lurid bunkmates blend with the backdrop of omnipresent fear "smoke and soot, . . . mephitic air, . . . clanking of shackles, amid curses and shameless laughter," and no egress (Pt 1, Ch 4; 69). Goryanchikov finds it unprecedented to be assigned a society in which it is next to impossible to obtain solitude or be able to just sit silently with one's own thoughts:

Could I ever have imagined the terrible and excruciating suffering of never being alone even for a single minute during all ten years of my imprisonment? Could I have imagined that at work I would always be under guard and that at home I would always be together with two hundred comrades, and that not once, not once would I be alone? (Pt 1, Ch 1; 11)[29]

But the trauma is not just about the congestion of bodies. Pitted against the unrequited lust for solitude is an equal and opposite, but just as unquenched, thirst for communion with others.[30] Goryanchikov's nobleman status exacerbates his isolation and automatically alienates him from the peasants, commoners, and those of the lower castes.[31] He in fact concedes that the imprisoned "gentleman" will never be considered by the others as "one of them" and that "[n]o matter how just, kind, and intelligent he is, he'll be hated and despised by the whole mass of convicts for years on end; they won't understand him, and—this is the most important thing—they won't trust him" (Pt 2, Ch 7; 263–64).[32] Despite this bleak reality, Goryanchikov conterminously yearns for both solitude and unification with others, but due to the very nature of the prison, neither oppositional void can ever be filled. In essence, loneliness *sans* solitude, like being both claustrophobic and agoraphobic at once, is a genotype of torture, which conceivably extracts as much (if not more) pain than the shackles, chains, or even the dreaded death-birch. It is the kind of suffering that Shneidman diagnoses in his case study of a thirty-year-old man who ultimately blew his brains out: there was an "inner disputation . . . between his needs for autonomy, inviolacy, privacy, independence, on the one hand, and on the other, his needs for friendship and affiliation," which he simply could not resolve.[33]

ABRUPT CONVULSIONS

Dead House, which is ruled by an arbitrary major and permeated by fear, is rife with euthanasic potential.[34] Once interred, inmates are perpetually aware of the potent Grim Reaper in the form of brutal floggings. Goryanchikov recounts how officials punish prisoners by flogging them to the brink of death in calculated intervals:

> If the number of blows prescribed for the crime is so high that the prisoner wouldn't be able to endure all of them in a single session, this number is divided into two or even three parts, depending on what the doctor says during the punishment itself—that is, depending on whether the prisoner is able to continue walking through the sticks or whether this will endanger his life. Usually, five hundred, a thousand, and even fifteen hundred blows were inflicted in one session, but if the sentence called for two or three thousand, its execution would be divided into two or even three parts. (Pt 2, Ch 3; 201)

The beatings hurt "terribly" and feel "like fire . . . as if your back is being fried on the hottest fire" (Pt 2, Ch 3; 202). Agonizing redundancy, where officers mete out beatings in intervals to permit a little healing, and then start anew while flesh is still raw, adds to the seductive potential of final release. Hospital doctors, standing by, signal when the victim verges on death, which, as the men realize, is an iffy judgment call:

> Men leaving the hospital for the second half of their punishment, once their backs had healed following the first half, were extremely grim, sullen, and untalkative on the day of their discharge and the day before. One noticed in them a stupor of the mind, a kind of unnatural absentmindedness. Such men didn't enter into conversations and for the most part didn't speak at all. (Pt 2, Ch 3; 201)

Such floggings transmit a terror that is "involuntary and insuperable," one which "crushes [a man's] entire moral being" (Pt 2, Ch 3; 200–1). The "unanimous verdict" was that with the birch, the "the severest of all punishments," one could "kill a man" with only 400 strokes and that "anything over five hundred will almost certainly kill him" (Pt 2, Ch 3; 202). None of this is mere conjecture because actual corpses attest to the efficacy of death by flogging. The seemingly invincible Orlov, "a famous robber" and "man with a terrible strength of will and a proud awareness of his strength," is evidence unto himself (Pt 1, Ch 4; 58). The inmates know that Orlov "had undergone in one go exactly half of the sticks to which he had been sentenced" and that "[t]he doctor stopped the execution of the punishment only when he observed that any further beating would inevitably bring about the prisoner's death" (Pt 1, Ch 4; 58). When this "passionate" individual returns to the hospital "half dead from the beating," with the worst wounds Goryanchikov had ever seen, the "only thing that annoy[s Orlov is] that his back [is] taking a long time to heal and that he couldn't obtain his discharge from the hospital as soon as he would have liked so that he could receive the remaining blows as soon as possible" (Pt 2, Ch 3; 201–2). Right after the first installment, this brute of a man becomes energized, has his "spirits revived," and is putatively dreaming of release (Pt 2, Ch 3; 202). Prisoners, who had seen with their own eyes that even the sturdy and seemingly immortal Orlov had "failed to survive the second half of his punishment," know that the post-flog grave was indeed a possibility (Pt 2, Ch 3; 202).

Prison cohorts, ones frailer than Orlov, intuit with every fiber of their being that corporal punishment could become their angel of mercy. The "stupor" and muteness following corporal punishment derive from the victims' conscious (or possibly unconscious) apprehension that beatings can deliver a fatalistic reprieve (Pt 2, Ch 3; 201). Inmate Alexander, who had been whipped throughout his childhood, leaps into his flogging with lusty gusto and even makes it into a little tryst. Knowing that he is "awfully good at playing dead," he is resolved to "trick" his oppressors and dance a teasingly lethal Barynya:

> [T]hey led me through the first thousand; it burned me, and I was screaming; they led me through the second, and I thought my end was coming: they had beaten me senseless; my legs weren't holding me up anymore and I crashed against the ground; my eyes became dead, and my face turned blue; I wasn't breathing, and I was foaming at the mouth. The doctor came up to me: "He's going to die any minute," he said. They carried me to the hospital, and I came back to life at once. (Pt 2, Ch 2; 191)

After Alexander fools them two more times, the infuriated floggers sharpen the pain so much so that in the fourth go around, "every stick [is] like a knife cutting [his] heart" and "every stick [feels] like three sticks" (Pt 2, Ch 2; 191). Unable to resist, he dupes them once again, making them "crazy with fury" such "[t]hat pitiful last thousand . . . [is] worse than the first three put together" (Pt 2, Ch 2; 192). Although he braggingly attributes his "success" to his having grown up "under the lash," his exclamation ("And why couldn't they beat me to death?") imparts displeasure with what he in his heart of hearts deems a failure—namely, his survival. Alexander and others know that they can commit "unheard-of-atrocities . . . in order to be executed and put out of their misery as soon as possible" (Pt 1, Ch 5; 82). There are and will be ample opportunities to expire in a prison where "almost every manifestation of the convict's free will is considered to be a crime," where it doesn't matter if that "manifestation" is large or small, and where even a mere blink can beget eternal rest (Pt 1, Ch 5; 83).

The Fatalistic

Durkheim classifies the "[i]mpulsive or automatic suicide" as resulting "from an abrupt and immediately irresistible impulse," which matches what Dostoevsky's Goryanchikov calls "a matter of convulsions" (SU, Bk 2, Ch 2; 165: *DH*, Pt 2, Ch 5; 83). The Dead House "convulsions" not only correspond to Durkheim's "impulsions," but also have kinship with those "strange" and "astonishing" murders by "common people," who go "temporarily amuck" and strive to self-destruct through paroxysms of crime (Pt 1, Ch 8; 111).

Goryanchikov witnesses "strange outbursts" whereby a prisoner might "suffer patiently for several years, submits, and endures the cruelest punishments, but then he suddenly snaps because of some trifle, because of some little thing, almost for no reason at all" (Pt 1, Ch 1; 18). Such outbursts happen (as Durkheim has put it) as "truly automatic," as occurring "[i]n the twinkling of an eye" and can be so unexpected that they even shock prison authorities who essentially have seen just about everything (SU, Bk 1, Ch 1:65). Goryanchikov observes:

> [A] convict can have led a peaceful and exemplary life for several years, even being made an elder for his praiseworthy behavior, when suddenly for no apparent reason (as if a demon had invaded him), he starts to act crazy, carouses frantically, runs amuck, and sometimes even commits an actual criminal offense, such as open disrespect for the higher authorities, or murder, or rape, and so on. (Pt 1, Ch 5; 83)

Goryanchikov traces the causes of this "sudden explosion" to quashed selfhood and to the convict's "anguished, convulsive manifestation of his personality, . . . an instinctive longing to be himself, . . . a desire to express himself, his crushed personality, a desire which appears suddenly and which climaxes in spite, fury, eclipse of reason, fits, convulsions" (Pt 1, Ch 5; 83).[35] By likening this impulse to a man "buried alive," who after awakening in his coffin struggles in futility to "fling" open the lid, Goryanchikov suggests that what belies that "anguished, convulsive manifestation of his personality" is partly the primal survival instinct (Pt 1, Ch 5; 83). A similar coalescing of suicide with vivification in the coffin also appears in *A Writer's Diary*, where Dostoevsky comments on the unnamed Elizaveta Aleksandrovna Herzen, daughter of Alexander Herzen, who slays herself by "soaking a piece of cotton wool in chloroform" and binding it onto her face.[36] In her last note, she writes: "I ask only that you not bury me until you have determined that I am completely dead, because it is most unpleasant to awaken in a coffin underground."[37] There, as in *Dead House*, the image of awakening in a hermetically sealed tomb is a life-death alloy or metonymic conflation of resurgent freewill with an oppositional force just as almighty—namely, the omnipresent thanatotic drive.

Durkheim explains that impulsive or automatic suicide is more irrational than even maniacal suicide, a type that derives from "hallucinations or delirious conceptions" (SU, Bk 1, Ch 1; 63):

> The abruptness recalls what has been mentioned above in connection with mania; only the maniacal suicide has always some reason, however irrational. It is connected with the patient's delirious conceptions. Here on the contrary the suicidal tendency appears and is effective in truly automatic fashion, not preceded by any intellectual antecedent. The sight of a knife, a walk on the edge of a precipice, etc. engender the suicidal idea, instantaneously and its execution follows so swiftly that patients often have no idea of what has taken place. (SU, Bk 1, Ch 2; 65)

Durkheim noticed that suicides and suicide attempts, be they impulsive or automatic, tend to surface in clusters. He calls this phenomenon "imitation" or "contagion" and relates "the well-known story of the fifteen patients who hung themselves in swift succession in 1772 from the same hook in a dark passage of the hospital" (SU, Bk 1, Ch 2; 97).[38] He tells how history confirms the phenomenon:

> In 1813, in the little village of Saint-Pierre-Monjau, a woman hanged herself from a tree and several others did likewise at a little distance away. Pinel tells of a priest's hanging himself in the neighborhood of Etampes; some days later two others killed themselves and several laymen imitated them. When Lord Castelreagh threw himself into Versuvius, several of his companions followed his example. (SU, Bk 1, Ch 4; 131)

"Imitation" or "contagion" approximates "the Werther effect," named after Johann Wolfgang von Goethe's novel *The Sorrows of Young Werther*, in which the protagonist, inflicted with *weltschmerz*, kills himself.[39] In its wake, this popular novel spawned a throng of copycats or as Kay Redfield Jamison points out, "young men were found dead by gunshot, dressed in blue frock coats and yellow waistcoats, with a copy of Goethe's novel nearby."[40] Some scholars, like sociology professor David P. Phillips, believe in the phenomenon of imitative "suggestion." Phillips, who coined the term "Werther effect," found a pattern of rising suicides after the dissemination of a suicide story.[41]

While Durkheim generally rejected the epidemiological significance of imitative suggestion as a factor influencing suicide rates, he acknowledged that it could hasten a death that would otherwise occur and might impact a few individuals in the immediate vicinity of a publicized suicide.[42] Noting that "[t]he frequency of such cases of contagion in prison is likewise affirmed by many observers," Durkheim states that while some statistics "prove that prisoners are in general unusually disposed to suicide[,] . . .imprisonment by itself develops a very strong tendency to suicide" (SU, Bk 1, Ch 4; 131: Bk 3, Ch 2; 345–46). Here Durkheim posits a seminal question—"[o]f what does this influence consist?"—which he answers:

> It seems due in part, certainly to cell life. But we should not be surprised if the community-life of the prison were apt to have the same effects. The Society of evil-doers and prisoners is known to be very coherent; the individual disappears completely and prison discipline has the same effacing tendency. Something similar to what we have observed in the army may take place. What confirms this hypothesis is that epidemics of suicide are frequent in prisons as well as in the barracks. (SU, Bk 3, Ch 2; 346n. 44)

Dead House has that "effacing tendency" plus "contagion," but inmates tend not to exactly copy each other but mint their own methodology. In her discussion of suicide epidemics in Russian prisons, Morrissey expounds upon the "astounding ingenuity: there was hanging (with towels, shirts); cutting (with glass, tin cans); poisoning (with home-made extracts derived from tobacco); burning (with the kerosene of a lamp)."[43] She adds that "[s]ome accounts were horrific in their laconic brevity" and cites the example of one prisoner, who "used her hair for a noose" and another who "ripped open an artery with his teeth."[44]

Dead House suicidal acts and attempts, not unlike those listed in Morrissey's book, are varied, inventive, and dependent on available resources. In Dead House, some prisoners guzzle death through vodka.[45] One prisoner, who "[d] ecide[s] to drink a jug of vodka which he had laced with snuff," becomes "ill at once" and starts vomiting blood, which damages his chest (Pt 1, Ch 4; 53). He winds up in the hospital "almost unconscious" with symptoms of tuberculosis and dies shortly thereafter (Pt 1, Ch 4; 53, 211). Gazin, whose vodka orgies make him so "vicious" that he actually "throws himself at people with a knife" is subdued by other prisoners: "[t]en men jump on him and beat him mercilessly until he loses consciousness" (Pt 1, Ch 2; 37–38). Essentially, they "beat him half to death[,] . . . [and then] lay him down on the bed planks and cover him with a sheepskin" so that he can sleep it off (Pt 1, Ch 2; 37). As a Polish prisoner tells Goryanckikov, Gazin is "terribly strong" and if it were someone else, this might have killed him (Pt 1, Ch 2; 37). Despite knowing full well that his drinking is the sequelae to a thrashing or even death, Gazin nevertheless persists in gulping that corrosive elixir. And even though Gazin has a "constitution like an ox," he begins to "succumb, . . . complain of various pains, [with] his health . . . noticeably deteriorating," and starts to frequent the hospital (Pt 1, Ch 2; 37, 51).[46]

In addition to inebriant binging, there is at least one prison attack and even a short-lived escape, either of which could produce the birch and the grave. Petrov comes perilously close to being one such fatality. He is the inmate who had suddenly stabbed his colonel "openly, in broad daylight" before coming to prison (Pt 1, Ch 7; 106). Once in Dead House, other prisoners divine a replay and Prisoner M even warns that Petrov, "the most determined and fearless," is "capable of anything" and would "stop at nothing if some whim enters his head" (Pt 1, Ch 7; 106). M admonishes that Petrov would "slice you up if the fancy takes him: he'll just slice you up without flinching and without remorse" (Pt 1, Ch 7; 106). In prison, Petrov, giving credence to the lore, almost does himself in by plotting to kill the major. But when Petrov is being led to his flogging, he is "saved by a miracle" because the major "[rides] away just before the punishment [is] due to begin" (Pt 1, Ch 7; 106). If this homicidal scheme had not been aborted, Petrov might have been sleeping under the sod.

Unlike Petrov, convict Lomov lacks an intervening *deus ex machina* when he suddenly stabs another prisoner, Gavrilka, with an awl "almost under the heart" (Pt 2, Ch 5; 242). Lomov knows that he had been sent to Siberia for murders that Gavrilka had committed, but this arguably palatable motive for vengeance is not what precipitates the incident. Rather, Lomov suddenly blows up in a jealous rage when Gavrilka starts gasconading about his affair with a "repulsive floozie" (Pt 2, Ch 5; 244). Although Gavrilka survives with just scratches, Lomov's sentence is increased and the prospect of death looms in the delivery of that "thousand blows" (Pt 2, Ch 5; 245).

While an escape might look like a desperate effort to retrieve life, Goryanchikov points out that it is more like an attempted dive into the grave from a prison where men tend to be "cowardly," where "supervision [is] especially strict and military," and where the location itself is treacherously "exposed and in the steppe" (Pt 2, Ch 9; 294). But most of all, it is predetermined that escapees, who either turn themselves in or get caught, wind up back in lockup and potentially face the death penalty.

In *Dead House*, two criminals indulge the temptation to break out and nearly fulfill prophesies of doom. One, named "A___v," is insolent and already predisposed to self-sabotage: he would not hesitate to "slit [a] throat for vodka" and "he would have continued spying and doing business by all sorts of underground means if he had been given his freedom" (Pt 2, Ch 9; 294). A___v finds a suitable cohort in the "vigorous" Kulikov, a convict in the special category, and they enlist from within: they anoint as their coconspirator the Polish guard, Koller, who is "capable of anything" and contains a "mute, concealed, [and] constant hatred" (Pt 2, Ch 9; 295–96). When the surmised denouement comes to fruition and A___v, along with Kulikov, surrenders, the other prisoners guess that one will receive a thousand lashes and that two will die. Although it unexpectedly turns out that the punishment is lighter than divined, it doesn't take A___v long to start flirting anew with his last rites: "he strut[s] about the hospital and [keeps] saying loudly that nothing could stop him now, that there was nothing he [isn't] prepared to do," and he thus mobilizes himself for a renewed effort to self-combust (Pt 2, Ch 9; 304).

The Fatalistic-Altruistic

Durkheim acknowledges that his suicide categories can syncretize in alloys. In Dead House, there exist fatalistic, suicidal undertakings that are mingled with altruism.

For Durkheim, the altruistic suicide occurs when "the ego is not its own property, where it is blended with something not itself, where the goal of conduct is exterior to itself, that is, in one of the groups in which it participates" (SU, Bk 2, Ch 4: 221). Regarding altruism in spiritual or religious spheres, Durkheim states that "the individual kills himself purely for the joy of sacrifice, because, even with no particular reason, renunciation in itself is considered praiseworthy" (SU, Bk 2, Ch 4; 223). He offers examples of the southern Jainists where "religious suicide was very often practiced"; Hindus where "the custom of seeking death in the waters of the Ganges or other sacred rivers was widespread"; Bhils, who, using "a rock from the top of which men cast themselves with religious motives, to devote themselves to Shiva"; the "fanatics who let themselves be crushed to death in throngs under the wheels of the idol Juggernaut"; the Japanese "who throw themselves into the water weighted with stones, or sink their ships and let themselves be gradually submerged while singing their idols praises"; the "sectarians of Amida" who "quietly allow themselves to die of hunger," while others ascend cliffs to "cast themselves head-foremost to the bottom of the abyss" (SU, Bk 2, Ch 4; 224). Durkheim explains that altruism is a transcultural, trans-religious phenomenon:

> We actually see the individual in all these cases seek to strip himself of his personal being in order to be engulfed in something which he regards as his true essence. The name he gives it is unimportant; he feels that he exists in it and in it alone, and strives so violently to blend himself with it in order to have being. He must therefore consider that he has no life of his own. Impersonality is here carried to its highest pitch; altruism is acute. (SU, Bk 2, Ch 4; 225)[47]

Durkheim notes that these "so-called martyrs" are frequently "revered" in their own cultures (SU, Bk 2, Ch 4; 225).[48] In distending the altruistic category to subsume "the death of some of the Christian martyrs," Durkheim states that "those neophytes who without killing themselves, voluntarily allowed their own slaughter, are really suicides." He elaborates:

> Though they did not kill themselves, they sought death with all their power and behaved so as to make it inevitable. To be suicide, the act from which death must necessarily result need only have been performed by the victim with full knowledge of the facts. Besides, the passionate enthusiasm with which the believers in the new religion faced final torture shows that at this moment they had completely discarded their personalities for the idea of which they had become servants. (SU, Bk 2, Ch 4; 227)

Durkheim's exegesis of those "passionately" seeking "death with all their power" and "behav[ing] so as to make it inevitable" evokes images of the "passion sufferer," which according to Marcia A. Morris, appear early among East Slavic Orthodox believers."[49] Although Morris concedes that "[s]cholars have defined passion-sufferers variously," she follows George P. Fedotov, who aligns them with "kenotic holiness," which is the passion sufferers' enactment of Christ though the "redeeming and purifying merit of suffering and death."[50] Fedotov asserts, "[i]n a correct, orthodox form, willing, self-offering nonresistance is needed to bring the victim into conformity with the suffering kenotic Christ."[51]

The individuals in Durkheim's treatise who enthusiastically "face final torture" and Fedotov's "kenotic" holy men, who by imitating Christ, pay homage to the "redeeming and purifying merit of suffering and death," are akin to the Bible-reading convict in *Dead House* (SU, Bk2, Ch 4; 227).[52] This unnamed convict, "distinguished by his meek behavior" and viewed as "a sort of holy fool," passes his time reading the Bible (Pt 1, Ch 2; 34). One day, after refusing to work, this imprisoned *yurodivy* goes for the major with a brick. Even though the blow misses its mark, the convict, after being "seized, tried and punished," perishes in the hospital (Pt 1, Ch 2; 34). While dying, he announces that "he meant no harm to anyone but only wanted to suffer" (Pt 1, Ch 2; 34).[53] Like many of those in Durkheim's altruistic classification, he is "remembered with respect" and like the East Slavic Orthodox passion-sufferer, has acquired his badge of veneration (Pt 1, Ch 2; 34).[54]

Significantly, Goryanchikov links the unnamed convict to the Old Believer from Starobudye, who, also esteemed amongst the prisoners, exhibits a similar martyr-like bent. Like Luka Kuzmich, Petrov, Akim Akimych, Sirotkin, Dutov, Balkushin, and Shishkov, all of whom exhibited suicidal behavior before prison, the Old Believer's pre-prison self-oblation is precisely what catapults him into Dead House. When some converts settled in his community and started to build a Edinover church, this Old Believer, "together with other fanatics, decided to 'stand up for the faith' " (Pt 1, Ch 3; 40). After incinerating the church, the Old Believer, as instigator, got precisely what he foresaw—deportation and penal servitude. His sacrifice, however, was huge because he, "a well-to-do tradesman" with a wife and children, had plenty of reasons to live. Yet, he went into exile "with fortitude, because in his blindness he considered it a 'martyrdom for the faith' " (Pt 1, Ch 3; 40).

George Howe Colt notes that the Old Believers had a history of "collective suicide."[55] He states that "[i]n the mid-seventeenth century, the Old Believers, a Russian Orthodox sect that insisted the Antichrist was to arrive in 1666, burned their villages around them" and "[i]n less than decade some twenty thousand had taken their own lives."[56] Like the zealots depicted in Durkheim's *Suicide*, the Old Believer in *Dead House* refuses to disavow his convictions and seemed to have "regarded his act and the 'martyrdom' he had taken on because of it as a glorious deed" (Pt 1, Ch 3; 40–41).

The ligature between the Old Believer and the unnamed convict becomes perspicuous when they figuratively collide: the narrator spies the Old Believer, who is "weeping" while "sitting on the stove (the same one on which the Bible-reading convict who had tried to kill the Major used to pray at night)" and, in implicit mimicry of his conjugate, he too is "reading prayers" (Pt 1, Ch 3; 41). Toward the close of the novel, Goryanchikov again ties the Old Believer to his Bible-reading doppelganger. Goryanchikov proclaims that the unnamed convict "who went crazy, the one who did nothing but read the Bible . . . and attacked the Major with a brick, . . . had invented a way out for himself in the form of voluntary, almost artificial martyrdom" and "desire to take suffering upon himself" (Pt 2, Ch 9; 261–62). In like fashion, Goryanchikov declares that the Old Believer from the Starobudye settlements knows of one "salvation, a way out: prayer and the idea of martyrdom" (Pt 2, Ch 9; 261). Using Goryanchikov as his mouthpiece, Dostoevsky thus identifies the unnamed convict and the Old Believer as men who strive to altruistically "strip [themselves] of [their] personal being in order to be engulfed in something which [they] regard[ed] as [their] true essence" (SU, Bk 2, Ch 4; 225).

The unnamed convict and the Old Believer evoke the tradition of those "ascetic heroes" who will ne'er return.[57] In exploring the "ascetic hero's" lack of reintegration back into society, Morris adapts Joseph Campbell's depiction of a "separation-initiation-return" path, whereby a literary hero "comes back from his mysterious adventure with the power to bestow boons on his fellow man."[58] She then contrasts this paradigmatic path of the canonical hero with that of the ascetic hero, who "fails to return" and instead "keeps his mysterious powers to himself."[59] The Old Believer, the unnamed convict, and "the religious ascetic[s who] seek to maintain [their] state of communion with the transcendent" are irreversibly torn from their own collectives.[60] In short, none can and will complete the heroic cycle by returning to their origins to "bestow boons on [their] fellow man."[61] As Durkheim finds, the inability to be at home or part of a community can inflame suicidal proclivities.

There is a distinction, however, between these two prison martyrs: the Old Believer technically endures life, while the unnamed convict consigns himself to the grave. Durkheim would understand this distinction because he felt that "[t]he beneficent influence of religion is . . . not due to the special nature of the religious conceptions," but rather due to the fact that it comprises a "society," which serves to provide "a sufficiently intense collective life" (SU, Bk 2, Ch 2; 170). Durkheim emphasizes that "[t]he more numerous and strong these collective states of mind are, the stronger the integration of the religious community and also the greater its preservative value" (SU, Bk 2, Ch 2; 170). The Old Believer epitomizes a being effectually brainwashed with that "preservative" of an "intense collective life" (SU, Bk2, Ch 2, 170). Historically, the Old Believers fortified their schismatic homogeneity when they rebelled against the liturgical reforms that Patriarch Nikon introduced in the middle of the seventeenth century. At that time, Old Believers settled in Starodubye, which became their shared religious venue. What tightened their coalition was their united front against religious persecution: in a cooperative endeavor, they fled Starodubye and settled on the island of Vetka. In 1764, however, Catherine II had them expelled from there as well, after which the group returned to home turf—Starodubye.[62] The Old Believer has thus imbibed the itinerant journey of social cohesion, which migrates within his very soul and psyche to Dead House and girds him with that Durkheimian prophylaxis—"beliefs and practices common" to his sect, ones which are "traditional and thus obligatory" (SU, Bk 2, Ch 2; 170). In contrast, the unnamed convict, who does "not belong to any schismatic sect," lacks allegiance with a shared faith, the very thing that Durkheim holds has a "moderating effect upon suicide" (SU, Bk 2, Ch 2; 170: DH, Pt 1, Ch 2; 34).

The unnamed convict terminates his own existence in what amounts to a solipsistic nondenominational sacrifice. Fifteen years later, Dostoevsky portrays another reality-based fictional suicide in "The Meek One." Like the unnamed convict, the meek one is interned by her pawnbroker-husband in a micro-prison of oppression, tyranny, and torment. While she "presse[s] the ikon to her bosom and [flings] herself out of the window," to escape her husband's coercion, in Dostoevsky's *Dead House*, the death-seeker does not resort to self-defenestration, but rather secures escape through a convulsive lunge at a lethal flogging.[63]

The fact that the Old Believer accepts a martyr life of imprisonment with "obvious fortitude" and the unnamed convict literally repudiates life is for

Dostoevsky a distinction without real difference (Pt 1, Ch 3; 41).[64] The doubling of these fatalistic-altruistic passion-sufferers broaches the overarching question: what does it really mean to *live*? The Old Believer and the unnamed convicted provide an answer. The Old Believer nurtures within "a profound incurable sorrow, which he trie[s] to hide from everyone" and which in the wee hours of the morning exudes in "quiet, restrained weeping" (Pt 1, Ch 3; 41). Although, over time, Dostoevsky came to view suicide as the product of incarcerating oneself in God-less universe, he always believed that the feet of the faithful had to be firmly planted in *terra firma* and that faith can and should inform robust interactions between and amongst flesh-and-blood beings. What Dostoevsky imparts through Goryanchikov is the aphorism that individuals who either live *solely* or die *solely* "in order to be engulfed in something" they regard as "true essence" fall into the same ditch: the figurative or literal tomb (SU, Bk 2, Ch 4; 225). That is, all forms of piacular offerings (be it a jump from the window with an ikon, a brick attack on the major, a stab in the chest of a fellow inmate, or a self-imposed prison martyrdom) equally propel the self into a larger something that translates into a nothingness, into an etherized nullity.

COLLECTIVE SUCCEDANEA

Durkheim holds that society is constituted by "the existence of a certain number of beliefs and practices common to all" and such "numerous and strong . . . collective states of mind" have a "moderating effect upon suicide" (SU, Bk 2, Ch 2; 170). Durkheim asserts that people "cling to life more resolutely when belonging to a group they love, so as not to betray interests they put before their own" (SU, Bk 2, Ch 3; 209–10). His antidote to suicide is thus "a cohesive and animated society" in which there is "a constant interchange of ideas and feelings from all to each and each to all" (SU, Bk 2, Ch 3; 210). By contrast, Dead House stands as an excessively regulated void crammed with a populace tantalized by a virtually inaccessible "collective credo" (SU, Bk 2, Ch 2; 159).

Throughout the novel, readers meet inmates who are famished for friendships and trying desperately, through blurting confessions or straining dialogue, to be heard so they can forge a salvational tie to something bigger than the "I."[65] These men, who are shoved together yet never alone, relish the chance to ritualistically bond in the bath house or embrace what becomes a fleeting reprieve in the form of a collective Christmas festivity:

> [E]ach convict had an unconscious feeling that by observing the holiday he was coming into contact with the whole world, that consequently he was not

altogether an outcast, a lost man, a piece of bread cut off from the loaf, and that prison wasn't different from the rest of life. (Pt 1, Ch 10; 135)[66]

These souls ache with chronic cognitive dissonance: on the one hand, they hunger for release from *forced cohabitation*, and on the other, they covet collective nutrients (Pt 1, Ch 2; 24).[67] Yet, why do some, like the Poles, manage to plod along and survive? Dostoevsky's and Durkheim's retort can be redacted into two words—collective succedanea. Either the convicts build their own collective subculture within the prison, share hopes of returning to their collective origins, or engorge collective nutrients through labor.

The Sub-society

Elizabeth A. Blake proffers an answer to the Pole enigma, one that would ring true for Durkheim.[68] In discussing how "Dostoevsky's desire to separate himself from Polish Catholic political exiles is reflected in the relatively little space he devotes to them in the first part of *House of the Dead*," she explains that "Goryanchikov frequently depicts the Poles as a collective group in his first impressions of the prison in which he emphasizes their exclusive nature."[69] Blake, Durkheim, and Dostoevsky penetrate the very quiddity of the Polish prisoner's life support system.

The Poles scrupulously keep themselves apart from the rest of the prison population: Goryanchikov relates that the Poles have "formed a completely separate family" and "shut [themselves] off . . . in a cold and inaccessible politeness" (Pt 1, Ch 4; 67: Pt 1, Ch 6; 96). In fact, the *Dead House*-Poles come across as a "tightly knit," cohesive subculture, one which lives and breathes as a unitary organism (Pt 1, Ch 4; 68). This is also apparent with respect to the stage show, which nearly all enthusiastically attend except the Old Believer and the Poles. When the Poles finally do show up and only for the "last performance," this comes after considerable coalitional deliberation, "after many assurances that the show [is] good and entertaining, and that there [is] no risk in going" (Pt 1, Ch 11; 155). When the prisoners unite to lodge a complaint, the Poles decide to participate, but do so as a caucus with Polish commoners "attach[ing] themselves to the noblemen" (Pt 2, Ch 7; 271).

While the Poles, like everybody else, are exiled from their families and community, they manage to construct and sustain a surrogate "collective credo" (SU, Bk 2, Ch 2; 159). Instinctively, the Poles accomplish what Durkheim prescribes—namely, they foster "a mutual moral support, which instead of throwing the individual on his own resources, leads him to share in the collective energy and supports his own when exhausted" (SU, Bk 2, Ch 3; 210).

The Shared Hope of Return

Unlike the Poles, other prisoners feed on morsels of hope that someday they will be able to walk out and rejoin their old hives. Goryanchikov tells us that from day one, he starts "to dream about freedom" (Pt 1, Ch 7; 99): it becomes his "favorite occupation to calculate, using a thousand different measurements and methods, how long it would be before my years of imprisonment were over" (Pt 1, Ch 7; 99). Admitting that he doesn't know whether the other prisoners think and "calculate" the same way, what strikes Goryanchikov as universal is "the astonishing unreality of their hopes" of reclaiming their gone domiciles (Pt 1, Ch 7; 99).

While all Dead House inmates have been ripped from their roots, many men cling to pipe dreams of eventual replantation. By way of example, the prisoner Nurra, one of the Caucasian mountain tribesmen, perseveres with a daily regimen of hope. He is "quite convinced that as soon as he ha[s] finished his sentence, he'd be returned to his home in the Caucasus, and he live[s] only for that hope" (Pt 1, Ch 4; 63). Goryanchikov acknowledges that if Nurra had been "deprived" of this hope of rejoining his settlement, "he would have died" (Pt 1, Ch 4; 63). Aley is similar. He nostalgically pictures his old Daghestan celebrations, envisions his beautiful sister, and in his mind's eye, sees his mother weeping over him. Although such life-affirming associations are gone, Aley aspires to rejuvenate them through periodic reverie.

As mentioned earlier, there are others, incarcerated for the most heinous crimes and chained to a wall for five to ten years, who ponder the shared mirage of relative reprieve in the form of joining other prisoners who live only in shackles. If these prisoners had been stripped of their goal of ending their "period of enchainment" as quickly as possible, they would simply perish or lose their minds (Pt 1, Ch 7; 100). Dostoevsky's narrator knows that "[n]o man who is alive can live without some goal" and that the divestiture of a shared mecca of betterment or of an eventual reversion to normalcy would spawn "misery [that] will often turn him into a monster" and goad him to self-offend (Pt 2, Ch 7; 262).

The Labor Nutrient

For those who cannot construct a prison micro-society or share what is often a mirage of improvement or a return home, there is yet another potential anodyne, one that Durkheim also prescribes. Both Durkheim and the *Dead House* narrator suggest that work has the potential to supply the collective spirit that traditional faith, family, and communities once yielded. Durkheim states that while "religion, the family and the nation" are "preservatives" against suicide, it is not due to "the special sort of sentiments encouraged by each" (SU, Bk 3, Ch 3; 378). Rather, it is because they are and can be "well integrated societies" (SU, Bk 3, Ch 3; 378).[70] In a changing world, where old institutional handholds are crumbling and units of cohesion unraveling, Durkheim turns to meaningful labor for succor: "[s]ince it consists of individuals devoted to the same tasks with solidarity or even combined interests, no soil is better calculated to bear social ideas and sentiments" (SU, Bk 3, Ch 3; 378). Consequently, "[i]dentity of origin, culture and occupation makes occupational activity the richest sort of material for a common life" (SU, Bk 3, Ch 3; 378).[71]

In *Dead House*, work becomes the "material for a common life" (SU, Bk 3, Ch 3; 378). It grants the prisoners a collaborative respite and chance to "cooperate in the same function" (SU, Bk 3, Ch 3; 378). While Goryanchikov calls labor a "compulsory task," which the convicts "look upon . . . with hatred," he, prefiguring Durkheim, also aligns work with self-preservation and even deems it the line between man and beast:

> [H]ow could all these men, who had experienced much, who had lived intensely and desired to live, but who were forcibly collected here into one swarming mass, who had been forcibly torn away from society and normal life, how could all these men be expected to settle down into a normal and regular existence here of their own free will and desire? Idleness alone would have engendered in them criminal qualities of which they hitherto had no conception. A man can't live without work and without lawful and normal property; he becomes depraved and turns into a beast. (Pt 1, Ch 1; 17–18)

Upon arrival, Goryanchikov predicts "that work could be [his] salvation" and makes it clear that although convicts cherish money, the occupational drive is not just propelled by remunerative lust: rather labor by itself restores a sense of humanity and spells the difference between life and death: "without work the convicts would have devoured one another like spiders in a glass jar" (Pt 1, Ch 7; 100: Pt 1, Ch 1; 18). Without having the prospect of "earning [the] kopek," convicts would cease to be: "they would die like flies (in spite of being provided with everything they needed), or commit unheard of atrocities—some out of boredom, others in order to be executed and put out their misery as soon as possible" (Pt 1, Ch 5; 82).

Ousted from familial hearths, the prisoners replace past collectives by forming what is essentially a salubrious guild within prison walls. Goryanchikov observes that even in winter, when convicts are shut in as soon as night falls, despite official bans on private industry and tools, "almost every barracks [is] transformed into an enormous workshop," and "almost everyone . . . would settle down to some form of work" (Pt 1, Ch 1; 18: Pt 1, Ch 4; 62). While some convicts arrive in prison without a trade, they learn how to be "cobblers, shoemakers, tailors, carpenters, locksmiths, engravers, and gilders" (Pt

1, Ch 1; 18). For example, Akim, who has acquired skills as "a carpenter, a cobbler, a shoemaker, a painter, a gilder, a locksmith," embodies the principle that enterprise can subsidize the soul with a will to live (Pt 1, Ch 2; 31). Aley, another case in point, possesses "a good deal of mechanical ability: he ha[s] learned how to sew clothes quite well, [is] excellent at making books, and later on he learn[s] carpentry tolerably well" (Pt 1, Ch 4; 66). As artisan, Aley becomes an integrant module within a broader alliance, which make "his brothers praise him" and feel "proud of him" (Pt 1, Ch 4; 66). The lone Jewish prisoner, Isay Bumshtein, a moneylender and jeweler, who "toil[s] away and earn[s] a kopek or two" and gets orders from the town, also secures himself a meaningful niche (Pt 1, Ch 1; 18). Through trades, each man plugs into a coterie and receives that reciprocal oomph in response.

While such vocations fortify each man's role in the prison microcosm, they also enable individuals to eschew hyperbolic individualism, a morbidity that Durkheim attributes to egoistic suicide.[72] Sushilov, who "ha[s not] learned any handicraft," instead latches onto Goryanchikov and literally vocalizes the anti-egoistic, life-affirming effect of what he concocts as his prison-specialty (Pt 1, Ch 5; 73). Sushilov carves out his identity as Goryanchikov's servant: he does Goryanchikov's laundry, boils his tea, runs his errands, takes his jacket to the menders, and greases his boots. This job not only endows Sushilov with a "main purpose in life" but also facilitates his release from miasmic egocentrism, which becomes audible when Goryanchikov describes his lackey's pronouns: "he joined his fate completely with mine and [takes] all my affairs on himself. He never [says,] for example, 'You have this many shirts, your jacket is torn,' and so on; instead, he always [says,] '*We* have this many shorts; *our* jacket is torn' " (Pt 1, Ch 5; 73). As such, work becomes the medium through which Sushilov and others become yokemates, not an "I" but a "we," not a "mine" but an "our."

Like Sushilov, other prisoners reclaim banished community through spurts of teamwork. While preparing for the inspector, the men go out "in droves to level the streets in the fortress, pull up tussocks, to paint the fences and posts, to do plastering work, to touch things up" and exhibit "ever-increasing fervor and excitement" (Pt 2, Ch 5; 242). When the prisoners partner to achieve a common goal, as when they cluster to lodge a complaint or to plan a stage show or to haggle over and purchase the new workhorse, Dead House surges with renewed vitality.[73]

Goryanchikov proclaims that penal labor has redeeming value because it is "rational enough" when it has "meaning and purpose" (Pt 1, Ch 2; 23). He says that when the men are engaged in activity with "sense and a value," they "seem to grow animated, and . . . exert every effort in order to finish the job as quickly and as well as possible" and feel as if "their self-respect [were] somehow at stake" (Pt 1, Ch 5; 114–15). Goryanchikov observes that "when the work [is] intrinsically useful and valuable" and when the assignment has a "fixed conclusion," the convicts act "as if something inspired them" and will do anything to "finish the task as quickly and efficiently as possible; it even seem[s] their self-esteem [is] somehow at stake" (Pt 1, Ch 6; 87–88). As Goryanchikov detects, at times, a convict would "attack his work task . . . with extraordinary zeal totally incommensurate with what was required, and [would begin] to work—to work as hard as he could, as if trying to suppress in himself something that had been stifling him and pressing on him from within" (Pt 2, Ch 5; 229–30). Both Goryanchikov and Durkheim attest to the fact that labor can help individuals stave off hyperbolic self-absorption with its accompanying, nearly irresistible, ravening to self-implode.

While Goryanchikov concedes that prison work can be salutary, he knows that it can also strike chords of pain. In a haunting segment of the novel, Goryanchikov, who is contemplating the impact of penal labor, attributes misery not to the unalleviated difficulty of the task itself, but to the fact of "it being *compulsory*, obligatory, done under the stick": he adds that "[i]n the world of freedom the peasant works, perhaps, incomparably harder, sometimes even at night, especially in the summer, but he works for himself and he works with a rational goal in view, and it's incomparably easier for him than for the convict who does compulsory work that is completely useless to him" (Pt 1, Ch 2; 23). Goryanchikov feels that since there is "necessarily an element of . . . torture, senselessness, humiliation, and shame in all compulsory work, penal work is incomparably more excruciating than any work done in the world of freedom" (Pt 1, Ch 2; 23). Such thoughts propel Goryanchikov into a downward spiral, where he ponders the kind of work that can induce the self-imposed death decree.

With respect to penal labor, Dostoevsky's narrator, beginning at the precipice, with the preservative value of work, descends to its degrading "compulsory" quality, and then drops into the abyss of unadulterated futility. This is one of the techniques that Joseph Frank ascribes to Dostoevsky's artistry:

> Dostoevsky's imagination at this point could not resist taking the eschatological leap that was to become so characteristic for him—the leap to the end condition of whatever empirical situation he is considering—and so, in order to dramatize the supreme importance of hope for human life, he deliberately *invents* a situation in which it is systematically destroyed.[74]

In his treatise on work, Goryanchikov, "leaping" down "to the end condition," digs to extract the mephitis that deflates hope, shatters meaning, and provokes self-homicide:

> The thought once occurred to me that if one wanted to crush and destroy a man completely, to punish him with the most terrible punishment, so that even the most fearsome murderer would tremble before such a punishment and dread it beforehand, all you'd have to do would be to make him do work that was completely and totally useless and senseless. . . [I]f you force him, for example to keep pouring water from one bucket into another and back again, to keep pounding sand, or to keep carrying a heap of soil from one place to another and back again, then I think he'd strangle himself after a few days or commit a thousand crimes, preferring to die rather than endure such humiliation, shame and torment. (Pt 1, Ch 2; 23)[75]

Goryanchikov implicitly concedes that without a surrogate collective, be it through formation of a prison coalition, shared hopes of returning to community, or grasping at the life raft of non-Sisyphean labor, a man might "strangle himself" or like some convicts did before prison and do while they are in prison, "commit a thousand crimes in order to die" (Pt 1, Ch 2; 23).[76] Once emptied of any and all collective stand-ins, Dead House inmates would look elsewhere. They would construct and predicate fellowship on something far vacuously darker—the renunciation of existence itself. Durkheim glosses this theory when he rebuts the contention that suicidal imitation is an *individual* phenomenon, that it "originate[s] in one or two individual cases which they merely repeat" (SU, Bk 1, Ch4; 131). Durkheim finds that contagious suicidal ideation "does not spring up in one particular person and then spread to others," but instead "is developed by the whole group, which, in a situation, desperate for all, collectively decides upon death" (SU, Bk 1, Ch 4; 131–32).[77] In short, for both Durkheim and Dostoevsky, when there is no "all," no "we," no community, then the "one," and the "I" secure collective succedaneum in self-homicide.

CONCLUSION: SLOUCHING TOWARD ZOSIMA

In *Suicide*, Durkheim seeks to understand societal cohesion by enlisting what is ostensibly the opposite—an individual's self-extrication from the social fabric. For Durkheim, those who deliberately and with finality sever their umbilical cord with the communal corpus hold the key to unlocking the secret of beneficent cohesion. Although *Suicide* was not published until well after Dostoevsky's death, the foreshadowing of Durkheim and the social collective (or lack thereof) constitute threads navigating readers through *Dead House*.

In *Dead House*, which predates *Suicide* by more than three decades, Dostoevsky illustrates Durkheim's concept of fatalistic suicide, which emerges in those contexts characterized by excessive regulation where a populous, forced to adhere to the same routine day after day, feel the absence of egress and of improvements. While many men, like Luka Kuzmich, Petrov, Akim Akimych, Sirotkin, Dutov, Baklushin, and Shishkov had self-destructive propensities before incarceration, excessive regulations, coercion, and futility aggravate these and goad prisoners to re-self-offend through "fatalistic" acts of and attempts at suicide. Dead House convicts know that their fortress is rife with euthanasic potential, that they can commit "unheard-of acts atrocities . . . in order to be executed and put out of their misery as soon as possible" (Pt 1, Ch 5; 82). Indelibly ingrained in their psyches is the icy fact that floggings can be conscripted to obtain their final release.

Durkheim acknowledges that his suicide categories can amalgamate into alloys, and Dostoevsky demonstrates how Dead House can breed the fatalistic-altruistic self-homicide hybrid. For Durkheim and Dostoevsky, an "individual [can] kill himself purely for the joy of sacrifice, because, even with no particular reason, renunciation in itself is considered praiseworthy" (SU, Bk 2, Ch 4; 223). In *Dead House*, the unnamed Bible-reading convict doubles with the Old Believer from Starobudye, both of whom exhibit self-sacrificial inclinations. The fact that the Old Believer endures his "exile with fortitude" and the unnamed convict literally extinguishes, life is for Dostoevsky not such a particularly significant distinction (Pt 1, Ch 3; 40). That is, Dostoevsky implicitly equates some forms of martyrdom with suicide, and thus has Goryanchikov suggest that individuals who live *solely* or die *solely* "in order to be engulfed" in some nebulous "something" they deem "true essence" end up with death or its simulacrum—living death (SU, Bk 2, Ch 4; 225).

In Dead House, prisoners ache with chronic cognitive dissonance where on the one hand, they yearn for release from *forced cohabitation*, and on the other, crave collective nutrients (Pt 1, Ch 2; 24). Yet, some inmates evade excoriation by forming their own collective subsociety, by sharing hopes of returning to their collective origins, or by fortifying themselves with collective labor. A residual question here is how do two specific survivors—narrator and author—fit into the schema? The response entails connecting Durkheimian ideas to not only Goryanchikov's evolution, but also to what will be for now a pre-glimpse at Dostoevsky's artistic trajectory.

For Durkheim, the "essential thing" is for individuals to enlist in a society "capable of supporting a sufficiently intense collective life," which will render "preservative value," lend meaning, and reinforce the will to live (SU, Bk 2, Ch 2; 170). Even though post-release Goryanchikov appears broken, misanthropic, and projects a demeanor of "suffering and weary exhaustion," in Dead House he harvested that "essential thing" that fuels incremental change and lets him seize at least a minim of "collective life" on the outside (Pt 1, Intro; 5).

For Goryanchikov, his prison bildungsroman is teaching Aley to read and write Russian, a task that fills him with pride: "Aley learn[s] to read superbly in a few weeks" and "learn[s] with fervor and enthusiasm" (Pt 1, Ch 4; 66). In fact, teacher and student "once read the whole of the Sermon on the Mount together," and Goryanchikov sees "color [come] into [Aley's] face" when his student says that what he liked best were the words, "[f]orgive, love, don't hurt people, and love your enemies" (Pt 1, Ch 4; 66–67). By giving these lessons, Goryanchikov bonds with Aley, who once "thr[ows] his arms around [his] neck and burst[s] into tears" (Pt 1, Ch 4; 67). Significantly, this also sweeps the tutor into a bigger brotherhood with Aley's siblings, who take "turns helping [Goryanchikov] and look on it as a happiness to be able to do so" (Pt Ch 4; 67). For Goryanchikov, Dead House's parting gift is not merely his vocation, but also the attendant realization that pedagogy can render collective preservation.

When Goryanchikov completes his ten-year sentence, his vocation migrates with him to the Siberian town of K where he lives a "morally irreproachable" life and earns his livelihood as a tutor (Pt 1, Intro.; 5). Although his existence is hermitic, as a teacher he is again able to bond with and positively impact others, which in its own way integrates him into K's social construct. This is evident in Goryanchikov's kindness toward and relationship with Katya, his landlady's granddaughter. When the narrator of the *Dead House* Introduction asks Katya if she posthumously "remembers her teacher," she "look[s] at [him] in silence, turn[s] to the wall and start[s] to cry" (Pt 1, Intro.; 7). By exclaiming that "even this man had been able to make someone love him," the narrator suggests that Goryanchikov's tenure in prison had not only awakened talent and ignited incremental change but also gifted him with the kind of labor that facilitated his post-prison participation in community life even if minimally (Pt 1, Intro.; 7).

Dostoevsky's own artistic trajectory parallels that of his *Dead House* narrator's development into the beneficent tutor. That is, like Goryanchikov, Dostoevsky himself exited Dead House with an "essential thing," but for the author it was his still somewhat inchoate genius as a writer and an ability to find self-preservation in his craft. Before serving his sentence in Omsk Fortress, Dostoevsky was just getting started. Dostoevsky's epistolary novel *Poor Folk*, lauded by Vissarion Belinsky as "revealing such secrets of life and characters in Russia as no one before him even dreamed of" and published in the *St. Petersburg Anthology*, launched his career.[78] Despite the scathing criticism of his next novel, *The Double*, and the ensuing strained relations with prominent Belinsky, Dostoevsky was beginning to spread his wings and hone his talent.[79] Once arrested and his death sentence commuted, the horrific conditions in Omsk could have halted Dostoevsky's advancement. Miraculously, he not only stayed alive but also exited with augmented creative wattage.

Just as Dead House becomes Goryanchikov's gymnasium on route to his teaching career, the Siberian prison became Dostoevsky's laboratory not only for the *Dead House* novel, but for future masterpieces. In Siberia, Dostoevsky resided in shackles, alongside a multicultural population from all parts of the Russian Empire. Thanks to Dr. Troitsky, in the hospital Dostoevsky could keep notebooks which he used to supplement his memories as he wrote his semiautobiographical masterpiece. But *Dead House* was not the sole progeny of his internment. During this era, Dostoevsky harvested lots of raw material, observing, memorizing, and most poignantly—listening to and really hearing the surrounding voices. It was here that Dostoevsky began to mature into what Bakhtin calls "the creator of the polyphonic novel," or the father of a "fundamentally new novelistic genre," one which refuses to "fit any of the preconceived frameworks or historico-literary schemes that we usually apply to various species of the European novel."[80] In Dead House, that very "plurality of *independent and unmerged voices and consciousness*," implanted themselves in Dostoevsky's brain, incubated, and later debuted as a "new novelistic genre."[81]

Essentially, prison did for Dostoevsky what it does for protagonist Goryanchikov: it primed the author for his post-release vocation, but for him it was one in which he would inculcate a "collective credo" through his craft (SU, Bk2, Ch 2; 159). What also sprang from Dostoevsky's Dead House experience was an epiphanic vision mingled with remorse over his early dallying in Western "isms" and a commitment to the sanctity of a Russian Christ, which became the entelechy of his later fiction. Several scholars, including Joseph Frank, have aptly noticed that *Dead House* is far more autobiographical than Dostoevsky's other fiction.[82] While Robin Feuer Miller has pointed out that "in his fiction Dostoevsky always sought to conceal his own voice as a matter of policy," *Dead House* veers from that "policy."[83] In *Dead House*, polyphony is frequently forsaken and the author's soliloquized voice, not muted, fuses with the narrator's in such a way that they orate in unison.

Intermittently, in *Dead House*, Dostoevsky's most passionate revelations are "not independent of" but also "merge" with that of his fictive ombudsman. Like Dostoevsky, Goryanchikov, a member of an educated, elite class, living cheek-by-jowl with peasant-convicts, "encounter[s] signs of the most refined spiritual development among the uneducated men suffering their lives away in this most oppressive of environments" (Pt 2, Ch 7; 262–63). His fraternization, although limited by his nobleman stature, culminates in the narrator-author's realization:

> It sometimes happened in the prison that you knew a man for several years and thought he was a beast, not a man, and you regarded him with contempt. And then suddenly a chance moment would arrive when some involuntary impulse

> revealed his soul, and you'd see in it such riches, such feeling and heart, such a vivid understanding of his own suffering and that of others, that it would be as if the scales had fallen from your eyes, and in the first moment you'd hardly be able to believe what you yourself had seen and heard. (Pt 2, Ch 7; 263)

In sync with his creator, Goryanchikov conveys that "[e]very man, whoever, he might be and however downtrodden he may be, nonetheless demands, even if instinctively and unconsciously, that respect be shown for his human dignity" (Pt 1, Ch 8; 115–16). These sentiments with respect to "feeling," "heart," and "suffering," which make everyone worthy of respect and dignity can endow humanity with that Durkheimian "intense collective life" (SU, Bk 2, Ch 2; 170). Empathic ruminations, once embryonic in *Poor Folk*, were decidedly quickened in Dead House and anticipate what would fully emerge in Dostoevsky's later masterpieces. They prefigure an overarching theme in *The Brothers Karamazov*—the "experience of active love"—along with Zosima's commendation of a life where we "actively and tirelessly" love and embrace our neighbors.[84] For Durkheim and Dostoevsky (and his Zosima), the energy of "active love" can yield the kind of collectivity that can empower us to repel what Durkheim calls the ubiquitous "suicidogenetic current" (SU, Bk 3, Ch 1; 323).

NOTES

1. Gier Kjetsaa, *Fyodor Dostoevsky: A Writer's Life*, trans. Siri Hustvedt and David McDuff (NY: First Ballantine Books, 1989), 87.

2. See Letter from Fyodor Dostoevsky to Mikhail Dostoevsky (December 22, 1849) in *Complete Letters*, trans. David Lowe and Ronald Meyer, Vol. 1 (MI: Ardis Publishers, 1988) [hereinafter *Letters* Vol. 1], 178 ("I was the sixth in line, people were summoned by threes, cons[equently], I was in the second row and had no more than a minute left to live.").

3. See Letter from Fyodor Dostoevsky to Mikhail Dostoevsky (January30–February 22, 1854) in *Letters* Vol. 1, 188 (writing from Omsk, he states, "[b]ecause of unstrung nerves I came down with epilepsy, but attacks occur rarely, however"); Kjetsaa, Ibid., 35 ("The evidence suggests that Dostoyevsky's epilepsy first made it appearance in Siberia."); Ibid., 101 ("When he had just returned from the prison clinic, he made a retort to an order, and the major is said to have implemented a punishment that triggered his first epileptic seizure."). See also Brian R. Johnson, "Intersecting Nervous Disorders in Dostoevsky's *The Insulted and the Injured, Dostoevsky Studies*, 16 (2012), 84 ("Dostoevsky's assertion that convulsive epilepsy first struck him while he was in prison is confirmed by virtually every source corresponding to that period."). But see Diane Oenning Thompson, "On the Koranic Motif in *The Idiot* and *Demons*," in *Aspects of Dostoevskii: Art, Ethics and Faith*, eds. Robert Reid and Joe Andrew (NY: Rodopi B.V. 2012), 116 (discussing a

conversation in which Dostoevsky "told some friends about his first epileptic fit which occurred after his release from prison camp"); James L. Rice, *Dostoevsky and the Healing Art: An Essay in Literary and Medical History* (MI: Ardis Publishers, 1985) (After meticulous research, he asserts that Dostoevsky's epilepsy began before Siberia.). Ibid., 6 ("[*K*] ondrashka was Dostoevsky's whimsical euphemism for an epileptic seizure (falling sickness—*paduchaia*), the first severe attack of which [Dr.] Yanovsky reports from July 1847."); Ibid., 10 (Dr. Yanovsky dates the first epileptic seizure "from July 1847, when by pure chance he encountered Dostoevsky being led by the arm by a policeman on St. Isaac's Square, shouting that he was dying, his head bent backward, convulsions beginning.").

4. Letter from Fyodor Dostoevsky to Andrey Dostoevsky (November 6, 1854) in *Letters*, Vol. 1, 201.

5. See Amy D. Ronner, *Dostoevsky and the Law* (NC: Carolina Academic Press, 2015), 211–76 ("Prisons of Coercion," showing how the United States Supreme Court is effectually recreating Dead House through its post-*Miranda* decisions, by revisiting the overarching thesis in Dostoevsky's *Dead House* and demonstrating that when prisons are stripped of free will and human dignity, the transmitted message detriments and flogs all—even those on the outside).

6. See Fyodor Dostoevsky, *Notes from the House of the Dead*, trans. Boris Jakim (MI: William B. Eerdmans Publishing Co., 2013), 108 (Goryanchikov describes how his only book, *The Bible*, was stolen from him by another convict, who secretly sold it to buy vodka). All citations are from this translation. Hereinafter, I will include the part and chapter number, as well as the page number from the Yakim translation, in parentheses in the text. Whenever the author is referring to the novel, she will use the italicized *Dead House*. When, however, she is referring to the prison itself, she will use the unitalicized version—Dead House.

7. Various commentators have discussed the impact prison camp had on Dostoevsky and how it shaped not just the autobiographical novel, *Dead House*, but also his insights into criminal justice and the psyches of people who commit crimes or are punished for crimes they did not commit. See Joseph Frank, *Dostoevsky: A Writer in His Time* (NJ: Princeton University Press, 2010), 185–222 (describing the four years Dostoevsky spent in prison and how it shaped *Dead House*); Amy D. Ronner, *Dostoevsky and the Law*, Ibid., 211–76 (analyzing Dostoevsky's *Dead House* and its salient message, one which pertains to today and the contemporary prison systems); Amy D. Ronner, *Law, Literature, and Therapeutic Jurisprudence* (NC: Carolina Academic Press, 2010), 89–149 (analyzing Dostoevsky's insights into criminals convicts and confessions); Nancy Ruttenberg, *Dostoevsky's Democracy* (NJ: Princeton University Press, 2008) (discussing how the Siberian prison inspired *Dead House* and affected Dostoevsky's philosophy and view of society). See also David McDuff, "Translator's Introduction" in Fyodor Dostoevsky, *The House of the Dead*, trans. David McDuff (NY: Penguin Books, 2003), 7 (noting that Dostoevsky wrote to his brother Mikhail "I got to know something of the convict population back in Tobolsk; here in Omsk, I was to live for four years in close proximity to it" and discussing how Tolstoy considered *Dead House* "the finest work in all of modern Russian literature"). In *Dead House*, Goryanchikov shows readers that there were innocent men in

prison and uses the example of Ilyinsky, the nobleman, convicted of parricide, who lost his nobility and government rank and was sentenced to deportation and penal servitude, yet is proclaimed innocent after serving ten of his twenty years when the "*real perpetrators*" came forth and confessed. Dostoevsky, *Dead House*, Ibid., 260. Goryanchikov opines on the "*full depth of tragedy in this fact of a young life ruined by such a terrible accusation*" and how it "*adds a new and extremely striking aspect in the overall picture of the House of the Dead.*" Ibid.

8. See David McDuff, "Translator's Introduction," *The House of the Dead*, Ibid., 2–3 (discussing how Dostoevsky started planning the novel while he was still in prison and how the kindly hospital doctor facilitated the process); Joseph Frank, *Dostoevsky: A Writer in his Time* (NJ: Princeton University Press, 2010), 193–94 (describing how Dostoevsky "would have suffered more if not for the kindness of the head of the fortress hospital, Dr. Troitsky" and how Dostoevsky "kept a notebook in the hospital in which he jotted down phrases and expressions"); Linda Ivanits, *Dostoevsky and the Russian People* (MA: Cambridge University Press, 2008), 39 ("Though Dostoevsky was not permitted to write while in prison, thanks to the good auspices of Doctor Troitsky and his assistant, A. I. Ivanov, during his stays in the hospital he managed to compile a notebook of roughly 500 popular sayings and turns of speech that caught his attentive ear.").

9. See McDuff, "Translator's Introduction," *Dead House*, Ibid., 14 ("The intensity of the suffering undergone by the writer seems to have been such that he was unable to approach its recollection in personal terms" and "[i]n order to write his memories down, he had to construct a 'novel,' with a fictitious narrator-hero."). But see Frank, Ibid., 364 ("The more convincing accepted view is that Dostoevsky introduced Goryanchikov primarily as a means of avoiding trouble with the censorship, and that he did not expect his readers to take him as more than a convenient device.").

10. See Ronner, *Dostoevsky and the Law*, Ibid., 215–26 (discussing how the Dead House "inmates are systematically stripped of free will, a process that Dostoevsky distills into three elements: excessive regulation, coercion, and futility").

11. Emile Durkheim, *Suicide: A Study in Sociology*, trans. John A. Spaulding and George Simpson (NY: The Free Press, 1951), 44 (hereinafter "SU"). All further citations are from this translation. Hereinafter, I will include the book and chapter number, as well as the page number from the Spaulding and Simpson translation, in parentheses in the text.

12. George Simpson, "Editor's Introduction," in Durkheim, *Suicide*, Ibid., 17 (explaining that Durkheim's "approach has been carried forward, tested, and applied further by his student and friend, Maurice Halbwachs, in *Les Causes du Suicide* [Paris, 1930] and he saw that there is no antithesis such as Durkheim posited, between the social and the psychological explanations of suicide, but that they are complementary"). Ibid., 26 ("[W]ith the unflagging ability Durkheim always showed in utilizing the findings of psychologic science, there is every precedent in his work for believing that he would strive to bring his sociological analysis into harmony with psychoanalysis."). See also Andrew Solomon, *The Noonday Demon: An Atlas of Depression* (NY: Scribner, 2015), 250 (stating that Durkheim's categories "have defined much modern thinking about suicide" and "[c]ontrary to beliefs of his time, Durkheim proposed that

though suicide is an individual act, its sources are societal." Solomon explains that according to Durkheim, "[a]ny single suicide is the result of psychopathology, but the relatively consistent appearance of psychopathological suicidality seems to be tried to social constructs." Ibid. See also Steven Lukes, *Emile Durkheim, His Life and Work: A Historical and Critical Study* (CA: Stanford University Press, 1973), 9 (discussing how Durkheim conceded that psychology and sociology are closely related and that sociology can assist psychological analysis even though he sought to present the two sciences as distinct).

13. Simpson, "Editor's Introduction," in Durkheim, *Suicide*, Ibid., 23. See also Durkheim, Ibid., 82 (acknowledging that humanity has "a tendency to renounce existence," but questions the belief that it is "a monomania . . . [or] a form of mental alienation or neurasthenia.").

14. Karl A. Menninger, *Man Against Himself* (NY: Harcourt Brace & World, Inc., 1966), 187.

15. Menninger, Ibid., 187.

16. Isaac Ray, *A Treatise on the Medical Jurisprudence of Insanity*, ed. Winfred Overholster (MA: The Belknap Press of Harvard University Press, 1962), 195.

17. Ray, Ibid., 195.

18. Durkheim says that "[t]he type of suicide actually the most widespread and which contributes most to raise the annual total of voluntary deaths is egoistic suicide" and the individual prone to egoistic suicide has "too keen a feeling for himself and his own value, . . .wishes to be his only goal, and as such an objective cannot satisfy him, [he] drags out languidly and indifferently an existence which henceforth seems meaningless to him." Durkheim, *Suicide*, Ibid., 356. In contrast, "[h]omicide depends on opposite conditions" and "is a violent act inseparable from passion." Ibid. Durkheim asserts that "for the same reasons, altruistic suicide and homicide may get along very well together" because "they depend on conditions different only in degree" and "[w]hen one is trained to think little of his own life, he cannot have much regard for another's." Ibid., 357. As for "anomy," it "begets a state of exasperation and irritated weariness which may turn against the person himself or another according to circumstances; in the first case, we have suicide, in the second, homicide. Ibid. He concludes that "for anomy, since it produces both homicide and suicide, whatever checks it checks both of these." Ibid., 359. He explains that "a man sensitive enough to moral discipline to renounce suicide out of respect for the public conscience and its prohibitions will be much less inclined to homicide which is more severely reproved and repressed." Ibid., 359.

19. Durkheim states that "the society of evil-doers and prisoners is known to be very coherent: the individual disappears completely, and prison discipline has the same effacing tendency." Durkheim, *Suicide*, Ibid., 346 n. 44. He adds that "[s] omething similar to what we have observed in the army may take place" and "[w]hat confirms this hypothesis is that epidemics of suicide are frequent in prisons as well as in barracks." Ibid.

20. Solomon points out: "there are plenty of what one might call unconscious suicides, in which someone lives carelessly and dies of the incaution—perhaps through mild suicidality and perhaps through simple boldness," that the "line between

self-destructiveness and suicide can be blurry," and that "people who push their own decay without obvious recompense are pro-suicidal." Solomon, Ibid., 259. See also Susan K. Morrissey, *Suicide and the Body Politic in Imperial Russia* (UK: Cambridge University Press, 2006), 291–92 (discussing how "[i]n the wake of 1905, many liberal commentators began to ponder whether the revolution itself constituted a kind of metaphysical (and literal) death-wish," and how "they developed an alternate vision of regeneration"). Morrissey points out that when Prime Minister P. A. Stolypin's dacha was bombed in 1906, several of the terrorist organizers were sentenced to death, including Natal'ia Klimova, who "pondered the meaning of her death, both the physical experience, and the spiritual consequences—the dissolution of her individual consciousness." Ibid., 292. In the wake of this, "the prominent liberal commentator A.S. Izgoev argued that the path toward terrorism was nothing other than a form of suicide by proxy." Ibid.

21. See Sigmund Freud, *The Psychopathology of Everyday Life*, trans. A. Brill (SC: Columbia, 1901) (chapter 8) (discussing self-inflicted injuries and their connection to suicide); Menninger, Ibid., 87–415; Edwin S. Shneidman, *The Suicidal Mind* (NY: Oxford University Press, 1996), 63; and Edwin S. Shneidman, "Orientations Toward Death," in Edwin Shneidman, Norman L. Farberow, and Robert Litman, *The Psychology of Suicide: A Clinician's Guide to Evaluation and Treatment* (NJ: Jason Aronson Inc., 1994), 10–11.

22. For this, Morrissey references Nada Boskovska even "though she only cites two cases as evidence," one in which "a blacksmith's wife hanged herself, and her husband was subsequently interrogated about the conditions of their marriage" and another in which "a man formally reported his daughter-in-law for constantly running away and threatening to kill herself" in hopes of "prevent[ing] himself or his son from being blamed should she one day be found drowned, hanged, or frozen." Morrissey, Ibid., 37. Morrissey opines "that many suicides . . . occurred within the context of domestic abuse [which] is plausible, though a direct causality cannot be demonstrated," but "[e] qually important is that contemporaries perceived a causal relationship." Ibid.

23. Fyodor Dostoevsky, *The Idiot*, trans. David McDuff (UK: Penguin Books, Ltd., 2004), 708. See William Mills Todd III, "Introduction," in *The Idiot*, Ibid., xxvi (discussing Dostoevsky's "theme of illness . . .-- epilepsy (the Prince), consumption (the Swiss girl, Marie and Ippolit) and self-destructiveness ('hara-kiri', Nastasya Filippovna)," which "come to dominate Parts Two, Three, and Four of the novel"). See also Murray Krieger, Dostoevsky's "Idiot": The Curse of Saintliness," in *Dostoevsky: A Collection of Critical Essays*, ed. Rene Wellek (NJ: Prentice Hall, Inc., 1962), 39. Krieger states that Myshkin "understands why again and again she has deserted Rogozhin after promising to marry him, in order to run off with Myshkin, only to be even more terrified of her feelings of guilt with the little saint whom she must in turn desert to seek her fated death once more at the hands of Rogozhin." Ibid., 46. He further points out that Nastasya's "final turn—and she knows it is to be the last one—is to Rogozhin." Ibid. *See also* chapter 2 of this book.

24. Shneidman, *The Suicidal Mind*, Ibid., 63.

25. Durkheim explains that this "derives from excessive regulation" where individuals see their "futures pitilessly blocked and passions violently choked by

oppressive discipline." Durkheim, *Suicide*, Ibid., 276 n. 25. He states, "that prison discipline has the same effacing tendency" whereby "the individual disappears completely." Ibid., 346 no. 44.

26. See also Letter from Fyodor Dostoevsky to Mikhail Dostoevsky (January 30, 1854) in *Letters* Vol. 1, Ibid., 187 (describing the physical discomforts in which his "foot got frostbitten," he "lived in a heap, all together, in one barracks," in which "in the summer the stuffiness is unbearable, in the winter the cold beyond enduring," and they were "like herring in a barrel," where "there's no room to turn around[,] . . . [and a]ll prisoners stink like pigs . . . shiver the whole night" with "[m]ountains of fleas, lice, and cockroaches").

27. See Letter from Fyodor Dostoevsky to Mikhail Dostoevsky (January 30, 1854) in *Letters* Vol. 1, Ibid., 184 ("I put on irons for the first time" and "[t]hey weighed about 10 pounds and it was extraordinarily awkward walking.").

28. Goryanchikov points out that "[e]ven the consumptives died before my very eyes with their shackles on," and that the officials would only remove the fetters from one consumptive patient, Mikhailov, after he was dead. Dostoevsky, *Dead House*, Ibid., 182. Goryanchikov recalls the "shackles clank[ing] loudly against the floor amid the universal silence" and "the sergeant outside in the corridor sending someone for the blacksmith" because [t] he dead man had to be unshackled." Ibid., 185.

29. See also Letter from Fyodor Dostoevsky to Natalya Fonvizina (January 1854) in *Letters* Vol. 1, Ibid., 195 ("I haven't been alone for a single hour. To be alone is a normal need, like drinking and eating, otherwise in this forced communism you'll become a misanthrope."); Letter from Fyodor Dostoevsky to Mikhail Dostoevsky (July 30, 1854), Ibid., 199 ("I live here in solitude; as is my custom, I hide from people . . . I was under guard for five years, and therefore it's the greatest pleasure for me to find myself alone sometimes.")

30. See Ronner, *Dostoevsky and the Law*, Ibid., 223–24 (discussing the cognitive dissonance of no aloneness with no sense of community).

31. See Dostoevsky, *Dead House*, Ibid., 262 ("I couldn't and even didn't know how to penetrate into the inner depths of this life, and . . . I sometimes found myself hating my fellow sufferers" and "even envied them . . . because, after all, they were among their own kind, their comrades, and understood one another."). See also Letter from Fyodor Dostoevsky to Mikhail Dostoevsky (January 30, 1854), in *Letters* Vol. 1, Ibid., 186 ("They are coarse people, irritable and spiteful. Their hatred of the nobility exceeds all bounds."); Letter from Fyodor Dostoevsky to Eduard Totleben (March 24, 1856), in *Letters* Vol. 1, Ibid., 251 ("I did not see and could not see for all of these 4 years anything cheerful, besides the blackest, most hideous reality. I had not a single being at my side with whom I could exchange even a single . . . word . . .and . . .my thieving comrades . . . took vengeance because I was from the nobility and an officer.").

32. See Ruttenburg, Ibid., 44 (describing Goryanchikov as "[e]ntirely cut off from his former life as a nobleman and landowner" and as "existing in a state of oppositional solitude . . . utterly estranged from those around him and thus as disarticulated from the social body"). Goryanchikov states that he "had comrades, noblemen like [himself], but this camaraderie didn't lift the whole burden from [his] soul" and "[e]

verything around [him] repelled [him], but there was nowhere to run." Dostoevsky, *Dead House*, Ibid., 259. He describes an event, which "made [him] understand how alienated [he] was and what a special case [he] was in prison." Ibid. When the men conspire to lodge a complaint, Goryanchikov tries to join them and finds them staring at him in "extreme amazement." Ibid., 269. Vasily Antonov even asks Goryanchikov, "What the fuck are you doing here?" and others start spewing insults at him. Ibid. Eventually, Kulikov "[takes] [Goryanchikov] by the arm and [leads] [him]out of the ranks." Ibid., Later when the men unite but exclude the noblemen, Goryanchikov tries to discuss his estrangement with Petrov and says that he wanted to be part of it "out of camaraderie." Ibid., 275. When Petrov responds, "But . . . how could you be our comrade?" Goryanchkiov realizes that he "would never be accepted by these men as their comrade—not even if [he] were to become a super-convict, not even if [he] were to be a convict for all eternity, not even if [he] were in the special section." Ibid.

33. Shneidman, *The Suicidal Mind*, Ibid., 119.

34. Goryanchikov explains that "[e]very convict, no matter how bold and reckless he may be, is afraid of everything in prison." Dostoevsky, *Dead House*, Ibid., 55. When describing the major's "violent hatred for M," Goryanchihkov says that the major persecuted him, and he would have made things extremely bad for M. if it hadn't been for the intercession of the prison governor." Ibid., 80.

35. See Morrissey, Ibid., 150 (discussing those who "explicitly framed the act of suicide as a means to affirm personal autonomy and self-sovereignty against external authorities"). Morrissey adds that "[t]he affirmation of dignity in the face of repression was integral to most prison suicides among populists, who seemed to perceive the act as both a protest against autocratic power and a demonstration of self-will over the impending loss of the self to madness or infirmity." Ibid., 279.

36. Fyodor Dostoevsky, *A Writer's Diary*, Vol. 1, 1873–1876, trans. Kenneth Lantz (IL: Northwestern University Press, 1994), 652.

37. Dostoevsky, *A Writer's Diary*, Ibid., 652. The suicide victim also states that "[i]f the suicide should not succeed then let everyone gather to celebrate my resurrection with glasses of Cliquot." Ibid.

38. Durkheim explains that "[*i*]*mitation exists when the immediate antecedent of an act is the representation of a like act, previously performed by someone else; with no explicit or implicit mental operation which bears upon the intrinsic nature of the act reproduced intervening between representation and execution.*" Durkheim, *Suicide*, Ibid., 129 (emphasis in original). Solomon discusses suicide and its relationship to contagion as well: "[s]uicide breeds suicide in social communities as well. The contagion of suicide is incontrovertible. If one person commits suicide, a group of friends or peers will frequently follow. . . Locations for suicide are used over and over again, carrying the curse of those who have died: the Golden Gate Bridge in San Francisco, Mount Mihara in Japan, particular stretches of railway lines, the Empire State Building. . . Public accounts of suicides also inspire suicidal behavior." Solomon, *The Noonday Demon*, Ibid., 250–51.

39. David. P. Phillips, "The Influence of Suggestion on Suicide: Substantive and Theoretical Implications of the Werther Effect," in *Essential Papers on Suicide* (NY:

New York University Press, 1996) [hereinafter *Essential Papers*], 290–313. See also Dostoevsky, *A Writer's Diary*, Ibid., p. 300 (discussing Goethe's Werther).

40. Kay Redfield Jamison, *Night Falls Fast: Understanding Suicide* (NY: Vintage Books, 1999), 278.

41. Phillips, in *Essential Papers*, Ibid., 290–313. When Phillips was a Harvard freshman, he was introduced to Durkheim's theory of suicide and Durkheim became one of his "sociological gods." Ibid., 290. Despite his reverence for Durkheim, Phillips sought to refute Durkheim's belief that imitative factors had no effect on the suicide rate. He concluded that the evidence indicates that the increase in suicides can be due to the influence on suggestion in suicide.

42. See generally Phillips, in *Essential Papers*, Ibid., 305 (discussing Durkheim's claim that "the effects of suggestion on suicide are only local" and that "suggestion serves merely to precipitate a suicide a little sooner than it would otherwise have occurred").

43. Morrissey, Ibid., 305.

44. Ibid. Morrissey states that "[t]he affirmation of dignity in the face of repression was integral to most prison suicides among populists who seemed to perceive the act as both a protest against autocratic power and a demonstration of self-will over the impending loss of the self to madness or infirmity." Ibid., 279. Discussing the views of the "Progressive doctor L. Prozorov" in roughly the first decade of the twentieth century, Morrissey states that Prozorov was "[d]eeply concerned about the 'infectiousness' of the prison" and felt that "[t]he question of prison suicides possesses a tremendous meaning due to its connection with the question of political suicides [. . .] and due to the great affinity of Russian everyday life at large, especially during reaction to the conditions of existence in prison." Ibid., 300 (quoting L. Prozorov, "Samoubiistva v. tiur 'makh I okolo tiurem po dannym 1906 I 1907 goda," *Meditsinskoe obozrenie* no. 12 [1908], 64, 75). Morrissey offers Prozorov's quote from a psychiatric textbook:

> The entire being of the patient is filled with a feeling of grief and horror, a consciousness of powerlessness and hopelessness in the present and an absence of hope for the future and the expectation of the most terrible and horrifying end. This constant feeling of spiritual burden, this eternal condition of fear and horror, this physical and mental powerlessness [. . .] produces an unbearable hopeless condition of the soul" and often culminates in suicide.

Ibid. (quoting L. Prozorov, "Samoubiistva prigovorennykh," *Meditsinskoe obozrenie* no. 12 [1911], 80). Morrissey also explains that "representations of prison suicide as an assertion of sovereign selfhood against political despotism were inherently unstable for the price of imprisonment was often physical and mental damage." Ibid. She adds that the physician Dimitrii Zhbankov "was ambiguous on this point . . . [and] although he described the prison suicide as a means to escape the executioner and thereby to avenge one's sentence, he characterized the primary motive as the 'consciousness of powerlessness and loss of faith in a better future.' " Ibid. (quoting D. N. Zhbankov, "Sovremennye samoubiistva," *Sovremennyi mir* no. 3 [1910], 39, 40).

45. See generally Menninger, Ibid., 160–84 (discussing alcohol addiction as a form of chronic suicide). See also Jan Fawcett, William A. Sheftner, Louis Fogg,

David C. Clark, Michael A. Young, Don Hedeker, and Robert Gibbons, "Time-Related Predictors of Suicide in Major Affective Disorders," in *Essential Papers*, Ibid., 599–611 (treatment of alcoholism as suicide preventer).

46. See generally Morrissey, Ibid., 31–33 (discussing "drinking to death" as suicide). Morrissey states that "[i]n the seventeenth century, church leaders explicitly associated 'drinking to death' with suicide" and "[t]he conflation of these two phenomena [,which] persisted for over two centuries[,] . . . provides one of the best illustrations of how intention came to be associated with moral conduct." Ibid., 31. She explains that "[l]ike suicides, . . . drunkards willfully harmed their bodies and ultimately destroyed their souls," but "[t]he potential for repentance and redemption existed, however, at least until death." Id., 33. Morrissey adds that in the eighteenth and early nineteenth centuries, "many suicides were attributed to drunkenness" and that in 1900, "the "the standard guide to parish practice was (mostly) unambiguous . . . [and] it affirmed that those who die from drunkenness cannot be categorized as suicides and must be accorded a full burial," but "drunken suicides could only be denied burial if it could be proven that the idea of suicide had originated when they were sober and that they drank deliberately to take their lives." Ibid., 228–29.

47. A. Alvarez, discussing martyrdom, human sacrifice, and Durkheimian "altruistic suicide, states "tribes as far apart as the Iglulik Eskimos and the inhabitants of the Marquesas islands believed that a violent death was a passport to paradise, which the Iglulik called the land of Day." A. Alvarez, *The Savage God: A Study of Suicide* (NY: W.W. Norton & Co., 1990), 73. He adds that one of the "extreme examples" of "altruistic suicide" is "Captain Oates, who walked out to his death in the Antarctic snow in order to help Scott and his other doomed companions." Ibid., 74.

48. See generally M. D. Faber, "Shakespeare's Suicides: Some Historic, Dramatic and Psychological Reflections," in *Essays in Self-Destruction*, ed. Edwin S. Shneidman (NY: Jason Aronson, Inc., 1967), 30, 33. Faber states that "the religiously or patriotically motivated suicide might be labeled what Durkheim called 'altruistic suicide' " and "[w]hether one destroyed himself for the sake of his friend, his master, his spouse, his nation, or his faith, he was sure to be extolled." Ibid., 33.

49. Marcia A. Morris, "Expedient Sanctity: The Making of a Russian Passion-Sufferer," in *Sanctity as a Story: Narrative (In) Variants of the Saint in Literature and Culture across the Centuries*, eds. Halszka Lelen and Peter Lang (2020). In her brilliant paper, Morris "examines two seventeenth-century versions of the *Life* of Ivan the Terrible's youngest son, the murdered passion sufferer Tsarevich Dmitrii Ivanovich (1582–1591), who is said to have died because he was an impediment to another man's royal aspirations." Ibid. She broadly proposes that "Dmitrii's hagiography treats sanctity not as the defining quality of a holy person but, rather, as a vehicle for promoting social stability."

50. Ibid. See George P. Fedotov, *The Russian Religious Mind: Kievan Christianity, The Tenth to the Thirteenth Centuries* (NY: Harper & Brothers, 1960), 109.

51. Fedotov, Ibid., 110. In defining "the kenotic Russian saint," he explains that "repentance is also the most serious thing: there is nothing of optimistic joyfulness or cloudless serenity about him." Ibid., 392.

52. Fedotov, Ibid., 110.

53. See Fyodor Dostoevsky, *Crime and Punishment*, trans. Richard Pevear and Larissa Volokhonsky (NY: Vintage Classics, 1992), 455, where Porfiry tells Raskolnikov that "there was a most humble convict in prison" who "sat on the stove at night reading the Bible" and then "out of the blue, he grabbed a brick and threw it at the warden" and "so he 'embraced suffering.' " Porfiry then links it to Mikolka, who likewise seems to crave suffering.

54. Morrissey discusses prison suicides and states that "[n]umerous memoirs depicted prison life as an ongoing struggle between despotic officials striving to assert absolute authority and prisoners striving to place limits on it." Morrissey, Ibid., 279. She adds that "political suicide also tapped into the principle of group solidarity" and that "it could function as a form of redemptive self-sacrifice, even a gift, for the general welfare of the collective." Ibid.

55. George Howe Colt, *November of the Soul: The Enigma of Suicide* (NY: Scribner, 2006), 84. See also Andrew Kahn, Mark Lipovetsky, Irina Reyfman, Stephanie Sandler, *A History of Russian Literature* (UK: Oxford University Press, 2018), 141 (excellent discussion of *Raskol* and Old Believer writing).

56. Colt, Ibid., 84. He elaborates that "[i]n these instances a collection of individual impulses seems to detonate simultaneously, often under the influence of a leader who acts as a sort of lethal pied piper." Ibid., 85. There are "other times," in which "a single suicide seems to set off a chain reaction in which the act of suicide is passed like a baton from despairing person to despairing person. Ibid.

57. See generally Marcia A. Morris, *Saints and Revolutionaries: The Ascetic Hero in Russian Literature* (NY: State University of New York Press, 1993).

58. Ibid., 4. Morris quotes the "path," which is described by Campbell whereby "[a] hero ventures forth from the world of common day into a region of supernatural wonder[;]" then "fabulous forces are there encountered and a decisive victory is won[;]" and finally, "the hero comes back from his mysterious adventure with the power to bestow boons on his fellow man." Ibid. (quoting Joseph Campbell, *The Hero with a Thousand Faces* (NJ: Princeton University Press, 1968), 30.

59. Morris, Ibid., 4.

60. Ibid., 5. Morris adds that the religious ascetic "experience is one which is achieved only after he has fully perfected himself" and that "[h]e cannot show others the road to perfection: each must find it for himself." Ibid. She adds that this ascetic hero "more often than not. . . withdraw[s] into a place of total seclusion such as a cave or a remote and wild area and avoiding all contract with others." Ibid.

61. Joseph Campbell, *The Hero with a Thousand Faces* (NJ: Princeton University Press, 1968), 30. See Morris, Ibid., 4–5 (quoting Campbell and discussing the ascetic hero's failure to "return").

62. See generally "Notes" in Fyodor Dostoevsky's *The House of the Dead*, Ibid., 61 n. 10. Durkheim discusses why religious minorities, who are fending off hate and oppression, like the Jews, have a lower suicide rate: "the reproach to which the Jews have for so long been exposed by Christianity has created feelings of unusual solidarity among them" and "[t]heir need of resisting a general hostility, the very impossibility of free communication with the rest of the population, has forced them to strict union among themselves." Durkheim, *Suicide*, Ibid., 160. As such, "each

community became a small, compact, and coherent society with a strong feeling of self-consciousness and unity" and "[t]he Jewish Church has thus been more strongly united than any other, from its dependence on itself because of being the object of intolerance." Ibid., 160. As such, the Jews have a "slight tendency . . . to suicide in spite of all sorts of circumstances which might on the contrary incline them to it" and "they owe this immunity in a sense to the hostility surrounding them." Ibid.

63. See Fyodor Dostoevsky, "The Meek One," *Notes from Underground, The Double and Other Stories*, trans. Constance Garnett (NY: Barnes & Noble Classics, 2003), 315, 357 (narrator exclaiming, "suddenly I saw she had got on the window and was standing there, her full height in the open window with her back to me, holding the ikon in her hand . . . but instead of turning back, took a step forward, pressed the ikon to her bosom, and flung herself out of the window"). In *A Writer's Diary*, Dostoevsky discusses "a seamstress [who] threw herself out of a fourth-floor window" and the newspaper accounts "added that she leapt and fell to the ground *holding an icon in her hands*. Ibid., 653. He adds, "[t]his icon in the hands is a strange and unprecedented feature in suicides." Ibid. See also Deborah A. Martinsen, "Introduction" in *Notes from Underground, The Double and Other Stories*, Ibid., xxxvi–xlii (providing a superb analysis of "The Meek One"). Martinsen explains how "the meek one chooses death" and elaborates on the significance of the ikon:

> Instead of accepting her husband's embraces, she clasps her family icon to her breast and steps out the window. The icon represents the Mother of God holding her divine son, thereby symbolizing familial love. Dostoevsky thus artfully contrasts the pawnbroker's predatory love with the meek one's love of family. He also charged her choice with a political message: the child of Russia refuses to be uprooted from her native soil.

Ibid., xli–xlii. See also Irina Paperno, *Suicide as a Cultural Institution in Dostoevsky's Russia* (NY: Cornell University Press, 1997), 182–83 (explaining that the suicidal "act itself was probably the result of an impulse, a momentary whim" and "[w]hat Dostoevsky's story communicated was that the act itself was inaccessible").

64. See generally Karl Menninger, Ibid., 87–143 (discussing covert human self-destruction, includes as examples asceticism and martyrdom).

65. While in Dead House it is apparently taboo for inmates to discuss their crimes, they tend to do that anyway and divulge all kinds of personal information. See Dostoevsky, *Dead House*, Ibid., 17 (A man falsely accused of parricide, talked about his father, and the "hereditary good health of his family."); Ibid., 30 (Russian nobleman, who "immediately told [Goryanchikov] about his 'case' "); Ibid., 65 (Aley goes on and on about his mother: "[s]he must have died by now grieving over me. I was her favorite son."); Ibid., 112–13 (Goryanchikov "lay idly and miserably on the plank bed" and heard the "story . . . about how Luka Kuzmich, for no other reason than his own amusement had 'taken out' a certain major."); Ibid., 128 (Inmate Baklushin tells the story of murder and how in the midst of a love triangle, "he shot one of the Germans . . . with a pistol."); Ibid., 146–47 (Varlamov tells his life story while being "tailed by a kind of hanger-on, an extremely small convict with a big head" who keeps interrupting and saying "He keeps telling lies . . . He keeps telling lies!"); Ibid., Ch 4; (While in the hospital, Goryanchikov hears the story of Akulka's

husband and how a man tortures and murders his wife.); Ibid., 243 (The Lomovs, accused of killing their farmhands, "themselves told the story, and the whole prison knew it.").

66. In the "cramped" bath house, Goryanchikov describes how Petrov "never left his side," and "rushed over to help [him] without [Goryanchikov] inviting him, and even offered to wash [him]." Dostoevsky, *Dead House*, Ibid., 123. Goryanchikov elaborates: "[a]fter having washed me, he led me back to the anteroom with the same ceremonies as before—that is, supporting me and taking all kinds of precautions at each step, as though I were made of porcelain . . . and only when he had totally finished with me did he plunge back into the bathroom to steam himself." Ibid., 127. Also, in *Dead House*, the Christmas festivities, along with a stage show, prompt the men to bond, become friendly, civil, and considerate. Goryanchikov remarks: "each convict had an unconscious feeling that by observing the holiday, he was coming into contact with the whole world, that consequently he wasn't altogether an outcast, a lost man, a piece of bread cut-off from the loaf, and that prison wasn't different from the rest of life." Ibid., 135.

67. See also John Jones, *Dostoevsky* (UK: Oxford University Press, 1983), 145 (Dostoevsky's "[p]rison life, imagined and realized, sometimes contracts into absolute embattled solitude.").

68. Elizabeth A. Blake, *Dostoevsky and the Catholic Underground* (IL: Northwestern University Press).

69. Ibid., 44. Blake points out that as "Goryanchikov's relationship with the Polish prisoners becomes progressively strained in *House of the Dead*, he distances himself from the Poles by supplying the reader with additional details about his disagreements with specific Polish prisoners." Ibid., 44–45. She adds that "[a]lthough the Polish accounts corroborate the growing estrangement between Dostoevsky and the Poles, Goryanchikov's narrative detailing alienation from the group does not correspond chronologically to Dostoevsky's experience in Omsk." Ibid., 45.

70. Durkheim explains that the ideal "occupational group has the three-fold advantage over all others in that it is omnipresent, ubiquitous and that its control extends to the greatest part of life." Durkheim, Ibid., 379. With respect to this, he goes into depth:

> Its influence on individuals is not intermittent, like that of political society, but it is always in contact with them by the constant exercise of the function of which it is the organ and in which they collaborate. It follows the workers wherever they go; which the family cannot do. Wherever they are, they find it enveloping them, recalling them to their duties, supporting them at need. Finally, since occupational life is almost the whole of life, corporative action makes itself felt in every detail of our occupations, which are thus given a collective orientation. Thus, the corporation has everything needed to give the individual a setting, to draw him out of his state of moral isolation; and faced with the actual inadequacy of the other groups, it alone can fulfil this indispensable office. Ibid.

Durkheim, however, concedes that for occupational activity to have this healthy influence, it has to be revamped so that it can "become a definite and recognized organ of our public life, instead of remaining a private group legally permitted, but politically ignored." Ibid.

71. In discussing Durkheim's treatise, *The Division of Labor In Society*, Lukes explains that Durkheim examines abnormal division of labor, which does not produce "organic solidarity" and "diagnos[es] the ills of capitalism, under three heads: anomic, inequality and inadequate organization." Lukes, Ibid., 172.

72. Durkheim emphasizes that "[e]xcessive individualism not only results in favoring the action of suicidogenic causes, but it is itself such a case." Durkheim, *Suicide*, Ibid., 210. He adds that "[i]t not only frees man's inclination to do away with himself from a protective obstacle, but creates this inclination out of whole cloth and thus gives birth to a special suicide that bears its mark." Ibid.

73. Goryanchikov describes the team effort to procure that new Gnedko whereby the men "began to bargain" and "[t]he bargaining was intense and prolonged; the asking price gradually came down while the offer went up" and [f]inally they began to laugh at themselves." Dostoevsky, *Dead House*, Ibid., 250. When "the new Gnedko was led into the prison with due honor, . . .there was [not] a single convict who, on this occasion didn't pat the horse on his neck or stroke his face." Ibid., 250–51. Goryanchikov says that when the "Gnedko was harnessed to the water cart, . . . all the men watched with curiosity to see how the new Gnedko would pull his barrel." Ibid., 251. Because the purchase was a collective endeavor, "the Gnedko soon became the darling of the prison" and "[a]lthough the convicts were rough men, they often used to go up to the horse and stroke him." Ibid. Durkheim explains how work can be a source of healthy solidarity:

[T]he worker, far from remaining bent over his task, does not lose sight of those cooperating with him, but

> acts upon them and is acted upon by them. He is not, therefore, a machine who repeats movements the sense of which he does not perceive, but he knows that they are tending in a certain direction, toward a goal that he can conceive of more or less distinctly. He feels that he is of some use. For this he has no need to take in very vast areas of the social horizon: it is enough for him to perceive enough of it to understand that his actions have a goal beyond themselves.

Emile Durkeim, *The Division of Labor in Society*, ed. Steven Lukes, trans. W. D. Halls (NY: Free Press, 2014), 291.

74. Frank, Ibid., 219.

75. See Durkheim, *The Division of Labor in Society*, Ibid., 291 ("[H]owever specialized, however uniform [the worker's] activity may be, it is that of an intelligent being, for he knows that this activity has meaning.").

76. In Greek mythology, Sisyphus was once King of Corinth, who was punished in Hades for betraying a secret of Zeus, and thus sentenced to forever roll a stone up a hill, only to have it roll back down. See generally Homer, *The Odyssey*, ed. and trans. Emily Wilson (NY: W.W. Norton & Co., Inc., 2018), 298. When Odysseus is amongst the dead, he describes:

And I saw Sisyphus in torment, pushing
A giant rock with both hands, leaning on it
With all his might to shove it up towards

A hilltop; when he almost reached the peak,
Its weight would swerve, and it would roll back down,
Heedlessly. But he kept on straining, pushing,
His body drenched in sweat, his head all dusty.

Ibid. In her glossary, Wilson calls Sisyphus "[a] consummate trickster who seduced his brother's wife and killed travelers and guests." Ibid., 574. She explains, "Sisyphus was condemned to punishment in the underworld: he had to roll a rock up a mountain, but every time, just before he reached the top, the rock rolled back down." Ibid. See also Edith Hamilton, *Mythology: Timeless Tales of Gods and Heroes* (NY: Little Brown, & Co., 1969), 298; *The Ultimate Encyclopedia of Mythology* (UK: Lorenz Books, 1999), 83 ("Zeus condemned Sisyphus to Tartarus to pay for his lifelong impiety" and "[f]or the rest of eternity he had to roll a block of stone to the top of a hill only to see it roll back again as it reached the crest."). But see Albert Camus, "The Myth of Sisyphus," in *The Myth of Sisyphus and Other Essays*, trans. Justin O'Brien (NY: Vintage Books, 1991), 123 ("Each atom of that stone, each mineral flake of that night-filled mountain, in itself forms a world. The struggle itself toward the heights is enough to fill a Man's heart. One must imagine Sisyphus happy.").

77. See Morrissey, Ibid., 279 (discussing how "[t]he affirmation of dignity in the face of repression was integral to most prison suicides among populists"). She adds that "[o]ne of the key sources of individual dignity was the collective of political prisoners" and that "political suicide also tapped into the principle of group solidarity: it could function as a form of redemptive self-sacrifice, even a gift for the general welfare of the collective." Ibid.

78. The *Poor Folk* manuscript excited writer Dmitry Grigorovich and poet Nikolai Nekrasov so much that, after spending the night reading it, they headed to the home of the great literary critic, Vissarion Belinsky to announce, "We've a new [Nikolai] Gogol" and Belinsky, initially dubious, said, "With the likes of you, Gogols are springing up like mushrooms." Kjetssa, Ibid., 42–44. See also David McDuff, "Introduction," in Fyodor Dostoyevsky *Poor Folk and Other Stories* (NY: Penguin Books, 1988), xi ("A new Gogol has appeared!" Nekrasov shouted, as he entered Belinsky's study holding the manuscript of *Poor Folk*"). Once Belinsky read the manuscript, he was instantly swayed: he could scarcely contain his enthusiasm for this "new talent . . .[whose] novel reveals such secrets of life and characters in Russia as no one before him even dreamed of." Frank, Ibid., 76. The *St. Petersburg Anthology*, edited by Nekrasov, published the novel and Dostoevsky, at a young age, rose to stardom. In a letter to his brother, Dostoevsky elaborates on his sudden popularity:

> I think my fame will never reach such an apogee as now. There's unbelievable admiration everywhere . . .Everyone is receiving me like a miracle. I can't even open my mouth without having it repeated in all corners that Dostoev[sky] said such-and-such . . . Dostoev[sky] wants to do such-and-such It would be impossible to like me more than Belinsky does.

Letter from Fyodor Dostoevsky to Mikhail Dostoevsky (November 16, 1845), in *Letters* Vol. 1, Ibid., 117.

79. Belinsky, who was already having reservations about Dostoevsky, scathingly criticized the next novel, *The Double*, by calling it "terrible nonsense" and saying that "[e]very new work of Dostoevsky is a further step down . . . I think, dear friends we may have hit bottom with this genius." Kjetsaa, Ibid., 53. In a letter to his brother, Dostoevsky says, "[b]ut here's what vile and painful: our own people, our kind Belinsky, and everyone are displeased with me for [*The Double*]. Letter from Fyodor Dostoevsky to Mikhail Dostoevsky (April 1, 1846) in *Letters* Vol. 1, Ibid., 124. See also, Ronner, *Dostoevsky and the Law*, Ibid., 90–97 (discussing the many critics of *The Double* who during Dostoevsky's life and right up until the present see the novel as a setback or failure). This disparagement by a cultural icon of Russian culture, along with growing ideological differences between Belinsky and Dostoevsky, led to a rift. In a letter to his brother, Dostoevsky writes, "[a] s for Belinsky, he's such a weak person that even in literary opinions he keeps changing his mind" but adds, "[o]nly with him have I retained my former good relations." Letter from Fyodor Dostoevsky to Mikhail Dostoevsky (November 26, 1846) in *Letters* Vol. 1 Ibid., 142. Later in life, Dostoevsky will write: "[t]he stinking little bug Belinsky . . . was precisely feeble and weak in his puny letter talent, and therefore cursed Russia and consciously brought her so much harm." Letter from Fyodor Dostoevsky to Nikolay Strakhov (April 23, 1871) in *Dostoevsky Letters* Vol. 3 (1878–1871), ed. and trans. David Lowe (MI: Ardis Publishers, 1990), 352.

80. Mikhail Bakhtin, *Problems of Dostoevsky's Poetics*, ed. and trans. Caryl Emerson (MN: University of Minnesota Press, 2009), 7. See also Kjetsaa, Ibid., 335 (discussing Bakhtin's "polyphony" and stating that Dostoevsky "disagreed with the notion that everything in a work of art must be easily comprehended and pleasantly obvious at whatever the price . . .: 'Let the readers do some of the work themselves,' he would say, defending the right to produce books that were difficult and intricate"); Robin Feuer Miller, *Dostoevsky and the Idiot* (MA: Harvard University Press, 1981), 9 ("Though the voices in a polyphonic composition may be heard separately, they are organically connected. They are composed and carefully orchestrated by a single consciousness that is carrying out a highly structured plan."). Victor Terras, *Reading Dostoevsky* (WI: The University of Wisconsin Press, 1998), 10 ("Bakhtin showed that Dostoevsky's text creates a polyphonic concert of living voices, one of which is the narrator's (which itself may well be dialogic!), rather than a homophonic narrative dominated by the narrator's voice."). Terras believes that Dostoevsky "will write elegantly only when the voice in question demands it . . . [and i]f one disregards the 'polyphony' argument, Dostoevsky's highly uneven narrative style, often distinctly colloquial, often journalistic, sometimes chatty, then again lyrical, solemn, or pathetic, places his work with the *roman-feuilleton* and may be legitimately seen as an aesthetic flaw." Ibid.

81. Bakhtin, Ibid., 6.

82. Frank, Ibid., 185–222 (discussing Dostoevsky's four years in prison and how that experience shaped *Dead House*). See also Jones, Ibid., 229–71 (analyzing the autobiographical nature of *Dead House*).

83. Robin Feuer Miller, Ibid., 91.

84. Fyodor Dostoevsky, *The Brothers Karamazov*, trans. Richard Pevear and Larissa Volokhonsky (NY: Farrar, Straus and Giroux, 2002), 56. See also, Ronner, *Dostoevsky and the Law*, Ibid., 204–10 (discussing the "experience of active love"). Dostoevsky explains that he "quite share[s] the ideas that [Zosima] expresses," and adds: "if I personally were expressing them, *on my own behalf*, I would express them in a different form and different language, but Zosima "*could not* have expressed himself in either a language or a spirit other than the one I gave him." Letter from Fyodor Dostoevsky to Nikolay Lyubimov (August 7, 1879) in *Letters* Vol. 5, ed. and trans. David Lowe (MI: Ardis Publishers, 1991), 130–31.

Chapter 3

Egoistic Self-Decimation in *Crime and Punishment* and *The Idiot*

In *Suicide*, Emile Durkheim states that "[e]xcessive individualism not only results in favoring the action of suicidogenic causes, but it is itself such a cause."[1] Durkheim, who was concerned with the connexity between the individual and society, recognized that egoism cuts two ways: on the one hand, it can promote moral and intellectual autonomy, which has its value. On the other hand, inordinate "me-ness" can backfire by not just alienating people from salutary collectives, like family, community, and faith, but also by inciting suicide epidemics. Dostoevsky, who saw egoism as a predominant symptom of nineteenth-century Russian pathology, depicted suicides and suicide attempts that prefigure Durkheim's egoistic typology.[2]

This chapter, using the Durkheimian lens, examines suicidogenic propensities in two Dostoevsky novels, *Crime and Punishment* and *The Idiot.* Arkady Ivanovich Svidrigailov's blast to the brain, Nastasya Filippovna's self-imposed death penalty, and Ippolit Terentyev's botched attempt are forms of egoistic self-decimation. This chapter concludes with a discussion of how Dostoevsky, like Durkheim, intuited the vacuity of a life untethered to anything beyond the self. In fact, Dostoevsky's cognizance of the human proclivity to egoistically hunger for oblivion became a galvanizing force in his creative process and evolving spiritual vision.

EGOISTIC INDIFFERENCE IN *CRIME AND PUNISHMENT*

Beginning in 1864, Dostoevsky endured one tragedy after another. His wife, Marya, died and then about three months later, the death of his beloved brother, Mikhail, delivered a staggering blow. Compounding this, his brother's family blamed Dostoevsky for the misfortune and the huge debt left behind. Dostoevsky responded by assuming the burden of paying creditors, caring for his brother's family, and keeping Mikhail's struggling journal, *Epoch*, afloat. When the journal went bankrupt, it saddled him with more debt. Consequently, in 1865, Dostoevsky found himself in dire financial straits, stalked by creditors, and fearful of landing in debtors' prison. Such desperation led him to sell a new work to Fyodor Stellovsky, a publisher with a bad reputation.[3] Dostoevsky agreed to accept 3,000 rubles for the edition, a negligible sum for such a popular author. More menacing, however, was the contract itself, which stated that if Dostoevsky failed to submit a new novel before November 1 of the following year, Stellovsky would receive a substantial windfall. Anna Grigoryevna Snitkina, who would become Dostoevsky's wife, describes what is conceivably one of the most unconscionable clauses in literary history:

> [T]he cruelest thing of all was the clause requiring Dostoevsky to deliver the new novel by 1st November, 1866. In case of non-delivery Dostoevsky was to pay a heavy fine; and should the novel not be delivered by 1st December of the same year, Dostoevsky was to lose his copyright, which would then to pass to Stellovsky in perpetuity.[4]

Stellovsky, who had every incentive to thwart Dostoevsky's fulfillment of his obligations, had done his due diligence: he had researched the extent of the debt, knew about the epilepsy that tended to derail the writer's schedule, and assumed that Dostoevsky, who had committed himself to writing *Crime and Punishment*, which was appearing serially, could not simultaneously complete two novels.[5]

By the end of September 1866, Dostoevsky was still plugging away on *Crime and Punishment* and had not even begun the contractual novel.[6] When he complained to writer friends that he could not finish a 200-page manuscript in a month, they offered to use Dostoevsky's plot and team up to help him finish the book. Because Dostoevsky could not ethically agree to sign off on work authored by others, he rejected that proposal.[7] Then his friend, Alexander Milyukov proposed that he hire a secretary.

The collaboration, which would change the course of Dostoevsky's life, began when a bright, twenty-year-old stenographer, Anna, stepped in to rescue him from Stellovsky's machinations.[8] Although Dostoevsky had some initial reservations about stenographers, he accepted Anna's assistance and embarked on *The Gambler* in early October. Nearly miraculously, they completed the novel on October 30, right on the cusp of the deadline.[9] Unbeknownst to Dostoevsky, however, Stellovsky had a back-up plan for blocking *The Gambler*'s timely delivery. The villain arranged to be absent from his office on that crucial day and left no staff willing to accept the work.[10] A lawyer acquaintance of Anna's mother advised the couple to deliver the manuscript to a notary public or police inspector and obtain a receipt.[11] Late in the evening, prior to the midnight deadline, Dostoevsky, armed with the receipt, planned a celebration.[12] Not only had Dostoevsky, with Anna's support, foiled Stellovsky's plot, but they had somehow managed to construct a fine piece of literature in only twenty-six days.[13] It is interesting that during the creation of *Crime and Punishment*, the Stellovsky-Damoclean sword dangled directly above Dostoevsky's writing table because throughout the novel, Rodion Raskolnikov's plight, which portends potential extinction, is also precarious.[14]

Raskolnikov: Crime as Potential Prequel to Egoistic Suicide

In *Crime and Punishment*, Rodion Raskolnikov bludgeons to death Alyona Ivanovna, an old moneylender:

> [H]e struck her again and yet again with all his strength, both times with the butt-end, both times on the crown of the head. Blood poured out as from an overturned glass, and the body fell backwards. He stepped aside, letting it fall, and immediately bent down to her face; she was already dead. Her eyes bulged as if they were about to pop out, and her forehead and her whole face were contracted and distorted in convulsion.[15]

When the victim's stepsister unexpectedly returns home, Raskolnikov, again wielding his axe, makes it a double murder and absconds with valuables. Fourteen days later, Raskolnikov surrenders to the police. While the novel entails a brutal murder of two women, the real focus is not on the crime itself, but on Raskolnikov's psychological anguish. The overarching question is whether Raskolnikov will accept responsibility, confess, and embark on a path toward spiritual regeneration or whether he will self-annihilate. As Dostoevsky writes in his notebook for *Crime and Punishment*, Raskolnikov is "passionately attached to both" options: hope, presented by Sonya, or "despair" and self-homicide, hypostatized as Svidrigailov.[16]

The psychiatrist Karl A. Menninger asserts what he feels is "obvious," that "aggressions against society lead to self-destruction in the sense of imprisonment, misery, and deprivation."[17] He thus incorporates criminality into his chapter on chronic suicide:

> In many individuals the impulse to commit crimes, which we can assume is a universal tendency, is irresistible, but such individuals cannot, on the other hand, escape the vengeance of their own consciences. Such individuals,

therefore, having yielded to their aggressive impulses, are obliged to surrender in the end to the threats of their own consciences if not to the intimidations of the law. This leads them, then, to seek punishment, to allow themselves to be caught, to commit provocative offenses or even "break into jail."[18]

While Menninger professes to be "somewhat dubious about the possibility of convincing the average American reader that criminality is actually self-destruction," Dostoevsky would not be counted as among the scoffers. In a letter to his publisher, Mikhail Katkov, Dostoevsky shares his plans to include in *Crime and Punishment* "a hint at the idea that legal punishment imposed for a crime frightens the criminal much less than lawmakers think, in part because [the criminal] himself psychologically demands it."[19] In his closing argument in *The Brothers Karamazov*, prosecutor Ippolit Kirillovich pounds this point, that "outraged nature and the criminal heart revenge themselves more fully than any earthly justice!"[20] Raskolnikov might have escaped detection and gotten away with murder, but with every step he sabotages such a result. Even before he confesses, there is something that impels Raskolnikov to do himself in, revisit the crime scene, make incriminating insinuations to a police clerk in a pub, and bring himself to the attention of Porfiry Petrovich, who is the examining magistrate working the case. For Raskolnikov, slaying the old moneylender, which would lead to "imprisonment, misery and deprivation," is his potential prequel to suicide.[21]

Attempting to figure out why Raskolnikov did what he did, scholars tend to adopt one of the perpetrator's spurious rationalizations for his offense.[22] The scholarship on the novel itself proffer essentially four possibilities, and as Dostoevsky intended, each one is discredited. Raskolnikov's first putative motive is personal: he murders Alyona simply because he hates her, which the novel substantiates to some extent. When we first see her through the starving ex-student's eyes, Alyona is repulsive and cadaverous: she is "a tiny, dried-up old crone, about sixty, with sharp, spiteful little eyes[,] . . . a small, sharp nose, . . . thickly greased" hair and a "long, thin neck . . . [that] resembled a chicken's leg" (CP, Pt I, Ch 8; 6). This repugnant portrait more than suggests that Raskolnikov is not particularly fond of his victim. It is even more accurate to say, as Raskolnikov does to Sonya, that Alyona is just a "useless, nasty, pernicious louse" someone whose humanity he tries to negate (CP, Pt 5, Ch 4; 416). When Sonya argues that she is not a louse but a "human being," Raskolnikov concedes that he "know[s]" this himself, that he is "lying" and that he "wanted to kill without casuistry, . . . to kill for [himself], for [himself] alone!" (CP, Pt 5, Ch 4; 416, 419).

Raskolnikov not only admits to Sonya that the murder is about himself, but he also beats himself over the head with that realization. This first happens when he visits Alyona. Although he feigns interest in pawning a watch, he is there to plan the attack. Throughout these dealings, he is nonemotional, business-like, even mechanical. This is Raskolnikov suppressing any emotional investment in his victim, whom he sees as a thing of neutrality—a nonperson. When Raskolnikov departs, he does not profess hatred for Alyona, but rather unleashes it all on himself: "Oh, God, how loathsome this all is! . . . But then, what filth my heart is capable of! . . . Above all, filthy, nasty, vile, vile" (CP, Pt 1, Ch 1; 9). If anything, what Raskolnikov reviles are his own brutal impulses—not this old lady, who is nothing to him.

Some psychologists and psychiatrists entertain a second but related theory: they attribute the murder to Raskolnikov's conflicted feelings towards his mother. For example, Kathleen Garber explains that Raskolnikov, viewing the "harsh, miserly old woman" as "the bad mother . . . who treats her stepsister shamefully," needs to "project inner destructiveness (the death instinct) and finds the old pawnbroker suitable for this purpose."[23] But Alyona is not the only candidate for the role of maternal scapegoat. Rather, as Louis Breger has pointed out, *Crime and Punishment* is chock full of mothers, like the landlady, who serves as the "bad" mother, "the source of food, shelter, and comfort, [. . .] whose care is bound up with anger, fear and guilt" and the landlady's maid, who serves as the "good" mother, who "attends to [Raskolnikov's] needs in a simple and straightforward manner."[24] If matricidal ire were the real trigger, Raskolnikov might have targeted a whole cluster of females in his vicinity, but the truth is that he is a sporadic equal-opportunity-misanthrope. In the novel, Raskolnikov expresses repulsion, intermittently pushing away everyone—both men *and* women—in his radius. If both loving and abhorring his mother has anything to do with the crime, it is more likely that he, unconsciously fusing her with his own ruptured psyche, seeks to unleash the death instinct on himself.

The third putative motive assigned to impoverished Raskolnikov is monetary. Raskolnikov tries to convince himself that murder plus robbery constitute an economic escape hatch. Some scholars, like I. Atkin, who call this a "social crime," argue that "[h]ad Raskolnikov not been a ragged, starving ex-student whose sister was about to prostitute herself for his benefit, no murder would have been committed, and his youthful ambitions would have taken a different course altogether."[25] For Atkin and others, Raskolnikov, who has "already been reduced to the lowest level of poverty," feeling "driven into a cage like a rat to starve to death," believes that only Alyona's bounty can set him free.[26] When Raskolnikov overhears a tavern conversation that leads him to think that the money grubber's riches can be used to better the poor, his motives become seemingly less self-centered and even altruistic. But over time, Dostoevsky (and Raskolnikov) debunks any and all economic justifications.

One of the few consistencies about Raskolnikov is that the destitute scholar, donned in rags and residing in a suffocating box, is not materialistic. Whenever he manages to get his hands on a few kopecks, he either gives or tosses them away. Sonya underscores this when she hypothetically asks Raskolnikov: "how is it that you could give away your last penny, and yet kill in order to rob!" (CP, Pt 5, Ch 4; 413). Further, in the murder's wake, Raskolnikov displays little interest in the spoils: he hides the purse and valuables under a brick and never bothers to retrieve them. At his trial, it emerges that Raskolnikov failed to "remember in detail all the things he had actually carried off but was even mistaken as to their number" (CP, Ep., Ch 1; 535). In fact, he had never once deigned to look in the purse, and after abandoning it, "some of the topmost bills, the largest, had become quite damaged" (CP, Ep., Ch 1; 536). Yes, Raskolnikov put himself through living hell, but surely it was not for his own, or humanity's, monetary enrichment.

The fourth putative motive is philosophical—Raskolnikov's Napoleonic theory—likely borrowed from Napoleon III's book, *The Life of Julius Caesar*, which was popular among the Russian intelligentsia at the time Dostoevsky was writing *Crime and Punishment*.[27] Commentators have suggested that Raskolnikov, suffering from deep-seated feelings of inferiority, confiscated an ideology prefiguring Nietzsche and killed to prove his own greatness and superiority.[28] In an article that Raskolnikov penned after leaving the university, he theorizes that there are certain people in the world who "are fully entitled to commit all sorts of crimes and excesses and to whom the law supposedly does not apply" (CP, Pt 3, Ch 5; 258). Even though Raskolnikov did not put his name on the article, but had merely initialed it, Porfiry, manages to locate and describe it:

> The whole point is that in his article all people are divided into the "ordinary" and the "extraordinary." The ordinary must live in obedience and have no right to transgress the law, because they are, after all, ordinary. While the extraordinary have the right to commit all sorts of crimes and in various ways to transgress the law, because in point of fact they are extraordinary. (CP, Pt 3, Ch 5; 259)

As Porfiry paraphrases such notions, he insinuates that his suspect might have committed a crime to prove himself to be that extraordinary Napoleonic hero: "Now then, sir, it really cannot be—heh, heh, heh!—that when you were writing your little article you did not regard yourself—say, just the tiniest bit—as one of the 'extraordinary' people" (CP, Pt 3, Ch 5; 265). Dostoevsky, however, has Raskolnikov poke holes in the Napoleonic motive. When Sonya asks him to explain the twisted philosophy, he proclaims that "It's all nonsense, almost sheer babble!" (CP, Pt 5, Ch 4; 415). Through dialogue with

Porfiry and again with Sonya, Dostoevsky leads readers to see that the crime was neither due to a personal vendetta against Alyona or raw matricidal rage, and it was surely not monetarily, altruistically, or philosophically driven. Rather, his wielding of that axe and making Alyona's "whole face contract and distort in convulsion" is a stroke along a self-destructive trajectory, one Durkheim would attribute to egoistical detachment and suicide theorist, A. Alvarez, similarly depicts as ingress into a "shut-off impregnable" realm, full of superstition and omen (CP, Pt 1, Ch 6; 77).[29]

Before the crime, Raskolnikov is a starving ex-law student, whose saintly sister, Dunya is on the brink of prostituting herself for his benefit by marrying a vile man with some wealth and social standing. Raskolnikov's room is like a "closet . . . located just under the roof of a tall, five-storied house" and is "more like a cupboard than a room" (CP, Pt 1, Ch 1; 3).[30] Because Raskolnikov is unemployed, in debt, and in arrears on his rent, his daily life consists of dodging his landlady and her maid, who live on the floor below. In addition, it is apparent that Raskolnikov tends to gravitate toward self-martyrdom. Like Nikolai Stavrogin of *Demons* who marries a lame *yurodivy*, Raskolnikov was engaged to his landlady's daughter, who died. Raskolnikov's friend Razumikhin explains that this fiancé, lacking a dowry "was not even good-looking . . . even homely . . . quite sickly," and Raskolnikov admits that "[if] she'd been lame or hunchbacked, [he] would have loved her even more" (CP, Pt 3, Ch 2; 217: Pt 3, Ch 3; 231).

Raskolnikov is not just trapped by his masochistic urges, poverty, squalid living conditions, and pesky people. "[I]n an irritable and tense state, resembling hypochondria," he also suffers from disorienting seizures while plotting murder (CP, Pt 1, Ch 1; 3). A sense of impending doom propels yet stymies him. Further, he displays an instability that "happens with certain monomaniacs when they concentrate too long on some one thing" (CP, Pt 1, Ch 3; 28). His state thus approximates what Durkheim denominates suicide-prone: excessive indulgence in "free inquiry," which "once proclaimed multiples schisms" and even "presupposes them and derives from them, for it is claimed and instituted as a principle only in order to permit latent or half-declared schisms to develop more freely" (SU, Bk 2, Ch 2; 159). In fact, Raskolnikov's name says it all, because in Russian *raskol* means split or schism.[31] As Razumikhin puts it, it is "as if there really were two opposite characters in him, changing places with each other" (CP, Pt 3, Ch 2; 215). The Raskolnikov enigma, and the reason that he is so difficult to pin down, is that he is indeed ruptured, perennially at war with himself, torn asunder by an internally repugnant craving for both salvation and oblivion. Raskolnikov's self-division predisposes him to self-decimation.

Raskolnikov fits Durkheim's melancholy typology, where the inflicted can "no longer realize sanely the bonds which connect him with people and things around him" and "sees everything as through a dark cloud" (SU, Bk 1; Ch 1; 63–64). Raskolnikov manifests symptoms of one verging on egoistic self-demise, which "spring[s] from [an] excessive individualism" that unplugs him from the "collective force" that is "one of the obstacles best calculated to restrain suicide" (SU, Bk 2, Ch 3; 209). Dostoevsky tells us that Raskolnikov is "so immersed in himself and had isolated himself so much from everyone" and "had decidedly withdrawn from everyone, like a turtle into its shell, and even the face of the maid who had the task of serving him . . . drove him to bile and convulsions" (CP, Pt 1, Ch 1; 3: Pt 1, Ch 3; 28).

Raskolnikov's self-imposed exile intensifies after the murder as he approaches the climactic choice between life and death. Dunya calls him an "unfeeling egoist" when he tells his mother and sister, "[w]hatever happens to me, whether I perish or not, I want to be alone" (CP, Pt 4, Ch 3; 313). Even Sonya, Raskolnikov's chosen catalyst for the confession that might lead him on the arduous path to rebirth, is someone he ambivalently repels. After telling her, "I may never see you again" and "I've broken with everything," Sonya hypothetically asks, "how can one live with no human being!" (CP, Pt 4, Ch 4; 316, 328: Pt 5, Ch 4; 421). Durkheim, in response to Sonya, would explain that such estrangement extracts all "reasons for existence" and then when "life is not worth the trouble of being lived, everything becomes a pretext to rid ourselves of it" (SU, Bk 2, Ch 3; 213).

Not only does Raskolnikov sequester himself, but he also replaces participation in conversation with eavesdropping. This begins prior to the crime, when Raskolnikov, "walks . . . like a man condemned to death," has "become lately superstitious," and enters what Alvarez portrays as the "world of suicide," which is "superstitious" and "full of omens" (CP, Pt 1, Ch 5; 62: Pt 1, Ch 6; 63).[32] Alvarez, who once tried to kill himself, explains that a person plotting to "take his own life[,] . . . enters a shut-off impregnable . . . world where every detail fits and each incident reinforces his decision."[33] Alvarez gives examples: "[a]n argument in a bar, an expected letter which doesn't arrive, the wrong voice on the telephone, the wrong knock at the door, even a change in the weather—all seem charged with special meaning," and thus "contribute" to the deed under deliberation.[34] While contemplating murder, Raskolnikov foists himself into the warp where everything is "charged with special meaning" where "[t]races of superstition remained in him for a long time almost indelibly," and where "he was always inclined to see a certain strangeness, a mysteriousness, as it were, in this whole affair, the presence as of some peculiar influences and coincidences" (CP, Pt 1, Ch 6; 63).[35]

The Alvarez-mindset becomes perspicuous in *Crime and Punishment*'s eavesdropping scene when Raskolnikov sits in the "wretched tavern" and overhears a conversation in which a student and a young officer are discussing Alyona (CP, Pt 1, Ch 6; 63). This "seem[s] strange" to Raskolnikov and "ha[s] an extreme influence on him" (CP, Pt 1, Ch 6; 66). When the two men propose disseminating Alyona's wealth to the poor, sick, and needy, Raskolnikov, pondering the "coincidence," asks himself, "why precisely now did he have to hear precisely such talk and thinking, when . . . *exactly the same thoughts* had just been conceived in his own head?" (CP, Pt 1, Ch 6; 66). He surmises that there is "indeed some predestination, some indication in it" (CP, Pt 1, Ch 6; 66). Not only is Raskolnikov adrift in that pre-suicidal murk of sigils and omens, but he, listening in on rather than engaging in, the banter, is already subsuming someone (or something) he has not yet formally met: this is Svidrigailov, who is the proficient eavesdropper, the ghost of egoistic indifference, and suicide incarnate.

Svridrigailov: Reified Egoistic Self-Homicide

Multiple scholars, including Edward Wasiolek, editor and translator of the *Crime and Punishment* notebooks, have called Svidrigailov an "embodiment of one side of Raskolnikov."[36] Breger, acknowledges that "[m]any commentators" have seen Svidrigailov as Raskolnikov's "double," concedes that "this seems to have been Dostoevsky's intention," and raises the bigger question: "[b]ut what, exactly, does Svidrigailov represent?"[37] For Breger, "Svidrigailov functions as a representation of impulse, unchecked by morality, as a man without God."[38] But Svidrigailov's amorality is just a point of embarkation.

Yes, Svidrigailov, a murderer, womanizer, and lecherous pedophile, is devoid of conscience, morals, or normative values. He is solitarily aweigh, unanchored to any collective ethos, which in Durkheim's view constitutes prime sustenance. Svidrigailov lacks any inkling of religion or life-affirming "beliefs and practices common to all" (SU, Bk 2, Ch 3; 170, 213). Svidrigailov is hydrophobic, which probably derives from his implicit spurning of the baptismal font, the basin in which old, sinful natures drown and then, resurrected by Christ, are reborn in a cleansed form.[39] His concept of eternity, not derived from any ism, is "one little room. . . something like a village bathhouse, covered with soot, with spiders in all the corners," and he demotes the Sistine Madonna to a mere "mournful holy fool" (CP, Pt 4, Ch 2; 289: Pt 6, Ch 4; 480).[40]

Svidrigailov is also untethered to the family unit: he says that his children "do not need [him] personally" and exclaims, "[a]fter all, what sort of father am I!" (CP, Pt 4, Ch 1; 291). The scholium, "what sort of husband am I," could logically follow his negated paternity. His wife Marfa Petrovna once plucked Svidrigailov out of debtor's prison, took him home to her estate "like some treasure," and loved him "very much" (CP, Pt 4, Ch 1; 285). But he reciprocated with apathy, rendering the marriage an otiosity: their union is memorialized in "an oral contract" that lets him stray and "cast an eye occasionally on the serving girls" (CP, Pt 4, Ch 1; 285: Pt 6, Ch 4; 472–73).

Svidrigailov is antisocial, a being walled off from fellowship, or as Raskolnikov tells him, "people don't want to have anything to do with you, they chase you away" (CP, Pt 4, Ch 1; 282). Durkheim opines that "[s]ocial man necessarily presupposes a society which he expresses and serves," but when this "dissolves, . . . [a]ll that remains is an artificial combination of illusory images, a phantasmagoria vanishing at the least reflection: that is, nothing which can be a goal for our action" (SU, Bk 2, Ch 3; 213). When an individual's arterial connectives to the élan vital disintegrate, "there is nothing more for our efforts to lay hold of, and we feel them lose themselves in emptiness" (SU, Bk 2, Ch 3; 213). It is thus unremarkable that Raskolnikov brands Svidrigailov "the emptiest and most paltry villain in the world" (CP, Pt 6, Ch 3; 472). Within Svidrigailov's vacuity, all deeds—be they good or bad—are interchangeable, and all that resides in his core is boredom and indifference. The parasitic void, moreover, does not merely goad Svidrigailov toward oblivion, but reduces its host into an abstraction—into suicide itself.

Interchangeable Deeds

The first mention of Svidrigailov occurs in Pulcheria Raskolnikov's letter to her son, in which readers get a glimpse not at immorality, but at the "emptiness" of unadulterated *a*morality. Svidrigailov is a mutation, incapable of discerning any boundary between good and evil. In her letter, Raskolnikov's mother states that while her daughter served as governess in Svidrigailov's house, he "conceived a passion for Dunya, but kept hiding it behind the appearance of rudeness and contempt for her" (CP, Pt 1, Ch 3; 32). Eventually, "he could not restrain himself and dared to make Dunya a vile and explicit proposition" (CP, Pt 1, Ch 3; 32). When his wife Marfa "chanced to overhear her husband pleading with Dunya," she blamed the governess, humiliated her by shipping her home in a "simple peasant cart," and "succeeded in accusing and besmirching [her] in all houses" until she became a pariah (CP, Pt 1, Ch 3; 32–33).

Suddenly, Svidrigailov did an about-face, presented his wife with proof of Dunechka's "complete innocence," which launched Marfa's campaign to "fully restore [her] honor" (CP, Pt 1, Ch 3; 33–34). Early in the novel, in a letter, Raskolnikov's mother alerts readers to Svidrigailov's redundant pattern, his agile shifting from evil to ostensible virtue. What belies this behavior, however, is an idiosyncratic deformity, one in which conduct does not ensue from any moral organ. Consequently, whatever Svidrigailov does, be it iniquitous or noble, is all the same to him. In her letter, Raskolnikov's mother naively speculates that Marfa's husband "repented, and probably [felt] sorry for Dunya," but as the plot thickens, it becomes patent that Svidrigailov can no more "feel" or "repent" than paraplegics can stand up and jog (CP, Pt 1, Ch 3; 33).

When Raskolnikov meets his sister's predator in the flesh, Svidrigailov states, "[b]ut you need only suppose that I, too, am a man, *et nihil humanum*" (CP, Pt 4, Ch 1; 281). His appropriation of Roman playwright Terence's phrase, *homo sum, humani nihil a me alienum puto* ("I am a man, nothing human is alien to me"), one that Ivan Karamazov's devil also utters, captures Svidrigailov in a nutshell.[41] He is indeed "*nihil humanum*," nothing human or human nothingness, and it is apodictic that all that is human *is* alien to him. When we learn of Svidrigailov's transgressions, including the murder of his wife, Svidrigailov himself along with circulating rumors convince us that he is devoid of remorse, with his "conscience . . . entirely at rest" (CP, Pt 4, Ch 1; 282). In short, *nihil* propels him, and he emptily acts with detachment.

Luzhin, who does distinguish between good and evil but chooses evil, says that Svidrigailov is "the most depraved and vice-ridden of all men of this sort," which rings true (CP, Pt 4, Ch 2; 298). Here the immoral Luzhin conjectures that there exists perfidy fouler than his own. Svidrigailov's is of the sort that disenables the process through which human beings make or reject axiological choices. In fact, Svidrigailov has no shame and therefore no difficulty owning up to his prior misdeeds. When Luzhin states that Svidrigailov "perhaps contributed to hastening his wife's death," the perpetrator is not so tentative (CP, Pt 4, Ch 2; 298). With chilling dispassion, Svidrigailov divulges to Raskolnikov that the task was "performed in perfect order and with complete precision" (CP, Pt 4, Ch 1; 282).[42] For him, that *coup de grace* is no different from discarding fusty chattel.

Svidrigailov, moreover, did not just commit uxoricide, but also provoked the suicide of his household serf, who hung himself, "driven or, better inclined towards a violent death by . . . [his master's] system of constant punishments and persecutions" (CP, Pt 4, Ch 2; 299).[43] To add to the litany, Svidrigailov, whose sensuality knows no bounds, persistently harasses and attacks women. Svidrigailov's wife "could not look upon him as anything other than a profligate and a skirt-chaser who was incapable of serious love" which he redundantly validates (CP, Pt 6, Ch 4; 473). On his estate, Svidrigailov pursued a pretty, young, serving girl, dark-eyed Parasha, who "burst into tears" and "raised the rooftops with her howling" (CP, Pt 6, Ch 4; 475). Further, he exults in his seduction of a lady, who was "devoted to her husband, her children, and her own virtues" (CP, Pt 6, Ch 4; 476). After "flatter[ing] her infernally" and manipulating her, "she, in her innocence, did not foresee any perfidy and succumbed inadvertently, without knowing, without thinking" (CP, Pt 6, Ch 4; 476). While this lady was soothing herself with the thought that she was still "innocent and chaste," her defiler, gutting her of her remaining self-respect, told her that she was a voluptuary, just like him (CP, Pt 6, Ch 4; 476).

The record discloses Svidrigailov's history of abusing and preying on young girls and Raskolnikov surmises that "it's this monstrous difference in age and development that arouses [his] sensuality" (CP, Pt 6, Ch 4; 480).[44] Apparently, when a "foreign woman named Resslich" gave Svidrigailev access to her niece, "a deaf and dumb girl of about fifteen, or even fourteen," he "cruelly abused" her and, like the serf, the child ended up killing herself (CP, Pt 4, Ch 2; 298).[45] Another Svidrigailov-saga makes Raskolnikov cry out, "stop your mean vile anecdotes, you depraved, mean, sensual man!" (CP, Pt 6, Ch 4; 482). This one started with Svidrigailov visiting a "so-called dance hall—a terrible cesspool," a place he likes "precisely with a bit of filth," and seeing "a girl of about thirteen, in a lovely dress, dancing with a virtuoso" (CP, Pt 6, Ch 4; 481). He initiated his pedophiliac grooming by sitting down next to the mother, letting her know that he has lots of money, and taking them home in his carriage. When he "discovered that they had neither stick nor stone," he offered not only to pay them but to help fund the "young lady's education" (CP, Pt 6, Ch 4; 482). Such overtures ignited what he intimates is an ongoing tryst and euphemistically refers to as an "acquaintance" (CP, Pt 6, Ch 4; 482).

Svidrigailov, who is fifty years old, plans to marry a girl who is almost sixteen in a match that "that rogue" Resslich "cooked . . . up" for him (CP, Pt 6, Ch 4; 479). Elaborating on his prurient attraction to this "unopened bud" in a "short dress," Svidrigailov confesses, "but to my mind those sixteen years, those still childish eyes, that timidity, those bashful little tears—to my mind they're better than beauty . . .[f]air hair fluffed up in little curls like a lamb's, plump little crimson lips, little feet—lovely!" (CP, Pt 6, Ch 4; 479–80). Svidrigailov instantly "took the [schoolgirl] on [his] knees without let[ting] her get down" and "kissed her all the time" while "mama . . . impresse[d] upon [her] that this, you see, is your husband, and it ought to be this way" (CP, Pt 6, Ch 4; 480).

While courting his little "lamb," Svidrigailov brought gifts worth "fifteen hundred roubles," and she embraced him, kissed him and told him that she "wished to have *only [his] respect*" and needs "nothing else . . . nothing, no presents" (CP, Pt 6, Ch 4; 480). Such a scene might entreat Dostoevsky readers to remember what the narrator says of Goryanchikov in *Notes from the House of the Dead*, that "even this man [has] been able to make someone love him."[46] If so, we might concoct some Pollyannaish theory that somewhere deep within Svidrigailov there might be a seed of redemptive virtue. By having Svidrigailov chalk up almost as many charitable deeds on his scorecard as those that make the flesh creep, Dostoevsky might even be tempting readers to buy into such delusional whitewashing. Afterall, with respect to

Dunya, Svidrigailov evinces proof of her innocence, later seeks to beg her forgiveness, and wants to offer her 10,000 rubles to "facilitate her break with Luzhin" (CP, Pt 4, Ch 1; 291). Also, by informing Raskolnikov that his wife Marfa left Dunya 3,000 rubles in her will, Svidrigailov seemingly gives her some sense of control over her future. Ultimately, he stops short of raping her and relinquishes the key that sets her free.

Moreover, after Katerina Ivanovna dies, Svidrigailov doles out charity: he covers Katerina's funeral expenses, orders memorial services to be held "punctually twice a day," places her children in a "proper" orphanage, and "settle[s] fifteen hundred roubles on each [child], for their coming of age" (CP, Pt 5, Ch 5; 435: Pt 6, Ch 1; 440–41). He also hands Sonya "three five-percent notes . . . for [herself] personally" not only to release her from the shackles of prostitution, but also to ensure that she has funds at her disposal when she accompanies Raskolnikov to Siberia (CP, Pt 6, Ch 6; 499). Further, before killing himself, Svidrigailov does not just toss his nubile fiancé to the wolves, but after explaining that due to some urgency he must leave St. Petersburg, gives the child "various bank notes worth fifteen thousand roubles in silver" (CP, Pt 6, Ch 6; 501).

In asking "what's the purpose of all this philanthropizing," Raskolnikov, rightfully distrustful, intuits that all Svidrigailov-deeds are nothing but neutral numbers scrawled on a blanched balance sheet (CP, Pt 5, Ch 5; 435). When Svidrigailov defends his offer to give 10,000 rubles to Dunya, he protests to Raskolnikov that it is "not to buy myself off, not to pay for the unpleasantness, but purely and simply to do something profitable for her, on the grounds that I have not, after all, taken the privilege of doing only evil" (CP, Pt 4, Ch 1; 292). For him, all doings, be they "profitable" or "evil," are equal and take on a life of their own, outside and apart from the actor, who is a bystander, a neutral accountant. Contrary to Svidrigailov's insistence that there is not "even a millionth part of calculation in [his] offer" to Dunya, for him everything is calculation (CP, Pt 4, Ch 1; 292). Suggesting that he "cannot find anything bad in depravity," he says point blank that "one must of course maintain a certain measure and calculation in everything, even if it's vile" (CP, Pt 6, Ch 3; 470–71). Svidrigailov considers all conduct as rudimentary bookkeeping with two columns—one of debited evil and the other credited good. This also becomes apparent when Svidrigailov offers to take Raskolnikov abroad and tells Dunya that her brother can avoid Siberia and that "as for the murder, he'll still have time to do many good deeds, so it will be all made up for" (CP, Pt 6, Ch 5; 492).[47]

According to "cool and calm" Svidrigailov, without such methodical tallying "man can only do evil to men in this world, and on the contrary, has no right to do even a drop of good, because of empty, conventional formalities" (CP, Pt 4, Ch 1; 292). What Svidrigailov perverts into the alternative, the "empty, conventional formalities" of others, antithetically derives not from vacuity, but rather from soulful ethology (CP, Pt 4, Ch 1; 292). His process is thus diametrically opposed to other living beings, who with hearts a beating, tap into their moral core to affirm that epithets, like right and wrong, resonate with meaning. Svidrigailov stores his deed-ledger in the coffers of "excessive individualism" where he "depends only on himself and recognizes no other rules of conduct than what are founded on his private interests" (SU, Bk 2, Ch 3; 209). Svidrigailov boldly proclaims "[e]veryman looks out for himself" and it is that selfism that leads him to finesse a hybrid column of debit-credits for his last posting—that of self-homicide (CP, Pt 6, Ch 4; 481).[48]

Boredom, Ghosts, and Eavesdropping

Durkheim could be speaking of Svidrigailov when he describes "exaggerated individuation" associated with egoistic suicide, which is "characterized" by boredom, by a state of prolonged "apathy," where the individual "drags out languidly and indifferently an existence which henceforth seems meaningless to him" (SU, Bk 3, Ch 2; 356). Svidrigailov could also serve as a specimen for Steve Taylor, who extracts the suicidal "*ectopic*" symptoms, which are the "individual's sense of detachment" and "*moral* insulation from others."[49] In Taylor's suicide theory, "[e]ctopia . . . produces in people a psychological detachment from the opinions, actions, and feelings of others, and the suicidal performances which arise from such situations are . . . private and 'self-contained.' "[50]

When Raskolnikov first meets ectopic Svidrigailov, this "unexpected visitor" introduces himself as a "depraved and idle person" and admits that aside from his sexual obsession with women and little girls, "there's not much that interests [him]" (CP, Pt 4, Ch 1; 281, 284, 291). Svidrigailov emphasizes that "nothing really occupies [him]" and that he is "not particularly interested in anyone's opinion" (CP, Pt 4, Ch 1; 284). While on Marfa's estate, Svidrigailov has no gumption to travel or go anywhere and even on the occasions that he and his wife quarrel, he stays poker faced, "silent for the most part" and does not even become "irritated"(CP, Pt 4, Ch 1; 284: Pt 6, Ch 4; 473). He paints a self-portrait of "a gloomy, boring man" who can "sit in the corner" without uttering a word "for three days" (CP, Pt 6, Ch 4; 479). Exposing the interiority of what will become Durkheim's conceptualized egoism, Dostoevsky injects ghosts, eavesdropping, and relentless ennui into Svidrigailov's morbific indifference.

While trying to coax Raskolnikov into helping him give Dunya 10,000 rubles, Svidrigailov blurts out what is perhaps the most ironic query in *Crime and Punishment*: "[i]f I died, for example, and left this sum to your dear sister in my will, is it possible that even then she would refuse it?" (CP, Pt

4, Ch 1; 292). It is no wonder that for Svidrigailov, an *inter vivos* gift is no different from a testamentary one because he is as close to dead as a living thing can be. We sense this even when he first materializes because there is a funereal "silence" in Raskolnikov's crypt-like room with a "buzzing" fly (CP, Pt 3, Ch 6; 278). Here Svidrigailov seems to emanate like a dybbuk from Raskolnikov's dream.

Svidrigailov, who communes with ghosts, is tantamount to the living dead. He postulates that ghosts "cannot appear to anyone but sick people," and "[t] he healthy man, naturally, has no call to see them, because the healthy man is the most earthly of men, and therefore he ought to live according to life here, for the sake of completeness and order" (CP, Pt 4, Ch 1; 289). For the "sick" man, however, when "the normal earthly order of his organism is disrupted, the possibility of another world at once begins to make itself known, and the sicker one is, the greater contact with this other world, so that when a man dies altogether, he goes to the other world directly" (CP, Pt 4, Ch 1; 289).

Svidrigailov is not one who can tread among the healthy and "live according to life here" with "completeness and order" (CP, Pt 4, Ch 1; 289). Since ghosts visit Svidrigailov, he is that "sick" man with a "disrupted" organism, who is so close to cadaverous that he is already floating in that "other world" (CP, Pt 4, Ch 1; 289). For example, Svidrigailov nonchalantly incorporates ghosts into his daily life. When his dead wife appears, she reminds him to wind the clock as she did "every week for seven years" (CP, Pt 4, Ch 1; 287). She, who "used to be good at reading cards," holds her deck and prepares to tell him his future (CP, Pt 4, Ch 1; 288). Svidrigailov even attempts to pique her jealousy by teasing her about his plans to remarry, and she responds predictably: "[t]hat's just like you . . . it won't be right for her or for you" (CP, Pt 4, Ch 1; 288). Similarly, when Svidrigailov's dead servant walks in, he reflexively tends to his old job and jumps to fetch his master's pipe. Svidrigailov is decidedly at home with the deceased and when he first drifts in and out of Raskolnikov's tomblike domain, his host posits that perhaps "[he] was only seeing a ghost," thereby equating him with a revenant (CP, Pt 4, Ch 2; 295).

Regarding the "causal relationships in the fabula of *Crime and Punishment*," Robert L. Belknap states that "[o]ne of the most common observations about the novel challenges the number of coincidences, chance meetings, and episodes of eavesdropping it contains."[51] Surely with respect to Svidrigailov, the consummate eavesdropper, who happens to hire the room adjacent to Sonya's, the coincidences are not, as Ernest Simmons suggests, a "blemish" in the novel, but rather serve to fortify it: they italicize Svidrigailov's role as a disembodied spirit, who can materialize anywhere and everywhere in St. Petersburg.[52]

Right from the outset, Svidrigailov informs Raskolnikov that he is "very bored." He later expounds on his superfluity: "if only I were at least something—a landowner, say, or a father, an uhlan, a photographer, a journalist . . . n-nothing, no profession!" (CP, Pt 4, Ch 1, 284: Pt 6, Ch 3, 469). As a man with no bonds and nothing to do, Svidrigailov wallows in a boredom that tumefies as he inches closer to effectuating his own demise. For Svidrigailov, predatory sexuality, which Raskolnikov brands "depravity," is his sole occupation, and it alone injects stimulation into his otherwise all-pervading lethargy (CP, Pt 6, Ch 3; 470). It is, as Svidrigailov says, "something that abides in the blood like a perpetually burning coal, eternally enflaming, which for a long time, even with age, one might not be able to extinguish so easily" (CP, Pt 6, Ch 3; 470). However, as Svidrigailov creeps closer to destination *nihil*, what little he has left, including his "enflamed" depravity, is progressively petering out (CP, Pt 6, Ch 3; 470). In the novel, there are three milestones along Svidrigailov's lethal itinerary: his final meeting with Dunya, his last voyeuristic nonevent, and his valedictory nightmares.

In the first milestone, when Dunya risks going alone to Svidrigailov's apartment to discover the truth about her brother, there is an intimation that her pursuer's sole raison d'etre, which "abides in his blood"—that "perpetually burning coal"—is starting to smolder (CP, Pt 6, Ch 3; 470). As Dunya enters his room, she immediately notes that "Svidrigailov's eyes [are] already shining with the same flame that had once so frightened [her]" (CP, Pt 6, Ch 5; 489). After learning of Raskolnikov's culpability, Dunya, "[a]lmost in a faint," falls onto a chair and Svidrigailov "sprinkle[s] her with water" (CP, Pt 6, Ch 5; 492). This effectuates a baptism of sorts where her passivity perishes, and what emerges is a strong, resistant, Dunya, who is reborn with a resolve to defend herself at all costs.

After Svidrigailov's ploy to woo Dunya with phony sound bites misfires, she finds herself trapped alone with her tormentor with no one in earshot of her cries for help. At this juncture, Svidrigailov drops the mask of ardent suitor and unveils his bare visage with "a spiteful and mocking smile . . . forcing itself to his still trembling lips" (CP, Pt 6, Ch 5; 493). But then when Svidrigailov beholds his captive, who, frenzied, enraged, and wielding a revolver, shrieks, "I hated you always, always," he comes face to face with what he lacks—affective faculties and intact emotionality (CP, Pt 6, Ch 5; 495). This, in turn, blasts him with a vision of his own mien of dispassion and moral bankruptcy.

When Dunya's attempts to shoot Svidrigailov fail, he no longer pursues her but chases death instead. He begs Dunya to finish the job: "You've got another cap left. Put it right; I'll wait" (CP, Pt 6, Ch 5; 496). At this turning point, Svidrigailov enters what the suicide theorist Taylor portrays as the tunnel of "submissive suicide," which differs from that of the death-seeking "thanatationist."[53] Taylor explains that "while the thanatationist is asking *Who am I?*, the submissive suicide is saying *I am dead.*"[54] As is characteristic of "submissive suicide," Svidrigailov begins to "*feel that he knows everything worth knowing*," and that "he is virtually dead anyway."[55] After Dunya tosses the revolver aside, "[i]t was as if something had all at once been lifted from his heart" (CP, Pt 6, Ch 5; 496). That "it" is the detritus of vitality. Svidrigailov realizes not only that he "had hardly felt" the sensation of "mortal fear," but that he, "deliver[ed] from another, more sorrowful and gloomy feeling," has been catapulted into a hole of "virtually dead," numbness (CP, Pt 6, Ch 5; 496).[56]

This final encounter with Dunya raises a nagging question: after putting cunning and energy into setting the trap, why does Svidrigailov suddenly give Dunya the key and let her go? The answer, like everything with Svidrigailov, has layers. It is not just because Svidrigailov realizes that Dunya can never love him. While admittedly Eugene Onegin differs from Svidrigailov in several respects, Dostoevsky's insights into Pushkin's "wanderer" supply a helpful analogue.[57] Deducing that Onegin "does not love anyone and is incapable of loving anyone," Dostoevsky postulates that if Tatiana had run off with him, he would have become "disenchanted the very next day and look[ed] mockingly at his infatuation."[58] What restrains Svidrigailov here is his ratification of what his wife Marfa suspected all along—that he, like Onegin, is "incapable of serious love" (CP, Pt 6, Ch 4; 473). While bragging to Raskolnikov about his "psychological anomaly," Svidrigailov proclaims, "let it be known to you that I no longer feel any love [for Dunya], none at all" (CP, Pt 4, Ch 1; 291). If Svidrigailov had successfully ensnared Dunya, he, like Pushkin's superfluous man, would have inevitably become "disenchanted" and reclaimed boredom "the very next day."[59] In fact, what prompts pimpish Resslich to secure him a replacement-bride is her clairvoyant cocksureness that Svidrigailov would inexorably "get bored, abandon his wife, and leave" (CP, Pt 6, Ch 4; 479). Along with his inability to love, Svidrigailov acknowledges that he is emotionally insensate and confesses that he "never [felt] a great hatred for anyone, never even wished especially to revenge [himself] on anyone" (CP, Pt 6, Ch 6; 505). In aborting his assault on Dunya, Svidrigailov, who can neither love nor hate, anticipates his exanimate quietus.

Moreover, it might be tempting for those readers with rose-colored glasses to attribute Svidrigailov's forfeiture of Dunya to a deeply interred tad of decency that precipitously bubbles up and impels him to put someone else's interests before his own. That "smile of despair," however, quashes such an interpretational pipe dream (CP, Pt 6, Ch 5; 497). Svidrigailov lets Dunya go because he has reached the dead end of "knowing everything worth knowing."[60] He is sinking into that "submissive-suicide" pit, where antinomies merge, where loving and hating are clones, and where defiling a victim or setting her free is a distinction without a difference.[61] In this trench, Svidrigailov's egoistic depravity dwindles and obnubilates until that "perpetually burning coal" recasts itself into a block of dry ice (CP, Pt 6, Ch 3; 470).

Svidrigailov's second milestone en route to his finale is his last eavesdropping episode, which like everything else, disappoints. Other than carnal indulgence, Svidrigailov mostly refrains from social interaction and instead listens in on or peeps at others from the outside. The scene in which Sonya reads the gospel to Raskolnikov is seminal in *Crime and Punishment,* and it makes sense that Svidrigailov is hauntingly present, "stealthily listening" behind the door (CP, Pt 4, Ch 4; 330). Sonya's reciting "loudly and rapturously" the part where Jesus commands, "Lazarus, come forth. *And he that was dead came forth,*" incubates in Raskolnikov's soul and gradually inducts his passage from confession toward spiritual regeneration, from virtual death to new life (CP, Pt 4., Ch 4; 328). Sonya's sermon also has affinity with the sacred ritual in Eastern orthodoxy, in which a Lazarus-like rebirth occurs in the divine womb of the baptismal font. When water covers the head, it is like being buried alive, but when the newly baptized emerges, it symbolizes ascension from the grave.[62] While this renascence might foreshadow Raskolnikov's course, the Lazarus scene conversely presages hydrophobic Svidrigailov's progressive descent from a semblance of life into the literal grave.[63]

Eric Naiman notes that "nearly all commentators of the Lazarus scene neglect to mention Svidrigailov listening behind the door, just as they inevitably pass over Sonia's erotic dream."[64] We might add that while *Crime and Punishment* scholarship is packed with suggestions that Raskolnikov's coffin-like abode matches his psyche, there is little to no mention of Svidrigailov's seemingly "empty" and "uninhabited" apartment as correlative to his vacant "excessive individuation" (CP, Pt 4, Ch 4; 330: SU, Bk 2, Ch 3; 213).[65] As Naiman suggests, from behind the door, Svidrigailov not only sates himself with the *Lazarus* rendition, but is possibly attune to Sonya's erotic fitful slumber, her "fever and delirium," her repeated "jump[ing] up," weeping, and handwringing(CP, Pt 4, Ch 4; 330).[66] Naiman says that this crucial scene with "the raising of Lazarus serv[es] both to incite and metaphorically to reflect rising sexual excitement" and that in "[r]eading the Bible aloud, Sonia raises not only Lazarus but Svidrigailov's flesh."[67] It is here that "empty" Svidrigailov, who is impervious to everything but lust, is fleetingly aroused from his long languid yawn: he "f[inds] the conversation amusing and bemusing, . . . like[s] it very, very much" and moves his chair so that he could "treat himself to a pleasure that was full in all respects" (CP, Pt 4, Ch 4; 331).

Svidrigailov's twinge of "pleasure" after overhearing the Lazarus dialogue contrasts with the total indifference he experiences in his last voyeuristic nonevent (CP, Pt 4, Ch 4; 331). Significantly, this happens shortly prior to his suicide after he checks into a "stuffy and small" hotel room (CP, Pt 6, Ch

6; 503). In this cubbyhole, which is nearly as constricted as Raskolnikov's crypt-abode, Svidrigailov orders a spartan meal of veal and tea. When the "ragamuffin" attendant asks if he wants anything else, Svidrigailov responds with the two words—"[n]othing, nothing"—that succinctly encapsulate all he has become (CP, Pt 6, Ch 6; 503). His nothingness is verified after he detects a "strange, incessant whispering" nearby, which "sometimes rose almost to a shout," and Svidrigailov reflexively plugs in with his gazing ears in a last-ditch effort to vicariously taste a morsel of human intrigue (CP, Pt 6, Ch 6; 503).

As Svidrigailov listens and peeps, an emotive fervor culminates behind the wall where one guest is "scolding and almost tearfully reproaching someone else" (CP, Pt 6, Ch 6; 503). With his "red, inflamed face, [this guest is] . . . standing in the pose of an orator" and "beating his breast with his fist, in a voice full of pathos" (CP, Pt 6, Ch 6; 504). He is accusing his "friend" of being a "beggar" and menacingly "claim[ing] that he had dragged him from the mud and could throw him out whenever he wanted" (CP, Pt 6, Ch 6; 504). The target of this scalding fury, however, appears frigidly nonplussed and antonymic to his riled-up assailant. He sits as frigid as a *corpus delicti*. He "look[s] like someone who has a great desire to sneeze but cannot manage to do so" and "from time to time" this "reproached" friend "glance[s] at the orator with dull and bovine eyes, but evidently ha[s] no idea what it [is] all about and most likely ha[s] not even heard any of it" (CP, Pt 6, Ch 6; 504). The watched catatonic form, who cannot muster enough energy for a mere sniffle, mirrors the "nothing, nothing" of his watcher. In his miscarried siege of Dunya, Svidrigailov's "eternally enflaming" depravity betrays him and here his scopophilia, his depravity's sole mate, is defecting as well.[68]

For an individual like Svidrigailov, for whom everything is sexualized, any event aurally or visually detected, even a prostitute's tutorial on the Gospel, can arouse, "amus[e] and bemus[e]" (CP, Pt 4, Ch 4, 331). Some psychoanalysts, like Otto Fenichel, disagree with Freud's psycho-medical theory that the "scopic drive" might lead to physical illness (like blindness) and instead posit that scopophilia can result in madness and retreat from reality.[69] Svidrigailov, with his voyeurism no longer delivering its jism, retires from his peephole with "indifference" and a "total loss of appetite" for anything associated with real life (CP, Pt 6, Ch 6; 504).[70]

From there, Svidrigailov traipses into a fantastical, nightmarish realm of "half slumber," which is not only his third milestone on the trail to denouement, but also the antipode to Raskolnikov's dream of the beaten mare (CP, Pt 6, Ch 6; 506). In Raskolnikov's dream, Mikolka is the owner of a wagon, hitched to a skinny horse, and he invites rowdies to pile in for a ride. Although it is obvious that the horse cannot drag the overloaded wagon, Mikolka beats the mare "pointlessly on the back with the crowbar" until "she heaves a deep sigh, and dies." (CP, Pt 1, Ch 5; 58). In the dream, however, child-Raskolnikov "tears through the crowd to the gray horse, throws his arms around her dead, bleeding muzzle, and kisses it, kisses her eyes and mouth" (CP, Pt 1, Ch 5; 58).[71] While the compassionate boy, who stars in the dream, is animate yet dormant within Raskolnikov, Svidrigailov's nightmares harbor no such kindred spirit.

In the sleazy hotel, Svidrigailov's "fragments of thought with no beginning, no end, no connection" concentrically swirl into dreams, ones in which he is the detached outsider peering in (CP, Pt 6, Ch 6; 506). At first, he is spying on pastural splendor: there are "fragrant flowerbeds," a "porch, entwined with climbing plants, filled with banks of roses," and a "stairway . . . adorned with rare flowers" (CP, Pt 6, Ch 6; 506). This mirage appears as an idyllic synesthesia of redolent color where everything quickens with ostensible life, where birds "chirp" and even "the bouquets of white and tender narcissus . . . in jars" thrive with their "long, bright green, fleshy stems" and "heavy, sweet scent" (CP, Pt 6, Ch 6; 506). Suddenly, the fallen incubus of mortal despair infiltrates the Edenic blur: Svidrigailov comes upon a girl in "coffin" where the "stern and already stiff profile of her face . . . seem[s] carved from marble" (CP, Pt 6, Ch 6; 507). This child's "smile on her pale lips," which is "full of some unchildlike boundless grief and great complaint," impugns itself (CP, Pt 6, Ch 6; 507). Svidrigailov not only knows that this is a suicide because "no icons, no lighted candles stood by the coffin, [and] no prayers were heard," but he also identifies the corpse as the fruit of his own depravity:

> Svidrigailov knew the girl . . . She was only fourteen, but hers was already a broken heart, and it destroyed itself, insulted by an offense that had horrified and astonished this young child's consciousness, that had covered her angelically pure soul with undeserved shame, and torn from her a last cry of despair, not heeded but insolently defiled in the black night, in the darkness, in the cold, in the damp thaw, while the wind was howling. (CP, Pt 6, Ch 6; 507)

Could this be a pang of guilt? Remorse? Is Svidrigailov "beside himself" like the "poor boy" in Raskolnikov's dream (CP, Pt 1; Ch 5; 58)? When it comes to Svidrigailov, the answers triplicate as no, no, no! As Svidrigailov once indicated, for him the child's suicide is nothing more than one of "those trivialities" that just tends to happen (CP, Pt 6; Ch 4; 474). From the image of the coffin, his mind does what it habitually does—turns to his balance sheet, nods first at the debit (the defiling of a child), and then shifts over to the putative credit (the rescuing of a child).

His nightmare thus foists him next into a "long narrow corridor" where he discovers "a girl of about five, not more, in a wretched little dress soaked through like a dishrag, who was shivering and crying" (CP, Pt 6, Ch 6;

508). After inferring that she is "an unloved child, beaten down, and terrorized by her mother," Svidrigailov enacts the bit part of good Samaritan (CP, Pt 6, Ch 6; 508). He methodically comforts her, puts her to bed, and swaddles her "head and all" in a warm blanket (CP, Pt 6, Ch 6; 509). Later when Svidrigailov returns to check on her, he beholds her nauseating metamorphosis from prelapsarian purity to sullied corruption as the "color[,] . . already spread[ing] over her pale cheeks . . . appears brighter and deeper than a child's red cheeks would ordinarily be" (CP, Pt 6, Ch 6; 509). Her mien, becoming "unchildlike," is deformed into "the face of a scarlet woman, the insolent face of a woman for sale, of the French sort" (CP, Pt 6, Ch 6; 509).

When the babe morphs into that "insolent" French whore, she mirrors the depravity of the dreamer, who is dropping further into chasmic nonbeing and becoming a "submissive suicide."[72] Svidrigailov has become the desiccated nonentity, who in Taylor's words, "knows everything worth knowing because, having established that for him life is over, knowledge that may once have been important (such as the state of his bank balance) is now irrelevant."[73] For Svidrigailov, "all is now known" and his "existence [is] . . . completely demystified and drained of possibility."[74] He is descending into the suicidogenic subterrain of "constricting horizons[,] . . . closing doors, blind alleys and cul-de-sacs."[75]

The rising water, which also rushes through his unconscious, will "flood all of the lower places," make "cellar rats . . . float up" (CP, Pt 6, Ch 6; 507). These nightmares evoke the disastrous St. Petersburg flood of the Neva in 1824 and signify the irreversibility of Svidrigailov's sinking, which is antithetical to baptismal emergence. These dreams also tie in to Alexander Schmemann's exegesis of water as not only "revealing . . . the meaning of Baptism" but also as being "the mysterious depth which kills and annihilates, the dark habitation of the demonic powers, the very image of the irrational, uncontrollable, elemental in the world."[76] On the brink of his self-imposed anti-baptism, Svidrigailov is no longer terrified by the prospect of being drenched because everything—even his lifelong aversion—is submerged in the annihilative "ectopic" font (CP, Pt 6, Ch 6; 507–8).[77] This comes across in the last meeting between Sonya and Svidrigailov. Sonya asks, "how can you go now, sir, in such rain," but he, brushing it off, rephrases it as his question: "to go off to America and be afraid of rain?" (CP, Pt 6, Ch 6; 500). For Svidrigailov, going to America and putting a gun to his head are one and the same. They equate with his pending act of obtunding everything he is and has been, which includes his intrinsic hydrophobia. When the tot-harlot reaches for Svidrigailov, he awakens to the prehension "that for him the game is irretrievably over and lost" and marches off for that egoistic "submissive" blast to the brain.[78]

Reification

Before shooting himself, Svidrigailov tells the man in the Achilles helmet that he's "off to foreign lands . . . to America" (CP, Pt 6, Ch 6; 511).[79] For Dostoevsky, "America" is a two-tiered concept: on one level, it denotes the agony that ensues when a Russian is voluntary or involuntary wrenched from the bosom of Mother Russia and ends up in a remote, inhospitable land.[80] On another level, it is one of Dostoevsky's pokes at Nikolai Chernyshevsky novel, *What Is to Be Done?*. Dimitry Sergeich Lopukhov, a character in that novel fakes his own death and runs off to the United States.[81]

The allusion to Lopukhov is not surprising because, as Joseph Frank has pointed out, after returning from exile, Dostoevsky "[took] up the polemical cudgels against *The Contemporary*," especially "the ideas . . . propounded by . . . its most notable and influential critic," Chernyshevsky, who sought to "establish a new ethics on the foundation of egoism."[82] Frank suggests that Lopukhov, who seeks "to prove the omnipresence of egoism," presented *Crime and Punishment*'s author with an ideal target for derision.[83] Moreover, Lopukhov's "going to America," which was conflated with ersatz self-demise, became a Dostoevsky buzzword for suicide.[84] By having the novel's bored, eavesdropping ghost repeat "America. . . America . . . America," Dostoevsky renders Svidrigailov as something more diffuse than a single egoist effectuating a single self-homicide and installs him as the personification of suicide itself (CP, Pt 6, Ch 6; 511). Svidrigailov as reified suicide comes across even before he physically shows up in the novel and he, the specter of suicide, continues to haunt Raskolnikov and Dostoevsky's readers from his grave.

Before Svidrigailov literally emerges, he is figuratively omnipresent as suicide pitches its tent in St. Petersburg and some inhabitants become like moths gravitating toward a candle flame.[85] The fiery sergeant Ilya Petrovich exclaims that "there are so many suicides spreading around—you can't even imagine" (CP, Pt 6, 8; 529). On top of this, St. Petersburg has clusters of drunkards and Dostoevsky, joined by multiple suicidologists, agree with Menninger's proposition that alcoholism can be a type of suicide.[86] As Menninger has noted, there are many who, like Marmeladov, "suffer from what seems to be an irresistible impulse to throw away all obligations and opportunities and bring their house of cards tumbling about their heads by getting drunk."[87] In fact, Marmeladov, whose drinking has not only driven Sonya into prostitution, but has further impoverished his consumptive wife and three small children, could be a case study in Menninger's chapter on chronic suicide. Marmeladov even knows that he is spinning his wheels in the gutter of self-ruin: "It is not joy I seek, but sorrow only . . . I drink, for I wish doubly to suffer!" (CP, Pt 1, Ch2; 16).

Self-flagellation and drinking are conflated when post-crime Raskolnikov is "lashed on the back with a whip by the driver of a carriage" (CP, Pt 2, Ch 2; 113). Unconsciously hankering for punishment, he "almost fall[s] under the horses' hoofs" (CP, Pt 2, Ch 2; 113). It is then disclosed that there is trend in St. Petersburg whereby people "pretend they're drunk and get under the wheels on purpose" (CP, Pt 2, Ch 2; 113). Suicide and alcoholism converge once again when one of the last things that Svidrigailov notices before pulling the trigger is a person "lying, dead drunk, in an overcoat, face down on the sidewalk" (CP, Pt 6, Ch 6; 510).

In *Crime and Punishment*, Marmeladov and other drunkards are not the only self-dynamitards in quest of suffering. Housepainter Mikolka also seeks to suffer, but he wields more direct methodology: he falsely confesses to Raskolnikov's crime, retreats to a shed where "he tie[s] his belt to a beam, [makes] a noose, and [is] standing on a stump trying to put the noose around his neck" (CP, Pt 2, Ch 4; 137). This transpires while Raskolnikov, the real perpetrator, is intermittently toying with the idea of ending it all, or, in Lopukhov's vernacular, considers "flee[ing] altogether . . . far away . . . to America" (CP, Pt 2, Ch 3; 127). Just as Razumikhim fears that his friend "might drown himself," Raskolnikov finds himself on the bridge, "as if peering intently into the water" until Afrosinyushka, hurling herself into the canal, ruptures his dark ripples of thought (CP, Pt 2, Ch 6; 168–69). After she is revived, Raskolnikov learns that this tradeswoman with her "long, yellow, wasted face and reddish sunken eyes," is known as a repeat attempter, who had before tried to hang herself, which is possibly her protest against an unjust world (CP, Pt 2, Ch 6; 169).[88]

Raskolnikov, who watches Afrosinyushka leap while he contemplates drowning himself, is overcome by a "strange feeling of indifference and detachment," where "[t]otal apathy" replaces his "former energy" (CP, Pt 2, Ch 6; 170). Here he resembles his doppelganger, nihil-Svidrigailov. Although Svidrigailov is not literally in attendance, he, inseparable from the suicidogenic impulse, is nevertheless present, entrenched in Raskolnikov's soul. What Sonya detects—that "gloomy catechism had become his faith and law"—becomes more visible as Raskolnikov deteriorates, as "moments, hours, and perhaps even days, full of apathy, . . . [come] over him" (CP, Pt 5, Ch 3; 418: Pt 6, Ch 1; 439). The "apathy" which "resemble[s] the morbidly indifferent state of some dying people," makes him "especially anxious about" Svidrigailov, who becomes suicide itself or that "it" contending for his soul (CP, Pt 6, Ch 1; 439).

After Svidrigailov physically arrives in St. Petersburg, Dunya predicts with "excessive fear" that "he's contemplating something horrible" (CP, Pt 4, Ch 3; 310). Her intuition is astute: Svidrigailov is not just "contemplating" suicide but is evolving into the veritable embodiment of that egoistic contemplation of "something horrible" (CP, Pt 4, Ch 3; 310). Raskolnikov himself is in mortal dread of his own declivity toward self-obliteration. He proclaims that he is "very afraid" of Svidrigailov as is Luzhin, who says that "if there was anyone he was seriously afraid of, it was—Svidrigailov" (CP, Pt 4, Ch 2; 294: Pt 4, Ch 3; 308). But it is not just Raskolnikov and Luzhin who are spooked by Svidrigailov, but various elements in the city seem to kowtow to and quake before him (or rather, before it). Raskolnikov notices that "Svidrigailov had not spent even a week in Petersburg, but everything around him was already on some sort of patriarchal footing" (CP, Pt 6, Ch 3; 466).

In fact, Svidrigailov, who seems to hold court in St. Petersburg, is ubiquitously present by hiding, ogling, or cocking his ears. Readers can sense this in the scene where Raskolnikov tells Sonya that "[i]t would be more just, a thousand times more just and reasonable, [for her] to jump headfirst into the water and end it at once" (CP, Pt 4, Ch 4; 322). After Raskolnikov's suggestion, it is as if that "something horrible"—Svidrigailov—is standing squarely in the room instead of merely "stealthily listening" in from an adjacent apartment (CP, Pt 4, Ch 4; 330). When Sonya asks "what would become of them" if she had decided "to end it all at once," Raskolnikov grasps "what [the] poor little orphaned children . . . and [the] pitiful half-crazed Katerina Ivanovna" meant to her (CP, Pt 4, Ch 4; 322). In concluding that "what has so far kept her from the canal is the thought of sin, and of *them, those ones*," Raskolnikov, prefiguring Durkheim, intuits that faith and familial bonds, those things that transcend the self, can repel the "something horrible," that egoistic eidolum with its ear pressed to Sonya's wall (CP, Pt 4, Ch 4; 323).

As Raskolnikov trudges toward the climactic choice between life or death, Svidrigailov dwindles as a person and ripens into an abstraction. In fact, the story begins to atavistically evoke the medieval *Sinai Paterick* where forces of good and evil fight for individual souls.[89] More and more, Svidrigailov, who is "suddenly appear[ing,]" "wooing around," and floating in and out of Raskolnikov's space, devolves into the quintessential egoistic abiosis (CP, Pt 5, Ch 5; 433: Pt 6, Ch 3; 469). He becomes the troubling thought that is "flashing in" Raskolnikov's mind, which "keeps hovering around him," drawing him "further into the corner," and "strik[ing] him terribly, to the point of horror" (CP, Pt 6, Ch 3; 463–64: Pt 5, Ch 5; 435).

Raskolnikov, who increasingly feels as if "he ha[s] become stuck, as it were on Svidrigailov," has internalized this thanatotic nemesis, which surfaces after Katerina's memorial service (CP, Pt 6, Ch 1; 439). Her service triggers Raskolnikov's acknowledgment that "there had always been something heavy and mystically terrible for him in the awareness of death and the feeling of the presence of death" (CP, Pt 6, Ch 1; 441). Shortly thereafter Svidrigailov, the alluring Last Summoner, strays into the deep recesses of Raskolnikov's psyche, not as a flesh-and-blood man, but as the cold option.

Raskolnikov senses that "here was something that called for immediate resolution, but which it was impossible to grasp or convey in words . . . Better Porfiry again . . . or Svidrigailov" (CP, Pt 6, Ch 1; 442). The prospect of ending it all, which incessantly "troubles him," forces Raskolnikov to see that "[m]aybe he'll have to face a struggle" and that Svidrigailov is "a whole way out" as opposed to "Porfiry's, which is a different matter" (CP, Pt 6, Ch 1; 447). Svidrigailov articulates this as well when he admonishes Sonya that "[t]here are two ways open for Rodion Romanovich: a bullet in the head, or Siberia" (CP, Pt 6, Ch 6; 500).

Porfiry is the Siberia option, which is the wholly "different matter" from what Svidrigailov portends. This comes across when the examining magistrate urges his suspect to "give [himself directly to life," imparts, "by God, life will carry you" (CP, Pt 6, Ch 2; 460). Convinced that the offender will ultimately accept responsibility, Porfiry doubts that Raskolnikov will heed Svidrigailov by "end[ing] this matter somehow differently . . . by raising his hand against himself" (CP, Pt 6, Ch 2; 462). Immediately after hearing Porfiry advocate God and life, Raskolnikov heads off to consult with opposing counsel, the godless Svidrigailov, the thing with "some hidden power over him" whose closing argument is an alluring swan song (CP, Pt 6, Ch 3; 462). From here on in, Raskolnikov's nutates from one pole to the other, from Porfiry to Svidrigailov, with Sonya's voice solmizing in his head. This physical pendulation to and from polar advisors, becomes the conceit for Raskolnikov's internecine tug of war between Svidrigailov's foredoomed "America" and Porfiry-Sonya's "implacable sentence" (CP, Pt 6, Ch 3; 463).

There is a point in the novel where Svidrigailov tells Raskolnikov, "You go right, and I'll go left," which foretokens the eventual route (CP, Pt 6, Ch 4; 483). In *The Brothers Karamazov*, Ivan says the same thing to Alyosha—"now you go right, I'll go left"—which alludes to the sinister direction of the devil.[90] Although Sonya is "tormented by fear at the thought that Raskolnikov might indeed commit suicide," he ultimately steers right to dodge Svidrigailov on the left. Raskolnikov recalls Sonya's words, "[g]o to the crossroads, bow down to people, kiss the earth, because you have sinned" (CP, Pt 6, Ch 8; 521, 525). It is only after learning of Svidrigailov's death that Raskolnikov confesses, and as Dostoevsky suggests, this might be his right turn into a "new" story (CP, Ep., Ch 2; 551).

EGOISTIC SELF-DECIMATION IN *THE IDIOT*

Dostoevsky wrote *The Idiot* during a turbulent period in his life. Dostoevsky married Anna Grigoryevna Snitkina, twenty-five years his junior, and in February 1867, two months later, they went abroad to dodge creditors.[91]

Although they planned to be away from Russia for just a few months, their exile spanned more than four years.[92] While he was working on *The Idiot*, Dostoevsky was constantly running off to gamble money or pawn possessions. Repeatedly evicted from their lodgings for nonpayment of rent, the impoverished couple moved multiple times between various cities.[93] Dostoevsky also endured regular epileptic seizures, including one just as his wife was going into labor with their first child.

During this difficult era, Anna's efforts to manage business and practical affairs were undermined by her husband's gambling.[94] Because of their poverty and indebtedness, Dostoevsky would dash off to the casino, lose his last kopeck, and pawn the remnants of their possessions, including their wedding rings, his winter coat, and his wife's earrings, broach, lace shawl, and spare frock.[95] After learning that Anna was pregnant, Dostoevsky, still unable to control his addiction, became more bent on scoring a big win at roulette.[96] When in March 1868, their first child, Sonya, was born, even that joy was short-lived because three months later the baby's death from pneumonia catapulted the couple into despair.[97] Despite their tragic loss, his gambling, the couple's incessant travels, and his repeated epileptic seizures, Dostoevsky managed to complete *The Idiot* in January 1869. Although Dostoevsky had hoped that *The Idiot* would alleviate the burden of their mounting debt, he realized that the novel, not a financial success, would probably fail to obtain a decent fee for book-form release.[98]

Dostoevsky's notebooks, the novel's putative precursor, mirror the erratic tumultuousness of his daily life. Repeatedly, Dostoevsky proposes and sketches characters, plots, and themes, and then in apparent frustrated recoiling, jettisons them and starts over. Edward Wasiolek captures the feverish "creative world" of the notebooks for *The Idiot*:

> The relationships between characters fluctuate from plan to plan: sisters are and are not sisters, nephews become sons, fathers become uncles. The Idiot is sometimes the son of the Uncle, sometimes the nephew, sometimes the foster son, sometimes illegitimate, and sometimes legitimate; acts are committed and die abortively in the next plan, or even a few lines later.[99]

As Wasiolek explains, "[f]rom August to December, 1867, Dostoevsky seemed to be looking for his novel more than writing it."[100] Shortly before sending the first part to his publisher, he destroyed most of what he had and basically started over from scratch. *The Idiot* of the notebooks could not be further from the novel's innocent, messianic Prince Myshkin. The prince's caustically villainous antecedent shape-shifts throughout the notes into a manipulating, conniving, demon, who commits rape, arson, and uxoricide. Robin Feuer Miller points out that although the almost saintly Prince Myshkin of the novel did not take shape until March 1868, there were "glimpses of the character" of the final version as early as October 22, 1867.[101] In a letter to his niece, Sofya Ivanova, Dostoevsky states:

> The main idea of the novel is to portray a positively beautiful person. There's nothing more difficult than that in the whole world, and especially now. All the writers, and not just ours, but even all the European ones, who ever undertook the depiction of a *positively* beautiful person, always had to pass. Because it's a measureless task. The beautiful is an ideal, and the ideal—both ours and that of civilized Europe—is far from having been achieved. There's only one positively beautiful person in the world—Christ, so that the appearance of this measurelessly, infinitely beautiful person is in fact of course an infinite miracle.[102]

Once Dostoevsky moved from the notebooks to the "measureless task" of the novel—that of portraying the "positively beautiful person"—readers tend to fixate on Prince Myshkin and other main hegemonic characters locked in a love quadrangle.[103] There is a tendency to focus primarily on Rogozhin, the dissolute merchant's son, Nastasya Filippovna, the self-condemned beauty, and Aglaya, who is infatuated with the prince, whom she idealizes into a pure spirit and designates her Pushkin-hero, her own "poor knight."[104] Due to the intensity of the intrigue, the prince, Rogozhin, Nastasya Filippovna, and Aglaya can eclipse others, like Ippolit, who for the first parts of the novel resides in the periphery. It is only later in the notes for *The Idiot* and in the novel's third part that the young nihilist, Ippolit, who threatens to sign his own death warrant, steps toward front stage.

The finished novel, in which atheism and Christian faith are perpetually competing, presents almost as many themes as life itself: it excavates the meanings of love, beauty, humility, innocence, guilt, repentance, and time.[105] Although the notebooks for *The Idiot* are vastly different from the end product, they disclose what ultimately resides at the novel's core: namely, the human suicidogenic propensities in a postlapsarian world where everyone is born irrevocably sentenced to death. In both the novel and notebooks, invocations of mortality, scaffolds, and guillotines abound. Rogozhin serves as the death blade; Nastasya Filippovna, craves death by proxy; and the consumptive Ippolit seeks to both stave off and hasten the inevitable. All three become thanatotic arteries converging in the body of *The Idiot*.

Death Banter

While immersed in roulette, Dostoevsky was filling the notebooks for *The Idiot* with iterations of death, arson, rape, murder, and self-homicide. Reading such preliminaries feels like a nightmarish plunge into a lake of fire and brimstone. Here is a sample:

> He rapes Mignon . . . sets fire to the house . . . he wants to blow his brains out . . . a sudden urge to play with fire or leap off a tower . . . [o]ut of boredom he sets fire to the house and rapes Umetskaia . . . [s]uicide . . .*[h]is mother hanged herself* . . . the baby dies . . . [y]es, I killed her . . . heads being cut off, about fingernails being torn out . . . a man about to be decapitated . . .the little coffin and the wife takes poison . . . But she did not forgive the rape of the heroine and she poisoned herself. . . . [s]he hanged herself . . . [s]he drowned herself . . . I'll hang myself in a fit of passion . . . [s]he dies or else kills herself . . perish on a Japanese dagger in a brothel . . . [s]he wants to poison herself . . . [h]e cut her throat because of her jealousy . . . shoot yourself . . . and all of a sudden he has no desire to live the uncle dies . . . [i]t can be foreseen that even if the Idiot is to die . . . shall he hang himself . . . the uncle wants to hang himself. . . He wants to kill the heroine . . . he wants to blow his brains out. . . She wants to poison herself . . shoot yourself . . .[h]e cut her throat because of jealousy . . [h]e wants to kill them . . .perhaps the Idiot will kill . . . she wants to kill herself. . . . I still have to die, for this is the one thing I can begin and end . . . [t]hey do let him shoot himself.[106]

Dostoevsky shapes this concatenation of mayhem, homicide, and *hara-kiri* into the society of *The Idiot*, one in which, as Durkheim puts it, "the fixed idea of death . . . without clear reason, has taken complete possession of the . . . mind" and is tied to "obsessive suicide" (SU, Bk 1, Ch1; 64). Besides Rogozhin, Nastasya Filippovna, and Ippolit, who are either delivering, embracing, or fearing death, the apparition of mortality pervades the novel: Prince Myshkin recollects Marie's dead body and the children "deck[ing] her coffin with flowers" (Id, Pt 1, Ch 6; 87). The novel sporadically references the widely publicized murder of the Zhemarins, a family of six in Tambov killed by an eighteen-year-old student, Vitold Gorsky.[107] Lebedev pontificates about death in his funereal drawing room, inhabited by his daughter Vera, "a young girl of about twenty, in mourning attire with a babe in arms, a girl of thirteen, also in mourning" (Id, Pt 2, Ch 2; 224). Blathering about "Revelation," Lebedev also proclaims, "after this will follow the pale horse and the one whose name is death, and after him Hell" (Id, Pt 2, Ch 2; 235). Lebedev also recounts how Nil Alexeyevich "gave up his soul to God," how "[h]e fell out of his carriage after a dinner . . . hit his temple on a post and, like a little child, like a little child, instantly departed the world" (Id, Pt 2, Ch 2; 236). Lebedev thus serves as a reminder of the lethal blade that can drop on any neck, anywhere, and at any time.

General Ivolgin sporadically alludes to death as well. The prince first piques the general's interest by mentioning his father, who "died a good twenty years ago," and his mother, who perished "six months later from a chill" (Id, Pt 1, Ch 8; 111,112). In one of the general's many farcical fabrications, he proclaims that he nearly fought a lethal duel with Myshkin's father over Myshkin's mother. He declares that we "put pistols to each other's heart and looked into each other's faces" (Id, Pt 1, Ch 8; 112). Elsewhere, he concocts a story to explain the trial of Myshkin's father, the late Nikolai Lvovich. While serving as acting commander, Lvovich reputedly dressed down a Private Kolpakov, who had been caught stealing, and threatened him with a flogging. Kolpakov returned to his barracks, lay down, and died. He is then "buried with the usual parade and tattoo of guns" and dutifully "removed from the lists" (Id, Pt 1, Ch 8; 114). Suddenly, six months later, he shows up in another battalion "as though nothing were the matter" (Id, Pt 1, Ch 8; 114). General Ivolgin stops yapping about finality only when he himself hits the dust. Wracked by shame, with a deflated self-identity due to his theft of Lebedev's wallet, Ivolgin goes "purple," his lips "turn blue," and with "slight convulsions run[ning] across his face," collapses from a stroke (Id, Pt 4, Ch 4; 589).[108]

At Nastasya Filippovna's soiree, General Yepanchin adds to the death-chatter by giving a self-serving confession about himself being "billeted in a suburb" with "a second lieutenant's wife" (Id, Pt 1, Ch 14; 174). This wizened widow had deceased relatives, had "buried her husband some forty-five years earlier," and once lived with a hunchback niece, who bit her hostess's finger and later died (Id, Pt 1, Ch 14; 174). In this tale, General Yepanchin besmirches the woman's last moment by berating her just as she is "depart[ing] from the world" (Id, Pt 1, Ch 14; 175). This inspires his remorseful ejaculation about the final summons that unexpectedly comes to all: "[o]nce she had had children, a husband, a family, relatives, all that had effervesced around her . . . and suddenly—a total void" (Id, Pt 1, Ch 14; 175). From there, he self-aggrandizes by claiming to have made amends by "at [his] own expense . . . [by] settl[ing] two chronically ill old women in the almshouse, with the object of softening the last days of their earthly life" (Id, Pt 1, Ch 14; 176).

The Yepanchin family also participates in the ongoing threnody. Aglaya recites the poem about the "poor knight," with "his mien . . . pale and gloomy" who "[a]s a madman . . . died" (Id, Pt 2, Ch 7; 293–94). She mentions Pushkin's untimely demise and asks the prince whether duels typically end with "one of them . . . certainly killed or wounded" (Id, Pt 3, Ch 3; 414). In talking about marriage, Aglaya's mother, Lizaveta Prokofyevna, snaps "[p]ut me in my coffin first and bury me in the ground, then marry off my daughter" (Id, Pt 2, Ch 12; 372). When this Yepanchin matriarch visits the ailing prince, she anticipates seeing a "dying man on his death bed," an event punctuated by Kolya's observation that she is infatuated with the macabre:

"No matter how hard I tried to assure you that the prince was almost well again, you wouldn't have wanted to believe me because it was far more interesting to imagine him on his deathbed" (Id, Pt 2, Ch 6; 283). In short, the chorus of *The Idiot* drones a dirge and as both Durkheim and Dostoevsky know, when that "fixed idea of death" takes hold, quests for self-extinction proliferate (SU, Bk 1, Ch 1; 64).

Guillotines and Scaffolds

The novel begins with Prince Myshkin, who returns to Russia after spending four years in a Swiss clinic for treatment of severe epilepsy. In Petersburg, he plans to visit the Yepanchin household to meet his distant relation, Lizaveta Prokofyevna. Guillotines and scaffolds, emblems of mortality, appear early during his visit. While waiting to be received, Prince Myshkin, apparently oblivious to social class distinctions, converses with the lackey footman about capital punishment. The prince describes the French guillotine, which is a "heavy thing, powerful," which makes a "head [fly] off so quickly you don't have time to blink" and chats about Legros's execution in Lyons (Id, Pt 1, Ch 2; 26). When the footman remarks, "[i]t's a good thing at least that the suffering is short," the prince correctionally opines that the guillotine lacks distractions and hope and thus can inflict the most extreme agony (Id, Pt 1, Ch 2; 26). He notes that other tortures can bring physical pain and discomfort, which "probably distract" from and mitigate the anguish (Id, Pt 1, Ch 2; 27). And in an autobiographical allusion to Dostoevsky's own trauma before the firing squad, the prince states: "perhaps the worst, most violent pain lies not in injuries, but in the fact that you know for certain that within the space of an hour, then ten minutes, then half a minute, then now, right at this moment—your soul will fly out of your body, and you'll no longer be a human being, and that is certain, the main thing is that its *certain*" (Id, Pt 1, Ch 2; 27).[109] It is anticipation of that which cannot be deflected that begets raw anguish. But the implicit concomitant truth, one implicit here, is that all beings, born sentenced to expire, implacably await certain cessation.

According to Prince Myshkin, even a twinkling of hope, albeit unrealistic, can potentially dilute the toxins in that impending "moment," where the "soul will fly out of the body" (Id, Pt 1, Ch 2; 27). He adds that one slaughtered by a bandit with "his throat cut at night" can pray for rescue "right up to the last moment" and asserts that there are "people whose throats have been cut," who are "still hoping, or running away, or begging for their lives" (Id, Pt 1, Ch 2; 27). Execution, which is *sui generis* due to its utter hopelessness, invokes the kind of "suffering and terror" of which "Christ spoke" and which the replica of Holbein's painting displayed in Rogozhin's house suggests (Id, Pt 1, Ch 2; 27). As the prince puts it, "here, all this final hope, with which it's ten times easier to die, is taken away *for certain*; the terrible torment remains, and there's nothing in the world more powerful than that torment" (Id, Pt 1, Ch 2; 27). When his conversation with the servant ends, the prince leaves a riddle dangling: how would an individual who has been pardoned after being sentenced to death describe that mindset right before that imminent blow? The prince implies that such a circumstance is so unusual that this one person who "know[s] everything" might not even exist (Id, Pt 1, Ch5; 78).[110]

When the prince meets the Madame Yepanchin and her three daughters, Alexandra, Adelaida, and Aglaya, he again seizes topic death and returns to his hypothetical of the pardoned man. But first Myshkin talks about a man who spent about twelve years in prison and "once tried to kill himself" (Id, Pt 1, Ch 5; 70). Through this anecdote, the novel creates a ligature between attempted suicide and an aborted execution, thereby foreshadowing that pivotal scene where Ippolit puts the pistol to his brow. From this mention of an attempted suicide, the prince reminisces about his encounter with a man sentenced to death by firing squad, who, like Dostoevsky himself, was reprieved while awaiting execution. On the brink of his demise, this man pondered: "What if I didn't have to die? What if I could get my life back—what an infinity it would be! And it would all be mine! Then I would make each minute into a whole lifetime, I would lose nothing, would account for each minute, waste nothing in vain!" (Id, Pt 1, Ch 5; 72). When Alexandra inquires whether this man accomplished his resolve once reprieved and thus, gifted that "eternal life," the prince answers "no," that "he didn't live like that at all, and wasted far too many minutes" (Id, Pt 1, Ch 5; 72). When this man's epiphany recedes into the past, he reverts to his trodden ways, back to pedestrian normalcy with its squandered minutes. The prince proffers this snippet about the pardoned man as proof "that it is impossible to live 'counting each minute' " and yet, he himself comes closest to attaining such an ideal (Id, Pt 1, Ch 5; 72).

Squandered moments, the sentenced man, scaffold and guillotine, assemble into a unifying conceit that unfolds in the novel. Shortly after his discourse on the plight of the pardoned man, the prince admits that he has actually seen an execution and suggests to Adelaida that she "paint the face of a condemned man a minute before the guillotine falls, while he is still standing on the scaffold and before he lies down on that plank" (Id, Pt 1, Ch 5; 77–78). He then suggests details: "[p]aint the scaffold so that only the last stair can be seen clearly and closely; the condemned man has stepped on to it: his head, white as paper, the priest holding out the cross, the man extending his blue lips and staring—and *knowing everything*" (Id, Pt 1, Ch 5; 77–78). From then on, the mortal face in the "minute before the guillotine falls" couples with the novel's presiding horologe, which relentlessly ticktocks in the background (Id, Pt 1, Ch 5; 75).

Supplementing the prince's tale of the sentenced man, Lebedev, the roguish drunkard, "pray[s] for the repose of the soul of Countess Du Barry," who was executed by the revolutionary tribunal in the late eighteenth century:

> When she saw that he was bending her down by the neck under the blade, pushing her under it, kicking her—the other laughing—she began to shout: "*Encore un moment, monsieur le bourreau, encore un moment!*" Which means: "Wait just one little moment, Mr. Executioner, just one!" And for that moment, perhaps the Lord will forgive her, because a *misere* worse than that is impossible to imagine for a human soul . . . Well that is the very personification of *misère*. (Id, Pt 2, Ch 2; 230–31)

The message conveyed here is that even the elite, like Marie-Jeanne Du Barry, once a favorite of Louis XV of France and according to Lebedev, who "reigned in place of the queen," did not escape the ineluctable "blade" that halts for no one (Id, Pt 2, Ch 2; 230).[111] Here and elsewhere, *The Idiot* tautologically proclaims that from the exact moment of nascency the clock is mercilessly palpitating, and that everyone will swiftly and steadily mount the scaffold where the broad knife is poised to willy-nilly lop off their heads.

The desperation to, and futility of, trying to arrest the blade or steal time abounds in the novel: the prince tells Roghozin about a "watch, a silver one, on a yellow bead chain" and the peasant, the thief in the night, who became so enamored with it that after "cross[ing] himself and saying a bitter prayer to himself," slashed his friend's throat and tried to pilfer time by "[taking] the thing for himself" (Id, Pt 2, Ch 4; 257). Another glimpse at the impossibility of toppling the reign of temporal irrefragability occurs in General Ivolgin's wishful yarn about Private Kolpakov, who miraculously materialized after his own burial. It is also present in that nanosecond before the epileptic fit, where the prince can embrace "boundless happiness," and has the revelation that "*there should be time no longer*" (Id, Pt 2, Ch 5; 265). The "knowing-everything" face of the pardoned man, the account of the stolen watch, the fable of the reincarnated private, and the fleeting vision prior to the ictal howl, which was "in itself worth the whole of one's life," add up to a treatise on time's dominion and the inescapable fact of mortality (Id, Pt 1, Ch 5; 77: Pt 2, Ch 5; 264). *The Idiot* as a whole thus dispatches the message that snatching time trinkets, along with all of the revelations, myths, prayers, and howls in the world, cannot stop the unstoppable ebb toward preordained interment.

To say that the citizenry of *The Idiot*, analogous to the pardoned man, fails to cherish what they do have—namely, each priceless moment—is a veritable understatement. Most of the characters, with their social climbing, avarice, vanity, excesses, prevarications, and selfishness, extinguish any possibility of "wast[ing] nothing," of "*knowing everything*," of "mak[ing] each minute into a whole lifetime" (Id, Pt 1, Ch 5; 72, 78). The tragedy inheres in the fact that they are purblind to the prince's potential not only to elevate consciousness, but to catalyze the kind of spiritual transformation that could help them savor little gems in life, the ones that truly matter. William Mills Todd III explains that instead of "appreciating [the Prince's] gentleness and sharing his ecstatic sense of joy, as in the passage on the donkey or in his story about the mother taking delight in her child," it is "his tragedy that very few characters, such as the Swiss children, can accept him in these terms" and what they do is "project their corruption and tortuous psychology on him."[112] In the society of *The Idiot*, the prince's sojourn becomes "pearls before swine."[113]

Death-Blade Rogozhin

Durkheim believes that murder and suicide are allies. He calls suicide a "transformed and attenuated homicide" and suggests that both sorts of perpetrators, "equally unable to play a useful part in society[,] . . . are consequently doomed to defeat" (SU, Bk 3, Ch2; 340–41). He elaborates:

> Where average morality has a ruder character and human life is less respected, he will revolt, declare war on society and kill, instead of killing himself. In short, the murder of one's self and of another are two violent acts. But sometimes the violence, which is their source, finding no resistance in the social environment, overruns it and then it becomes homicide. Sometimes, incapable of outward expression because of the public conscience, it reverts to its source, and then the same person from whom it springs is its victim. (SU, Bk, 3, Ch 2; 341)

Durkheim could be profiling Rogozhin, the outsider, who plays no "useful part in society," and is loaded with aculeate violence that "find[s] no resistance" in his "social environment" (SU, Bk 3, Ch 2; 340–41). Like the guillotine, Rogozhin serves as the blade ready and eager to deliver the final stroke. From his first encounter with the prince right up to the scene where the two antonymic beings sit vigil over Nastasya Filippovna's corpse, Rogozhin portends extinction.[114]

In the novel's opening, the prince, an ethereal man in his mid-twenties on a train to St. Petersburg, meets two characters, Rogozhin, a debauched merchant's son, and Lebedev, the meddling bureaucrat. They share a third-class compartment and instantly start revealing details of their private affairs. The "fair-haired" prince, with eyes that are "large, blue and fixed" and a face that is "pleasant, delicate and lean," seems to radiate light and innocence (Id, Pt 1, Ch 1; 6). Carrying his meager possessions in a bundle, he lacks the sophistication to detect "the utterly casual, inappropriate and idle nature" of Rogozhin's interrogation (Id, Pt 1, Ch 1; 7).

The prince is not just *sitting* "opposite" Rogozhin, but the two are opposites, both in appearance and by nature, which is what Rogozhin stresses when he later tells the prince, "we differ in everything" (Id, Pt 1, Ch 1; 1: Pt 2, Ch 3; 244). In stark contrast to the prince, Rogozhin is "swarthy," has "black curly hair," "fiery eyes," and "thin lips," which are "constantly creased in a kind of brazen, mocking and even cruel smile" (Id, Pt 1, Ch1; 1). Unlike the prince, he already has wealth along with a grasp of and flair for iniquity. What is "especially striking," moreover, is his "deathly pallor" and how his conversation is peppered with words of destruction and darkness (Id, Pt 1, Ch1; 6). While the orphaned prince, who had spent years adrift in epileptic idiocy, has practically no past, no comprehension of evil, and seems to just drop from the sky as *tabula rasa*, Rogozhin has a concrete family history, one replete with death, violence, and combustibility. The prince has a talent for reading faces and sees Rogozhin's "gloomy face" as his predominant feature (Id, Pt 1, Ch 1; 17). Later, while speaking to Ganya, the prince senses that the "gloomy one" serves as dispenser of death and prophesies that Rogozhin "might marry Nastasya Filippovna and a week later, perhaps, cut her throat" (Id, Pt 1, Ch 4; 43).

On the train, it becomes apparent that the Rogozhin culture is one of physical brutality: in a voice of "alarm" and "agitation, Rogozhin tells of how he ran away after his father "nearly thrashed him to death" (Id, Pt 1, Ch 1; 11–12). After the prince naively inquires, "did you do something to make him angry," Rogozhin, who is passionately infatuated with Nastasya Filippovna, confesses to having used his father's money to buy her pricey earrings. Then "like a man who has been damned," Rogozhin dreads returning home to paternal wrath (Id, Pt 1, Ch 1; 17). What comes into play here is what Durkheim has said about the seemingly "contrasting phenomena" of homicide and suicide, which actually "conceal a fundamental identity" and derive from a "single predisposition which itself inclines no more one way than the other" (SU. Bk 3, Ch 2; 340). On the train, Rogozhin, the proverbial cutthroat, exposes the cognate inclination toward self-homicide: "[t]o tell the truth, I was just about ready to throw myself in the water right there on the spot" (Id, Pt 1, Ch1; 17). But Rogozhin, whom Durkheim would call "the ruder character," is one who "cannot resign himself, confess his impotence, and . . . withdraw from the fight by withdrawing from life," but invariably will "revolt, declare war on society and kill, instead of killing himself" (SU, Bk 3, Ch 2; 341). Shortly after tinkering with the idea of self-demise ("why didn't I die right there and then?"), Rogozhin reclaims what is rightfully his—bestial violence—and threatens to thrash Lebedev (Id, Pt 1, Ch 1; 15). When Lebedev states, "[i]f you thrash me, it means you'll have placed your seal on me," he brands Rogozhin the chief inflictor of excruciation (Id, Pt 1; Ch 1; 16).

As the novel progresses, Rogozhin becomes more linked to death's blade. He owns a knife "with a blade three and a half vershoks long, and of corresponding width," which he treats as if it were a cherished bodily appendage (Id, Pt 2, Ch 3; 253). When the prince picks up the treasure, Rogozhin "seize[s] it with ill-tempered vexation" and puts it out of reach (Id, Pt 2, Ch 3; 253). Nastasya Filippovna likens Rogozhin to the Moscow murderer, who "also lived in the same house as his mother and also bound a razor in silk to cut someone's throat" (Id, Pt 3, Ch 10; 531). She claims that when she was in the house, "it seemed to [her] that somewhere under a floor-board . . . was hidden a corpse . . . surrounded by bottles of Zhdanov fluid" (Id, Pt 3, Ch 10; 531).[115] The slasher Rogozhin is intrigued by the prince's account of the peasant who "cut his friend's throat in one stroke" (Id, Pt 2, Ch 4; 257, 260). After exchanging crosses with the prince, Rogozhin promises, "[t]hough I took your cross, I won't cut your throat for your watch!" (Id, Pt 2, Ch 4; 257, 260). When Rogozhin corners the prince with his "right hand raised," his blade ejects almost reflexively and the only thing that "save[s] the prince from the inevitable blow of the knife that was already descending on him" was his "terrible, unimaginable howl" prior to his seizure (Id, Pt 2, Ch 4; 274).

When Rogozhin appears with his "rabid smile," he is depicted as a lone stalker, who is as ubiquitous as the Grim Reaper (Id, Pt 2, Ch 5; 274). His "pale face" periodically "fleet[s] into view" and then vanishes like a "vision" (Id, Pt 3, Ch 2; 405). He is a mere "impression of a crooked smile" and "a pair of eyes" (Id, Pt 3, Ch 2; 405). He is "[t]he crunch of quiet footsteps on the gravel" and the approach of a "man whose face it [is] hard to make out in the darkness" (Id, Pt 3, Ch 3; 423). Ippolit, who is gradually perishing, envisions ghostly Rogozhin slithering into his room, sitting "silently" by his sick bed, "trying to frighten" and "torment" him (Id, Pt 3, Ch 5; 451). Rogozhin thus insinuates himself into Ippolit's terminal illness to become an apparition. He creeps into his consumptive delirium and becomes what "chills" spines and makes "knees tremble" (Id, Pt 3, Ch 6; 478–79).

The lone stalker is present, yet concealed, when the prince, heading for a dacha retreat, arrives from Moscow by train. Upon "disembarking from the carriage," the prince "suddenly fancie[s] that he [sees] the strange, hot gaze of someone's eyes in the crowd" (Id, Pt 2, Ch 2; 223). What follows shortly thereafter is a tour of Rogozhin's lodgings. This "unpleasant" and "gloomy" abode with its precious knife is virtually interchangeable with its occupant (Id, Pt 2, Ch 3; 239). As the narrator reveals, houses (and Rogozhins) "of this genre" are tomblike with "thick walls and exceedingly few windows" and ground floors, like prisons, with windows that "sometimes have bars" (Id, Pt 2, Ch 3; 239). It is also telling that in structures, like Rogozhin's, members of the *Skoptsy* reside on the ground floor, which typically houses a moneychanger shop and where the amassing of wealth substitutes for indulgence in sexual pleasure.[116] The *Skoptsy* practice castration and evoke the religious sect that Kondraty Selivanov founded in the latter half of the eighteenth century.[117] According to Richard Peace, these "[c]astrates were an extreme development of the sect of the Flagellants whose asceticism led them to believe that the kingdom of heaven could only be achieved through castration" and Rogozhin and his family are connected to flagellation and sterility.[118] In fact, the rattling image of Rogozhin's brother severing the tassels from the sheath over his father's coffin is suggestive of the castrated *Skoptsy*.

Nastasya Filippovna also links Rogozhin to the *Skoptsy* by guessing that one day he might join them:

> And as you're a completely uneducated man, you'd have started to pile up money, and, like your father, you'd have settled down in this house with its *Skoptsy*; you might even have gone over to their faith yourself in the end, and you'd have loved your money so much that you'd have piled up not two but ten millions, and died of starvation on your money sacks, because for you everything is passion, you turn everything into passion. (Id, Pt 2, Ch 3; 250)

Peace speaks of it as somewhat "bizarre" that Rogozhin, who is thought to represent "sensual passion," is so "strongly identified with the sect of the Castrates" and even has a Christian name, Parfen, which deriving from the Greek *Parthenos*, means "virgin."[119] When Nastasya Filippovna calls Rogozhin a man of "strong passions," it is not a misnomer, but a precise characterization of a primitive being, but one devoid of *sexual* passion (Id, Pt 2, Ch 3; 251). When Nastasya Filippovna denies having had sex with Rogozhin, she bolsters his fundamental asexuality, which is corroborated by what happens when the two rendezvous: they engage not in sex, but in violence.[120] Rogozhin flagellates Nastasya Filippovna until she turns "black and blue" and then flagellates himself through fasting and self-humiliating pleas for forgiveness (Id, Pt 2, Ch 3; 246).

Moreover, Rogozhin's ligation with the Castrates serves to inject into the novel a more all-embracing prodrome. Menninger calls self-castration a form of "focal suicide" and points out that the Castrates of Russia, believing that "when the world contained 144,000 Skoptsi the millennium would be at hand," sought to "secure new converts."[121] Missionaries worked to spread the sect "among the beggars and other lowly elements of society [by] convincing them or bribing them to accept the new religion" and they even "forcibly mutilated" some people.[122] The *Skopsy*, with their self-induced sterility, do not merely implicate a "focal suicide," but impend something larger—namely, the potential, forcible extinction of the human race. Implicit in this is the sense that Rogozhin, who is all about murder and violence, does not just menace the well-being of specific people, like the prince, Nastasya

Filippovna, and Ippolit. As a lethal outsider, he is alienated from faith and community and emblemizes the sort of congenital anomaly that can spread and potentially slash humanity to smithereens.

The prince equates Rogozhin with his cinerary abode when he tells him that the "gloomy place . . . bears the physiognomy of your whole family and the whole of your Rogozhin way of life" (Id, Pt 2, Ch 3; 242). Rogozhin's brother, whose wife died, stays in a wing. Rogozhin's room is "dark," and "[a]long the walls, in tarnished gilt frames, hang several oil paintings," which are "dark and soot begrimed" (Id, Pt 2, Ch 3; 242). When the prince meets Rogozhin's mother, she too is enshrouded in darkness and wears "a black woolen dress, with a black kerchief at her neck" and "[b]eside her [is] another small, clean old woman . . . also dressed in mourning" (Id, Pt 2, Ch 5; 260). In a portrait, Rogozhin's father looks blighted as if he has one foot in the grave: he is displayed with "greyish beard, a yellow, wrinkled face, and a suspicious, reserved and sorrowful gaze" (Id, Pt 2, Ch 3; 242). At times, Rogozhin himself appears as if he is in a stage of rigor mortis: Rogozhin "turn[s] so pale and [goes] so rigid that for a time he look[s] like a stone statute, staring with an immobile and frightened gaze" (Id, Pt 2, Ch 3; 240).

The adjectives enshrouding Rogozhin conjure up torture, gaunt geldings, and decay: he is "a kind of minor, fleeting convulsion," an "exceedingly strange and turbid gaze," "a face . . . contorted in a malicious, mocking smile," the recollection of "something recent, painful, and somber," and "a grim and terrible look" (Id, Pt 2, Ch 5; 245–49). He, who "has no trace of beauty," represents a brutal physical force, suggestive of what is conveyed in the dead Christ in Hans Holbein the Younger's picture, *The Body of the Dead Christ in the Tomb* (Id, Pt 3, Ch 6; 475). Ippolit describes the copy of the painting which hangs in the Rogozhin gallery:

> [I]n Rogozhin's painting there was no trace of beauty; this really was the corpse of a man who had endured endless torments even before the cross, wounds, tortures, beatings from the guards, beating from the mob while he carried the cross and fell beneath it, and, at last, the agony of the cross which lasted six hours (by my calculations, at least) . . . ; nothing has yet had time to go stiff, so that on the face of the dead man one can even see suffering. (Id, Pt 3, Ch 6; 475–76)[123]

It is as if the painting, which demotes Christ to a butchered carcass, has the potential to annul faith in Christ and in his resurrection. The impersonal, entropic forces of nature that have ravaged what is, according to Ippolit, just a "corpse of a man" envelope Holbein's scene (Id, Pt 3, Ch 6; 475). When the prince first sees Holbein's Christ, he exclaims, "[s]ome people might lose their faith by looking at that painting" and Rogozhin confirms that he himself is "losing" faith (Id, Pt 2, Ch 4; 255).[124] The painting and its owner thus coalesce to imply that the monstrous, potent lethality, which seemingly subjugates Holbein's Christ, is devouring Rogozhin and concretizing him into the death blade hanging over the corrupt kingdom of *The Idiot*.

When Rogozhin is not portrayed as solitary stalker, he arrives as the head honcho of a pack of unruly rogues, which underscores his role as chief expiry. After Nastasya Filippovna visits the Ivolgin apartment to meet the family and invite them to her soiree, Rogozhin, who is "gloomily and irritably preoccupied," follows (Id, Pt 1, Ch 10; 132). He comes with his raucous gang of "ten or twelve people" who, "hav[ing] had a good few many," behave "disgracefully" (Id, Pt 1, Ch 10; 131). At the subsequent soiree, hints of degeneration precede Rogozhin's arrival: there are "jerky, feverish, frenzied words," along with ominous "disorder" and the abrupt "loud, resonant ringing of the bell" (Id, Pt1, Ch 15; 182). While the Roghozhin cohorts are practically the same, there are disreputable and brutal add-ons. One such newcomer is like a member of a demolition crew, which further reinforces Rogozhin's office as the head death-deliverer: this underling is a "fisted gentleman, who "display[s] . . . an enormous fist, sinewy, knotted, covered in a kind of reddish down," such that it becomes "clear to everyone that if this profoundly national object were to land on its target without error, it would reduce it to a jelly" (Id, Pt 1, Ch5; 185).

At the party, Rogozhin brings a dirty bag of money, which helps foment a scandal, one that Mikhail Bakhtin likens to a "carnivalised netherworld" where "the image of *fire*" plays a central role:

> In European carnivals there was almost always a special structure (usually a vehicle adorned with all possible sorts of gaudy carnival trash) called "hell," and at the close of carnival this "hell" was triumphantly set on fire . . . Characteristic is the role of "moccoli" in Roman carnival: each participant in the carnival carried a lighted candle ("a candle stub"), and each tried to put out another's candle with the cry "Sia ammazatto!" ("Death to thee!").[125]

The party, in which attendees play Ferdyshchenko's parlor game and confess "the worst of all the bad things" they have ever done in their lives, serves up fire and a charcuterie of assorted societal vices, like money-grubbing, self-aggrandizement, vanity, and vengeance (Id, Pt 1, Ch 13; 166).[126] Here Rogozhin supplements the menu with that twisted kind of "love" that seeks ownership of its object. At the party, Nastasya Filippovna "seize[s] the tongs, rake[s] two smouldering logs, and as soon as the flames leap up," tosses Rogozhin's parcel of lucre into the fire (Id, Pt 1, Ch 16; 201). According to Bakhtin, carnival-fire tends to "simultaneously destroy and renew the world," but the incendiary scandal in *The Idiot* lacks even a cinder of dualism.[127] Whenever death-blade Rogozhin is present, there are no shades of renewal, only infernal allusions to the biblical legacy of the Fall with its pyrexia, sins, disease, and death. In fact, Nastasya Filippovna's party climaxes in "carnivalistic" pandemonium: a serpentine "long, thin tongue of flame licks the parcel" while "flame [shoots] upward" (Id, Pt 1, Ch 16; 203). Then when Nastasya Filippovna prepares to dash off with her chosen slayer, Rogozhin yelps not words of love, but of lust for a possession: "[s]he's mine! It's all mine!" (Id, Pt 1, Ch 16; 199).[128] General Yepanchin appropriately spews: "[t]his is a Sodom, a Sodom!" (Id, Pt 1, Ch 16; 199).

Nastasya Filippovna: Egoistic-Anomic Death by Proxy

Menninger might have renamed the "Sodom" of *The Idiot* "man against himself."[129] Suicide makes a cameo appearance when there is news that Yevgeny Pavlych's uncle, Radomsky, shot himself at dawn.[130] It also surfaces when Aglaya confesses to having had suicidal ideation at age thirteen: "I thought of poisoning myself . . . and then writing all about it in a letter to my parents, and also imagined how I would lie in my coffin, with everyone weeping over me and blaming themselves for having been so cruel to me" (Id, Pt 3, Ch 8; 497). What Aglaya describes is what suicidologist Charles William Wahl gives as one motive for suicide—the desire to punish a parent or a sibling, or the "extrapolation of them."[131] Wahl's specimen is Tom Sawyer, who, like Aglaya, imagines punishing a "depriving figure," but he would do it by "drowning himself in the Mississippi" after thinking "to himself how sad and piteous a spectacle he would make when his body would be brought into his aunt's presence . . . and how consequently sorry and remorseful she would be."[132] According to Wahl, fantasies, like Tom Sawyer's and Aglaya's, are "ubiquitous among children" who are "totally impotent physically and mentally," and prone to deny "the infinitude and irreversibility of death."[133] *The Idiot*, however, does not expound much on Radomsky's uncle's self-homicide or Aglaya's juvenile fantasies of self-poisoning. It does, however, yield a full psychoanalytic history of Nastasya Filippovna, who courts "the infinitude and irreversibility of death," and fits the Durkheimiam hybrid—an egoistic-anomic self-homicide.[134]

The notebooks for *The Idiot* refer to Mignon and Umetskaia. Mignon, whom Dostoevsky took from Johan Wolfgang von Goethe's *Wilhelm Meister's Apprenticeship*, has a tragic childhood of loss and abandonment.[135] She is kidnapped, enslaved to a wicked circus master, and endures abuse from her foster family. Olga Umetskaia, however, was a real person whom Dostoevsky read about in the Russian newspapers and even mentions in an 1867 letter to Apollon Maykov.[136] The Umetskys beat and starved their fifteen-year-old daughter, who responded by setting fire to the family estate.[137]

When Olga was charged with arson, she didn't deny the crime, but after trial, the jury felt sympathy for her pain and acquitted her.

In his notebooks, Dostoevsky wrote, "Mignon's history is altogether like that of Olga Umetskaia."[138] As his notes progress, Mignon recedes while Umetskaia advances as the Nastasya Filippovna prototype. Katherine Bowers has pointed out that "aspects linked to Umetskaia appear in *The Idiot*" and are "most readily visible in Nastas'ia Filippovna's gothic-inspired history, in which she is violently orphaned by fire, isolated through misfortune, and exploited by an unscrupulous guardian."[139] Further, Umetskaia attempted suicide at least twice, and Nastasya Filippovna is hell-bent on getting herself annihilated.

Unresolved Mourning and the Quest for an Executioner

As discussed in this book's introductory chapter, death "through the services of someone else," a timeless concept dating back at least as far as Socrates, threads its way through the works of multiple suicide theorists, including Freud, Menninger, Shneidman, Durkheim, and Colt.[140] Freud has explored "half-intentional self-destruction," a phenomenon that Menninger expands into "self-destruction . . . by proxy."[141] Shneidman calls it "subintentioned death" and Durkheim names it "embryonic suicide" and points to people who flirt with excessive risk (SU, Introduction, 46).[142] Colt employs the nomenclature of "victim-precipitated homicide," along with an aspiring "murderee" who:

> completes suicide by getting someone else to kill them, becoming what Aldous Huxley called a "murderee." Like the Christian martyrs who goaded the Romans into executing them or the angry young men who engage in "suicide by cop," they provide someone or something else into striking the final blow. . . . [S] ociologist Marvin Wolfgang might call them examples of "victim-precipitated homicide." In his 1950s study of murder in Philadelphia, Wolfgang stated that 150 of 588 consecutive homicides were cases of victim-precipitated homicide, many of them husbands who attacked their wives, provoking their wives into murdering them.[143]

Colt explains how this need to be the "murderee" can be so overpowering that it can propel individuals to "horrific" extremes.[144] He gives the example of a German man who "responded to an internet posting seeking someone willing to be 'slaughtered,' whereupon he was stabbed to death, carved into pieces, and eaten, over a period of months, by a . . . computer technician."[145]

Dostoevsky was apparently aware of the intensity of the proxy-phenomenon and knew that there exist such "murderees" who, like Nastasya Filippovna, find executioners to do them in. Durkheim also understands that there are those who "intentionally toy with death" and acknowledges that although suicide is a "social fact," each "victim . . . gives his act a personal stamp which expresses his temperament, the special conditions in which he is involved, and which consequently cannot be explained by the social and general causes of the phenomenon" (SU, Bk 2, Ch 6; 277–78). For Nastasya Filippovna, the "personal stamp" on her "victim-precipitated homicide" is "incomplete mourning" embedded in egoistic-anomie (SU, Bk 2, Ch 6; 277–78).[146]

In egoistic suicide, perpetrators are torn from the social fabric in such a way that their "own goals" become "preponderant over those of the community" and Nastasya Filippovna's biography epitomizes the very confluence of events that can promote self-homicide (SU, Bk 2, Ch 3; 209). Nastasya Filippovna's loss of hearth, home, and family at a tender age frayed her bond with the community, which according to Durkheim is a vital defense against suicide. Nastasya Filippovna's descent into "me-ness" began after her family was ruined. Although saddled with enormous death, her father, Barashkov, managed through "back-breaking" labor to whip his small farm into decent shape (Id, Pt 1, Ch 4; 47). Cheered "inordinately" by this upswing, he visited his district chief's town to try to resolve matters with creditors, but in his absence his farm burned down, and his wife died in the blaze (Id, Pt 1, Ch 4; 47).

Nastasya Filippovna was only seven years old at the time. The peripeteia incinerated not just her home and life as she knew it, but also claimed her main staple, her maternal nourishment. About a month later, Nastasya Filippovna and her sister were orphaned when her father, unable to bear the catastrophe, "went mad" and "died of a fever" (Id, Pt 1, Ch 4; 47–48). Not long thereafter, Nastasya Filippovna's sister perished from whooping cough. In the language of Durkheim, Nastasya Filippovna was "thrown back onto herself" and thrust into a life "without attachment to some object, which transcends and survives" the self (SU, Bk 2, Ch 3; 210). Aglaya articulates this when she accuses Nastasya Filippovna of being "self-loving to the point of insanity," a condition Durkheim ties to morbific self-destruction (Id, Pt 4, Ch 8; 661). Durkheim states that when egoistic malaise sets in, when "we have no other object than ourselves," we cannot evade "the thought that our efforts will end in nothingness" and "lose courage to live, that is, to act and struggle, since nothing will remain of our exertions" (SU, Bk 2, Ch 3; 210). For adult Nastasya Filippovna, "it [is] as though in place of a heart she ha[s] a stone; and her feelings [have] withered and died once and for all" (Id, Pt 1, Ch 4; 53). In fact, Nastasya Filippovna, who "live[s] mostly alone" and has "few acquaintances," could be the poster child of egoistic typology (Id, Pt 1, Ch 4; 53).

Another aspect of Nastasya Filippovna's "personal stamp" is what some theorists designate "incomplete morning" or "unresolved grief," which is rooted in both Freud's *Mourning and Melancholia* and Durkheim's concept of anomie.[147] Freud states that "mourning is regularly the reaction to the loss of a loved person, or to the loss of some abstraction which has taken the place of one, such as fatherland, liberty, an idea, and so on."[148] In melancholia, some of the same influences are at work, but "instead of a state of grief," it develops into "a morbid pathological disposition" that can spell the loss of the will to live.[149] Its "distinguishing mental features are a profoundly painful dejection, abrogation of interest in the outside world, loss of the capacity to love, inhibition of all activity, and a lowering of the self-regarding feelings to a degree that finds utterance in self-reproaches and self-revilings, and culminates in a delusional expectation of punishment."[150] For Durkheim, anomie, a close cousin, "throws open the door to disillusionment and consequently to disappointment" and can likewise culminate in self-murder (SU, Bk 2, Ch 6; 285).

The social historian Howard Kushner's hypothesis about "incomplete mourning" draws from "[b]oth Durkheim and Freud, [who] would have agreed that . . . suicide is often accompanied by a combination of unresolved grief, an exaggerated belief in the hopelessness of one's condition, fear of conspiracies by others, and a wish for revenge."[151] Kushner finds that the death or disappearance of a parent, especially before or during puberty, frequently figures in severe depression and self-inflicted death.[152] The novelist William Styron commends Kushner's work and gives an account of his own "lurch down pathways toward doom," which he attributes to "incomplete mourning" of his mother, who died when he was thirteen.[153] Styron writes that when there is "unresolved mourning," the afflicted "has, in effect, been unable to achieve the catharsis of grief, and so carries within himself through later years an insufferable burden of which rage and guilt, and not only dammed-up sorrow, are a part, and become the potential seeds of self-destruction."[154]

Nastasya Filippovna, who didn't just lose *a* parent at any early age, but saw the fruit of her father's "backbreaking" toil smolder into ash, and unexpectedly lost mother, father, and then sister, is possibly one of the more hyperbolic cases of "incomplete mourning" on record.[155] Like Freud's pathological melancholic, Nastasya Filippovna utters "self-reproaches and self-revilings" chronically throughout the novel.[156] The prince, who diagnoses Nastasya Filippovna as being "deeply convinced that she is the most fallen, the most depraved creature in the whole world," states that "[s]he has tortured herself too much with the consciousness of her own undeserved shame!" (Id, Pt 3, Ch 8; 506). In the showdown between rivals for the prince's affection, Aglaya tells Nastasya Filippovna that she can "love only her own disgrace and the constant thought that [she was] disgraced" and has "been humiliated" (Id, Pt 4, Ch 8; 661–62). At her soiree, Nastasya Filippovna's self-denigration corroborates both the prince's diagnosis and Aglaya's allegations. It is supposed to be Nastasya Filippovna's special day, but instead of celebrating, she, working herself up into a frenzy, hurls barbs at herself: she claims to "have no shame," calls herself "a concubine," a "shameless hussy," a "woman of the streets," a "loose woman" and after the prince pledges his love for her, she tells him, "later you would [begin] to despise me" (Id, Pt 1, Ch 16; 199–200). She shouts, "I'm going on the streets . . . you heard, that is my place if not there, then I'll be a washerwoman!" (Id, Pt 1, Ch 16; 204).

Anomic-Egoism

Anomie is the other fiend adrift in Nastasya Filippovna's egoistic murk of despond. Anomie helps fuel her courtship of self-effacement, and it is enmeshed in one of Dostoevsky's recurrent themes—that of the "accidental family," which begets "disorder" and "fragmentation."[157] It is telling that Nastasya Filippovna, whose family was wiped out, kept getting one new "accidental" substitute after another. Durkheim recognizes that anomic suicide and egoistic suicide "have kindred ties" and states that they can operate independently or together (SU, Bk 2, Ch 5; 258). While both egoistic and anomic types "spring from society's insufficient presence in individuals, the sphere of its absence is not the same in both cases" (SU, Bk 2, Ch 5; 258). Egoistic suicide, which is a deficiency of "truly collective activity," deprives the individual "of object and meaning" (SU, Bk 2, Ch 5; 258). In those afflicted with anomie, however, "society's influence is lacking in the basically individual passions," which leaves them "without a check-rein" (SU, Bk 2, Ch 5; 258). Durkheim points out that "every disturbance of equilibrium . . . is an impulse to voluntary death" and "whenever serious readjustments take place in the social order," people inch closer to anomic self-destruction (SU, Bk 2, Ch 5; 246). In "times of rapid change" and when a "family catastrophe . . . affects the survivor," individuals, like Olya, the young suicide in *The Adolescent*, and most markedly Nastasya Filippovna, become "less resistant" to suicide (SU, Bk 2, Ch 5; 259).[158]

Nastasya Filippovna's anomie was jumpstarted by a virtual earthquake—a major "family catastrophe" (SU, Bk 2, Ch 5; 259). This was followed by a tsunami of "serious readjustments," which lapsed into sequential aftershocks that gyrated into a "disturbance of equilibrium" (SU, Bk 2, Ch 5; 246). In the wake of her parents' death, Nastasya Filippovna and her sister became dependents of Totsky and were effectually impressed into a flimsy, fleeting "accidental" family unit. Change, however, instantly hit when Totsky, bowing out of the configuration, forgot about the girls, and left for Europe. Nastasya Filippovna was thus effectually hurled into a slightly different matrix when Totsky's estate manager, a retired German official, added the children to his own large family. What might have been a moratorium from disruptive jolts was short lived, however, when the death of Nastasya Filippovna's sibling subtracted from the calculus the last piece of her old life.

There was, moreover, another "considerable change" in "the little girl's upbringing" five years later, when Totsky checked in and spied "delightful" Nastasya Filippovna, who was "some twelve years old, playful, intelligent and promising unusual beauty" (Id, Pt 1, Ch 4; 48). Totsky, the "unerring connoisseur," hired a "respectable elderly governess," with a "progressive education," to reside in the house and educate Nastasya Filippovna (Id, Pt 1, Ch 4; 48). After four years of this new arrangement with a Swiss tutor, who taught her French and sciences and enhanced her education, Nastasya Filippovna was again uprooted (Id, Pt 1, Ch 4; 48). In accordance with her "foster" father's instructions, the governess exited and a Totsky neighbor from a distant province entered to "fetch" Nastasya Filippovna and whisk her off to the distant hamlet of Otradnoye (Id, Pt 1, Ch 4; 48). There Nastasya Filippovna received another makeshift family, one comprised of the "childless widow," housekeeper, and chambermaid, along with a reconstructed identity as a kept woman in a gilded cage, where she was surrounded by "musical instruments, an exquisite young ladies' library, pictures, prints, pencils, brushes, paints and a wonderful little greyhound" (Id, Pt 1, Ch 4; 48–49). Next Nastasya Filippovna experienced the most tonitruous rumble, one which upheaved her foundational ipseity when Totsky, who was *in loco parentis* and her longtime benefactor, suddenly turned into her seducer.

When adult Nastasya Filippovna shows up in St. Petersburg to derail Totsky's marriage to some rich, beautiful woman of high society, what her defiler beholds is egoistic-anomie in the shape and voice of a "completely different woman, not at all resembling the one he had hitherto known and had left in the hamlet of Otradnoye" (Id, Pt 1, Ch 4; 49). As discussed in the next chapter in connection with Stavrogin of *Demons*, anomie can percolate under a veneer of apathy or, as it is with Nastasya Filippovna, it can vent as unconstrained rage. In fact, the altered, adult Nastasya Filippovna sounds like Durkheim's description of notes left behind by anomic suicides, which "contain blasphemies, violent recriminations against life in general, sometimes threats and accusations against a particular person to whom the responsibility for the suicide's unhappiness is imputed" (SU, Bk 2, Ch 6; 284). Nastasya Filippovna is "laughing in [Totsky's] face and stabbing him with the most venomous sarcasms" as she tells him "directly that she had never had anything for him in her heart but the most profound contempt, contempt that rose to the point of nausea, and had begun immediately after her initial astonishment" (Id, Pt 1, Ch 4; 50). Nastasya Filippovna is, as Durkheim has put it, packed with an "emotion" that "is over-excited and freed from all restraint," a "passion" that "no longer recogniz[es] bounds" (SU, Bk 2, Ch 6; 287).

Durkheim points out that incensed anomics are capable of murder, of "killing [themselves] after having killed someone else whom [they] accuse of having ruined [their] li[ves]" (SU, Bk 2, Ch 6; 285). Totsky, with his "sureness of vision," is staring ballistic anomie in the face and knows that Nastasya Filippovna "had long ago ceased to value herself" and is "capable of ruining herself, irrevocably and hideously with Siberia and penal labour, as long as she [can] treat outrageously the man for whom she [feels] such inhuman revulsion" (Id, Pt 1, Ch 4; 51). Totsky also realizes that he could be "murdered and bloodied and injured, or spat in the face in public in front of everyone," and that these things could "happen to him in such an unnatural and unpleasant manner" because his malefactor has "studied him, and consequently knew where to strike him" (Id, Pt 1, Ch 4; 52).

At her soiree, Nastasya Filippovna ratifies Totsky's forebodings after she takes repeated verbal stabs at him and then runs off with her lethal blade, Rogozhin. The *hara-kiri* mentioned in the notes for *The Idiot* crystallizes when Ivan Petrovich Ptitsyn tells Totsky about the Japanese practice:

> [T]hey say that something of this kind happens among the Japanese. . . The man who has been insulted apparently goes up to his insulter and says to him: "You've insulted me, so I've come to slit open my belly in front of you," and with these words, he really does slit open his belly in front of his insulter's eyes and it would seem, experiences a sense of extreme satisfaction, as though he had really obtained his revenge. (Id, Pt 1, Ch 16; 205)

Ptitsyn's *hara-kiri* disquisition describes Durkheim's anomic suicide, the kind "preceded by . . . some violent outbursts," and where "anger" and the resultant "state of acute over-excitation . . . tends to seek solace in acts of destruction" (SU, Bk 2, Ch 6; 285). It also anticipates Freud, who states that "impulses to suicide in a neurotic turn out regularly to be self-punishments for someone else's death" and that "thoughts of suicide" are really "murderous impulses against others redirected upon [the self]."[159] Further, Wahl points out that the "most painful" suicidal motive arises in individuals, who seek to extinguish or reduce self-blame through "an act of self-punishment" or attempt "to expiate the fantasied act of murder (death wishes) by operation of the talion law."[160]

Anomic *hara-kiri*, which Totsky deems an "excellent" comparison, also fits Nastasya Filippovna's polysemous love-hate for Aglaya, whose belly she'd like to kiss, but also "slit open" along with her own (Id, Pt 1; Ch 16; 205). The letters that Nastasya Filippovna writes to Aglaya have four purposes: they disclose idolatry of what she has lost, compulsive self-abasement, shattered equilibrium, and yearning for death. First, the worship of Aglaya that Nastasya Filippovna expresses in her letters is histrionically passionate.[161] Nastasya Filippovna asserts, "[w]e are two opposites, and I am so much out of your rank" (Id, Pt 3, Ch 10; 529). Aglaya represents a state so different from her own, that Nastasya Filippovna is moved to jealousy as well as an oxymoronic amorous loathing (Id, Pt 3, Ch 10; 529). After all, Aglaya has an intact life-affirming collective intact, her tightly knit family, complete with sisters, and respectability to boot. She, thus, embodies everything that Nastasya Filippovna feels she can never recoup. While Nastasya Filippovna, who was essentially deprived of innocence and childhood, yearns for extinction, virginal Aglaya is the oppositional vibrant, non-suicidogenic girlish celebrant of life.

Second, the letters do not merely divulge Nastasya Filippovna's idealization of Aglaya as the person she might have been—a "radiant spirit," who "cannot hate," rises "above all insult, above all personal anger," and "can love without egoism" (Id, Pt 3, Ch 10; 530). The letters give Nastasya Filippovna another weapon for self-abasement, which she redundantly denies:

> [d]o not think, either that I am abasing myself by writing to you like this or that I am one of those creatures that enjoy abasing themselves, even though they do it out of pride. But I know that I cannot abase myself even in a fit of pride. And of self-abasement I am incapable, because of the purity of my heart. So, therefore, I am not abasing myself at all. (Id, Pt 3, Ch 10; 531)

Nastasya Filippovna's string of denials indicates that she is on the threshold of other "abasing" episodes before perfecting the penultimate "self-abasement," the renunciation of life itself.

Third, for egoistic-anomic Nastasya Filippovna, the letters serve as a confessional in which she can expose her shattered equilibrium, one in which burning love copulates with oppugning odium. But it is the hatred and her worst self that Nastasya Filippovna unleashes in her climactic blow out with Aglaya. Sarcastically jabbing at Aglaya's respectability, Nastasya Filippovna asks, "have you come to see me without your governess," lances her with the accusation, "[y]ou wanted to personally ascertain whether he loves me more than you, because you are horribly jealous," and then slices at her with threats to "com-*mand*" the prince to desert his fiancé and marry her instead (Id, Pt 4, Ch 8; 664–65). But Nastasya Filippovna's campaigns to destroy others (like Totsky) inevitably invert into *hara-kiri* and self-inflicted trauma: after tormenting Aglaya, Nastasya Filippovna becomes "almost crazed" with "her face contorted and her lips parched," has an "outburst . . . so violent that she might perhaps have died," and then swoons (Id, Pt 4, Ch 8; 666–67). As Durkheim explains, anomic individuals "always attack [themselves] in excess of anger, whether or not [they have] previously attacked another" (SU, Bk 2, Ch 6; 285).

Four, Nastasya Filippovna's correspondence with Aglaya contain her love letters to death and exposes her aspirations of becoming "murderee."[162] She writes, "I shall soon be dead" and "I have renounced the world" (Id, Pt 3, Ch 10; 531). She conjures up images of euthanasic Rogozhin with "two dreadful eyes," whose "house is dark and tedious," and who owns "a razor wrapped in silk, like that Moscow murderer" (Id, Pt 3, Ch 10; 531). Knowing that Rogozhin "loves [her] so much that he cannot possibly prevent himself from hating [her]," Nastasya Filippovna states, "I would kill him out of fear," but instead she relies on the fact that "he will kill [her] first" in a "victim precipitated homicide" (Id, Pt 3, Ch 10; 531).[163]

Nastasya Filippovna plans to resolve her unresolved mourning, which is bottled up with her fury against Totsky, by turning it against herself through recruiting her executioner. While ranting about how Totsky would visit her in the hamlet of Otradnoye and "stay for a couple of months of the year, to disgrace, outrage, infuriate, deprave, and leave," she admits to suicidal ideation: "a thousand times I wanted to hurl myself into the pond, but I was base, I didn't have the courage" (Id, Pt 1, Ch 16; 200). Immediately after this, she turns to her blade and asks, "well, and now . . . Rogozhin, are you ready?" (Id, Pt 1, Ch 16; 200). She thus rebuffs light, life, forgiveness, faith, and the prince, who is the "kind, honest, good" man of her dreams, the one who can assure her, "You bear no guilt," and instead she dashes toward dark, nightmarish Rogozhin and his tomblike marital chamber (Id, Pt 1, Ch 16; 200). In accepting Rogozhin's proposal, Nastasya Filippovna says, "I have to go to my ruin anyway" and "I'll marry you though I might as well be drowning myself" (Id, Pt 2, Ch 2; 252). The prince, who agrees, tells Rogozhin, "to put it bluntly you may cut her throat and she understands that only too well now" (Id, Pt 2, Ch 3; 249).

Right before her death, Nastasya Filippovna is reading Gustave Flaubert's *Madame Bovary*, which features Emma's grisly and prolonged self-murder by arsenic: Emma "vomit[s] blood," with her "limbs . . . contorted, her body covered with brown blotches," and starts to "scream horribly."[164] Nastasya Filippovna's egoistic-anomic mission, however, is consummated with quick, clean, efficient sterility: the Rogozhin blade sinks into Nastasya Filippovna's flesh, "right under her left breast," and it is as if "the blow [went] straight to the heart" because "only about half a tablespoonful of blood flowed out from her chemise" (Id, Pt 4, Ch 11; 712). Nastasya Filippovna's "incomplete mourning" is completed in "motionless slumber," and the noises that Durkheim attributes to anomie, "violent recriminations against life in general," and "threats and accusations against a particular person to whom the responsibility for the suicide's unhappiness is imputed," are silenced in a room of "deathly" quiet, where the only thing to be heard is the buzzing of a fly (Id, Pt 4, Ch 11; 708: SU, Bk 2, Ch 6; 284).

Ippolit: Egoistic Thanatophobia

In the later notes for *The Idiot*, Dostoevsky comes to see Ippolit as "the main axis of the whole novel" and the question, "to die or not to die," as integral to a fictive populous that blabs incessantly about death, guillotines, scaffolds, and executions.[165] To reiterate, Durkheim asserts that suicide can be caused "solely by the fixed idea of death which, *without clear reason*, has taken complete possession of the patient's mind" (SU, Bk 1, Ch 1; 64). But the "patient" Ippolit, who is mired in death, actually does have *clear reason* for it: he is consumptive and like the condemned man climbing the scaffold, "know[s] for certain" that soon his "soul will fly out of [his body" and he will no "longer be a human being" (Id, Pt 1, Ch 2; 27). While Ippolit's attempted self-homicide fits within Durkheim's egoistic typology, it too has a "shade all [its] own" (SU, Bk 2, Ch 6; 278). Nastasya Filippovna's "personal stamp" on her egoistic suicide amalgamates as "incomplete mourning," anomie, and the desire to be "murderee," but what impels Ippolit to put a gun to his head is quite different: it is egoistic thanatophobia enmeshed in a deep-seated need to do the impossible—to joltingly renew life through the exorcism and conquest of death (SU, Bk 2, Ch 6; 277).[166]

The first mention of Ippolit, who seems to have no identity apart from illness, comes from Kolya, who relates that the consumptive is getting "worse" and that he "was in bed this morning" (Id, Pt 1, Ch 12; 153). Because Dostoevsky's first wife, Marya, had tuberculosis, he was intimately familiar with the progression of the disease. In 1863, Dostoevsky and his wife had settled in Moscow where a doctor was caring for Marya on her death bed.[167] During this time, Dostoevsky dutifully attended to Marya, who daily became more irritable and moodier, and thus had a temperament resembling that of "terribly touchy" Ippolit.[168] Seventeen- or eighteen-year-old Ippolit is all about himself, his disease, his dying: he has a "constantly irritated expression on his face, where disease had placed its terrible marks" and is "as thin as a skeleton, pale yellow, his eyes glittered, and two red spots burned on his cheeks" (Id, Pt 2, Ch 8; 302). Ippolit, who "cough[s] without cease" and whose "every word, every breath, almost, [is] accompanied by wheezing," is "clearly in a very advanced stage of consumption" and has "no more than two or three weeks left" (Id, Pt 2, Ch 8; 302).

Solipsism

From the outset, Ippolit is linked not just to terminal disease, but also to a potential self-imposed death: Kolya tells the prince that Ippolit would "do better to die as soon as possible" and says that "[i]f I were in his place I'd certainly want to die" (Id, Pt 1, Ch 12; 155). Like some people who lean toward egoistic suicide, Ippolit, the eldest son of the captain's widow, has tenuous family ties. Because his mother neglects him, Ippolit has landed in an "accidental family" and Kolya's mother helps him "with money, clothes, linen and everything" (Id, Pt 1; Ch 12;157).[169] Kolya notes that if Ippolit had the resources, he would detach himself even more by renting "separate lodgings" and would renounce his family altogether. But his detachment goes further and sporadically involves a resolve to shut out feeling and empathy. This becomes apparent when Ippolit, who professes to believe that "human beings are created in order to torment on another," visits Surikov, who is grieving over his infant's dead body (Id, Pt 3, Ch 6; 461–62). Ippolit "inadvertently" smiles and starts blaming this impoverished man for the tragedy (Id, Pt 3, Ch 6; 461–62). Later, when Ippolit involuntarily starts to "feel" a "painful" and "strange contemptuous pity" for Surikov, something "he did not want to feel at all," he shoves that back to reenter his cocoon of self-imposed insensibility (Id, Pt 3, Ch 6; 462).

Ippolit's illness, which not only secludes him and limits his participation in human activities, gives him ample time to become what Durkheim calls "self-preoccupied" and prone to "self-absorption" (SU, Bk 2, Ch 6; 279). Durkheim maintains that certain people who extricate themselves from the affairs of the world become entrenched in themselves and compensate for external activity by developing an active inner life. Ippolit admits that he "deliberately spent whole days locked in [his] room, though [he] could have gone out like everyone else" (Id, Pt 3, Ch 5; 458). He reveals his proclivity to project his funk on others and states that he cannot "endure" what he sees as "that poking, bustling, eternally, preoccupied, gloomy and anxious mass of human beings that scurr[y] about [him] on the pavements" (Id, Pt 3, Ch 5; 458). He brags that he has "broke[n] off all [of his] social contacts and abandoned all friends" (Id, Pt 3, Ch 6; 461). Tellingly, he replaces the familial word "home" for the more generic one, "household" (Id, Pt. 3, Ch 6; 461). Finally, he portrays himself as a "recluse," who "lock[s himself] away and completely separate[s himself] from the family's room" (Id, Pt 3, Ch 6; 461).

Ippolit fits the egoistic typology that Elder Zosima describes in *The Brothers Karamazov*: the man "in our age," who "seeks seclusion in his own hole, . . . withdraws from the others, hides himself, . . . and ends by pushing himself away from people and pushing people away from himself."[170] Zosima's discussion is consistent with Durkheim's description of how egoism emulates the "condition of melancholic languor" and "relaxes all springs of action":

> The moment the individual becomes so enamoured of himself, inevitably he increasingly detaches himself from everything external and emphasizes the isolation in which he lives, to the point of worship. Self-absorption is not a good method of attaching oneself to others . . . Reflection . . . has about it something

> personal and egoistic; for it is only possible as a person becomes detached from the outside world, and retreats from it into himself. And reflection is the more intense, the more complete this retreat. (SU, Bk 2, Ch 6; 278–79)

Ippolit, who is practically immobilized and can seldom do more than get out of bed, has become "enamored" not just with himself, but also with his own protracted process of dying. He stares at the "accursed" Meyer's Wall and states, "I've lain on that pillow so long, and have looked out of that window so long, and have thought so much . . . A dead man has no age, you know. I thought about that . . . when I woke up one night" (Id, Pt 2, Ch 10; 345: Pt 3, Ch 5; 458). The tuberculosis, which has claimed him, has "detached" him "from the outside world" and made him "retreat from it into himself" (SU, Bk 2, Ch 6; 279).

Durkheim could be diagnosing Ippolit when he says, "if [consciousness] separates itself too radically from other beings" it "creates nothingness within by creating it without, and has nothing left upon which to reflect but its own wretched misery" (SU, Bk 2, Ch 6; 279). In *The Brothers Karamazov*, Elder Zosima speaks of egoistic isolation and comes to the same conclusion: "everyone now strives most of all to separate his person, wishing to experience the fullness of life within himself, and yet what comes of all his efforts is not the fullness of life but full suicide, for instead of the fullness of self-definition, they fall into complete isolation."[171] This selfism annoys Lizaveta Prokofyevna about Ippolit. Even though he is "really dying," he "keeps on making speeches," and these speeches all center on Ippolit, Ippolit's illness, Ippolit's "wretched misery," and Ippolit's imminent death (Id, Pt 2, Ch 9; 334: SU, Bk 2, Ch 6; 279). Wallowing in his infirmity, Ippolit states: "As soon as I get home today, I shall go to bed . . . [and] in two weeks time, as I know, I shall die . . . I would like to say a few words to you in farewell" (Id, Pt 2, Ch 9; 334). When Lizaveta Prokofyevna orders him to "go to bed," Ippolit invokes that menacing "nothingness" and replies, "If I go to bed, then I won't get up again until I'm dead" (Id, Pt 2, Ch 9; 334).

Significantly, Ippolit, along with another facet of "nothingness," is present when Prince Myshkin encounters the group of young nihilists, which Dostoevsky satirizes.[172] But young-nihilist Ippolit, who unplugs from family and community, finds no common ground with this gang either. As Joseph Frank points out, unlike the angry nihilists, Ippolit is not revolting against "the iniquities of the social order."[173] Instead, he is railing against nature itself, which "is very given to mocking" and against the postlapsarian landscape, which is inundated with suffering and death (Id, Pt 2. Ch 10; 346). Ippolit bewails the fact that "today is the last time I shall be out in the fresh air and among people, for in two weeks' time I shall certainly be in the earth" (Id, Pt 2, Ch 9; 335). He laments that "here are these people, and they will never exist anymore, never" and notes that when "you're dead, introduce yourself as a corpse" (Id, Pt 2, Ch 10; 345). But because for Ippolit, only Ippolit exists, and because Ippolit equates Ippolit with suffering and death, his revolt is tragically one against himself.

For Durkheim, the very "idea of God" which "presents itself in all details of existence and makes individual wills converge to one identical goal," bestows the kind of "cohesion and vitality" that can fend off self-annihilative impulses (SU, Bk 2, Ch 2; 159). By calling Ippolit an atheist, Lizaveta Prokofyevna intimates that part and parcel of immersion in solipsistic "nothingness within" leads to that "nothingness without," which is repudiated faith (SU, Bk 2, Ch 6; 279). Lizaveta Prokofyevna's accusations become credible when Ippolit reflects on the painting of Holbein's Christ, displayed "in one of the most gloomy chambers of [Rogozhin's] house" (Id, Pt 3, Ch 6; 475). He notes that painters, who are in "the habit of depicting Christ, both on the cross and when taken from it," tend to add that "nuance of extraordinary beauty" connotative of irretractable faith (Id, Pt 3, Ch 6; 475). But, for Ippolit, Holbein's rendering does otherwise. It inspires him to blaspheme and own the "blind, dark, and speechless" forces of Nature as his Truth:

> [I]f this is really what the corpse looked like (and it certainly must have looked just like this) when it was seen by all his disciples, his chief future apostles, by the women who followed him and stood by the cross, indeed by all who believe in him and worshipped him, then how could they believe, as they looked at such a corpse, that this martyr would rise from the dead. (Id, Pt 3, Ch 6; 476–77)

Prince Myshkin, who acknowledges that the Holbein painting has the potential to extinguish faith, nevertheless leaves the Rogozhin habitat with his reverence for Christ intact. In stark contrast, Ippolit is supplicated not before Christ, but before the insuperable "laws of nature," which amount to a "dark, brazen and senseless eternal force, to which everything is subordinate" (Id, Pt 3, Ch 6; 477). He says that the people in the Holbein painting "who surrounded the dead man . . . must have felt a terrible anguish and perturbation that evening, which had smashed all their hopes and almost all their beliefs in one go," and he himself expresses affinity with those "part[ing] in the most dreadful fear" (Id, Pt 3, Ch 6; 477). Ippolit is thus disengaged from the very faith that Durkheim, Dostoevsky, and Prince Myshkin know can facilitate self-transcendence and help stave off suicidogenic forces.

While Nastasya Filippovna's "incomplete mourning" is a component of her propulsion to wed death's blade, Ippolit's reach for that "dark, brazen and senseless" demise stems from an internally discordant state of elated-mourning (Id, Pt 3, Ch 6; 477).[174] Here Eros and Thanatos take up the cudgels (Id, Pt 3, Ch 6; 477). Ippolit swings from extolling the richness of life, in which it is possible to partake of the prince's "drink to the health of the sun," and "live for the happiness of all people, for the revelation and the proclamation of truth," to the diametric pole—that of self-prostration before sheer nothingness (Id, Pt 3, Ch 4; 434: Pt 2, Ch 10; 346). Right after praising life, Ippolit welcomes death and says, "It's time I went" and that "if this consumption hadn't happened along, I'd have killed myself" (Id, Pt 2, Ch 10; 347). Throughout the novel, Ippolit ambivalently aches for, yet evades, sleep, which he hopes, yet fears, can lull him into "motionless slumber" (Id, Pt 4, Ch 11; 708).

When Lebedev quotes Hamlet's "To be or not to be," he fastens it to Ippolit, who "doesn't want to go to sleep!" (Id, Pt 3, Ch 4; 429). Ippolit's state of "to be or not to be" is one in which two instincts are ceaselessly warring. His condition foretokens Freud, who conceives of the battle between Eros, "the self-preservative instinct . . . assigned to the ego," and Thanatos, the death drive, the "task of which is to lead organic matter back into the inorganic state."[175] In Freud's view, most behaviors, including suicide, can be explained as the product of the relentless jousting of the life and death drives. In fact, the prince's dacha-gathering turns into a virtual Freudian symposium. The lecturer-guests pontificate on "the need to drink and eat, that's to say, the instinct for self-preservation" a "law" which is "as normal as the law of destruction, and perhaps, of self-destruction, too" (Id, Pt 3, Ch 4; 436–37). When Lebedev "seize[s] avidly on [this] paradox," and calls it a "profound one, a true one," he effectually steps up to the podium as keynote speaker, proclaiming that "the law of self-destruction and the law of self-preservation are equally strong in mankind!" (Id, Pt 3, Ch 4; 437).

In this Freudian congregation, Ippolit serves as both specimen and pulpiteer. By "pull[ing] Kolya's silver watch towards him" and "cast[ing] an avid look at its hands," Ippolit lectures through kinesics to remind everyone that he, the embodiment of embattled self-preservation and self-destruction, is the condemned man, one for whom the ticktock is gradually lapsing (Id, Pt 3, Ch 4; 437). Ippolit, however, wants to both halt and hasten the clock at once. He fears death with such intensity that he wants to just get it over with, bring it on himself. Ippolit depicts one of the "more recondite" suicidal motives that Wahl says is "magical" and "actuated to achieve irrational, delusional and illusory ends."[176] Wahl states that some people court "suicide as an aid in coping with overpowering thanatophobia, or fear of death."[177] For such individuals, self-slaughter "serves as a reaction formation to the morbidly feared eventuality of death by embracing it rather than running from it."[178]

Wahl's concept of the thanatophobic "embrace" of dreaded death coheres with Durkheim's egoistic suicide, in which individuals are "isolated," where "the ties uniting [them] with others are slackened or broken," where their "main task" becomes "self-observation and self-analysis" (SU, Bk 2, Ch 6;

279, 281). Wahl explicates how egoism can facilitate the thanatotic trumping of Eros and states that those who morbidly fear death tend to apotheosize themselves into abstractions, like "immortality and omnipotence."[179] Such self-deification enables individuals to "entertain and effect an act of self-destruction without the sense of self-preservation horror which it so commonly induces in others."[180]

Ippolit displays this sort of defiant self-inflation when he ceremoniously unveils his "My Necessary Explanation," with the "Epigraph, *Apres moi le deluge*" (Id, Pt 3. Ch 5; 449). Ippolit displays his regalia, an "official-sized package, stamped with a large red seal," vows that "[w]ith the first rim of the sun, [he] shall lie down" (Id, Pt 3, Ch 5; 448). Ippolit's suggestion that his self-imposed slumber is in a class by itself because it will aberrantly occur at sunrise is quite significant. Since sleeping at night abides by the normative human rhythm and because the Orthodox religion conceives of death as a "falling asleep in the Lord," Ippolit's distinctive chosen hour enables him to nihilistically thumb his nose at nature, humanity, and faith in one pop.[181] Then Ippolit self-glorifies into "the great and mighty angel in the book of Revelation" and proclaims "[t]omorrow 'there shall be time no longer'" (Id, Pt 3, Ch 5; 448). The egoistic chords in his suicidal overture become even more audible when Ippolit self-chastises, "[t]here's too much that's personal in it . . . too much about myself, really" and Lebedev "hiss[es]" back, "[y]es, sir, too damn interested in yourself" (Id, Pt 3, Ch 5; 456).

When Ippolit performs his pre-suicide recital of "My Necessary Explanation," what he lays bare is his multifaceted egoistic death wish. In this performance, Wahl's concept of thanatophobia, with its attendant self-aggrandizement, fuses with Ippolit's need to shock himself out of his cachexia. He reveals his drive hasten the death he so fears through the juxtaposition of opposites: he ponders the things in life that he dreads losing, like "look[ing] at trees," and then contrarily expresses his resolve to not just submit, but instead take matters into his own hands. In in his words, this "man who has been condemned to death," knowing that he has "only two weeks left to live," believes that "it's not worth living for two weeks" (Id, Pt 3, Ch 5; 451–52). Unlike the condemned man on the scaffold, however, Ippolit has deluded himself into believing that he has the power to quash ineluctability by becoming both the guillotine and its victim.

Entomophobia

In "My Necessary Explanation," the thanatophobia metamorphosizes into entomophobia when Ippolit describes his dream of a "horrible creature, some kind of monster . . . like a scorpion, but not a scorpion, more loathsome and far more horrible" (Id, Pt 3, Ch 5; 454). This vile "reptile," like Rogozhin or some scorpion of seppuku, crawls into Ippolit's room "*on purpose*" and is gunning for him and him alone, making him "dreadfully afraid that it would sting [him]" (Id, Pt 3, Ch 5; 454). This reptile, which climbs the wall and even "touches [Ippolit's] hair with its tail," causes the consumptive to "leap up" in sheer terror (Id, Pt 3, Ch 5; 455). It becomes clear though that this is only Ippolit's bugaboo and no one else's because when his mother and her friend enter the room, they are "calmer," "not afraid" and even try to "catch the loathsome thing" (Id, Pt 3, Ch 5; 455).

Ippolit's "mystical terror," however, is foisted onto his dog, Norma, who has been dead for five years (Id, Pt 3, Ch 5; 455). This resurrected dream-Norma is "trembling in every limb" and revving up for a fight to the finish (Id, Pt 3, Ch 5; 455).[182] Moreover, seeking to preserve her master's life, Norma is "dreadfully fierce," "bare[s] her terrible teeth, open[s] her enormous red jaws, position[s] herself, . . . pluck[s] up her courage, and suddenly grab[s] the reptile in her teeth"(Id, Pt 3, Ch 5; 455). The dream becomes a contest between equals, where the poisonous monster is pitted again protective Norma. While Peace states that "battle between the long-dead Norma and the 'scorpion' may be taken as a dream representation of the struggle between normality and disease," it more closely reflects the Freudian "paradox," the very one Lebedev calls "profound,"—namely, that "the law of self-destruction and the law of self-preservation are equally strong in mankind" (Id, Pt 3, Ch 4; 437).[183] Incidentally, immediately after Lebedev speaks in the idiom of Eros and Thanatos, he ties self-destruction to the devil and to Ippolit's vile reptile by rambling on about that "terrible spirit," with its "tail" and "horns" (Id, Pt 3, Ch 4; 437).

Lebedev's devil resembles Ippolit's diabolical creepy crawly, who similarly has a "tail" plus a hornlike protrusion consisting of "two fingers thick around the head" that stick up "like two strong needles" (Id, Pt 3, Ch 5; 454). Further, Lebedev's demon is reminiscent of the forces depicted in Ippolit's rant about Holbein's Christ and smashed faith: a death "so terrible," and "laws of nature so powerful" (Id, Pt 3, Ch 6; 476). That is, when Ippolit describes Holbein's Christ, he babbles about a "blind, dark, and speechless creature," an "enormous and repulsive tarantula," and connects it to death-blade Rogozhin, who seemingly creeps into his room, "stare[s] at [him] in silence," and impinges on his solitary, feverish consumptive delirium (Id, Pt 3, Ch 6; 477). In Ippolit's dream, all monster forms and lethal forces, including Rogozhin, come together. They are crammed into the conceptualized death drive and when Thanatos prevails, "all . . . hopes and almost all . . . beliefs" are "smashed . . . in one go" (Id, Pt 3, Ch 6; 477).

Significantly, the battle between Norma and the creature ends indeterminately: although Norma appears to swallow the creature, it continues to move. Eventually, the creature stings Norma's tongue while "the chewed-up reptile is still moving" (Id, Pt 3, Ch 5; 456).[184] Ippolit awakens to a cliff hanger, in which neither Norma nor the scorpion are officially proclaimed winner. The implication is that self-preservative and self-destructive drives are in dead heat and that the sparring in the Aceldama of Ippolit's psyche is irresolute. Ippolit himself confirms this when turning to Thanatos, he states, "the idea . . . that it was not worth living for a few weeks began to really overpower me," and then, turning to Eros, states, "I knew positively that I had consumption and that it was incurable . . . [b]ut the clearer my understanding, the more frantically did I want to life; I clung to life and wanted to live at whatever cost" (Id, Pt 3, Ch 5; 457).

Russian Roulette

Seeking release from conflictive vacillation, Ippolit lands on what he claims is a "complete decision," which involves his "hopeless pistol" (Id, Pt 3, Ch 7; 480). Rather than resort to Rogozhin-ism, commit "some atrocity" and kill someone else, which is the Durkheimian flipside of self-homicide, Ippolit's egoistic death-drive is pointed squarely at his own temple (Id, Pt 3, Ch; 7; 480).[185] As in Durkheim's egoistic and Wahl's thanatophobic suicides, before acting, Ippolit inflates "me-me-me" and delusively proclaims his "omnipotence."[186] He asserts, "I still have the power to die," and then, seeking conquest, dons the crown of free will: "suicide may possibly be the only action I can still begin and end of my own free will" (Id, Pt 3, Ch7; 484). The act that ensues, however, is unfree and as indeterminate as the contest between Norma and the "loathsome" creature (Id, Pt 3, Ch 5; 455).

After saying "farewell to Man," Ippolit pulls the pistol from his pocket, but at the very second Keller rushes over to abort the mission, the mission anticlimactically self-aborts (Id, Pt 3, Ch 7; 489). The reason "the sharp, dry click of the trigger [is] heard, but no shot follow[s]" is because the pistol has no firing cap (Id, Pt 3, Ch 7; 490). After the misfire, there is debate, which again anticipates not only Freud, who acknowledges the existence of "purposive accidents," where people secure unconscious ways to unleash their death drive, but also Menninger who sweeps "purposive accidents" into his category of "focal suicide," in which individuals concoct ways to self-injure.[187]

In *The Idiot*, however, the discussion of "purposive accidents" turns topsy-turvily into a suggestion that Ippolit's forgetting of the cap, the act that *spared* his life, was "purposive" self-preservation, rooted in the unconscious desire *not* to self-injure. Ippolit, in fact, bolsters this as a possibility when he claims that he did not insert the cap because he feared that "the gun might go off in his pocket by accident" and protests, "I forgot by complete accident, not on purpose" (Id, Pt 3, Ch 7; 490–91). Here Keller warns: "Gentlemen, if any of you ever again, out loud, in my presence expresses any doubt that the cap was forgotten on purpose, and tries to assert that the unhappy young man was merely indulging in playacting—then you'll have me to deal with me" (Id, Pt 3, Ch 7; 490–91). Despite these blanket denials of a "purposive accident," there is nothing unequivocal about Ippolit's flopperoo. Even before he whips out the pistol, his spectators bicker over whether Ippolit will go through with it. Vera exclaims, "[b]ut he is going to shoot himself in a moment," while dissenters mutter, "he won't shoot himself" (Id, Pt 3, Ch 7; 483). Putting in his two cents, Yevgeny Pavlovich states, "if I were in your place . . . I would purposely refrain from shooting myself, just in order to tease them" (Id, Pt 3, Ch 7; 487). These commentators sound like a chorus in Greek drama and as the figurative furies of equivoque, they chant a mixed message before protagonist Ippolit enacts his version of Russian roulette.

Russian roulette and Durkheim's concept of egoistic "depression and melancholy" are habitual bedfellows (SU, Bk 2, Ch 3; 214). Taylor homes in on this when he discusses "thanatation," whereby those craving relief from suicidal thoughts, boredom, and fatigue risk life in order to confirm and "reinvest" it "with meaning and purpose."[188] Taylor adds that suicidal acts by thanatationists are "*necessarily* ordeals," which tend to be " 'game-like' and may be described as 'ludenic.' "[189] One of his examples is Graham Greene, who suffered from chronic depression and whose autobiography reveals how playing Russian roulette was therapeutic for him because it shocked him (at least temporarily) out of numbness and inertia.[190]

Does Ippolit know that the gun lacks a firing cap at the very moment he pulls the trigger? Whether he doesn't know, or he purposively forgot, is essentially irrelevant because either way, Ippolit is fuddled in consumptive ambivalence. As Erwin Stengel has pointed out, "*[m]ost people who commit suicidal acts do not either want to die or to live: they want to do both at the same time.*"[191] Ippolit, like the "ludenic" player of Russian roulette, is afloat in the fog of "I want to die-live," "sleep-awake," or "I don't know" when he delivers that adrenergic "dry click" with his pistol of "hopeless" renewal (Id, Pt 3; Ch 7; 490). After the gun fails to fire, Ippolit falls into Keller's arms "as though unconscious, perhaps imagining that he [is] already dead," then sits up, "not understanding what [is] happening, and looking around at all with a senseless gaze" (Id, Pt 3; Ch 7; 490). From there, Ippolit starts sobbing "in a hysterical fit," collapses, and becomes "truly unconscious" (Id, Pt, 3; Ch 7; 490–91). The misfire thus effectuates a cathartic pseudo-death.

In Taylor's view, Russian roulette lets the thanatationist "exorcise death and, in the short run at least give[s] the individual a feeling of having conquered it."[192] He states that it is "rare for survivors of even the most dangerous attempts to try to kill themselves again at the first opportunity" because the attempter is convinced "that a 'death' has in fact taken place and that 'someone different' has arisen from the ashes."[193] The idea is that the attempter, like the pardoned man on the scaffold, has "arisen" as a new being who aspires to "make each minute into a whole lifetime" (Id, Pt 1, Ch 5; 72, 78). While Ippolit pontificates about Holbein's picture, he casts doubt on Christ's resurrection, but his egoism, infused with a delusional sense of his own omnipotence, has given him enough moxie to take a shot at self-resurrecting into the man-God. Ippolit does not lodge another attempt to blow his brains out and thus fits the pattern of the thanatationist, who in imitation of the mythic phoenix, seeks to rise, and in a sense, has arisen from the ashes.

Antipodal Revitalization

Ippolit, however, is familiar with a form of revitalization that is more effective than playing Russian roulette with a "hopeless pistol" (Id, Pt 3, Ch 7; 480). Durkheim asserts that individuals can be jolted out of that dark egoistic trance and morbid absorption in the "contemplation of emptiness" by something more sustaining than pressing a gun barrel to the brow (SU, Bk 2, Ch 6; 280). Durkheim defines the cure: through forging "ties [that] unite [the self] with others," through giving of the self "to blend in fecund union with another being," through "mixing with people," and through truly being "affected by something other than [the self]," individuals can obtain or recoup the collectivity that bestows the will to live (SU, Pt 2, Ch 6; 279–81).

Dostoevsky's thoughts about life affirmation are consistent with those of Durkheim. James P. Scanlan implies this, saying that Dostoevsky "wished to understand the condition of being human" and "[w]hatever subject he took up—religion, art, the state, history, morality—he was interested above all in its human significance and specifically in what clues he could find in it to the question of what it means to be human."[194] For Dostoevsky, what it means to be human (or a moral being) equates with what Ruben Apressyan calls "*agape*," which he defines as the "compassionate, benevolent, careful, loving attitude toward others."[195] What Dostoevsky's consumptive desperately needs is a reciprocating *agape*, or what Durkheim's prescribes as reinfusion of life from the outside world or a bonding with someone or something other than the "me." This need is apparent in Ippolit's impulse to share "My Necessary Explanation" with the budding nihilist Aglaya. The prince tells Aglaya that "he wanted us all, not only you, to praise him" and elaborates: "It's just that he probably wanted us all to surround him and tell him that we love and respect him very much, and wanted us all to implore him to remain alive" (Id, Pt 3, Ch 8; 497). What is tragic, however, is that Ippolit's illness bars him from that nourishing mingling with others and effectually places what he so needs out of reach.

Ippolit, however, gets just a teaser-taste of *agape*, along with the restorative experience of being "affected" by something outside the self. This occurs when his illness gives him a little reprieve and lets him emerge from hibernation to perform a virtuous deed. Every step along the way, Ippolit puts the interests of others before his own, and does so despite repeated physical obstacles. When a pocketbook drops out of passerby's threadbare coat, Ippolit retrieves it and, even with his ravaged lungs, chases after the owner. Then Ippolit, who is "dreadfully out of breath," climbs the seemingly "infinite" staircase and enters a room where its inhabitants are "reduced by poverty to that degrading condition in which disorder finally overcomes all attempts to fight it" (Id, Pt 3, Ch 6; 463, 465). Even after the man in the room "pounce[s] on" him with "rabid fury," frail Ippolit presses on to deliver the lost purse, which contains documents and last deeds and turns out to be the family's lifeline (Id, Pt 3, Ch 6; 465).

After reuniting the item with its owner, Ippolit is distracted from his chronic self-fixation and takes an interest in someone else's "plaintive discourse" (Id, Pt 3, Ch 6; 467). Ippolit learns how a series of misfortunes brought the unemployed medic to St. Petersburg, where he ended up spending all his savings, pawning "his wife's last rags," and lacking "bread" to feed his newborn infant (Id, Pt 3, Ch 6; 468). Ippolit promises to try to help by locating his school mate, Bakhmutov, whose uncle is the state councilor, the very one who can undo this man's devastation. Consequently, with a "cough [that]had begun to torment [him] again," Ippolit trudges forth to Vasily Island to find, Bakhmutov, who happens to be a person of whom he is not especially fond (Id, Pt 3, Ch 6; 469).[196] Due to Ippolit's altruistic exertions, the family is rescued: the medic gets a new post, receives a "travelling allowance, and even a cash advance"(Id, Pt 3, Ch 6; 470).

When Bakhmutov thanks his friend for letting him participate in the delivery of such a blessing, Ippolit essentially articulates Durkheim's conviction that inactive "inner meditation" yields morbific egoism and that "[a]ll movement is, in a sense, altruistic in that it is centrifugal and disperses existence beyond its own limitations" (SU, Bk 2, Ch 6; 279). Ippolit tells Bakhmutov that "whoever attacks individual 'charity,' . . . attacks the nature of man[, and that] [i]ndividual kindness will always remain, because it is a need of the personality, a living need for the direct influence of one personality on another" (Id, Pt 3, Ch 6; 470–71). Ippolit expounds: "In sowing your seed, sowing your 'charity,' your good deeds in whatever form, you give away a part of your personality and absorb part of another" (Id, Pt 3, Ch 6; 472). But Ippolit understands that his physical deterioration excludes him from feasting at the banquet of charitable giving: "when I have only two months left, and if I should terribly want to do one good deed that would require much work, much running about and fuss, . . . then in that case I suppose I would have to refuse it because of the lack of time remaining to me" (Id, Pt 3, Ch 6; 473).

Ippolit is thus tantalized by what Durkheim knows "man cannot live without"—namely that salvific "attachment" to that "which transcends and survives" the self—and he knows that "the reason for this necessity is a need we must have not to perish entirely" (SU, Bk 2, Ch 3; 210). But Ippolit is physically incapable of pursuing salubrious reciprocity, which entails "giving away part of [his] personality and absorb[ing] part of another" and of truly pursuing the kind of transcendence that resists suicide (Id, Pt 3, Ch 6; 472: SU, Bk 2, Ch 3; 210). Instead, Ippolit is the condemned man, imprisoned in melancholic egoism, which, according to Durkheim, is so "contradictory to human nature" and "too uncertain to have chances of permanence" (SU, Bk 2, Ch 3; 210).

CONCLUSION: A PARDON FROM THE EGOISTIC GUILLOTINE?

Both *Crime and Punishment* and *The Idiot* proffer a potential pardon from the egoistic guillotine, but in each novel, hope presents itself quite differently. While in *The Idiot*, it couches itself as "might have been," in *Crime and Punishment*, it conjugates as "might be."

Mikhail Bakhtin, who states that "almost all of Dostoevsky's novels have a *conventionally literary, conventionally monologic* ending" is not the only scholar to find that this is "especially characteristic" in *Crime and Punishment*.[197] Others have faulted *Crime and Punishment*'s "epilogue" for its radical departure from the preceding dialogical style.[198] But to some extent, the deceased Svidrigailov keeps the dialogue audible throughout the ostensibly "monologic ending." Because Svidrigailov is perhaps as close as Dostoevsky ever comes to creating pure allegory, even after the character itself has gone the way of all flesh, he is nevertheless figuratively zoetic. As the personification of egoistic self-demise, Svidrigailov continues to infect Raskolnikov, eavesdrop inside prison walls, and participate in the ongoing elenchus.

As specter, Svidrigailov accompanies Raskolnikov to Siberia where he spars with Sonya for dominion over the prisoner's soul. When Raskolnikov first lands in Siberia, he regrets not killing himself, feels no remorse, and even mimics Svidrigailov by telling himself, "[m]y conscience is clear" (CP, Ep., Ch 2; 544).[199] While asking himself, "[w]as there really such a force in his desire to live, and was it so difficult to overcome it," Raskolnikov consults the wraithy tutor of egoistic nihility: how did "Svidrigailov, who was afraid of death, overcome it?" (CP, Ep., Ch 2; 544–45). In addition, Raskolnikov, who "torment[s Sonya] with his contemptuous and rude treatment," cannot see that she, trying to fend off the tenacious Svidrigailov, "might herald a future break in his life, his future resurrection, his future new vision of life" (CP, Ep., Ch 2, 543, 545). Sonya, however, builds the only conceivable conduit between the convict and his new society. The prisoners all "come to love" Sonya, even though they "kn[ow] . . . that she had followed *after him*" and she becomes their shared sentiment: "when she [comes] to see Raskolnikov at work, or [meets] a party of convicts on the way to work, they would all take their hats off, they would all bow to her" (CP, Ep., Ch 2; 546). For Raskolnikov, still isolated, still clamoring after the Svidrigailov option, Sonya's bonds with the others presents an "insoluble" riddle (CP, Ep., Ch 2; 546).

According to Durkheim, people "cling to life more resolutely when belonging to a group they love, so as not to betray interests they put before their own" (SU, Bk 2, Ch 3; 209). In the prison in *Notes From the House of the Dead*, which is a virtual suicide incubator, some inmates manage to plod along and endure by forging a "cohesive and animated" community within that "irregular hexagon" (SU, Bk 2, Ch 3; 210).[200] In the *Crime and Punishment* prison, however, Raskolnikov rebuffs fraternization. For Raskolnikov, there is a "terrible and impassable abyss . . .between him and all these people," and "[i]t [is] as if he and they belong to different nations" (CP, Ep., 2; 545). Raskolnikov, who once told Svidrigailov "people don't want to have anything to do with you, they chase you away," finds himself in precisely that predicament (CP, Pt 4, Ch 1; 282). Sickened with Svidrigailov-cyanosis, Raskolnikov is "disliked and avoided by everyone," and they want to kill him and even accuse him of "being godless" (CP, Ep., Ch 2; 546). After "one convict fl[ies] at him in a perfect frenzy," Raskolnikov dons his Svidrigailov-like pallor of indifference (CP, Ep., Ch 2; 546). He "wait[s] . . . calmly and silently" with frozen eyebrows where "not a feature of his face trembl[es]" (CP, Ep., Ch 2; 546).

But eventually, there is the epiphanic transformation. This occurs shortly after an illness when Raskolnikov dreams in the prison hospital that the "whole world [is] doomed to fall victim to some terrible, as yet unknown and unseen pestilence" (CP, Ep., Ch 2; 547). There are newly spawned "microscopic creatures that lodge themselves in men's bodies," and those who "receive them into themselves immediately bec[ome] possessed and mad" (CP, Ep., Ch 2; 547). The pathology is egoism, one in which "[e]veryone [becomes] anxious, and no one [understands] anyone else, and where each person thinks that "the truth is contained in himself" (CP, Ep., Ch 2; 547). Those afflicted with Svidrigailov-neuropathy lack moral fibers and can "not agree on what to regard as evil, what as good" and do not "know whom to accuse, whom to vindicate" (CP, Ep., Ch 2; 547). Due to infectious selfism, everything ceases "because everyone offer[s] his own ideas, his own corrections, and no one [can] agree" (CP, Ep., Ch 2; 547). While there are a few, chosen "to begin a new generation of people and a new life, to renew and purify the earth," no one can see or hear them (CP, Ep., Ch 2; 547–48). The dream exposes the far-reaching implications of nihil-Svidrigailovism, which does not sate itself with a single blast to a single brain, but pestilentially "spread[s] further and further" to rescind all existence (CP, Ep., Ch 2; 547).[201]

After the dream, discarnate Svidrigailov starts to back off and concede defeat. When Raskolnikov realizes that he hasn't seen Sonya in a while, he suddenly worries about someone other than himself and asks about her. When Sonya, who was ill, learns that Raskolnikov "missed her and was so concerned about her," she sends him a note that stirs emotion and makes his heartbeat "heavily and painfully" (CP, Ep., Ch 2; 548). Emerging from his pre-suicidal anesthesia, Raskolnikov starts to feel and care for another being. After Sonya recovers and visits Raskolnikov at his worksite, "it [is] as if something lifted him and flung him down at her feet," and Sonya knows that this is the catharsis: "she [understands,] and for her there [is] no longer any doubt that he love[s] her, love[s] her infinitely and that at last the moment ha[s] come" (CP, Ep., Ch 2; 549).

It is not until Raskolnikov ousts Svidrigailov, the voice of egoistic suicide, along with "*all* those torments of the past," and discovers that "instead of dialectics, there is life," the epilogue becomes truly "monologic" (CP, Ep., Ch 2; 550). Picking up the *New Testament*, Raskolnikov not only begins to plan his future with Sonya, but also joins his community. Dostoevsky informs us that "all the convicts, his former enemies, now look at him differently," and that "[h]e even addresse[s] them himself and ha[s] been answered amiably" (CP, Ep., Ch 2; 550). As such, Raskolnikov's choice to "give [himself] directly to life" gradually leads him to cohere with the collective (CP, Pt 6, Ch 2; 460). As Durkheim teaches, it is the very "interchange of ideas and feelings" that has a "moderating effect upon suicide" (SU, Bk 2, Ch 3; 210). As Dostoevsky implies, for Raskolnikov this might turn into a "new account . . . of a man's gradual renewal, the account of his gradual regeneration, his gradual transition from one world to another" (CP, Ep., Ch 2; 551).

By ending with one "man's gradual renewal" in *Crime and Punishment*, Dostoevsky holds out a glimmer of "might be," which is the possibility that Svidrigailov, the embodied impulse toward self-decimation, is something that can be vanquished (CP, Ep., Ch 2; 551). *The Idiot*, however, is bleaker. Perhaps this is because Dostoevsky wrote *The Idiot* during a turbulent time in his life when his gambling addiction had flared up with raw intensity. In their book on "subtle suicide," Church and Brooks provide a case study of an addict, whose "gambling got worse with time," who kept borrowing money, "spirals downward" into "the subtle suicide zone," and ends up taking his own life.[202] No matter how this man's "family tried to support . . . and understand what was going on, [this gambler] kept up his self-defeating and self-destructive behavior patterns."[203] A perusal of Dostoevsky's letters and Anna

Dostoevsky's diary during this era, reveals an addiction that could have simulated just such a "downward spiral" into the "subtle suicide zone."[204] In one of many entries in his wife's diary, Anna bewails the fact that Dostoevsky's gambling has escalated into a matter of life and death:

> I was ill again. Fedya looked so miserable. Then about one o'clock he took the one louis we had, and I gave him a five-franc note I had saved up, and he went off to the tables. We have now altogether five florins; but we owe for three days' meals, and to-morrow we have to pay rent for the rooms; but how? Fedya came back saying he had lost everything. . . . We sat in still greater grief. What should we do now, what could we pawn?[205]

Dostoevsky's letters and his wife's memoir paint a picture of sheer desperation in which a gambling intoxication, like Marmeladov's dipsomania, threatened to haul away life's staples, like food, clothing, and shelter. The couple, repeatedly evicted from lodgings for nonpayment of rent, move from place to place while Dostoevsky pawns the remnants of their possessions. What was transpiring in Dostoevsky's life while he is "looking for his novel" invokes Menninger, who relegates addiction to a form of "chronic suicide" and speaks of individuals "bring[ing] their house of cards tumbling about their heads."[206] In what could conceivably be a passage lifted out of *The Idiot*, Menninger inserts into his addiction analysis a reference to the "gallows" and the "condemned man who remarked on the way to his execution, 'This is certainly going to be a lesson to me.' "[207]

For Dostoevsky, the implicit lesson is that the ubiquitous death drive can engender its opponent—the Eros of creativity. While in the throes of his self-destructive binge, which effectually condemned him to the roulette gallows, Dostoevsky, whose creative process was electrified, filled the notes for *The Idiot* with a menagerie of thanatotic specimens.[208] The executions, deaths, arson, rape, murder, and self-homicide of the notebooks surface in the finished novel as a zeitgeist of scaffolds, guillotines, and timepieces ticking away finite mortal breaths. What resides at the core of *The Idiot* is a disclosure of human suicidogenic propensities in a postlapsarian world where everyone is born irrevocably sentenced to death. It is a society where "the fixed idea of death . . . has taken complete possession the mind," which, according to Durkheim, tends to spawn "obsessive suicide" (SU, Bk 2, Ch 3; 210).

Durkheim elaborates on the perils of "[e]xcessive individualism," and Dostoevsky shows what happens when inordinate "me-ness" extricates individuals from salutary collectives, like family, community, and most importantly—faith (SU, Bk 2, Ch 3; 210). The world of *The Idiot* resembles the one in Raskolnikov's Siberian nightmare, where everyone is "doomed to fall victim to some terrible, as yet unknown and unseen pestilence" (CP, Ep., Ch

2; 547). Egoistic-anomic "murderee," Nastasya Filippovna, perishes at the hands of her chosen executioner.[209] About two weeks later, thanatophobic Ippolit, who sought to joltingly renew life by dabbling in Russian roulette, perishes "in dreadful agitation" and in doing so "somewhat earlier than expected," it is evident that his effort to dictate his own final moment has failed (Id, Pt 4, Ch 12; 715). Rogozhin, also lysed, is condemned to fifteen years of penal labor in Siberia. Kolya, who is "too reflective for his years," could himself be on an egoistic trajectory (Id, Pt 4, Ch 12; 715). As for Aglaya, she elopes with a wealthy "émigré, a Polish count, who "captivate[s her] with the extraordinary nobility of a soul tormented by suffering for his fatherland" (Id, Pt 4, Ch 12; 717–18). It turns out, however, that her Polish count is a fraud: he is "not . . . a count at all, and if he really [is] an émigré, then he is one with an obscure and ambiguous past," plus his supposed "colossal fortune" is "completely imaginary" (Id, Pt 4, Ch 12; 717–18). He nevertheless manages to lure Aglaya to "the Catholic confessional of some famous *pater*, who . . . take[s] possession of her mind to the point of frenzy," and who, in conjunction with her betrothed, ruptures her bond with her loving family, the collective that had always sustained her (Id, Pt 4, Ch 12; 718). Moreover, for Dostoevsky, who disliked Catholics, such a conversion could be a fate worse than death.[210]

While the ending of *The Idiot* appears to suggest that overpowering Thanatos is nothing but a quixotic fantasy, the novel is nevertheless not devoid of hope. For Raskolnikov's "gradual transition from one world to another" is a cogitable "might-be," although it "would not be given him for nothing" and would have to be "dearly bought, . . . paid for with a great future deed" (CP, Ep., Ch 2; 551). In *The Idiot*, Dostoevsky posits potential antidotes to self-destructive proclivities, but does it through "might-have-beens." One counteractant is the silent prayer of the condemned man, who after being deposited on the scaffold, is on the brink of his demise and vows if he can "get his life back," he "would make each minute into a lifetime, . . . would lose nothing, would account for each minute, waste nothing in vain" (Id, Pt 1, Ch 5; 72). All well and good, but what does that mean? As Dostoevsky suggests in *The Brothers Karamazov*, it means living with "active love" and is what Apressyan has described as that "compassionate, benevolent, careful, loving attitude toward others."[211] In *The Idiot*, Ippolit gets a teasing taste of active loving, of "making each minute into a lifetime," when he emerges from his sickbed of egoistic contemplation to rescue an impoverished medic and his family (Id, Pt 1, Ch 5; 72). This altruistic deed, countering his self-annihilative impulses, enables him to "give away part of [his] personality and absorb part of another," or in the language of Durkheim, permits him to "disperse existence beyond its own limitation" (Id, Pt 3, Ch 6; 472: SU, Bk 2, Ch 6; 279). Sadly, his physical infirmity blocks him from pursuing the beneficent path of protracted charitable giving—the one that might have been his.

In *The Idiot*, there is yet another sparkle of possible propitiation, one emanating from the prince, who is the product of Dostoevsky's effort to perform "the measureless task" of portraying "a positively beautiful person."[212] Dostoevsky has said, "[t]here's only one positive beautiful person in the world—Christ," and throughout his fiction and in *A Writer's Diary*, he pays homage to his Russian savior, not just as some unattainable abstraction, but as a mentor who can be integrated into daily life.[213] Yet, in *The Idiot*, it is paradoxically the "positively beautiful person," who reverts to an "incurable" idiocy with "complete derangement of the mental organs," and winds up back in the sanitarium (Id, Pt 4, Ch 12; 716).[214]

But more disheartening than Prince Myshkin's ultimate internment in his old Swiss haunt is that he, with unfaltering faith, had the potential to guide those around him toward self-preservation and redemption. In fact, his "might-have-beens" are perhaps the most profound tragedy of *The Idiot*: he might have derailed Nastasya Filippovna's egoistic-anomic quest for death by proxy, might have alleviated Ippolit's thanatophobia, and might have persuaded Rogozhin to trade his blade for the cross. But the populous of *The Idiot*, blind and deaf to what the prince has to offer, either end up in the grave, in prison, or sadly, stuck in life unchanged. Unlike the epilogue to *Crime and Punishment*, with its hint of "transition," the *The Idiot* epilogue monologically relates that "Lebedev, Keller, Ganya, Ptitsyn and many other characters of [Dostoevsky's] story live as before" and "have changed little" (Id, Pt 4, Ch 12; 715). In a sense, Dostoevsky intimates that what Durkheim denominates "egoism" can lead either to a solitary coffin bereft of "icons . . . lighted candles . . .and prayers" or to an inane subsistence in languid stasis (CP, Pt 6, Ch 6; 507).

NOTES

1. Emile Durkheim, *Suicide: A Study in Sociology*, trans. John A. Spaulding and George Simpson (NY: The Free Press, 1951), 210 (hereinafter in the text, it is "SU"). All further citations are from this translation. Hereinafter, I will include the book and chapter number, as well as the page number from the Spalding translation, in parentheses in the text.

2. See Donald A. Nielsen, "Dostoevsky in the Mirror of Durkheim," in *Durkheim: The Durkheimians and the Arts*, eds. Alexander Riley, W. S. F. Pickering and William Watts Miller (NY: Berghahn Books, 2013), 98 (discussing how both Durkheim and Dostoevsky, who saw "egoism as one of the central symptoms of Russia's current malaise," were "fascinated by the question of the relationship between individual and society").

3. See Letter from Fyodor Dostoevsky to Anna Korvin-Krukovskaya (June 17, 1866), in *Fyodor Dostoevsky Complete Letters*, trans. David A. Lowe (MI: Ardis Publishers, 1989), Vol. 2, [hereinafter *Letters* Vol. 2], 200 ("I was in such bad financial circumstances that I was forced to sell the copyright to everything I had written earlier, all at once, to a speculator, Stellovsky, a rather bad person."). See also Geir Kjetsaa, *Fyodor Dostoevsky: A Writer's Life*, trans. Siri Hustvedt and David McDuff (NY: Fawcett Columbine, 1987), 178 (calling Stellovsky a "crude speculator").

4. Anna Gregorevna Dostoevsky, *Dostoevsky Portrayed by His Wife: The Diary and Reminiscences of Mme. Dostoevsky*, trans. S. S. Koteliansky (NY: E.P. Dutton & Co., 1926), 20.

5. Anna Dostoevsky, Ibid., 21. See also Amy D. Ronner, *Dostoevsky and the Law* (NC: Carolina Academic Press, 2015), 25.

6. Anna Dostoevsky, Ibid., 21 ("Knowing the sickly state in which Dostoevsky nearly always was, Stellovsky counted on the chance that he would not have the time or the energy to execute two works simultaneously, and then, according to the agreement, he would acquire the copyright of Dostoevsky's works for ever."). See also letter from Fyodor Dostoevsky to Alexander Milyukov (July 10–15, 1866) in *Letters* Vol. 2, Ibid., 208 ("I haven't *gotten down to work* on the novel for Stellovsky . . . Stellovsky worries me to the point of torture; I even dream of him.").

7. See Anna Dostoevsky, Ibid., 21 ("Dostoevsky preferred paying a fine or even losing his copyrights to signing his name to a work which he had not written.").

8. Dostoevsky writes, "I am now hiring a stenographer, and although, as before, I look over what I've dictated three times and redo it, nonetheless the stenography shortens the work nearly by half." Letter from Fyodor Dostoevsky to Nikolay Lyubimov (November 2, 1866) in *Letters* Vol. 2, Ibid., 211. He explains that "[o] nly by that means was I able to finish in *one* month, ten signatures for Stellovsky; otherwise I wouldn't have written even five." Ibid.

9. See Letter from Fyodor Dostoevsky to Apollinaria Suslova (April 25, 1867) in *Letters* Vol. 2, Ibid., 227 (describing his "stenographer, Anna Grigorievna Snitkina . . . [as] a young and rather attractive girl, . . . with an extraordinary kind and clear character," and explaining that the work went wonderfully well" and "[t]he novel *The Gambler* . . . was finished . . . in twenty-four days").

10. See Joseph Frank, *Dostoevsky: A Writer in His Time* (NJ: Princeton University Press, 2010), 516–17. According to Frank, when Dostoevsky tried to deliver the manuscript to Stellovsky's home, he "was told that [he] had left for the provinces, nor would the manager of his publishing firm accept it." Ibid., 516–17. The problem was that "[b]y this time it was too late for a notary, and the police officer of the district would not be returning to his office until ten o'clock in the evening." Ibid., 517. Dostoevsky, however, "just managed to meet his deadline two hours before its expiration." Ibid.

11. Anna Dostoevsky, Ibid., 28 ("I asked mother to go to see a friend of hers, a lawyer" and he "advised that the manuscript should be delivered either to a Notary Public or to the police inspector of the district where Stellovsky resided, and that an official receipt should be taken for it.").

12. Anna Dostoevsky, Ibid., 29 ("Dostoevsky was very glad, and said that he wished in celebration of the safe delivery of the manuscript to give a dinner at a restaurant to his friends (Makov, Strakhov, Milyukov), and invited me to join them.").

13. Anna Dostoevsky, Ibid., 29 ("Thus, from 4th to 29th October, in twenty-six days, a novel [*The Gambler*] of seven folios, in a two-columned Stellovsky edition, had been written.").

14. Anna Dostoevsky, Ibid., 21 ("Dostoevsky at that time had been absorbed by his work on *Crime and Punishment* (running as a serial then), and in view of the great interest it aroused among the public, he wished to complete it to the best of his ability. And then to deliver ten folios of a new novel!")

15. Fyodor Dostoevsky, *Crime and Punishment*, trans. Richard Pevear and Larissa Volokhonsky (NY: Vintage Books, 1993), 77 (hereinafter in the text, it is "CP"). All citations are from this translation. Hereinafter, I will include the part and chapter number, as well as the page number from the Pevear and Volokhonsky translation, in parentheses, in the text.

16. Fyodor Dostoevsky, *The Notebooks for Crime and Punishment*, trans. Edward Wasiolek (IL: University of Chicago Press, 1967) [hereinafter *The Notebooks for Crime and Punishment*], 244.

17. Karl A. Menninger, *Man Against Himself* (NY: Harcourt, Brace & World, Inc., 1966), 203

18. Ibid. See also Fyodor Dostoevsky, *Crime and Punishment*, Ibid., 70 (Raskolnikov is "occupied with one question: why almost all crimes are so easily detected and solved, and why almost all criminals leave such an obviously marked trail.").

19. Menninger, Ibid., 201. Letter from Fyodor Dostoevsky to Mikhail Katkov in *Letters* Vol. 2, Ibid., 175.

20. Fyodor Dostoevsky, *The Brothers Karamazov*, trans. Richard Pevear and Larissa Volokhonsky (NY: Farrar, Straus and Giroux, 1990), 717.

21. Menninger, Ibid., 203.

22. See Amy D. Ronner, *Law, Literature, and Therapeutic Jurisprudence* (NC: Carolina Academic Press, 2010), 89–149 (Dostoevsky and Therapeutic Confessions). See Ibid., 93 (Arguing that "Dostoevsky's anguished protagonist is consumed with the need to confess, a condition that actually predates his contemplation of the crime"); Ibid., 117 ("The real truth, and indeed the kernel of Dostoevsky's wisdom, is that Raskolnikov commits the crime because he needs to confess.") Ibid. ("Raskolnikov's problem before the murder is that any confession he might make would be ethereally devoid of content. So, in essence, Raskolnikov murders to fill his confession with substances.").

23. Kathleen Donnellan Garber, "A Psychological Analysis of a Dostoyevsky Character: Raskolnikov's Struggle for Survival," *American Journal of Psychoanalysis* 38 (1978), 16. In killing Alyona, Raskolnikov "commits a symbolic suicide. It was not her death he really sought so much as relief from his intolerable rage at the introjected 'bad mother' from whom he learned the concept of 'bad self' and self-contempt." Ibid.

24. Louis Breger, *Dostoevsky: The Author as Psychoanalyst* (NY: New York University Press, 1989), 23. See also Jeffrey C. Hutzler, "Family Pathology in

Crime and Punishment," *American Journal of Psychoanalysis* 38 (1978), 337 ("[A] fter murdering the pawnbroker and her daughter (symbolically mother and sister?) Raskolnikov realizes that in this act he has cut himself off from his mother and sister.").

25. I. Atkin, "Raskolnikov: The Study of a Criminal," *Journal of Criminal Psychopathology* 5 (1943), 255 (analyzing Raskolnikov "as a living being who is at odds with his environment" and discussing the social determinants of crime"). See also Dostoevsky, *Crime and Punishment*, Ibid., 256 (Razumikhin states that according to the socialists, "crime is a protest against the abnormality of the social set-up" and "that if society itself is normally set up, all crimes will at once disappear.")

26. Atkin, Ibid., 356. Porfiry, the examining magistrate, suggests an economic motive for the crime: "can it be that you yourself would venture—say, in view of certain worldly failures and constraints, or somehow for the furtherance of all mankind—to step over the obstacle? . . . well, for instance, to kill and rob? . . ." *Crime and Punishment*, Ibid., 265.

27. Frank, *A Writer in His Time*, Ibid., 489 (discussing how "Raskolnikov had become fascinated with the majestic image of such a Napoleonic personality who, in the interests of a higher social good, believes that he possesses a moral right to kill"). See also William Burnham, "The Legal Context and Contributions of Dostoyevsky's *Crime and Punishment*," *Michigan Law Review*, 100 (2002), 1231 (suggesting that the "selfish" or Napoleonic" theory comes from Napoleon III's 1865 book).

28. See Atkin, Ibid., at 271 (suggesting that we follow the "fuller development of Raskolnikov's ideas by Nietzsche[,]" who "also envisages a society which is divided into two distinct classes, an aristocratic ruling caste (the 'free spirits') and an inferior slave class" and that Raskolnikov's theory is thus seen as foreshadowing . . . the ideology of a fascist society").

29. A. Alvarez, *The Savage God: A Study of Suicide* (NY: W.W. Norton & Co., 1990), 144.

30. Raskolnikov's mother likens Raskolnikov's apartment to a "coffin" and says, "I'm sure its half on account of this apartment that you've become so melancholic." *Crime and Punishment*, Ibid., 231.

31. Richard Pevear, "Foreword," in Fyodor Dostoevsky, *Crime and Punishment*, Ibid., xv ("His name comes from the word *raskolnik*, meaning 'schismatic,' one who has split away from the body of the Church; but he is also divided against himself.").

32. Alvarez, Ibid., 144. He explains that "[t]he logic of suicide is different" and that "[i]t is like the unanswerable logic of a nightmare, or like the science-fiction fantasy of being projected suddenly into another dimension." Ibid. While "everything makes sense and follows its own strict rules[,] . . . everything is also different, perverted, upside-down." Ibid.

33. Alvarez, Ibid.

34. Alvarez, Ibid.

35. Alvarez, Ibid.

36. Wasiolek, *The Notebooks for Crime and Punishment*, Ibid., 8 (Svidrigaylov . . . is for the most part . . . an embodiment of one side of Raskolnikov, an ironic expression of that bronze man that Raskolnikov admired."). See also Carol

Apollonio, *Dostoevsky's Secrets: Reading Against the Grain* (IL: Northwestern University Press, 2009), 64 (discussing Svidrigailov as one of Dostoevsky's "best-known doubles").

37. Breger, Ibid., 43.

38. Ibid. ("Raskolnikov aspires to be a Bronze Man, a Napoleon whose actions are not constrained by the fears and weaknesses of those made of flesh and blood; Svidrigailov is meant to be such a creature.").

39. See Alexander Schmemann, *Of Water & The Spirit: A Liturgical Study of Baptism* (NY: St. Valdimir's Seminary Press, 1974). Schmemann points out "that it is precisely *water* which reveals to us the meaning of Baptism" and that "[n]ot only does Baptism *begin* with the blessing of water, but it is this blessing alone that reveals all dimensions of the baptismal mystery." Ibid., 38–39. See, generally, John Meyendorff, *Byzantine Theology: Historical Trends and Doctrinal Themes* (NY: Fordham University Press, 1974). Meyendorff states that "[t]he Byzantine ritual of Baptism has inherited from Christian antiquity the strong initial emphasis on exorcism" and elaborates that the "deliberate renunciation of Satan, the sacramental expulsion of the forces of evil from the soul . . . imply a passage from slavery under the 'prince of this world' to freedom in Christ." Ibid., 134–35. He states that "[i]mmersion is indeed the very sign of what baptism means: 'The water destroys the one life, but shows forth the other; it drowns the old man and raises the new.' Ibid., 194 (quoting Nicholas Cabasilas, *loc. cit.*, 9:532B). He adds that " '[d]rowning cannot be meaningful signified other than through immersion." Ibid. See also John Anthony McGuckin, *The Orthodox Church: An Introduction to Its History, Doctrine, and Spiritual Culture* (UK: John Wiley & Sons, Ltd., 2011), 285 ("In the liturgical rite of Orthodox baptism . . . the candidate is led to the font where solemn prayers of blessing over the water are said "and "[t]he font is large enough to hold water completely to cover the person to be baptized."). Ibid. ("After the immersion, . . . the service moves on to a focus on the royal and priestly dignity that has been conferred on the New Creature.").

40. See Apollonio, Ibid., 54. She points out that "[i]n the Russian tradition, the bathhouse (*bania*) serves not only as a place for attaining physical cleanliness and ritual purification, but also as a privileged space for demonic forces" and that "Dostoevsky builds on the association . . . in *Crime and Punishment*, for example, where Svidrigailov's hell is located in a bathhouse." Ibid. As for the Sistine Madonna, Dostoevsky and his wife went to the Dresden gallery to see it and Dostoevsky "considered this painting to be one of the masterpieces of European art." Ronald Meyer, "Notes" in Fyodor Dostoyevsky, *Demons*, trans. Robert A. Maguire (NY: Penguin Books, 1971–72), 798 n. 42.

41. See Fyodor Dostoevsky, *The Brothers Karamazov*, Ibid., 639 (the devil says, "Satan *sum et nihil humanum a me alienum puto*," which is also adapted from Roman playwright Terence [190–159 BC]).

42. With respect to his wife's death, Svidrigailov says, "the medical experts diagnosed apoplexy, the result of bathing after a heavy meal and almost a full bottle of wine, and they could not have discovered anything else." *Crime and Punishment*, Ibid., 282. Later, Dunya accuses Svidrigailov of poisoning his wife. Ibid., 495. Raskolnikov's mother believes that Svidrigailov caused his wife's death by giving her

a "terrible beating" and then explains that she went to the bath house and "as soon as she got into the water, she suddenly had a stroke!" Ibid., 228.

43. When Svidrigailov is talking about his servant's ghost, he says "It's his revenge on me because we had quarreled badly just before his death." Ibid., 288.

44. The name, Svidrigailov, has a negative connotation. When Raskolnikov spots a "very foppishly dressed" man stalking a young girl, he approaches him and shouts, "Hey, you—Svidrigailov!" As Oliver Ready points out, "Svidrigailov was a surname familiar to Russian readers of the 1860s from the journal *The Spark* where the 'Svidrigailov' type was satirically presented as a provincial 'man of obscure origin with a filthy past and a repulsive personality that is sickening to any fresh, honest gaze and worms its way into your soul.' " Oliver Ready, "Notes," in Fyodor Dostoevsky, *Crime and Punishment*, trans. Oliver Ready (NY: Penguin Books, 2015), 528 (quoting Boris Tikhomirov, *'Lazar'! Gryadi von': Roman F.M. Dostoevskogo 'Prestuplenie i nakazanie' v sovremennom prochtenii; Kniga-kommentarii* ['Lazarus! Come Forth': F. M. Dostoevsky's novel *Crime and Punishment* Read in the Light of Its Time: A Commentary] (St. Petersburg: Serebryanyi vek, 2006)).

45. According to Luzhin, "the girl was found hanging in the attic." Dostoevsky, *Crime and Punishment*, Ibid., 298. Later Svidrigailov implies that the child drowned herself when he tells Raskolnikov, "[t]his same Resslich who rents me the room . . . the same one they say, about the girl, in the water, in winter . . ." Ibid., 479). Also, when he dreams of the girl in the coffin, he thinks, "the girl was a suicide—by drowning." Ibid., 507.

46. Fyodor Dostoevsky, *Notes from the House of the Dead*, trans. Boris Jakim (MI: William B. Eerdmans Publishing Co., 2013), 7. See R. E. Richardson, "Svidrigailov and the 'Performing Self' " *Slavic Review* 46 (1987), 540–42 (defending Svidrigailov). Carol Apollonio does a brilliant job as advocate for Svridrigailov, especially with respect to his interactions with women. Carol Apollonio, Ibid., 81–84. She states that "whenever we witness [Svidrigailov] in contact with a real girl or listen carefully to his stories, we realize that he always lets the girl go unharmed" and "let's her go satisfied, in good spirits, and well supplied with the means to avoid a life of prostitution." Ibid., 81.

47. Svidrigailov, for whom good and evil are just quantities for tallying, tells Dunya "that an isolated evildoing is permissible if the main purpose is good. A single evil and a hundred good deeds!" Dostoevsky, *Crime and Punishment*, Ibid., 490.

48. See Dostoevsky, *Crime and Punishment*, Ibid., 148–49 (Luzhin, echoing the Svidrigailov philosophy, says, "[l]ove yourself before all, because everything in the world is based on self-interest.")

49. Steve Taylor, *Durkheim and the Study of Suicide* (UK: The MacMillan Press, Ltd., 1982), 173.

50. Taylor, Ibid., 172.

51. Robert L. Belknap, *Plots* (NY: Columbia University Press, 2016), 115. He points out that some of the "coincidences . . . relate to the real world Dostoevsky was describing" and serve to "enhance the oppressiveness of the setting," and thus, "St. Petersburg becomes a city whose inhabitants cannot escape one another." Ibid., 117.

52. Ernest J. Simmons, *Dostoevsky: The Making of a Novelist* (NY: Vintage Books, 1962), 87 (explaining that "[c]oincidence is an ever-present trap for weary novelists, and in this respect Dostoevsky nodded rather frequently in *Crime and Punishment*").

53. Taylor, Ibid., 166–73.

54. Taylor, Ibid., 168. With respect to Taylor, all italicized phrases are in the original.

55. Taylor, Ibid., 167, 169.

56. Taylor, Ibid., 169.

57. Fyodor Dostoevsky, *A Writer's Diary*, Vol. 2 (1877–1881), trans. Kenneth Lantz (IL: Northwestern University Press, 1994), 1289.

58. Ibid.

59. Ibid.

60. Taylor, Ibid., 167.

61. Taylor, Ibid. 167–68.

62. Meyendorff, Ibid., 192 (With respect to Orthodox baptism, he states: "through his natural birth, man inherits a defective form of life—bound by mortality, inevitably sinful," and "[t]he alternative to this 'fallen' state is 'life in Christ,' which is true and 'natural' human life."). See also McGuckin, Ibid., 285, 287 (In "Orthodox baptism, . . . the candidate is laid under the waters and brought up high again," and "after baptism, . . . this new being "understand[s] that from that moment a life of merciful compassion, as detailed in the evangelical teachings of Jesus, is the expected master plan of the rest of a disciple's career.")

63. In the scene in which Svidrigailov "sprinkle[s] Dunya with water," she, "started and came to her senses," and seems to be reborn as an assertive being capable and willing to defend herself. Dostoevsky, *Crime and Punishment*, Ibid., 492.

64. Eric Naiman, "Gospel Rape," *Dostoevsky Studies*, 22 (2018), 37.

65. For discussion of Raskolnikov's closet-like habitation, see Ronner, *Law, Literature and Therapeutic Jurisprudence*, Ibid., 110–11.

66. Naiman, Ibid., 37.

67. Naiman, Ibid., He adds that "Dostoevsky paradoxically produced a profoundly pornophonic text" where "[f]lesh becomes word, but the erotic affect and the sense of erotic compulsion remain." Ibid.

68. Scopophilia, a term rooted in Ancient Greek, meaning a tendency to look at or examine, describes the process of deriving sexual pleasure from watching erotica as opposed to engaging in an actual relationship. See generally *Voyeurism: A Medical Dictionary, Bibliography, and Annotated Research Guide to Internet References*, eds. James N. Parker, M. D. and Philip M. Parker, PhD (CA: ICON Group International, Inc., 2004), 38 (defining voyeurism as "[a] paraphilia characterized by repetitive looking at unsuspecting people, usually strangers, who are either naked, in the act of disrobing or engaging in sexual activity, as the method of achieving sexual excitement"). See also Otto Fenichel, *The Psychoanalytic Theory of Neurosis* (NY: W.W. Norton & Company1945), 71 (defining "[s]coptophilia" as the sexualization of the sensations of looking" and as "analogous to touch eroticism")

69. Fenichel, Ibid., 177. According to Freud, *schaulust*, the pleasure of looking, a partial instinct innate to the formation of personality in childhood, might be sublimated either into aesthetics, looking at art objects, or into an obsessional neurosis. See Sigmund Freud, "The Sexual Aberrations," *On Sexuality: Three Essays on the Theory of Sexuality and other Works,* trans. James Strachey (NY: Penguin Books, 1991), 69 ("Visual impressions remain the most frequent pathway along which libidinal excitation is aroused; indeed, natural selection counts upon the accessibility of this pathway . . . when it encourages the development of beauty in the sexual object" and such looking can "be diverted ('sublimated') in the direction of art. . ."). Freud also believed that voyeurism and exhibitionism go hand in hand: "[e]very action of perversion is thus accompanied by its passive counterpart" and as such "anyone who is an exhibitionist in his unconscious is at the same time a *voyeur.*" Ibid., 81. See also Jacques Lacan, *The Four Fundamental Concepts of Psychoanalysis*, trans. Alan Sherman (NY: W.W. Norton & Co., 1998), 182 (developing the concept of the "gaze," which links the pleasure of voyeurism to fixating on "the other" who is not the "self," stating that the "scopic drive" is ambiguous, and that "[t]he gaze is this object lost and suddenly re found in the conflagration of shame, by the introduction of the other").

70. Dostoevsky, *Crime and Punishment*, Ibid., 504 (When "the ragamuffin . . . came back with the tea and veal, . . . Svidrigailov . . . could not eat even a single bite for total loss of appetite.")

71. See Ronner, *Law, Literature, and Therapeutic Jurisprudence*, Ibid., 115–17 (suggesting that there are four Raskolnikovs in this dream and that the third, the "boy-Raskolnikov, who compassionately leaps forth to try to spare a life" is the "most important in the quadrille"). See Pevear and Volokhonsky "Notes" in *Crime and Punishment*, Ibid., 555 n. 30 ("in his poem 'Before Evening' from the cycle *About the Weather* (1859), Nikolai Nekrasov (1821–1877) describes a scene of a horse being beaten 'on its meek eyes' ").

72. Taylor, Ibid., 168, See also Frank, *A Writer in His Time*, Ibid., 505 (For Svidrigailov "there is no natural innocence left in the world: everything he touches turns into the corruption of unashamed vice.")

73. Taylor, Ibid., 168.

74. Ibid., 172.

75. Ibid.

76. Schmemann, Ibid., 39.

77. Taylor, Ibid., 173 (stating that there is a "tendency to define [*ectopic*] in terms of physical isolation, whereas [it] refers to the individual's moral insulation from others"). He explains that such "an individual submits to death because he comes to realise [that] he has never been really alive." Ibid., 175.

78. Ibid., 168.

79. See Richard Peace, *Dostoevsky: An Examination of the Major Novels* (UK: Bristol Classical Press, 1992), 51 (discussing the significance of the Achilles helmet). He points out that "in the figure of the Jew wrapped up in the soldier's great coat, we have one of the persecuted dressed up as one of the persecutors." Ibid. According to Peace, this is "reinforced by the detail of the Achilles helmet," which is an "obvious

reference to the hero who is apparently unvanquishable, until his one fatal flaw has been discovered" and thus, Svidrigailov becomes "*both* monster and victim, *both* oppressor and oppressed." Ibid.

80. In *Demons*, Kirilov and Shatov set out on an emigrant ship for the United States, where they hired themselves out as "labourers to an exploiter." Dostoevsky, *Demons*, Ibid., 154. They "worked, got soaked with sweat, suffered and wore [themselves] out, until . . . they fell sick." Ibid. The "exploiter . . . cheated them[,] . . . beat [them] more than once" and they ended up with no work and "lay[ing] around on a floor in some horrible little town for four straight months." Ibid. Dostoevsky himself knows the misery of being uprooted from Russian soil. See, generally, Letter from Fyodor Dostoevsky to Apollon Maykov (August 16, 1867) in *Letters* Vol. 2, Ibid., 250 (describing his self-imposed exile abroad during the time he sought to escape creditors in Russia). In this letter, Dostoevsky calls Europe an "alien land," where there is "not a Russian face, Russian books, or Russian thoughts" and writes, "[r]eally, I can't even understand how a Russian abroad, if only he has feelings and sense, can fail to notice this and feel it painfully." Ibid. Dostoevsky, who was distressed by self-exile in Europe is implicitly aware of the reality that leaving for America, a much more remote and inaccessible land, had to multiply that stress to the nth degree.

81. See Michael R. Katz and William G. Wagner, "Introduction" in Nikolai Chernyshevsky, *What Is to Be Done?* trans. Michael R. Katz (NY: Cornell University Press, 1989), 33 (stating that "the most fascinating literary response provoked by *What Is to Be Done?* appeared shortly after the novel was published—Dostoevsky's brilliant *Notes from Underground* (1865)"). See also "Introduction" in Fyodor Dostoevsky, *The Crocodile*, trans. S. D. Cioran (NY: Ardis Publishers, 2013), xi (stating that "[m]any critics at the time of the publication of 'The Crocodile,' as, indeed, is the case even today, believed that Dostoevsky had written a vicious and cowardly lampoon on Chernyshevsky"). But see Fyodor Dostoevsky, *A Writer's Diary*, Vol. 1 (1873–1876) trans. Kenneth Lantz (IL: Northwestern University Press, 1994), 152 (rejecting the accusations that the " 'Crocodile' is an allegory—the history of Chernyshevsky's exile—and that [Dostoevsky] wanted to lampoon him," and calling that theory "too isolated and too farfetched to gain much currency"). In Dostoevsky, *Crime and Punishment*, there are other references to Chernyshevsky. See *Crime and Punishment*, Ibid., 132 (Razumikhin saying "we'll go to the Palais de Cristal" which Chernyshevsky believed was the ideal living space for communal society); Ibid., 371 (Lebezyatnikov saying "that a man insults a woman with inequality if he kisses her hand" and "[n]ow, I am explaining to her the question of freedom of entry into rooms in the future society," which refer to Vera Pavlovna's feminist words and to discussion of free access to rooms in *What Is to Be Done?*); Ibid., 377 (Lebezyatnikov saying "I have only loved you, but now I respect you, because you have been able to protest," which parodies Lopukhov's words to Vera Pavlovna when he discovers that she has been having an affair).

82. Frank, *A Writer in His Time*, Ibid., 249, 370.

83. Ibid., 401–2.

84. See also Fyodor Dostoevsky, *The Adolescent*, trans. Richard Pevear and Larissa Volokhonsky (NY: Vintage Books, 2003), 71 (Kraft, who commits suicide,

refers to going to America); Dostoevsky, *The Brothers Karamazov*, Ibid., 264 (When Ivan speaks of suicide, he tells Alyosha, "when I'm thirty and want to smash the cup on the floor, then . . . wherever you may be, I will still come to talk things over with you once more . . . even from America.").

85. *Crime and Punishment*, Ibid., 247 ("moth flying into the candle-flame"), Ibid., 340 ("Have you ever seen a moth near a candle? . . . [H]e'll keep circling around me, circling around me, as around a candle; freedom will no longer be dear to him.")

86. Menninger, Ibid., 160–84 (alcohol addiction as a form of chronic suicide). See also Jan Fawcett, William A. Sheftner, Louis Fogg, David C. Clark, Michael A. Young, Don Hedeker, and Robert Gibbons, "Time-Related Predictors of Suicide in Major Affective Disorders," in *Essential Papers on Suicide*, eds. John T. Maltsberger and Mark J. Goldblatt (NY: New York University Press, 1996), 599–611 (treatment of alcoholism as suicide preventer); Susan Morrissey, *Suicide and the Body Politic in Imperial Russia* (UK: Cambridge University Press, 2006), 31–33 (discussing "drinking to death" as suicide).

87. Menninger, Ibid., 161. In fact, Dostoevsky, had planned to write a novel, *The Drunkards*, in which he would explore alcoholism along with "all its ramifications, primarily pictures of families, the raising of children in that environment, and so on and so forth." Letter from Fyodor Dostoevsky to Andrey Kraevsky (June 8, 1865) in *Letters* Vol. 2, Ibid., 163.

88. See Howard I. Kushner, *Self-Destruction in the Promised Land* (NJ: Rutgers University Press, 1989), 109–11 (discussing the differences between male and female suicides). He points out that "[b]oth men and women historically have internalized social roles and gender-specific values and it would be absurd to contend that these were not manifested also in self-destructive behaviors." Ibid., 109. He adds that "[a] ttempting suicide . . . has been viewed as a legitimate strategy for women to gain attention for their grievances." Ibid., 110. He elaborates that "to the extent women have been taught that their intrinsic value can be reduced to their bodies, they have also learned to use their bodies to get what they want." Ibid. See Susan Morrissey, "Suicide," in *Dostoevsky in Context*, eds. Deborah A. Martinsen and Olga Maiorova (UK: Cambridge University Press, 2015), 136 ("Olya's suicide in *The Adolescent* features a cry for justice."). See also Erwin Stengel, *Suicide and Attempted Suicide* (NY: Jason Aronson, Inc., 1974), 78 (defining successful and unsuccessful suicide attempts). Stengel states that "[f]ailure may be due to any of the following causes: the sense of purpose may not have been strong enough; or the act may have been undertaken half-heartedly because it was not quite genuine; the subject was ignorant of the limitations of the method; or he was lacking in judgement and determination through mental illness." Ibid.

89. See generally excellent discussion in Andrew Kahan, Mark Lipovetsky, Irina Reyfman, and Stephanie Sandler, *A History of Russian Literature* (UK: Oxford University Press, 2018), 62–65 (discussing the hagiographic collections in the medieval period and the *paterik* stories).

90. Dostoevsky, *The Brothers Karamazov*, Ibid., 264. See also Ibid., 787 n. 36 ("The left is the 'sinister' side associated with the devil, especially in depictions of the Last Judgment.").

91. Frank, *A Writer in his Time*, Ibid., 531–48 (discussing the couple's "escape and exile").

92. Ronner, *Dostoevsky and the Law*, Ibid., 26–28.

93. Edward Wasiolek, "Introduction," in *The Notebooks for The Idiot* (NY: Dover Publications, 1967) [hereinafter *The Notebooks for the Idiot*], 1–20. Wasiolet states: "Devoured by a passion for gambling and then by guilt, humiliated by poverty, driven by deadlines, choking on foreign air, alarmed and disgusted by political currents, forced to move restlessly from apartment to apartment with a pregnant wife, and forced to bear the shock of the death of his three-month-old daughter—these comprise Dostoevsky's physical and spiritual environment during the eighteen months *The Idiot* was in the making." Ibid., 3–4.

94. Kjetsaa, Ibid., 193–228 ("marriage and flight"). After pointing out that "[s] everal commentators have, nevertheless, viewed this marriage as one of the most important in Russian literary history," Kjetsaa states, "[o]ver the years her persevering endurance and pragmatism enabled her to cope with the problems of everyday life in such a way that he was able to devote himself exclusively to his literary work." Ibid., 200. See also Letter from Fyodor Dostoevsky to Anna Dostoevskaya (May 6, 1867) in *Letters* Vol. 2, Ibid., 231–32 ("I could have won 300, because it was already in my hands but I took a risk and lost it . . . if one is prudent, that is, if one is as though made of marble, cold, and inhumanely cautious, then definitely, *without any doubt*, one can win *as much as one wishes*."); Letter from Fyodor Dostoevsky to Anna Dostoevskaya (May 9, 1867), in Ibid., 238 ("We'll leave for Switzerland and I'll get down to work quickly . . . perhaps this is even all for the best: I'll be rid of that cursed thought, the monomania, about gambling."); Letter from Fyodor Dostoevsky to Anna Dostoevsky (May 10, 1867) in Ibid., 239 ("I ought to have stopped and left . . . so as to calm my excited nerves (moreover, I have the observation (a most accurate one) that I can't be calm and cool at gambling for *more than a half hour at a time*).") Letter from Fyodor Dostoevsky to Anna Dostoevskaya (May 24, 1867), in Ibid., 243 ("Anya, dear, my friend, my wife, forgive me, don't call me a scoundrel! I have committed a crime, I have lost everything that you sent me, everything, down to the kreuzer . . . gambling is hateful to me."); Fyodor Dostoevsky to Anna Dostoevskaya (September 24, 1867), in Ibid., 269 ("Anya, dear, I'm worse than a beast! Last night . . . I had winnings of 1300 francs, clear. Today—not a kopeck. Everything! I lost everything!"); Letter from Fyodor Dostoevsky to Anna Dostoevskaya (November 5, 1867), in Ibid., 290 ("Oh darling, you shouldn't even allow me to get at the roulette wheel. As soon as I touch it, my heart stops, and my arms and legs tremble and go cold.") Letter from Fyodor Dostoevsky to Anna Dostoevskaya (March 23, 1868) in *Fyodor Dostoevsky Complete Letters*, trans. David A. Lowe (MI: Ardis Publishers, 1990), Vol. 3 [hereinafter *Letters* Vol. 3], 60 ("My dear angel . . . I lost everything as soon as I arrived, in a half hour I had lost everything."); Letter from Fyodor Dostoevsky to Anna Dostoevskaya (April 16, 1871) in Ibid., 339–40 ("My priceless one, my eternal friend, my heavenly angel, you realize of course, that I lost everything, the whole 30 thayers that you sent me . . . I'm not a scoundrel, just a passionate gambler."). See also Anna Dostoevsky, Ibid., 61 ("I saw Fedya standing at the head of my bed. He was terribly upset. I

understand that he must have lost all the ten louis; and so it turned out."); Ibid., 63 ("But Fedya implored me to give him at least two louis . . . so that he could go to the tables and get relief."); Ibid., 69 ("My apprehensions came true: Fedya returned home in the greatest despair. He said he had lost all, and began begging me to give him two more louis . . . He fell on his knees before me, imploring me to give him two more louis."); Ibid., 73 ("But Fedya asked me for five louis just to try his luck . . . Not to give him money was impossible."); Ibid., 99 ("Feyda . . came in very pale and fell on his knees before me. . . . He said that all was at an end, that he had lost everything. . . This affected me terribly."); Ibid., 101 ("Fedya . . . came home soon; he had lost. . . He was in complete despair, he said that he had ruined me and that all was lost.").

95. See Letter from Fyodor Dostoevsky to Apollon Maykov (August 16, 1867) in *Letters* Vol. 2, Ibid., 256 ("I began losing the last of my money . . . I started pawning my clothing, Anna Grigorievna pawned *everything* of hers, her last things.") Letter from Fyodor Dostoevsky to Anna Dostoevskaya (November 6, 1867), in Ibid., 291 ("I pawned both the ring and the winter coat and lost everything."); Letter from Fyodor Dostoevsky to Apollon Maykov (March 2, 1868) in *Letters* Vol. 3, Ibid., 47 ("[E]verything, up to the last rag, mine and my wife's has been pawned."); Letter from Fyodor Dostoevsky to Apollon Maykov (May 18, 1868) in Ibid., 76 ("I myself have *almost* nothing, and . . . I even pawned my clothes and my wife's.") Letter from Fyodor Dostoevsky to Nikolay Strakhov (February 26, 1869) in Ibid., 140 ("[T]he last of our linen has been pawned now."). See also Frank, *A Writer in His Time*, Ibid., 541 ("Dostoevsky himself was astonished at Anna's extraordinary tolerance of his failings, even when this meant pawning not only their wedding rings but the earrings and brooch he had given her as a present and, as a last resort, Dostoevsky's overcoat and Anna's lace shawl and spare frock.").

96. In a letter to his wife, Dostoevsky writes: "in a half hour I had lost everything. Forgive me, Ana, I have poisoned your life! And in addition, I have Sonya." Letter from Fyodor Dostoevsky to Anna Dostoevskaya (March 23, 1868) in *Letters* Vol. 3, Ibid., 60.

97. See Letter from Fyodor Dostoevsky to Pavel Isaev (Pasha) (June 9, 1868) in Ibid., 80 ("God has struck me a blow . . . I'm so depressed and sick at heart that it would be better to die."); Letter from Fyodor Dostoevsky to Apollon Maykov (June 22, 1868) in Ibid., 81–82 ("[T]he further along the time goes, the more painful the recollection and more vividly the image of my late Sonya presents itself to me. There are moments that are unbearable."). See also Kjetsaa, Ibid., 219 ("The period that followed [the death] was almost unbearable. The couple wept, and the neighbors would beat on the walls in an attempt to make them stop.").

98. See Letter from Fyodor Dostoevsky to Nikolay Strakhov (February 26, 1869) in *Letters*, Vol. 3, Ibid., 139 ("I sense that compared to *Crime and Punishment* the effect of *The Idiot* on the public is weaker."); Letter from Fyodor Dostoevsky to Vera and Sofya Ivanov (May 7, 1870) in Ibid., 254 ("The novel [*The Idiot*] turned out to be unsatisfactory.").

99. Wasiolek, "Introduction," in *The Notebooks for the Idiot*, Ibid., 7–8. For a superb discussion of the Notebooks for *The Idiot*, see Robin Feuer Miller, *Dostoevsky*

and the Idiot: Author, Narrator, and Reader (MA: Harvard University Press, 1981), 46–89.

100. Wasiolek, "Introduction," in *The Notebooks for the Idiot*, Ibid., 4.

101. Miller, *Dostoevsky and the Idiot*, Ibid., 65. See also Ibid., 68 (pointing to the entry in March, 1868, "Christian love—the Prince"). But see Wasiolek, "Introduction," Ibid., 5 (suggesting that the idea of "creating a positively good man . . . did not come until after Dostoevsky had been through at least six plans, and as late as a month before he submitted the first part of the novel to the publisher").

102. Letter from Fyodor Dostoevsky to Sofya Ivanova (January 13, 1868) in *Letters* Vol. 3, Ibid., 17. See also Letter from Fyodor Dostoevsky to Apollon Maykov (December 31, 1867) in *Letters*, Vol. 2, Ibid., 297 ("I've been tormented by one idea for a long time . . . This idea is to *depict an absolutely wonderful person*. I don't think there can be anything harder than that, especially in our time.").

103. Letter from Fyodor Dostoevsky to Sofya Ivanova (January 13, 1868), in *Letters* Vol. 3, Ibid., 17.

104. Fyodor Dostoevsky, *The Idiot*, trans. David McDuff (NY: Penguin Books, 2004), 293–94 (Aglaya reciting her "poor knight") (hereinafter in the text, "Id"). All further citations are from this translation. Hereinafter, I will include the part and chapter number, as well as the page number from the McDuff translation, in parentheses in the text.

105. See generally Lisa Knapp, "Myshkin" and Sarah J. Young, "Nastas'ia Filippovna" in *A Dostoevskii Companion: Texts and Contexts*, eds. Katherine Bowers, Connor Doak, and Kate Holland (MA: Academic Studies Press, 2018) for excellent discussions of some of the many motifs at work in *The Idiot*.

106. *The Notebooks for The Idiot*, Ibid., 29–46, 50–56, 60–73, 77–89, 93–120, 123–30, 135–46, 149–58, 165–232, 236–47.

107. *The Idiot*, Ibid., 26 ("Have you had occasion to follow the murder of the Zhemarin family in the newspaper?"); 330 ("This puts me in mind . . . of the recent famous defence of the lawyer who, pleading as an excuse the poverty of his client, who had murdered six people in one fell swoop."); Ibid., 332 ("[E]ven you, Yevgeny Pavlych could say just now that even the defence counsel at the trial declared that there's nothing more natural than to murder six people because of one's poverty."); Ibid., 393 ("Not long ago everyone was talking and writing about that dreadful murder of six people . . . and about the strange speech of the defence counsel."). See also Ibid., 226 n. 3 ("In 1868 Dostoyevsky read a story in the newspaper *The Voice* about the murder in Tambov of a family of six by an eighteen year-old student" and "Dostoyevsky considered the murderer, Vitold Gorsky, a typical representative of 'nihilist' youth."); Katherine Bowers, "Ol'ga Umetskaia and *The Idiot*," in *A Dostoevskii Companion*, Ibid., 277 (discussing how "Dostoevskii incorporated other newspaper items into *The Idiot*, many of them accounts of murders").

108. See Deborah A. Martinsen, *Surprised by Shame: Dostoevsky's Liars and Narrative Exposure* (OH: The Ohio State University Press, 2003), 65–91. In a superb analysis of General Ivolgin's "narratives of shame and identity," Martinsen points out that "[b]y having Ivolgin's stories originate in circumstances that recall his shame, Dostoevsky establishes the connection between shame and lying." Ibid., 65.

109. In Fyodor Dostoevsky's Letter to Mikhail Dostoevsky (December 22, 1859), in *Fyodor Dostoevsky Complete Letters*, trans. David Lowe and Ronald Meyer (MI: Ardis Publishers), Vol. 1, [hereinafter *Letters* Vol. 1], 178, Dostoevsky describes his near execution:

> [W]e were taken to Semyonov Square. There we were all read the death sentence, allowed to kiss the cross, had sabers broken over our heads and our pre-death attire put on (white shirts). Then three people were stood against the stakes for the carrying out of the execution. I was the sixth in line, people were summoned by threes, cons[equently], I was in the second row and had no more than a minute left to live. . .Finally a retreat was sounded, the ones tied to the stake were led back, and it was announced that His Imperial Majesty was granting us our lives. Then the real sentences followed.

See also Fyodor Dostoevsky, *Crime and Punishment*, Ibid., 73 ("It must be the same for men being led out to execution—their thoughts must cling to every object they meet on the way. . ."); Dostoevsky, *The Brothers Karamazov*, Ibid., 717 (In the prosecutor's closing argument, he states that Dmitri "felt . . . something similar to what a criminal feels on the way to execution, to the gallows.").

110. Dostoevsky writes in his letter to Mikhail Dostoevsky (December 22, 1849) in *Letters* Vol. 1, Ibid., 178: "I remembered you, brother, and all of your family; at the last moment, only you were in my mind, only then did I realize how much I love you, my dear brother!" See also Fyodor Dostoevsky, *Crime and Punishment*, Ibid., 186 (describing a "new, boundless sensation of a sudden influx of full and powerful life" as like "the sensation of a man condemned to death who is suddenly and unexpectedly granted a pardon").

111. Dostoevsky wove into the novel, references to other executions and to the death penalty. Throughout Part 3, Chapter 5, Ippolit refers to himself as a man condemned to death and there is a discussion of how ironic it would be to execute Ippolit if he committed murder since his death is already preordained. See also *The Idiot*, Ibid., 449 (Ippolit tells the prince "I believe you're collecting materials on the death penalty."); Ibid., 608 (reference to the agonizing death of Stepan Glebov, who was "impaled on the stake in the time of Peter the Great"); Ibid., 618 (allusion to the decapitation of Sir Thomas More).

112. William Mills Todd III "Introduction" in *The Idiot*, Ibid., xxvii.

113. *Matthew* 7:6 ("Give not that which is holy unto the dogs, neither cast ye your pearls before swine, lest they trample them under their feet, and turn again and rend you.").

114. See Peace, Ibid., 86 (Rogozhin's name links him both with the schismatics and with a cemetery: "death is his role in the novel.").

115. See *The Idiot*, Ibid., 531 n. 1 ("a reference to the murderer Mazurin, who killed a jeweler with a razor," who bound the handle in silk "to improve its grip" and "filled two bowls with Zhdanov fluid . . . in order to hide the smell.").

116. See *The Idiot*, Ibid. 239 n. 1 ("Many *skoptsy* lived in the large cities of Russia, where they occupied the status of merchants and had a reputation for amassing wealth because of their 'incapacity for all other enjoyments,' according to a contemporary observer.").

117. See *The Idiot*, Ibid. 239 n. 1.

118. Peace, Ibid., 85. See also Menninger, Ibid., 251–53 (discussing the "self-castration" of the "Skoptsi sect of Russia). Menninger explains that the "Skoptsi constitute a Russian religious sect of considerable size, founded about 1757" and it was "estimated to have included over 100,000 members." Ibid., 251. He explains that the "Skoptsi believe that Adam and Eve, our first parents sinned by entering into sexual relationship, and that the only way to atone for the evil and avoid further sin is to destroy the potency of human beings." Ibid., 252. Their founder, Szelivanov, believing that the "offending member . . . was the organ of procreation, . . . mutilate[d] his body with a blazing iron" and "baptized hundreds in the same way." Ibid., 252. Menninger also discusses "psychotic self-mutilation," as a form of "focal suicide," one he calls a "very weak . . . attempt at self-healing." Ibid., 271. He states that "[i]n all instances sexuality is identified with the genitals and since these patients are psychotic, and therefore very direct and undisguised in their logic, they do the obvious thing of ridding themselves of the guilty part of their body." Ibid., 270. He adds that "the self-mutilations of psychotic patients resemble the self-mutilations of the fanatical religious sects" and that "[t]he psychotic person, however, mutilates himself without regard for the net reality gain, e.g., he freely offers up—or rather throws away—his genital organs or highly prized symbolic substitutes for them, e.g., the eyes." Ibid., 271, 273.

119. Peace, Ibid., 85.

120. In *The Idiot*, in her confrontation with Aglaya, Nastasya Filippovna asks, "Why has she treated me as if I were a loose woman?" and "[a]m I a loose woman?" Ibid., 666. Then she says, "[a]sk Rogozhin, he'll tell you!" Ibid.

121. Menninger, Ibid., 252.

122. Ibid.

123. See Frank, *A Writer in His Time*, Ibid., 549 (giving an account of the Dostoevskys visiting the Basel Museum, in which Holbein's painting of the Dead Christ is on display, which intrigued Dostoevsky so much that wanted to get a very close look at it). According to Frank, "this chance visit to the Basel Museum was to have momentous consequences for the creation of *The Idiot*, in which the canvas of Holbein the Younger plays an important symbolic role," because "[n]o greater challenge could be offered to Dostoevsky's own faith in Christ the God-man than such a vision of a tortured and decaying human being." Ibid.

124. See Michael M. Ossorgin VIII, "Holbein's Visually Polyphonic Dead Christ Reveals Contrasting Perspectives in Dostoevsky's *The Idiot*," *Dostoevsky Studies* 21 (2017), 51 ("explain[ing] the special capacity of Holbein's Dead Christ to suggest conflicting messages about Christ's death" and stating that Dostoevsky "uses Holbein's painting to create a dialogue about faith and resurrection among Ippolit, Rogozhin, and Myshkin").

125. Mikhail Bakhtin, *Problems of Dostoevsky's Poetics*, ed. and trans. Caryl Emerson (MN: University of Minnesota Press, 1984), 126, 145.

126. See Robin Feuer Miller, "Dostoevsky and Rousseau: The Morality of Confession Reconsidered," in *Dostoevsky New Perspectives*, ed. Robert Louis Jackson (NJ: Prentice-Hall, Inc., 1984), 82, 89 (explaining that "the confessions told at Nastasya

Filippovna's nameday party contain the same bracing mix of vanity, self-justifications and lies as did the confessions of Valkovsky or the Underground Man" and that "[o]nce again Dostoevsky engages in a direct polemic with Rousseau and his *Confessions*.")

127. Bakhtin, Ibid., 126.

128. See Raskolnikov's dream of the beaten mare. *Crime and Punishment*, Ibid., 58 (Mikolka cries, "It's my goods!").

129. Menninger's book on suicide is called *Man Against Himself*. Menninger, Ibid.

130. *The Idiot*, Ibid., 409 ("This morning your uncle shot himself! . . . [T]hree hundred and fifty thousand roubles of state funds are missing, they say, though other say it's five hundred thousand."); Ibid., 416–17 (Yevgeny Pavlych's uncle . . .[s] hot himself this morning at dawn . . . A respected old fellow, seventy years old, an Epicurean—and exactly as she said—it was public money, a whacking sum!"); Ibid., 431 ("[t]omorrow morning at the crack of dawn I'm going to St. Petersburg on this unhappy business (about my uncle you know); imagine: it's all true and everyone knows it except me.").

131. Charles William Wahl, "Suicide as a Magical Act," in *Clues to Suicide*, eds. Edwin S. Shneidman and Norman L. Farberow (NY: McGraw-Hill Book Company, Inc., 1957), 25.

132. Ibid., 25.

133. Ibid., 25. See also Isaac Ray, *A Treatise on the Medical Jurisprudence of Insanity*, ed. Winfred Overholster (MA: The Belknap Press of Harvard University Press, 1962), 269 ("[A] girl but little over ten years of age, who being reproved for some trifling indiscretion, cried and sobbed bitterly, went upstairs and hung herself in a pair of cotton braces" and there was "a boy twelve years old, who hung himself by fastening the handkerchief to a nail in the wall and passing a loop of it around his neck for no other reason than because he had been shut up in his room and allowed only dry bread as a punishment for breaking his father's watch.").

134. Wahl, Ibid., 25.

135. Katherine Bowers, "Ol'ga Umetskaia and *The Idiot*," in *A Dostoevskii Companion*, Ibid., 275.

136. Letter from Fyodor Dostoevsky to Appollon Maykov (October 9, 1867) in *Letters*, Vol. 2, Ibid., 180 ("I'm just dying to get to Russia. I wouldn't let the Umetskys' case by without having my word; I'd publish it. As soon as I arrive, I'll go around in person to the courts and so on.").

137. Bowers, Ibid., 274–75 ("The press reported on the sensationalist details that emerged in the course of the trial, painting a picture of monstrous parents who tormented and abused their children" and "Dostoevskii was able to follow the trial from Geneva in the Russian newspapers.").

138. *The Notebooks for The Idiot*, Ibid., 32.

139. Bowers, Ibid., 276 ("In Nastas'ia Filippovna's fiery gaze we see Ol'ga Umetskaia grown up as Dostoevsky might hope she would: a survivor of abuse, a product of suffering, but a woman with her soul intact, still capable of trust and love.").

140. Plato, "Phaedo," in Plato, *The Last Days of Socrates*, trans. Hugh Tredennick and Harold Tarrant (NY: Penguin Books, 2003), 121.

141. See Sigmund Freud, *The Psychopathology of Everyday Life*, trans. A. A Brill (SC: Columbia, 1901) (Chapter 8, Erroneously Carried-Out Actions) ("[M]any apparently accidental injuries happening to such patients are really self-inflicted . . . brought about by the fact there is a constantly lurking tendency to self-punishment . . . [and] that the psychic conflict may end in suicide can never be excluded in these cases."); Menninger, Ibid., 317 ("[S]self-destruction [can be] obtained (usually) by proxy, i.e., at the hands of a second party.").

142. Edwin S. Shneidman, *The Suicidal Mind* (NY: Harcourt, Brace & World, Inc. 1966), 62 (also calling it "manifestations of indirect suicide"). See also Edwin S. Shneidman, "Orientations Toward Death," in *The Psychology of Suicide: A Clinicians Guide to Evaluation and Treatment* eds. Edwin S. Shneidman, Norman L. Farberow and Robert E. Litman (NJ: Jason Aronson, Inc., 1994), 10 (discussing behaviors in which individuals "play an indirect, covert, partial, or unconscious role in hastening [their] own demise").

143. George Howe Colt, *The November of the Soul: The Enigma of Suicide* (NY: Scribner, 2006), 275.

144. Ibid., 275.

145. Ibid., 275–76.

146. Ibid., 275. The concept of "incomplete mourning," which will be discussed later, comes from Howard I. Kushner, *Self-Destruction in the Promised Land: A Psychocultural Biology of American Suicide* (NJ: Rutgers University Press, 1989). See also William Styron, *Darkness Visible: A Memoir of Madness* (NY: Vintage Books, 1992) (adopting Kushner's theory and applying it to his own suicidal depression).

147. See generally Kushner, Ibid.

148. Sigmund Freud, "Mourning and Melancholia," in *A General Selection from the Works of Sigmund Freud*, ed. John Rickman, M.D. (NY: Anchor Books, 1989), 125.

149. Ibid.

150. Ibid.

151. Kushner, Ibid., 119. Kushner explains that "[f]or Durkheim, the loss resulted from an individual's social and cultural alienation," and "for Freud, the loss resulted from disconnection from one's self." Ibid. Kushner, however, feels that "neither explained to anyone's satisfaction . . . why the type of loss that they described did not always result in suicide." Ibid. He thus delves into "[t]wo case studies, those of Meriwether Lewis and of Abraham Lincoln," both of whom "experienced extreme loss," but one killed himself and the other did not. Ibid., 120. His theory is that Lewis and Lincoln "serve as compelling examples of the proposition that the success or failure of [strategies for dealing with loss] depends upon a confluence of historical possibilities and personal experience as both connect with psychological and constitutional factors." Ibid.

152. Kushner explains that "[l]oss of a parent or a sibling during childhood, increases the risk of incomplete mourning, because children often are removed from the mourning process by those who wish to protect them from the horrors of death." Ibid., 77–78. He adds that "children as much as adults are ambivalent toward those to

whom they are closest" and due to "both their weaker position and paradoxically their belief in the magic of wishes, children often feel more responsible for loss than adults do." Ibid., 78. If, however, "they are also shielded from rituals of mourning, this feeling of guilt intensifies" and "[w]hile their immediate reaction may be the repression of the unhappy event in their childhood, they remain particularly vulnerable to object loss later in life." Ibid.

153. Styron, Ibid., 79. He explains that although "the genetic roots of depression seem now to be beyond controversy, . . . an even more significant factor was the death of my mother when I was thirteen." Ibid.

154. Ibid., 79–80 (adding that Kushner "argues persuasively in favor of this theory of incomplete mourning").

155. See Styron, Ibid., 79 "[T]his disorder and early sorrow—the death or disappearance of a parent, especially a mother, before or during puberty—appears repeatedly in the literature on depression as a trauma sometimes likely to create nearly irreparable emotional havoc.")

156. Freud, "Mourning and Melancholia," Ibid., 125.

157. Fyodor Dostoevsky, *A Writers Diary* 2, Ibid., 1041–42. Dostoevsky explains that "the accidental nature of today's Russian family consists in the loss among contemporary fathers of any common idea about their families—an ideal common to all fathers that binds them together, an idea in which they could believe and could teach their children to believe, passing on to them this faith for the rest of their lives." Ibid.

158. Olya, the daughter of Arkady's neighbor, who commits suicide after a merchant rapes her and she mistakenly ends up in a brothel where women reject and humiliate her, has been divested of her dignity, identity, and trust in humanity. See Fyodor Dostoevsky, *The Adolescent*, trans. Richard Pevear and Larissa Volokhonsky (NY: Vintage Classics, 2004), 171–77 (summarizing the trauma that preceded her suicide). While Nastasya Filippovna's rage is vented at Totsky and herself, Olya is uncontrollably furious at the world.

159. Sigmund Freud, *Totem and Taboo*, trans. and ed. James Strachey (NY: W.W. Norton & Co., 1989), 191 n. 63. See also Freud, "Mourning and Melancholia," in *A General Selection from the Works of Sigmund Freud*, Ibid., 133 ("We have long known that no neurotic harbors thoughts of suicide which are not murderous impulses against others redirected upon himself, but we have never been able to explain what interplay of forces could carry such a purpose through to execution.").

160. Wahl, Ibid., 26.

161. Nastasya Filippovna's letters even have shades of lesbianism. While it is apparent from other works, like in *The Adolescent* and *Netochka Nezvanova*, that even in nineteenth-century Russia, Dostoevsky was not skittish about portraying same-sex relationships. But in *The Idiot*, Nastasya Filippovna's gushing over Aglaya transcends eroticism. For excellent discussions of homosexuality in Dostoevsky's works, see Susanne Fusso, *Discovering Sexuality in Dostoevsky* (IL: Northwestern University Press, 2006), 42–68 and Michael Katz, "Dostoevsky's Homophilia/Homophobia," in *Gender and Sexuality in Russian Civilization*, ed. Peter I. Barta (UK: Routledge, 2001), 239–53. In her chapter, "Dostoevsky's Comely Boy: Homoerotic Desire and Aesthetic Strategies in *A Raw Youth*," Fusso mentions Petya Trishatov from *The*

Adolescent and prisoner Sirotkin from Dostoevsky's *Notes from the House of the Dead*, in her discussion of homosexuality in Dostoevsky's works. Ibid., 42. She says that Sirotkin, whom Dostoevsky calls "khoroshen'kii mal'chik' ("pretty boy") . . . does not ply any of the prisoners' moneymaking trades, but he always seems to have sums of ready cash and new clothes, gifts from other prisoners" and that "[o] ne can only conclude that Sirotkin represents that 'other means' of satisfying sexual desire—male prostitution." Ibid. See also Fyodor Dostoyevsky, *Netochka Nezvanova*, trans. Jane Kentish (UK: Penguin Books, 1985) (portraying the passionate relationship between Netochka and Katya).

162. Colt, Ibid., 275.

163. Colt, Ibid., 275.

164. Gustave Flaubert, *Madame Bovary*, trans. Margaret Mauldon (UK: Oxford University Press, 2004), 284. See Anna Dostoevsky, *Dostoevsky Portrayed by His Wife*, Ibid., 85–86 (July 1867) (describing how the couple stopped at a book shop and "took two volumes of . . . *Madame Bovary*, of which novel Turgenev had said that it was the best work in the whole literary world for the last ten years").

165. *The Notebooks for The Idiot*, Ibid., 236.

166. For discussion of "victim-precipitated homicide" and "murderee," see Colt, Ibid., 275–76.

167. In a letter, Dostoevsky explains that he is moving to Moscow, that his wife's health is very bad" and "[s]he has been terribly ill for two months." Letter from Fyodor Dostoevsky to Varvara Konstant (November 10, 1863) in *Letters* Vol. 2, Ibid., 75.

168. See Letter from Fyodor Dostoevsky to Varvara Konstant (January 10, 1864) in *Letters* Vol. 2, Ibid., 85 ("Marya . . . has become irritable to the highest degree because of her illness" and "has death on her mind constantly: she grieves and is reduced to despair."). See also Ignat Avsey, "Fyodor Dostoevsky's Life," in Fyodor Dostoevsky *Humiliated and Insulted*, trans. Ignat Avsey (UK: One World Classics Ltd., 2008), 369–70 (stating that Marya's "suffering and moodiness are reflected in the description of Marmeladov's wife in *Crime and Punishment* and in Ippolit in *The Idiot*").

169. For discussion of "the accidental family, see Fyodor Dostoevsky, *A Writers Diary* 2, Ibid., 1041–42.

170. Dostoevsky, *The Brothers Karamzov*, Ibid., 303.

171. Ibid.

172. See Frank, *A Writer in His Time*, Ibid., 582 ("The thematic motif of religious faith is what saves the episodes involving Myshkin's encounter with the group of so-called Young Nihilists from becoming merely an acrid satire against the radicals of the mid-1860s.").

173. Frank, Ibid., 582. Frank explains that "Dostoevsky wisely focuses the spotlight on the dying young consumptive Ippolit Terentyev, who detaches himself from the group to rise to major heights and become the first in the remarkable gallery of metaphysical revels that Dostoevsky-created." Ibid. He explains that Ippolit, "anticipating Kirillov in *Demons* and Ivan Karamazov, [is revolting against] a world in which death, and hence immitigable human suffering, is an inescapable reality." Ibid.

174. For a discussion of "incomplete mourning," see Kushner, Ibid., 77–78.

175. Sigmund Freud, "The Ego and the Id," in *A General Selection from the Works of Sigmund Freud*, Ibid., 224. See also Sigmund Freud, *Civilization and Its Discontents*, ed. James Strachey (NY: W.W. Norton & Company, Inc. 1962), 66 ("I drew the conclusion that besides the instinct to preserve living substance[,] . . . there must exist another contrary instinct seeking to dissolve those units and to bring them back to their primaeval, inorganic state" and "[t]he phenomena of life could be explained from the concurrent or mutually opposing action of these two instincts.").

176. Wahl, Ibid., 22–23, 26.

177. Ibid., 26.

178. Ibid.

179. Ibid., 26–27.

180. Ibid., 27.

181. See Dostoevsky, *The Brothers Karamazov*, Ibid., 784 n. 3 (In "Orthodox understanding, death is a 'falling asleep in the Lord"); Ibid., 164 (In reference to the expectation of Zosima's death, the narrator says,"[e]veryone expected something immediate and great upon the elder's falling asleep").

182. Peace, Ibid., 124 n. 13 (connecting Norma's name with "[b]eauty is normality, health").

183. Peace, Ibid., 124.

184. In this scene, the "chewed up reptile . . . is emitting from its half-crushed body a large quantity of white fluid." *The Idiot*, Ibid., 456. See Peace, Ibid., 124 (stating that "the detail of the white juice on the tongue of 'normality' has much more relevance for Myshkin's disease of epilepsy than it has for Ippolit's consumption" and thus, "the condition of Myshkin is being compared with that of Ippolit").

185. Durkheim states the seemingly "contrasting phenomena" of homicide and suicide . . . "conceal a fundamental identity" and derive from a "single predisposition which itself inclines no more one way than the other." Durkheim, *Suicide*, Ibid., 340.

186. Wahl, Ibid., 27.

187. Freud, *The Psychopathology of Everyday Life*, Ibid. (Chapter 8, Erroneously Carried-Out Actions); Menninger, Ibid., 229–350.

188. Taylor, Ibid., 166–67.

189. Ibid.

190. Ibid., 152–53. See also Colt, Ibid., 274 ("For Novelist Graham, who suffered from manic depression and toyed with suicidal thoughts throughout his life, Russian roulette seemed to be an attempt to shock himself from numbness."). Taylor points to Sylvia Plath who "confessed to a friend that a recent car 'accident' she had survived had been quite deliberate" and "having survived, she was then able to write freely about the act because it was behind her." Taylor, Ibid., 153. As Taylor explains, "The car crash, like the previous suicidal attempt, became 'another death' that she had 'come through.' " Ibid.

191. Stengel, Ibid., 87 (emphasis in original).

192. Taylor, Ibid., 153.

193. Taylor, Ibid., 148, 150.

194. James P. Scanlan, *Dostoevsky the Thinker* (NY: Cornell University Press, 2002), 9.

195. Ruben Apressyan, "The Practices of Mercy" in *Dostoevsky's Brothers Karamazov*, eds. Predrag Cicovacki and Maria Granik (Germany: Universitatsverlag Winter Heidelberg, 2010), 116.

196. Ippolit says that during his school years, he and "this Bakhmutov" were in "perpetual conflict" and states, "[s]everal times during those several years [Bakhmutov] approached me; but each time I snubbed him morosely and irritably." *The Idiot*, Ibid., 469.

197. Mikhail Bakhtin, *Problems of Dostoevsky's Poetics*, Ibid., 39–40. See also M. M. Bakhtin, "Discourse in the Novel," in *The Dialogic Imagination*, trans. Caryl Emerson and Michael Holquist (TX: University of Texas Press, 1981), 349 (discussing the more dialogic approach in Dostoevsky's novels in which "the life experience of the characters and their discourse may be resolved as far as plot is concerned, but internally they remain incomplete and unresolved").

198. See e.g. Simmons, Ibid., 153 ("The epilogue is manifestly the weakest section of the novel, and the regeneration of Raskolnikov under the influence of the Christian humility and the love of Sonya is neither artistically palatable nor psychologically sound."). But see Belknap, Ibid., 128 ("[I]n the epilogue, Dostoevsky brings the entire novel together" and "[t]he social, historical, and scientific certainties that had led Raskolnikov to the murder are linked with the sicknesses from which he suffered through most of the novel."). See also Michael Holquist, "The Gaps in Christology: *The Idiot*" in *Dostoevsky New Perspectives*, Ibid., 127 (stating that "Raskolnikov's conversion experience is bodied forth as an abrupt shift to another narrative strategy" but that "the significance of [this] is to recapitulate the drama of Christian redemption").

199. Svidrigailov tells Raskolnikov that this "own conscience is entirely at rest." *Crime and Punishment*, Ibid. 282.

200. Dostoevsky, *Notes from the House of the Dead*, Ibid., 8.

201. In *The Idiot*, Dostoevsky hints at an egoistic pandemic through revealing the violent "Rogozhin way of life," connected with the *skopets* residing on his ground floor. *The Idiot*, Ibid., 242. If victorious, the *skopsy*, with self-induced sterility and zealous recruiting of converts, likewise portend the extinction of "everyone and everything." *Crime and Punishment*, Ibid., 547 (quoting Raskolnikov's dream). Lebedev also gives readers a sense of where what Durkheim calls "excessive individualism" leads when he talks about men "who even resorted to cannibalism," and the one, who "announced of his own accord and without any compulsion that . . . he had killed and eaten personally and in the deepest secrecy sixty monks and several lay infants." Durkheim, *Suicide*, Ibid., 210; *The Idiot*, Ibid., 439. Here what is implicit is that the suicidogenic impulse can, as in Raskolnikov's dream, "spread further and further" to spawn a cult of "devourer[s] of mankind," who thrash about in a self-extinguishing world in which "everything is permitted." *Crime and Punishment*, Ibid., 547; *The Idiot*, Ibid., 438; *The Brothers Karamazov*, Ibid., 69.

202. Michael A. Church and Charles I. Brooks, *Subtle Suicide: Our Silence Epidemic of Ambivalence about Living* (CA: Praeger, 2009), 71–72.

203. Ibid., 73.

204. Ibid., 71.

205. Anna Dostoevsky, Ibid., 94. See also endnotes 90–92 in this chapter (letters and writings by Dostoevsky's wife describing the gambling addiction).

206. Wasiolek, "Introduction," in *The Notebooks for the Idiot*, Ibid., 4.; Menninger, Ibid., 161.

207. Menninger, Ibid., 162.

208. Richard J. Rosenthal, "Gambling," in *Dostoevsky in Context*, Ibid., 148 ("During the eight years when he was addicted to roulette, Dostoevsky . . . appears to have been simultaneously at his most creative and self-destructive.").

209. Colt, Ibid., 275.

210. See *The Idiot*, Ibid., 633 (Prince Myshkin calls Catholicism an "unchristian faith," which "preaches a distorted Christ, slandered and desecrated by it, the opposite of Christ!"); *The Brothers Karamazov*, Ibid. 246–64 (the Grand Inquisitor); Letter from Fyodor Dostoevsky to Nikolay Strakhov (May 30 1871) in *Letters* Vol. 3, Ibid., 360 ("[I]n the West Christ has been lost (through the fault of Catholicism), and because of that the West is declining exclusively because of that."). See also Denis Dirscherl, *Dostoevsky and the Catholic Church* (IL: Loyola University Press, 1986), 121 (explaining how commentators have called Dostoevsky the enemy of Jesuits); Robin Feuer Miller, *The Brothers Karamazov: Worlds of the Novel* (CA: Yale University Press, 1992), Ibid., 45 (Dostoevsky scathingly indicts, through Smerdyakov the kind of reasoning applied to ethological issues that he believed to be typical of the Jesuits, whom he despised."); Ibid., 69 (In discussing the "Grand Inquisitor," Miller states that "[h]ere Dostoevsky welds together his dislike of the Catholic Church and socialist thought, which he believed were both moving toward atheism and the enslavement of man."); Ronner, *Dostoevsky and the Law*, Ibid., 180–85 (analyzing the Grand Inquisitor and discussing how "Dostoevsky . . . despised Catholics [and especially Jesuits]").

211. Dostoevsky, *The Brothers Karamazov*, Ibid., 56; Apressyan, Ibid., 116.

212. Letter from Sofya Ivanova (January 13, 1868) in *Letters* Vol. 3, Ibid., 17.

213. Ibid.

214. Ibid.

Chapter 4

Anomy in *Demons* and *The Brothers Karamazov*

This chapter turns to anomy, which Durkheim says is egoism's affiliate because it too derives from "the disease of the infinite."[1] Durkheim, however, explains that the disease "does not assume the same form in both cases" (SU, Bk 2, Ch 6; 287). In the egoist, "reflective intelligence is affected and immoderately overnourished," whereas in the anomic "emotion is over-excited and freed from all restraint" (SU, Bk 2, Ch 6; 287). Thus, the egoist "is lost in the infinity of dreams," whereas the anomic "[is lost] in the infinity of desires" (SU, Bk 2, Ch 6; 287).

Durkheim finds that anomic self-homicide abounds when "serious adjustments take place in the social order," when "religion has lost most of its power," and when there is a deviation from the "moral and material regimen" (SU, Bk 2, Ch 5; 246, 255, 262). Riddled with "disturbances of the collective order," such conditions reduce individuals to states of "irritation and exasperated weariness" in which they "necessarily tend to seek solace in acts of destruction" (SU, Bk 2, Ch 6; 284–85). This Durkheimian paradigm matches the nihilism, immorality, and godlessness that Dostoevsky depicts in his novels, *Demons* and *The Brothers Karamazov*, the focal points of this chapter. In *Demons* the nihilist, Pyotr Verkovensky, orchestrates a revolutionary upheaval that plummets the town into chaotic ruin. In *The Brothers Karamazov*, atheists, the devil, and champions of perfidy also turn Skotoprigonevsk into the venue of fratricide, miscarried justice, and foreboded cannibalism. In both novels, the societal equilibrium is jolted and those irreversibly anomic either hang or shoot themselves.

In *Demons*, the enigmatic Stavrogin churns with pent-up rage and in Durkheim's words with a "passion, [which] no longer recognizing bounds, has no goal left" (SU, Bk 2, Ch 6; 287). Preaching that "[w]hoever dares to kill himself is God," Aleksey Nilych Kirillov fits a bizarre Durkheimian amalgam: he is the anomic-egoistic-altruistic seeker of pseudo-deific death.[2] In *The Brothers Karamazov*, Mitya Karamazov plans to end his life at "the first hot ray of 'golden-haired Phoebus' in the morning," and Ivan Karamazov considers "smash[ing] the cup on the floor."[3] But Pavel Smerdyakov is the one who achieves self-annihilation. Armed with the credo, "everything is permissible," Smerdyakov is, as Durkheim would put it, "freed from all restraint" and thus, he kills before killing himself (BK, Bk 5, Ch 5; 263: SU, Bk 2, Ch 6; 287).[4]

This chapter closes with a discussion of Dostoevsky's implicit grasp of the propensity for anomic amorality, godlessness, and nihilism to form an unholy alliance that inevitably incinerates everything that matters. Then, anticipating this book's final chapter, this one posits that Dostoevsky's cognizance of the proverbial anomic trinity—amorality-atheism-nihilism—compelled him to masterfully animate those who evince the counteractive impulsions of "active love" (BK, Bk 2, Ch 4; 56).[5]

THE ANOMIC FACES OF *DEMONS*

After completing *The Idiot*, Dostoevsky conceived of an idea for a new novel titled "Atheism," which grew into a plan to write "The Life of a Great Sinner."[6] Although that novel never materialized, it gave Dostoevsky raw material, which he integrated into three novels, *Demons*, *The Adolescent*, and *The Brothers Karamazov*.[7]

Demons was published serially in 1871–1872, but homesick and craving reunion with Mother Russia, Dostoevsky started the novel while in exile abroad. In a letter to Nikolai Strakhov, Dostoevsky writes: "[t]he idea for this novel has existed in me for three years already, but earlier I was afraid to set to work on it while abroad; I wanted to be in Russia for it."[8] Dostoevsky dreaded debtors' prison and suspected that due to his poor health he wouldn't "be able to endure even a half a year in public incarceration," and thus felt trapped in the "cursed foreign land."[9] During this time, desperate for money, Dostoevsky was vexed by assorted physical ailments, including respiratory difficulties, hemorrhoids, headaches, and stomach pains.[10] On top of that, his epileptic fits, which had increased in frequency, occluded his work.[11] As Edward Wasiolek puts it, these years in Europe were "sheer misery" with his persistent fits, his wife's poor health, his daughter Liuba's teething, the French being "routed at Sedan," ugly weather, and Paris being "under siege by the Prussians" while "Dostoevsky [was] under siege by penury, delays, nonunderstanding editors and lost letters."[12]

In creating *Demons*, Dostoevsky drew not just from his fervent faith in the Russian Christ, but also from both present and past, from current events along with his own early, ill-fated participation in the Petrashevsky circle. While in exile, Dostoevsky kept abreast of current events in Russia, yet feared estrangement from the creative energy that could ensue only from the font of the motherland. This is what Dostoevsky articulates in numerous letters, especially in one to Apollon Maikov: he states that although he is going "through *three* Russian newspapers to the last line *daily* (!)" and receiving Russian journals, he fears "los[ing] touch not with the age, not with the knowledge of what's happening in Russia," but "los[ing] touch with the *living stream of life*."[13] The sources for *Demons* are not just "The Life of a Great Sinner" and the author's own yearning for and ever-intensifying exaltation of Russia as "the *living stream of life*," but also what Geir Kjetsaa calls a burgeoning "Russian messianism."[14] That is, one of Dostoevsky's predominant goals in later life was to "to proclaim 'the Russian Christ' " and "remind the Russian people of its God-bearing mission."[15] Although Ivan Pavlovich Shatov of *Demons* struggles with faith, Dostoevsky nevertheless sympathizes with him when he "babble[s] in a frenzy" that he "believes in Russia, . . . in her Orthodoxy, in the body of Christ . . . [in] the Second Coming [that] will occur in Russia" (D, Pt 2, Ch 1; 281). But as taken up in this chapter's conclusion, there is more to *Demons*' temporal transcendence because it, like mythological Janus, has two faces, one looking back at the past and the other forth to the future.

Before Dostoevsky went abroad with his new wife, he was shaken by the news of Dimitry Karakozov's attempt to assassinate Tsar Alexander II, which he saw as an outright attack on Russia, one that presaged further unrest.[16] While in Europe reading Russian newspapers and journals, Dostoevsky feared revolutionary upheaval from young people influenced by ideas imported from Europe. Then in 1869, Anna's younger brother Ivan Snitkin, a student at the Moscow Agricultural College, visited the Dostoevskys and bore crushing news. His friend, Ivan Ivanov, who had once helped the Dostoevskys prepare for their voyage to Europe, had been brutally murdered by a gang of five led by Sergei Nechaev.[17] As Edward Wasiolek points out, "Nechaev, the conspiracy, the murder of Ivanov, and the trial of the Nechaevists—all these had an enormous impact on Dostoevsky, dredging up all his fears for the future of Russia, reinforcing his conviction that the godless liberalism that had betrayed him in the forties led to destruction and chaos, and justifying his irrational and ungenerous disgust with Belinsky."[18]

In response, Dostoevsky decided to write a "pamphlet novel" directed against the radicals and the group spearheaded by the young agitator, Nechaev, who was responsible for Ivanov's murder.[19] Before slaughtering his former comrade, Nechaev, a nihilist, had returned from abroad where he had dedicated himself to the cause of the anarchist leader, Mikhail Bakunin.[20] Bakunin urged the formation of multiple independent groups of five to mount a terrorist attack on Russia, which was scheduled to climax on the ninth anniversary of the abolition of serfdom.[21] These nihilist threats, along with Ivanov's murder, fueled Dostoevsky's resolve to write a political novel, in which he would boldly and "fervently" voice his opinions.[22] In his Letter to Apollon Maikov, Dostoevsky writes: "The nihilists and Westernerizers will start yelling about me that I'm a *reactionary*! . . . But to hell with them—I'll state all my opinions down to the last word."[23]

While the novel's character, Pyotr Verkhovensky, is predicated on Nechaev, Dostoevsky did not aim to replicate reality exactly. In a letter to Mikhail Katkov, Dostoevsky explains, "my Pyotr Verhkhovensky may not resemble Nechaev at all; but I think that in my stunned mind there has been created by imagination the person, the type that corresponds to that villainy."[24] Dostoevsky plucked other *Demons*' characters from the social-political milieu as well, like Granovsky, Uspensky, and Miliukov, whose names are strewn through his notebook.[25] For example, Stepan Trofimovich Verkhovensky is largely modeled on Timofei Nikolaevich Granovsky, who was a history professor at Moscow University, a Western liberal, and friend of Alexander I, but there are also elements of Herzen, Nikolai Vladimirovich Stankevich, and Vissarion Grigoryevich Belinsky blended into his character.[26] Virginsky has shades of Pyotr G. Uspensky, a Nechaev accomplice, and likewise resembles Aleksandr P. Miliukov, the writer and teacher whom Dostoevsky chastised in later letters.[27] The template for Semyon Yegorovich Karmazinov is unmistakably Ivan Turgenev, the author of *Fathers and Sons*.[28] Dostoevsky caricatures him as a vain, narcissistic phony, who tries to ingratiate himself with villainous Pyotr.

But as the novel progresses, the anomic aristocrat, Nikolai Vsevolodovich Stavrogin, eclipses Pytor, Stepan, the socialists, nihilists, and liberals in relative importance to become a focal point. A ghost from the past, he likely dates to Dostoevsky's Petrashevsky days.[29] In 1847, young Dostoevsky began to frequent Friday-night meetings of the utopian socialist Mikhail Butashevich Petrashevsky.[30] While the attendees discussed literature, they also debated controversial issues, like the emancipation of the serfs and judicial and censorship reforms. They spoke of French socialist manifestos and Dostoevsky read aloud Belinsky's banned letter, which scathingly attacked Nikolai Gogol's defense of serfdom.[31] Dostoevsky became more entrenched in these perilous gatherings when Nikolai Speshnev, a radical member of the Petrashevsky circle, organized a secret society, whose goal was to foment Russian revolution.[32] The members, who swore a loyalty oath, aimed to spread the seeds of discontent within government and to infiltrate those "students dissidents, peasants, and soldiers," who were disgruntled and eager for change.[33] Dostoevsky signed on and his reading of Belinsky's banned letter was what lead to his arrest, confinement in the Peter and Paul Fortress, his near-execution, and eventual internment in Omsk Fortress. The Petrashevsky society became the added taproot for *Demons* and Speshnev is the likely prototype for Stavrogin, whom Dostoevsky calls a "gloomy," "tragic," "villain."[34]

Stavrogin: Anomic "Psychache"

Durkheim speaks of torture as an "[i]nextinguishable thirst" and explains that "[a]ll man's pleasure in acting, moving, and exerting himself implies the sense that his efforts are not in vain and that by walking he has advanced" (SU, Bk 2. Ch 5; 247–48). Durkheim hypothetically asks what happens to people who do "not advance when [they] walk toward no goal, or—which is the same thing—when [their] goal is infinity" (SU, Bk 2, Ch 5; 248). His implicit answer is that they turn into an anomic Stavrogin, "condemned" to a "state of perpetual unhappiness" (SU, Bk 2, Ch 5; 248).

Durkheim has pointed out that aristocrats are predisposed to anomic suicide because "superfluity" and "[w]ealth . . . by the power it bestows, deceives [individuals] into believing that [they] depend on [themselves] only" and that this "exalt[ation of] the individual," tends to "arouse the spirit of rebellion which is the very source of immorality" (SU, Bk 2, Ch 5; 254). Stavrogin has lost faith in God, is filled with pent-up rage, and bears kinship not just with the real-life Speshnev but also with literary characters like Pushkin's Evgeny Onegin and Mikhail Lermontov's Pechorin.[35] In a letter to Nikolai Lyubimov, Dostoevsky portrays Stavrogin as a type of superfluous man, whom he sees as a "whole social type . . . *our* type, a Russian, a person idle not out of a desire to be idle, but who has lost touch with everything native and most important, faith: a degenerate *out of ennui*, but a conscientious person who makes every convulsive, martyr-like effort to be renewed and to begin believing again."[36] Stavrogin also flashbacks to a portion of Porfiry Petrovich's interrogation in *Crime and Punishment* in which Raskolnikov expounds on those who "whip themselves" and "impose various public penances on themselves."[37]

Demons' readers, of course, must contend with the unreliable narration of Anton Lavrentyevich G_v, who vacillates between acting as a chronicler and an omniscient narrator.[38] Like it or not, as shape-shifting as he may be, Anton feeds the readers information about Stavrogin in three ways: he provides a glimpse at his childhood, accounts of his conduct, and perspectives of third parties. These perspectives create the cumulative portrait of an anomic suicide who has "neither enthusiasm, religious, moral or political faith, nor any of the military virtues" (SU, Bk 2, Ch 6; 284). On Durkheim's reading, Stavrogin's anomy is about "anger and all the emotions customarily associated with disappointment," which engender an "exasperated weariness" that ultimately finds closure in self-strangulation (SU, Bk 2, Ch 6; 284).[39]

Childhood: The Onset

Stepan Trofimovich Verkhovensky played a significant role in Stavrogin's upbringing and in instilling his suicidal inclination. Although Dostoevsky professed to love and respect Stepan Trofimovich the forties idealist, this comic-tragic character is flawed and fits the mold of a recurrent Dostoevsky theme—that of the "accidental family," which spawns "disorder" and "fragmentation."[40]

Early in *Demons*, the chronicler tips off readers to the fact that Stepan is left a widower with a five-year-old boy, Pyotr, whom he has only seen twice in his life, "the first time when he had been born, and the second time . . . in Petersburg, where the young man was preparing to enter the university" (D, Pt 1, Ch 1; 29). Oddly, even though Stepan has neglected his own son, he is the one whom Varvara Petrovna selects to be Stavrogin's "accidental" father, taking on "the education and entire intellectual development of her only son" (D, Pt 1, Ch 2; 44). Stepan accepts the job, not out of any passion or aptitude for child-rearing, but primarily out of self-interest: he clings to his tortured bond with Stavrogin's mother and appreciates the convenience of living on her estate. At this point, Stavrogin's father, the general, lives apart from the family while his effectually abandoned and vulnerable eight-year-old, is delivered into Stepan's histrionic arms.

Stepan Trofimovich, who has never taken control of his own life, fails to assume an adult role with his charge. Instead, he uses the boy to fill his own needs by making him into a friend, confident, and therapist. Stepan repeatedly awakens "his ten-or-eleven-year old friend at night," for the "sole purpose of tearfully pouring out his wounded feelings to him or revealing some family secret, without noticing that this was simply improper" (D, Pt 1, Ch 2; 44). Such late-night expulsions cleave deep into Stavrogin's tender psyche: Stepan is a virtuoso at "reaching into his young friend's heart" to "pluck the deepest chords and evoke in him the first, still vague sense of that eternal, sacred anguish which some elected souls, once having tasted and known it, would never again exchange for some cheap gratification" (D, Pt 1; Ch 2; 45). The narrator suggests that the redundant shocks led to an emotional overload that caused him to shut down yet retain a simmering anger (D, Pt 1; Ch 2; 44). Young Stavrogin becomes gutted of interest in and feeling for those around him, or as the chronicler puts it, although Stavrogin "knew that his mother loved him very much, . . . he didn't really love her very much at all" (D, Pt 1; Ch 2; 44).[41]

Stepan not only numbs his charge, he also jumpstarts the process of weaning Stavrogin from the "regulative force [that] must play the same role for moral needs which the organism plays for physical needs" (SU, Bk 2, Ch 5; 248). Durkheim posits that "[e]ither directly and as a whole, or through the agency of one of its organs, society . . . alone has the power to stipulate law and to set the point beyond which the passions must not go" (SU, Bk 2, Ch 5; 249). Pressed into Stepan's arms at night, Stavrogin is blasted with angst and impelled to process what budding brains rarely can process: the reversed roles of adult and child. Stepan has effectually unanchored Stavrogin from societal moorings, from the "exterior" that fosters equilibrium and tempers impulses. The chronicler opines that "[t]here are . . . lovers of . . . anguish who prize it more than its most radical gratification" (D, Pt 1, Ch 2; 44–45). The early infusions from Stepan Trofimovich, the 1940s idealist, induct Stavrogin into a suicidogenic cabal populated with such restless seekers of "anguish" (D, Pt 1, Ch 2; 45).

Conduct: Nose, Lips, Ears, Eyes, Plus a Duel

When Varvara Petrovna tells Stepan Trofimovich that her adult son "has experienced . . . many ups and downs in his life," that she has noticed not just "something strange, something peculiar," but also "a certain chronic restlessness and a tendency towards special inclinations," she is limning what Durkheim depicts as anomy and what suicidologist, Edwin S. Shneidman, coins as "psychache" (D, Pt 1, Ch 3; 111).[42] Durkheim states that sociological well-being hinges on "needs" such that "[n]o living being can be happy or even exist unless his needs are sufficiently proportioned to his means" (SU, Bk 2, Ch 5; 246). When "needs require more than can be granted, or even merely something of a different sort, they will be under continual friction and can only function painfully" (SU, Bk 2, Ch 5; 246). Shneidman analogously pinpoints "*needs*" as the crux of psychological health.[43] He concludes that "[i]n almost every case suicide is caused by pain, a certain kind of pain—*psychological* pain," which he names "*psychache*" and it invariably stems from "thwarted or distorted psychological *needs*."[44] Other scholars concur that "thwarted psychological needs" can cause the restlessness, hopelessness, despair, agitated anger, and desperation behind most self-inflicted deaths.[45]

What Stavrogin's mother senses is "a certain chronic restlessness," what Durkheim defines as needs "under continual friction," and what Shneidman calls "*psychache*" all belie Stavrogin's subversive behavior towards others and towards himself (SU, Bk 2; Ch 5; 246).[46] Stavrogin's anomie is distinguishable from Durkheim's suicidal egoism. The suicidal egoist withdraws from collective activity, but in the anomic, "society's influence is lacking in the basically individual passions" such that the person has no "check-rein" (SU, Bk 2, Ch 5; 258). Stavrogin's self-sabotaged career evinces the absence of restraint as does his outrageous conduct when he returns to Skvoreshniki. Once back in Skvoreshniki, he lashes out at society by taking pokes the nose, ears, lips, and eyes, which are receptors that assimilate data from the contextual sphere. Further, all such episodes entail self-throttling, a pattern that culminates in a potentially fatal duel that is a form of embryonic suicide.

Louis Breger points out that "Stavrogin comes into the novel from a wild and dissolute past life, a life of whoring, gambling, fighting and murderous duels," and misdeeds that reach Skvoreshniki as rumors.[47] Varvara Petrovna gets wind of the fact that her son "had suddenly taken up a life of almost mad dissipation," that "he had become a bully of sorts, attaching himself to people and then insulting them for the pleasure of it" (D, Pt 1, Ch 2; 46). Eventually, she learns that after fighting duels, her son loses his rank as an officer and is abruptly ejected from the elite regiment. Even when Stavrogin somehow rebounds by getting promoted to officer, he resigns his commission, "hook[s] up with the dregs of the Petersburg population," and wallows in wanton self-debasement, which Stepan Trofimovich likens to that of Prince Harry "roister[ing] with Falstaff, Poins, and Mistress Quickly" (D, Pt 1, Ch 2; 46–47).[48]

When Stavrogin returns home to Skvoreshniki, his "gross outrages," beginning with one directed at Pavel Pavlovich Gaganov's nose, substantiate the rumors (D, Pt 1, Ch 2; 49). Gaganov "had the innocent habit of accompanying his every word with a vehement 'No indeed they won't lead me by the nose!' " (D, Pt 1, Ch 2; 50). At a polite gathering, Stavrogin's attack on Pavel's proboscis ignites scandal: Stavrogin, "who [is] standing by himself to one side and to whom no one was paying any attention, suddenly walk[s] up to Pavel Pavlovich, seize[s] him unexpectedly but firmly by the nose with two fingers and manage[s] to drag him two or three steps across the room" (D, Pt 1, Ch 2; 50).

While dragging Pavel Pavlovich by the nose, Stavrogin appears to be on automatic pilot (D, Pt 1, Ch 2; 50). Then when Stavrogin comes out of it and realizes what he has done, he takes an extra jab at society by "show[ing] no embarrassment, but on the contrary, giv[ing] a malicious and happy smile" (D, Pt 1, Ch 2; 50). Gilding the lily, he mutters an all-too "casual apology," shrugs his shoulders, and walks out, which makes the narrator conclude that "[a]ll of this was . . . an ugliness that was calculated and deliberate, . . . and therefore constituted a deliberate and unbelievably insolent affront to our entire society" (D, Pt 1, Ch 2; 50–51).

After this "insolent" tug at the societal nose, the community wants "this dangerous brawler, this Petersburg bully [to] be restrained" to "protect[] the peace of the entire decent circle of people in [the] town from harmful infringements" (D Pt 1, Ch 2; 51). Yet, unrestrained and unrestrainable, Stavrogin takes another swipe by escalating from nose to lips. When Stravogin is invited to Madame Liputina's birthday party, he surmises that her husband, Liputin, "as the local liberal, was thrilled by the [nose] scandal and sincerely thought that this was precisely the way to act towards the senior members of the club" (D, Pt 1, Ch 2; 53). Already revved up for agitating more scandal, but this time amongst the liberals, Stavrogin attends. Rather than indulging in the "generous spread *zakusi* and vodka," Stavrogin binges on Liputin's wife by suddenly "put[ting] his arm around her waist, in front of all the guests, and kis[sing] her on the lips, some three times in a row, with genuine gusto" (D, Pt 1, Ch 2; 53). Once done, he triumphantly leaves behind a "dumbstruck husband," and again, a "general commotion" (D, Pt 1, Ch 2; 53).

Stavrogin next graduates from the lips to the ear, and it is here that the self-destruction inherent in these episodes becomes glaringly apparent. This siege takes place when the governor, Ivan Osipovich, offers Stavrogin, his relative, an opportunity to make amends by apologizing to Gaganov and other club members and then save face by going abroad. With "his eyes fastened on the floor," Stavrogin listens to the governor "with knitted brows, as if trying to overcome an acute pain," and seems to be containing his wrath (D, Pt 1, Ch 2; 55). But when the governor diffidently asks Stavrogin "what impels you to commit such unbridled acts, which are beyond the bounds of all accepted conventions and rules," salvo ensues (D, Pt 1, Ch 2; 55). "Something cunning and mocking gleams in Stavrogin's eyes" as he anticipates a new chance to not only offend, but also self-castigate (D, Pt 1, Ch 2; 55). Instead of "confiding the interesting secret" in a whisper, which Stavrogin's slouch seems to promise, he "suddenly seize[s] the upper part of [the governor's] ear in his teeth, and clamp[s] down on it rather firmly" (D, Pt 1, Ch 2; 56). After hearing the governor "gasp," Stavrogin resorts to animal behavior and "bit[es] down even harder" (D, Pt 1, Ch 2; 56). Ending up "locked in a special cell, with a special guard at the door," however, only whets Stavrogin appetite for an added chance to vent rage and zap himself (D, Pt 1, Ch 2; 56). Stavrogin "set[s] up a frenzied pounding on the door with his fist, [tears] the iron grating out of the small window, . . . smash[es] the glass and cut[s] up his hands" (D, Pt 1, Ch 2; 57). While doctors attribute this to *belaya goryachka* (brain fever or delirium tremens), Stavrogin's behavior derives from insanity's lookalike—the anomic "state of disaggregation" that "agitates," and "exasperates." In psychological parlance, it is "psychache" that compels Stavrogin's self-inflicted excruciation (SU, Bk 3, Ch 3; 382).[49]

This lust for pain is frequently a precursor to anomic death. It surfaces again when Ivan Shatov slaps Stavrogin "on the cheek with all his might" (D, Pt 1, Ch 5; 225). Despite the blow from Shatov's "large, weighty, [and] bony fist," which "grazed the left corner of the lip and upper teeth, causing Stavrogin to bleed, he just seizes up and declines to strike back (D, Pt 1, Ch 5; 225). Perplexed, because the Stavrogin he thinks he knows is the sort who "would have killed the offender right on the spot, without further ado," the narrator nevertheless unravels the mystery:

> It seems to me that if there were a man, for example, who would seize a red-hot iron bar and squeeze it in his hand in order to test his toughness, and then, for a whole ten seconds had tried to overcome the unbearable pain and ended by overcoming it, then this man, it seems to me, would have endured something like what Nikolay Vsevolodovich experienced for these ten seconds. (D, Pt 1, Ch 5; 226, 228)

Albeit iron-willed, Stavrogin appreciates Shatov's blow because it comes with the perk of public humiliation. By refraining from reflexive retaliation, Stavrogin can kill several birds with one stone: he can savor the gnawing throb of cheek and mouth, fully degust Shatov's insult, and ballyhoo his shameful dishonor right in his mother's drawing room. Moreover, his martyr-like paean to discomfort is consistent with a later episode, in which Stavrogin lets his abscessed tooth (possibly knocked loose when Shatov walloped him) fester rather than let a doctor lance it in time.[50]

After sniping at nose, lips, and ears, Stavrogin aims to poke society in the eyes and impose on himself the self-degrading "burden that no one else can bear" by publicizing his marriage to Marya Timofeyevna Lebyadkina (D, Pt 2, Ch 3; 321). Even before Varvara Petrovna learns that Marya is her son's wife, she fears her, senses that she "is fated to play an extraordinary role in [her] life," and thus sees blitzkrieg in the offing (D, Pt 1, Ch 5; 187). Not only is Marya crippled, mentally feeble and delusional, with daily "nervous attacks" that "knock out her memory," but she is also hobbled by her lower-class rank and is thus considered an unsuitable bride for the aristocrat (D, Pt 1, Ch 4; 159: Ch 5; 187). Stavrogin points out that the quasi-clandestine marriage is "completely legal" and "if it has not come to light until now," that is because the only three who know about it, Kirillov, Pyotr, and Lebyadkin, have vowed to "say nothing" (D, Pt 2, Ch 1; 271).

When Varvara Petrovna asks her son if this "unfortunate, crippled woman" is his wife, Stavrogin seals his lips, gives "a kind of slow, condescending smile," and kisses his mother's hand (D, Pt 1, Ch 5; 202). Guarding yet savoring this delectable yet shameful secret of his ill-suited marriage, Stavrogin aims to whip it out at an opportune time to maximize shock and self-degradation. Shatov hits the nail on the head when he shouts, "[y]ou got married out of passion for inflicting torment . . . Stavrogin and a pitiful, dim-witted, destitute cripple!" (D, Pt 2, Ch 1; 282). In doing so, Shatov sums up Stavrogin's quest to inflict shame, anguish, and pain on himself.

Stavrogin's "passion for inflicting torment" on not just his circle but also on himself culminates in his duel with Gaganov's son, which fits what suicide theorists, including Socrates, Sigmund Freud, Karl A. Menninger, Shneidman, Michael A. Church, Charles I. Brooks, and Durkheim, categorize as a stand-in for the overt act of attempted self-murder (D, Pt 2, Ch 1; 282).

As early as 399 BC, Socrates talks about death through the "services of someone else."[51] Much later, Freud refers to "half-intentional self-destruction" or "purposive accidents" where individuals secure unconscious ways to unleash the death drive.[52] Building on Freud and tacitly conjuring the image of Nastasya Filippovna's leap into the arms of Rogozhin in *The Idiot*, Menninger describes how the "unconsciously determined purposes of . . . self-destruction [can be] obtained (usually) by proxy."[53] In Shneidman's lexicon, such acts constitute "manifestations of indirect suicide" or "subintentioned deaths" by those "set on premature self-destruction," who "imprudently put themselves in harm's way."[54] Church and Brooks name the phenomenon "subtle suicide" by people "living 'on the edge' " and engaging in "risky behaviors, self-neglect, carelessness and negative mood states."[55] Durkheim's embryonic suicide similarly encompasses people who imperil their own lives by jousting with "mortal risks" (SU, Introduction, 45–46).

In the censored and originally unpublished chapter "At Tikhon's," Stavrogin mentions dueling and divulges the sort of emotivity at work in embryonic suicide. In the manifesto, Stavrogin shares with Bishop Tikhon, he states that "every time [he] stood facing [his] opponent in a duel, waiting for him to fire, [he] would experience the same feeling of shame and frenzy" and that he "often sought" this sensation because "it is the strongest of all feelings" (D, At Tik 2; 764). Whether we call this a lunge at "subintentioned" death through the "services of someone else," "suicide by proxy," or "subtle suicide," it is evident that Stavrogin's duels intoxicatingly deliver doses of craved "shame and frenzy" (D, At Tik 2; 764).[56] The narrator implies this as well when he likens Stavrogin to the Decembrist Mikhail Lunin, who reputedly engaged in reckless and frivolous dueling and sought to give his opponents a chance to experience the sensation of standing in front of a gun.[57] Although the narrator somewhat distinguishes Stavrogin from Lunin, the pre-duel mindset revealed to Tikhon in the omitted chapter approximates that of the Decembrist, who "purposely sought out danger all his life . . . [and] revel[ed] in the sensation of it" (D, Pt 1, Ch 5; 226).[58]

Stavrogin's Lunin-like flirtation with death occurs after Gaganov seeks to restore the family honor that was damaged when his father was dragged by the nose. When Gaganov challenges his nemesis to a duel, Stavrogin selects Kirillov to be his second, an apt choice. Kirillov is obsessed with death and betrothed to suicide. Stavrogin's choice suggests that there is an affinity between the dueler and Kirillov, who both court their own expiry. This comes across in the duel itself. Like the Decembrist, Stavrogin "revel[s] in the sensation of danger," and even heightens it by deliberately firing into the air (D, Pt 1, Ch 5; 226). When Gaganov's bullet "grazes the soft flesh" of Stavrogin's "finger joint," he wraps the wound and invites the next round (D, Pt 2, Ch 3; 318). After Gaganov fires again and the bullet hits his adversary's cap, Stavrogin "fires into the grove" and manages to survive (D, Pt 2, Ch 3; 320). His retreat signifies that he achieved what he came for—a brush with death.

But the duel, the aborted embryonic suicide, brings no sigh of relief, and instead incites Stravogin's anger as he seemingly "gallop[s] off" in defeat (D, Pt 2, Ch 3; 320). Kirillov's goal is to end his life, and he shares his expertise with Stavrogin, who is all about "endur[ing] something that no one else would endure, and seek[ing] out burdens that no one else can bear" (D, Pt 2, Ch 3; 321). By asking Stavrogin, "[i]f you yourself didn't want bloodshed, why did you give him the chance to kill you," Kirillov aligns himself with suicide theorists and thus equates the duel with attempted self-homicide (D, Pt 2, Ch 3; 322).

Tikhon: The Suicide Manifesto

Although Shatov says that Stavrogin's marriage to the cripple and his intent to broadcast it is "precisely" where "shamelessness and senselessness reache[s] the point of genius," he is mistaken because this seeker of "eternal, sacred anguish" has ammo far more ballistic tucked away in his back-pocket (D, Pt. 1, Ch 1; 282: Pt 1, Ch 2; 45). Stavrogin is simply not satisfied with just assailing the societal nose, ears, lips, and eyes. By delivering a calculated smite to Tikhon, Stavrogin aspires to vent rage on Russian faith. The *Notebooks for Demons*, in which Dostoevsky wrote that the "Prince [Stavrogin] will visit . . . Tikhon and [deliver] an insult to him," the prequels to "At Tikhon's," and clues in the excluded chapter itself all bolster the sharing of the manifesto as just such an outright attack.[59]

While "At Tikhon's" never made it into Dostoevsky's novel, it has ligatures to earlier episodes, which indicate that this seeker of "eternal, sacred anguish" aspires to expose a deed so base that it will incite a grisly reprisal (D, Pt 1, Ch 2; 45).[60] In dialogue with Shatov, Stavrogin invokes the seventeenth-century Don Cossack Stenka Razin (D, Pt 2, Ch 1; 281), who led a Cossack rebellion and was eventually quartered publicly on Red Square.[61]

Right after mentioning Stenka Razin, Shatov asks Stavrogin whether he has ever "seduced and debauched children" (D, Pt 2, Ch 1; 281), thereby hinting at what will be the *coup de grace* in Stavrogin's crusade to quarter himself.[62] Once Stavrogin denies having harmed children, Shatov diagnoses Stavrogin's spiritual disease. Shatov attributes Stavrogin's episodic outbursts, like biting the governor's ear and his shameless marriage to Marya, to "surges of carnality" that are fueled by his superfluity as an "idle, footloose, son of a landowner" (D, Pt 2, Ch 1; 282). An unspoken question hovers: what is next for Stavrogin? This anomic "landowner's son," who has "lost the distinction between evil and good," who has "stopped recognizing [his] own people," answers by making a pilgrimage to the Elder Tikhon. Once there, he makes Tikhon a witness to his self-destruction. (D, Pt 2, Ch 1, 283).

As prefigured in his session with Shatov, the censored chapter, "At Tikhon's," contains Stavrogin's account of raping a child who ultimately commits suicide. Joseph Frank suggests that this chapter's omission meant that Dostoevsky "could not give us the book as he had originally conceived it," and thus, "Stavrogin remains a far more enigmatic and mysterious figure than he was initially meant to be."[63] The missing chapter, however, is neither essential to the novel as published nor to solving the Sphinx-like riddle of Stavrogin. Stavrogin's divulgence of secrets fits into right into his pattern of flogging society, igniting scandals, and disgracing himself.

Stavrogin's arrival at the monastery and Tikhon's first reactions signal what is in store. In the Russian Orthodox tradition, confession was both venerated and suspect.[64] In old Russia, sinners often bowed down and whispered their sins into the ears of the Russian soil, rather than to priests.[65] Although the custom changed with time, it remains alive in the requirement that authentic confessions be oral—not written.[66] Carol Apollonio suggests that "[g]iven the demonic function of paper and writing in the novel, the fact that Stavrogin's confession is written compromises its integrity," which Stavrogin confirms by "grin[ning]" while fondly patting the scripted narrative in his pocket (D, At Tik 1; 751).[67] Readers are thus primed not to see Stavrogin as someone sincerely seeking an "indissoluble bond" with a spiritual guide.[68] Rather, readers should expect to see what they have seen all along. The confession will thus serve as an addendum to the litany of Stavrogin's antics, but this one aims to besmirch the sacred.

Stavrogin's behavior and Tikhon's reactions suffice to dissuade readers from viewing this escapade as a heartfelt inaugural step toward repentance. Stavrogin first ensures that Tikhon knows of his notorious scandals, then he admits that he does not have a sincere agenda by exclaiming, "I really don't know why I've come here" (D, At Tik 1; 755). Once the stage is set, Stavrogin dramatizes his suffering amidst the "theatrical works" that adorn Tikhon's cell (D, At Tik 1; 755). After whining about "hallucinations," driveling about his "wild and incoherent" revelations that "actually did seem to be the product of a deranged mind," claiming to sense evil beings or demons inside and around him, and indicating that he might even consult a doctor, Stavrogin suddenly retracts it all by yelping, "it's all rubbish, dreadful rubbish. It's just me in different guises, and nothing more" (D, At Tik 1; 756, 757). Packed with "eternal, sacred anguish," "psychache," and "thwarted needs," Stavrogin intimates that he is on the brink of giving society a swift kick in the gut (D, Pt 1, Ch 2; 45).[69] For this one, however, his chosen victim is an icon of Russian faith. Nonetheless, by looking on "questioningly" with a "vague smile" and repeatedly lowering his eyes, Tikhon indicates that he is not fooled for a second (D, At Tik 1; 757).

The document that Stavrogin delivers to Tikhon, which seems to "have been printed secretly by some Russian printing press" and "resemble[s] a manifesto," does precisely what Apollonio suggests: it becomes "associate[d] with the novel's many other paper products, particularly the political leaflets whose ostensible purpose is to stir up revolutionary activity among the local factory workers" (D, At Tik 2; 761).[70] The manifesto, which resembles nihilistic propaganda, is also a suicide note in which Stavrogin discloses his anomy and recurrent rageaholic bouts: "[e]very situation in my life in which I have ever happened to find myself, however unspeakably shameful, utterly degrading, vile and, most importantly, ridiculous, has always aroused both boundless anger and unbelievable pleasure in me" (D, At Tik 2; 763).[71] Here he exposes not only his anomic rage but also his shamefully pleasurable agenda before Tikhon.

In a meticulous self-indictment, the manifesto charges Stavrogin with "shameful, utterly degrading, vile" deeds, and it is so graphic and self-indulgent that it attempts to onanistically arouse his "boundless anger and unbelievable pleasure" (D, At Tik 2; 763). Stavrogin repeatedly alludes to Rousseau's *Confessions* and blames himself for Matryosha's unjust thrashing.[72] He brags of trysts with and schemes to victimize women and boasts of purloining the salary from a fellow lodger, a poor, overworked clerk, who needed it to support his family. Eventually, Stavrogin whips out the big shocker—his courtship of Matryosha, her rape, and suicide. In doing so, he hopes to unnerve Tikhon and provoke him to decry this as the most unspeakable sin against God.

With respect to suicide notes, psychiatrist Erwin Stengel and others have found that although "[t]here is no evidence that [they] are more truthful than other communications made under emotional stress," the authors "[a]lmost invariably. . . aim at eliciting certain emotional responses from survivors."[73] Stavrogin, however, is troubled that his "manifesto" does not get the anticipated response. His other jabs at society (the nose, lips, and ears) ostensibly worked: they left spectators appalled, aghast, dumbfounded. Tikhon, however, responds in a completely different manner. Becoming editor and literary critic, the Elder calmly asks the author if it would be "possible to make some corrections in this document," observing that the narrative is "comical" and will excite laughter (D, At Tik 2; 778, 782). A dejected Stavrogin gripes: "I don't see any sign of revulsion or shame in you. You don't seem to be disgusted!" (D, At Tik 2; 779). Tikhon concedes that "there is not, nor can there be a greater or more dreadful crime than the one . . . committed with this maiden," but proceeds to deflate Stavrogin's grandiose ploy to mortify (D, At Tik 2; 780). He likens the crime to "inevitable peccadilloes of youth" and the "old men who sin the same way, and even imperturbably and playfully" (D, At Tik 2; 780). By trivializing child rape as a commonplace, he undercuts Stavrogin's efforts to shock and deprives him of his claim to uniqueness.

Sparing no effort to make Tikhon's skin creep, Stavrogin next unbosoms his grandiose plan to disseminate the manuscript not just to "the police and local authorities," but all over Russia and abroad (D, At Tik 2; 777). Unperturbed, Tikhon acknowledges that Stavrogin just wants to debase himself and explains that the manifesto will not only make people hate him but will also excite "universal" laughter (D, At Tik 2; 782). Tikhon says that instead of publishing that "ugly" and "ridiculous" manifesto, there is another way to appease relentless lust "for martyrdom and self-sacrifice" (D, At Tik 2; 782–85). He suggests that Stavrogin relinquish worldly life for five to seven years to live as a monk in the spirit of true repentance.

Tikhon's response is not what Stavrogin sought. Psychiatrists Viggo W. Jensen and Thomas A. Petty have studied the impact of such dashed expectations. They point out that "[i]n the preparations for and in the execution of the suicidal act are expressed not only the wish to die but the wish to live and to be saved by [a chosen savior]," but "[i]f the behavior of the one chosen for the rescue is not what the suicidal person expects or hopes it will be, death is probable or inevitable."[74] After Stavrogin rejects the bishop's alternative, his chosen Tikhon experiences a painful facial spasm and clairvoyant epiphany, which is suggestive of Zosima in *The Brothers Karamazov*, who foresees ineluctable tragedy and bows down to Dmitry Karamazov in his cell. At that moment, Tikhon senses with every fiber of his being that Stavrogin inevitably stands "so close to the most dreadful crime," a "fresh crime as a way out" (D, At Tik 2; 787). Stavrogin says, "perhaps I can't hold out and in my rage, I'll commit a new crime," thereby foreboding his own anomic death (D, At Tik 2; 787). After Stavrogin calls Tikhon a "damned psychologist," this editor-critic-monk can add thanatologist to his resume because he knows that the manifesto is a swan song (D, At Tik 2; 787).

Stavrogin: A Nihil

Calling Dostoevsky's novels "polyphonic," Mikhail Bakhtin states that what "unfolds . . . is a plurality of consciousness with equal rights and each with its own world, that combine but are not merged into the unity of events."[75] In the manifesto that Stavrogin delivers to Tikhon, he indicts himself, but by "unfolding . . . a plurality of consciousness," third parties add their own charges.[76] Shatov, who struck Stavrogin "because of [his] degradation . . . because of [his] lie," brands him a self-defacer and liar (D, Pt 2, Ch 1; 267). When Shatov's wife, Marie, comes home to give birth to Stavrogin's baby, she shouts "Nikolay Stavrogin is a scoundrel!" (D, Pt. 3, Ch 5; 657). In *Demons*, other voices, like those of Marya, Lizveta Nikolayevna Tushina, and Darya Pavlovna Shatova, chime in, "combine," and convict Stavrogin of being a fraudulent nihil.[77]

Marya Lebyadkina, whom Joseph Frank calls "one of Dostoevsky's most poetic and enigmatic creations," effectively rips off Stavrogin's mask to bare the face of an imposter.[78] Despite her supposed inability to distinguish between reality and dream, Marya acts as a holy fool (*yurodivy*) and sees with sibylline precision.[79] In fact, as Stavrogin tries to cajole her to become his accomplice in a self-imposed martyrdom, she sounds like a skilled, but also oracular, psychoanalyst. By first focusing on the failings of Stavrogin's "disgusting" social caste, which has "so much wealth and so little joy," Marya puts her finger on the nub of anomy—superfluity (D, Pt 2, Ch 2; 305).

Marya also finds her suitor's fantasy of retreat to Switzerland with her "disgusting" and even laughable. While Marya may not be fully rooted in reality, she turns the tables and tells Stavrogin that he is the delusional one and that his charade, his proposed Christ-like sacrifice, is "improbable" (D, Pt 2, Ch2; 307). Like Tikhon, who found Stavrogin's manifesto comical, Marya ends up "bursting" with laughter (D, Pt 2, Ch 2; 307). Marya next ties Stavrogin to Grishka Otrepyev, one of three pretenders to the throne in the Time of Troubles.[80] Like Otrepyev, who masqueraded as Dmitry, Ivan the Terrible's son, Stavrogin is a sham—an owl disguising itself as a falcon and prince. Marya tells Stavrogin, "you're just an owl and a filthy little shop-keeper" (D, Pt 2, Ch 2; 308).[81] She elaborates: "[a]s soon as I saw your awful face when I fell and you picked me up—it was as if a worm had crawled into my heart: it's not *him*, I thought, not *him*! My falcon would never be ashamed of me in front of a society lady" (D, Pt 2, Ch 2; 308). What she detects here is the truth—namely, that her marriage is just Stavrogin's ploy to heap shame on himself.

As her final clap of thunder, Marya denigrates Stavrogin's manhood and predicts doom. The Stavrogin that first walked in was cocksure that he, the dashing aristocrat, could easily woo and manipulate this lower class, feeble cripple. Marya proves herself not only impervious to Stavrogin's masculine charisma but also adept at gaining the upper hand. Marya orders him to leave and then impliedly insults his phallus when she cries out "I'm not afraid of your knife" (D, Pt 2, Ch 2, 308). In this context, the knife serves as a double entendre because Marya divines her own demise, which will occur after Stavrogin's tosses money to her assassin, the knife-wielding Fedka.[82]

Marya's exposure of Stavrogin as a fraudulent impostor and her disparagement of his "knife" also foreshadow the anti-climactic tryst between Stavrogin and Liza. After Stavrogin tosses Fedka his purse and sits back while Pyotr orders Marya's murder, Stavrogin, the reputed "ladies' man," feels empowered to claim his prize, Liza (D, Pt 2, Ch 6; 412). But after the "complete failure" of their rendezvous, Liza echoes Marya when she calls Stavrogin a feckless impostor who needs a nurse (D, Pt 3, Ch 3; 587).[83] Moreover, like Marya and Tikhon, Liza responds to Stavrogin's plea—"I love you more now than yesterday"—by telling him that his "strange confession" is hogwash (D, Pt 3, Ch 3; 577). After Stavrogin proposes that Liza elope with him, she (again like Marya) refuses to submit to his "experiments" and delusions of redemption (D, Pt 3, Ch 3; 577). Like Marya, Liza sees through his antics and knows that Stavrogin uses others as helpers in his campaign to inflict pain on himself.

Liza's ridicule further stokes Stavrogin's chronic zeal for flagellation: he begs, "[t]orment me, punish me, vent your anger on me" (D, Pt 3, Ch 3; 581). Aspiring to be quartered, Stavrogin taunts his chosen executioner: "I knew I didn't love you, and I ruined you" (D, Pt 3, Ch 3; 581). Like Marya, Liza refuses to take the bait. Instead, she dislodges Stavrogin's mask, tells him he's "not capable of anything," denounces him as a nothing, and refuses to be a "sister of mercy" to a "legless, armless creature" (D, Pt. 3, Ch 3; 580, 581). Her words rhyme with those of the more docile Darya, who also sees through Stavrogin's façade and suggests that all he wants is a "superannuated sick nurse" (D, Pt. 2, Ch 3; 325).[84] The verdicts of Shatov, Marie, Marya, Liza, and Darya prefigure Stavrogin's last letter in which he sentences himself to death. The psychologist Henry Murray calls those who are pre-suicidal "dead to the world," meaning that a "person's primal springs of vitality have dried up, as if he were empty or hollow at the very core of his being."[85] Murray could be talking about Stavrogin, who tells Darya that "everything" (which necessarily includes himself) is "always shallow and flaccid," and brands himself as "dead to the world" (D, Pt 3, Ch 8; 746).

The Bullet or The Rope?

Durkheim's big question is worth reiterating here: what happens to those who "do not advance when they walk toward no goal, or—which is the same thing—when [their] goal is infinity?" (SU, Bk 2, Ch 5; 248). Stavrogin's mask-like pallor and his last letter to Darya provide the answer. Psychiatrist Lawrence S. Kubie explains that "[a] not infrequent suicide is carried out from behind a mask of '*belle indifference*,'' which "sometimes forms only after the decision to commit suicide has been reached in *secret*."[86] Kubie calls this a "suicidal purpose masked by an hysterical pseudoeuphoria," and in *Demons* by repeatedly comparing Stavrogin's face to a mask, the narrator suggests that behind the pallor of "indifference" is a death-bound man.[87] As Stavrogin comes closer to his final destination, he writes a letter to Darya, in which he implies that he has rejected the "*living stream of life*," states that "[i] n Russia, I'm not tied by anything," and recalls Shatov saying "that he who loses ties with his earth, also loses his gods, that is, all his goals" (D, Pt 3,

Ch 8; 745, 746).[88] In this letter, Stavrogin also tells Darya that even with "so much loving pouring out on to me . . . from your beautiful soul," you will not be able "to establish some goal for me" (D, Pt 3, Ch 8; 746). He knows that he has hit rock bottom and that not even love can fill his unfillable emptiness.

Stavrogin portrays his life as nonlife, one of aimlessness in a "gorge" where "mountains cramp one's sight and thought" (D, Pt 3, Ch 8; 744). Bereft of goals, Stavrogin projects a future for himself as a "citizen of the Canton of Uri," who self-exiles in "a very boring place" where it is "somber" and "everything is just as foreign as everywhere else" (D, Pt 3, Ch 8; 744). Durkheim might say that Stavrogin is doing time, self-interned in "perpetual unhappiness" and "exasperated weariness" (SU, Bk 2, Ch 5; 248: Ch 6; 284). As Stavrogin puts it, because his feelings are "too shallow" and his "desires too weak," he has dwindled to a state below nihility, where "[n]ot even negativity pours forth from [him]" (D, Pt. 3, Ch 8; 745). Shneidman would define his condition as suicidal because it features two demons: "elevated perturbation," which is "[a]nguish or disturbance . . . caused by pain," and "lethality," which is "the likelihood of an individual's being dead by his or her own hand in the near future."[89] Stavrogin's letter throbs with "psychache" and exposes lethality: he tells Darya, "I know I should kill myself, wipe myself from the face of the earth like a nasty insect" (D, Pt 3, Ch 8; 746).[90] Stavrogin lets her know that for him, death is a done deal and that the only remaining question is—how? This is where the "Werther effect," or "imitative suggestion," comes into play.[91]

Although Durkheim rejects the epidemiological significance of imitative suggestion as a factor affecting suicide rates, he recognizes it as a phenomenon that can hasten a death that would otherwise occur in someone who sees or knows of a suicide.[92] Durkheim explains that "*imitation exists when the immediate antecedent of an act is the representation of a like act, previously performed by someone else*," and stresses that "no imitation can exist without a model to imitate" (SU, Bk 1, Ch 4; 129, 133).[93] In the course of the novel, two imitative models present themselves to Stavrogin—the bullet and the rope.

The bullet option presents itself when Stavrogin joins a group trip to see the "blessed prophet Semyon Yakovlevich" (D, Pt 2, Ch 5; 361). While en route they learn that the "body of a guest who had shot himself had just been discovered in one of the hotel rooms" and decide to "have a look" at the dead boy (D, Pt 2, Ch 5; 362). The boy's widowed mother, sisters, and aunts had sent the nineteen-year-old to town to "make various purchases" for the dowry of his older sister, who was getting married (D, Pt 2, Ch 5; 363). Entrusting him with "four hundred roubles, which had been saved up over the course of decades," the family had "sent him off with endless, edifying admonishments, prayers and signs of the cross" (D, Pt 2, Ch 5; 363). Although "until then, the boy had been decent and reliable," once left to his own devices, he went on a wild binge (D, Pt 2, Ch 5; 363).

When he arrived in town, the boy did not go to his relative's home as instructed, but instead checked into a hotel and dashed off to a club, in hopes of finding some gambling or a card game. When that prospect fizzled, he returned to his room and although it was already close to midnight, ordered champagne, Havana cigars, and a six- or seven-course meal. Because he got drunk on the champagne and sick on the cigars, he did not touch the food and instead lapsed into an "almost unconscious state" (D, Pt 2, Ch 5; 363). The next morning, he ran off to a gypsy camp, got drunk again, returned to the hotel two days later, and slept it off. When he awoke, he asked for a cutlet, an expensive bottle of wine, grapes, paper, ink, and the bill. Then with a "calm quiet and pleasant" demeanor, he shot himself "directly into the heart" at the stroke of midnight (D, Pt 2, Ch 5; 363). On the table, he left a handwritten note stating that "no one should be blamed for his death" and that he had "shot himself because he had 'blown' four hundred roubles" (D, Pt 2, Ch 5; 262).

Under the Durkheimian lens, this is a suicide due to the traumatic and irreversible rupture of the boy's bond with his lifeline, the family that had not only raised him, fed him, but had also imbued him with a moral foundation and faith. The suicide theorist Eric Marcus would relegate it to his category of "public humiliation, scandal," which encompasses individuals who believe that they have disappointed others, "feel trapped by their circumstances," and "see suicide as their only way out."[94] Stavrogin undoubtedly remembered the image of the boy's corpse "half-reclining in a corner of the sofa" because the entire party had studied it "with avid curiosity" and discussed it at length (D, Pt 2, Ch 5; 364).[95] Kirillov's death, which likewise invites imitation, offers the bullet as a viable imitative model. Although Stavrogin did not witness the self-professed "man-God" shoot himself, he knows of it and even mentions it in his last note to Darya: the "magnanimous Kirillov couldn't tolerate the idea and he shot himself" (D, Pt 3, Ch 8; 746).

Matryosha, the raped child who hangs herself, provides the rope model. In Stavrogin's manifesto, he describes his rape of Matryosha, which begins with him kissing her little feet and climaxes with the child pouncing on him in "utter rapture" (D, At Tik 2; 767). Days later, Stavrogin returns to the crime scene to encounter his victim's "shriveled" face and "big reproachful eyes" (D, At Tik 2; 770). Stavrogin opines that "[m]ost likely she thought, when all was said and done, that she had committed an unspeakable crime, and a mortal sin—that 'she had killed God' " (D, At Tik 2; 768). Matryosha takes her own life because of her perceived alienation from faith and loss of her nexus to the Russian Christ. Ultimately Matryosha retreats into an enclosure while Stavrogin sits and waits in a room by the window. Then later, he walks to Matryosha's tiny retreat, stands on tiptoe, and peeks through a crack only to discover what he has already guessed—that the child has hung herself. Years later while abroad, Stavrogin buys a picture of a young girl "very much resembling Matryosha," and displays it on his mantel (D, At Tik 2; 774). Stavrogin contends that he "didn't glance" at it and even left it behind (D, At Tik 2; 774). Although purchasing the picture reveals his desire for self-retribution, it was unnecessary because Matryosha's image was embalmed in his memory (D, At Tik 2; 774).

Like "magnanimous" Kirillov or the boy who betrayed his family, Stavrogin can choose the bullet. Or like Matryosha, who believed she had betrayed God, he can grab the rope. On the expedition to the holy fool, Semyon Yakovlevich, a group member sums up what will become Stavrogin's options in the form of a query: "why [have] people in our country taken to *hanging* and *shooting* themselves so frequently, as if they'd lost their roots, as if the floor had slipped out from under their feet?" (D, Pt 2, Ch 5; 364). At one point, Stavrogin admits to considering the suicidal gun: he tells Kirillov that he "understands shooting [oneself]," and divulges that "[he] sometimes imagined doing it [himself]" (D, Pt. 2, Ch 1; 261). But in his last letter to Darya, it is apparent that Stavrogin rejects Kirillov's mode. He writes, "I . . . will never believe an idea to the same extent as [Kirillov] did" and "[n]ever, never shall I shoot myself" (D, Pt 3, Ch 8; 746).

In the end, Stavrogin borrows from both models—the rope and the gun. At the hotel, the boy's fatal shot was quick and seemingly painless: the chronicler points out that "death must have occurred instantaneously" because "there was no sign of the death agony in his face" and "his expression was calm, almost happy" (D, Pt 2, Ch 5; 364). Although Stavrogin emulates Matryosha by going into a small room to hang himself, he also borrows monads from the gun-model. Stavrogin leaves a note, which, like the boy's, states, "[n]o one is to blame, I did it" (D, Pt 3, Ch 8; 748). Also, by "thickly" soaping his cord, Stavrogin strives to evade "death agony" and make finality as "instantaneous" as possible (D, Pt 3, Ch 8; 748: Pt 2, Ch 5; 364).

Kirillov: The Anomic-Egoistic-Altruistic Man-God

Although not an actual member of Pyotr's gang, Kirillov has a posthumous role in the mayhem. He intends to shoot himself, promises to await Pyotr's signal, and leave a suicide note assuming blame for sorted vile deeds. Like Stavrogin, Kirillov is also rife with anger, "irritation and exasperated weariness," the symptoms of anomy that "necessarily tend to seek solace in acts of destruction" (SU, Bk 2, Ch 6; 284–85). Kirillov has not only purged himself of the bonds that yield a healthy "moral and material regimen," but has also estranged himself from Russia and exhibits egoism to the nth degree (SU,

Bk 2, Ch 5; 262). There is, moreover, an altruistic facet to Kirillov, which ties into Durkheim's point that "egoism and altruism themselves, contrary as they are may combine their influence" (SU, Bk 2, Ch 6; 289). What emerges from Kirillov's suicidogenic psyche is an anomic-egoistic-altruist who seeks to become Man-God by lodging a bullet in his brain.

When readers first meet Kirillov, they learn that he is a civil engineer, a profession that entails applying scientific and mathematical logic to design, construct, and operate structures to facilitate modern life and communications. Liputin claims that Kirillov has "returned from abroad" in hopes of being useful to the community by "obtain[ing] a position on the construction of our railways bridge" (D, Pt 1, Ch 3; 102). Yet, for someone who chooses a productive profession, Kirillov, contrarily dedicates his life to one mission—demolition. Liputin states that Kirillov "rejects the principle of morality altogether, and is holding to the latest principle of general destruction in the name of ultimately good purposes," while Stepan Trofimovich calls out Kirillov's hypocrisy: "you want to build our bridge, and at the same time you announce that you stand for the principle of universal destruction" (D, Pt 2, Ch 1; 105–6). In doing this, Stepan sees Kirillov's contradictions and foresees what will be Kirillov's undermining of his own objectives.

Not only does the engineer impugn himself, but he pushes others away and resists what Durkheim deems essential—the "moral and material regimen" stemming from family and other nurturant bonds (SU, Bk 2, Ch 5; 262). Aside from a brother, who has been dead for seven years, Kirillov, a solitary bachelor, mentions neither paramour nor blood kin. Until Marya returns to town to give birth, Kirillov even shuns Shatov, with whom he shared a traumatic ordeal in America.[96] Kirillov admits to self-imposed exile, boasts that he has "seen few people for four years," has "conversed little for four years," and has "tried not to meet people, for [his] own purposes" (D, Pt 2. Ch; 105). As such, he has estranged himself from everyone, from the Russian people.

Although Kirillov rarely mingles, when he does, observers are left with the impression that he is "deranged," "mad," "insane," or a "maniac" (D, Pt 1, Ch; 3 130: Pt 2, Ch; 6; 394: Pt 2, Ch 1; 275). Shatov calls it a deplorable state, for which he blames both America and Stavrogin. This is not surprising because Dostoevsky intermittently portrays America as a punitive or lethal destination, and it is Kirillov's visit there that helps launch his suicide fixation. This emerges in a conversation in which the chronicler states that Kirillov "seems to be demented on the subject of atheism," and Shatov responds by attributing this to his "lying around too long in America" (D, Pt 1, Ch 4; 152–53). Shatov and Kirillov had fled Russia for the United States so that they could "try out for [themselves] the life of the American worker and in that way to learn from [their] *personal* experience the condition of a human being in the most difficult of social conditions" (D, Pt 1, Ch 4; 153–54).[97]

After hiring themselves out as laborers to "an exploiter," they were cheated, beaten, "suffered," and "wore [themselves] out" (D, Pt 1, Ch 4; 154). When they became ill, Stavrogin sent Shatov a hundred rubles to fund a return trip.

After the debacle, Shatov came home to embrace Russia as the "*living stream of life*."[98] He wrested himself from Pyotr's influence, branded the nihilists "paper men," and slammed their ideas as "lackeyism of thought" (D, Pt 1, Ch 4; 152).[99] On the other hand, Kirillov left America drenched by the Styx of death and infected with that "animal hatred for Russia which has eaten into [his] organism" (D, Pt 1, Ch 4; 153). He is proud of not having "the slightest knowledge of the Russian people" and not only speaks poor Russian, but even brags that it "doesn't matter to [him]" (D, Pt 1, Ch 3; 104, 129).[100] When the suicide note that Pyotr foists on him includes French phrases, Kirillov rejoices and pledges to even "sign it again in French" (D, Pt 3, Ch 6; 688). Pyotr observes that Kirillov wanted to sign his suicide note in Russia. This, however, does not come from his fealty to the motherland, but instead is enmeshed in his goal of substituting himself for the "idea" of a Russian Christ.[101] Shatov also blames Stavrogin for aggravating Kirillov's abysmal condition: While Stavrogin was "implanting God and the motherland in [Shatov's] heart," he was conversely poisoning Kirillov, "validating lies and slander in him" and driving his "rational faculties to the point of frenzy"(D, Pt 2, Ch 1; 275).

America and Stavrogin also instigate Kirillov's excessive asceticism, which suicidologists, like Karl Menninger, see as a gradual march toward death. In the previous chapter, there is a discussion of Svidrigailov's suicide and its conflation with America, which became Dostoevsky's synonym for self-induced suffering or death.[102] Poisoned by America (and also by Stavrogin), Kirillov subsists as a virtual hermit, has stopped sleeping at night, and is practically starving himself to death: he admits, "I don't eat much, it's always tea" (D, Pt 1, Ch 3; 125).[103] In agreeing to serve as Stavrogin's double in the duel with Gaganov, "[p]oor, almost destitute" Kirillov looks like abstinent recluse, whose sole indulgence are his "treasured weapons," and among these "expensive" icons to deity-death is his "six-chambered *American* revolver" (D, Pt 2, Ch 1; 260) (emphasis added).

On his terminal ("American") mission, Kirillov resembles what Menninger describes as the chronically suicidal, self-proclaimed "ascetic" who "voluntarily condemns himself to a life of hardship, starvation, and flagellation."[104] Quibbling with Menninger's concept of chronic suicide because it is about "self-defeating ways of continuing to live," Shneidman prefers to label self-imposed austerity a "subintentioned death," or a "way of stopping the process of living."[105] But be it Menninger's "self-destructive urge in asceticism" or Shneidman's "race toward withdrawal and self-abnegation," Kirillov is figuratively bound for America.[106] In fact, right before his shot to the head,

Pyotr eggs him on and says "the best thing is for you to regard yourself as a Columbus now" (D, Pt 3, Ch 6; 676). In doing that, Pyotr strokes Kirillov's ego by comparing him to the discoverer of the New World.

Obsessive Suicide with "Good Reason"

Kirillov is not just bound for, but also bound up with America, which becomes apparent when he expounds his suicide philosophy to the chronicler, Stavrogin, and Pyotr respectively. With each sermon, however, the ramifications of self-homicide broaden.

First, Kirillov tells the chronicler that he is "collecting observations" and pondering "the reasons for the increase in incidents of suicide in Russia" (D, Pt 1, Ch 3; 104). Kirillov's findings uncannily parallel those of Durkheim, who states that there exist both "*impulsive or automatic suicide*," the execution of which "follows so swiftly that patients often have no idea of what has taken place," and "*obsessive suicide*," which is prolonged, caused "by the fixed idea of death, which . . . has taken complete possession of the . . . mind" (SU, Bk 1, Ch 1; 64–65). If Kirillov had been conceived after Durkheim, this Russian suicide theorist might have signed on as the sociologist's disciple. According to Kirillov, there are "those who kill themselves either from some great sorrow, or from anger, or the crazy ones" (D, Pt 1, Ch 3; 127). Like Durkheim's "impulsive or automatic" suicides, these are the quickies by individuals who "don't think about pain very much," and "do it suddenly" (D, Pt 1, Ch 3; 127). On the other hand, Kirillov speaks of people, who, like Durkheim's "obsessives," delete themselves "for good reason" and tend to "think a lot" (D, Pt 1, Ch 3; 127).

Kirillov believes that the "good-reason" category could encompass everyone if it were not for the two "prejudices": namely, the fear of pain and of the "next world" (D, Pt 1, Ch 3; 127).[107] He argues that everyone's "goal" should be the conquest of these fears, which will spell the "[f]ull freedom" that "come[s] only when it makes no difference whether to live or not to live" (D, Pt 1, Ch 3; 127). Kirillov proclaims that "whoever doesn't care whether he lives, or doesn't live . . . will be the new man." Having killed God, he will thus be God (D, Pt 1, Ch 3; 128). Consequently, everything will change: "the world will change, and deeds will change, and thoughts, and all feelings" (D, Pt 1, Ch 3; 128). While Kirillov does not explain here, he clearly associates "change" with the ouster of God.

The Anomic-Egoistic-Altruist

In taking up the topic with Stavrogin, Kirillov fleshes out what he means by God's death as the trigger for change in "deeds" and "thoughts" and "all feelings" (D, Pt 1, Ch 3; 128). In his apocryphal view, one reminiscent of Svidrigailov's *modus vivendi*, the moral censor simply defects. Kirillov explains the mindet: not only is dying of hunger or abusing a little girl "good," but every human picklement is adrift in neutrality and can be adjectively slapped with the word, "good." He elaborates, "someone who bashes in that man's head for the child, that's good too; and someone who doesn't bash in his head, that's good too. Everything is good, everything" (D, Pt 2, Ch 1; 263). His code of behavior lacks an arbiter of good and evil and thus, human beings can and will do whatever they do with impunity.

Kirillov explains that individuals who embrace the goodness of everything can hyperbolically personify what Christ "taught"—that "all are good" (D, Pt 2, Ch 1; 264). Those imbued with inordinate power can shatter rules, stop the clock, and become like Apocalyptic angel "swear[ing] that time will no longer exist" (D, Pt 2, Ch 1; 262).[108] Welded to Kirillov's philosophy is the notion that the "man-God" will dethrone Christ and "bring about the end of the world" (D, Pt 2, Ch 1; 264).[109] When the chronicler responds by telling Kirillov that "[i]f it doesn't matter whether one lives or doesn't live, then everyone will kill himself," what he does is define that big change as a suicide pandemic (D., Pt 1, Ch 3; 128). But the chronicler and readers later see that the "change" of which Kirillov speaks goes beyond the foreseeable rash of self-homicides. It inevitably bursts into an apocalyptic firestorm of rage and destruction.

Kirillov delivers the third installment of his suicide homily to Pyotr, but significantly in doing so, he unleashes the anomic anger, which is the core of his self-annihilation. Quite early in the novel, Kirillov sits "as if his feathers had been ruffled" and appears "to be angry at something" (D, Pt 1, Ch 3; 102). But as he moves closer to effectuating his own demise, he gets worse. He is in what Durkheim calls a "state of acute over-excitation" and exhibits the kind of skyrocketing tantrum that is the earmark of anomy (SU, Bk 2, Ch 6; 285). Kirillov's ersatz suicide confession resembles the anomic notes that Durkheim describes as "contain[ing] blasphemies" and "violent recriminations against life in general" (SU, Bk 2, Ch 6; 284). In his note, Kirillov wants to harangue "the whole world" and "curse . . . everyone" (D, Pt 3, Ch 6; 686–87). He even takes a spit at the motherland, by relishing the non-Russian, French phrases exhorting revolution and death.[110]

But before venting that rage on Russia, the world and himself, he goes for Pyotr. When Pyotr visits him to discuss the suicide pact, he tells Kirillov that he has avoided him because he has "become very angry of late" (D, Pt 2, Ch 6; 415). As the fatal day draws near, Pytor visits Kirillov again to remind him of his promise to "write and sign anything" he dictates (D, Pt 3, Ch 4; 615). Then Kirillov tells Pyotr, "the only one thing I feel very bad about" is that at the moment of death, "I'll have a reptile like you beside me," and warns him of his explosive anger (D, Pt 3, Ch 4; 617). Shortly thereafter, the convict, Fedka, who inhabits Kirillov's abode, enacts his host's fury by violently striking Pyotr "as hard as he could" on the face four times with a "blow" so "dreadful" that it causes its target to "suddenly crash full length on the floor" (D., Pt 3, Ch 4; 621). Essentially, lawless Fedka, who has become the figurative tenant of Kirillov's psyche, personifies his host's anomic wrath. Kirillov's fury crescendos right up until the moment of self-expungement. Before suicide, "Kirillov [keeps] his eyes fixed on [Pyotr] with angry loathing" and shortly before pulling the trigger, he lunges forth with "animal-like rage" to deliver a rabid bite to Pyotr's "little finger," that causes "almost unbearable pain" (D, Pt 3, Ch 6; 676, 689, 692).

In addition to displaying fury, Kirillov discloses his egoism as he presents his suicide theories to Pyotr. Kirillov and his ideas illustrate Durkheim's contention that anomy and egoism are "merely two different aspects of one social state," making it "not surprising that they should be found in the same individual" (SU, Bk 2, Ch 6; 288). The kind of egoism inherent in Kirillov is indeed the focus of Donald A. Nielsen's essay, "Dostoevsky in the Mirror of Durkheim."[111] Nielsen believes that the self-professed "man-God," who "remains a victim of his own egoistically driven metaphysical strivings," is one of multiple Dostoevsky characters who "isolate [themselves] from society and humanity . . . [and] become involved increasingly in the workings of his inner life to the point where [they] irritably resist the intrusion of others into [their] private world."[112] Like *The Idiot*'s egoist Ippolit, Kirillov is mired in death, has "detached" himself "from the outside world," and "retreat[ed] . . . into himself" (SU, Bk 2, Ch 6; 279).

Before his lethal bullet, Kirillov flaunts free will and spews a litany of egoistic soundbites at Pyotr: "If [God] does not exist, then all will is mine, and I am obliged to proclaim self-will" (D, Pt 3, Ch 6; 683). After Pyotr informs Kirillov that he is nothing special and states, "you're not the only one to kill yourself; there are many suicides," Kirillov replies that lowly folks "do it without reason" (D, Pt 3, Ch 6; 683). What elevates him above the hoi polloi is that he alone is doing it for "good reason . . . for self-will. I'm the only one" (D, Pt 3, Ch 6; 683). When Pyotr suggests that if he sought to flaunt self-will, he would do it by killing someone, the aspiring man-God remarks that unlike murder, which is the "the lowest point" of self-will, his deed alone—that of self-murder—is self-will at its "highest" (D., Pt 3, Ch 6; 684). He explains that only reason people have invented God is to live without killing themselves, but he—deific Kirillov—is the sole foregoer. As "the only one who hasn't felt like inventing God for the first time," he can egoistically inflate and be God (D, Pt 3, Ch 6; 684).

In addition to the hybrid, anomic egoism, Kirillov's suicide contains altruism. Durkheim holds that altruism occurs when "the ego is not its own property, where it is blended with something not itself, where the goal of conduct is exterior to itself, that is one of the groups in which in which it participates" (SU, Bk 2, Ch 4; 221). Typically, that altruistic leap into oblivion happens when individuals feel commanded to take their own life as a religious sacrifice or as a fanatical pledge of allegiance to some cult. Yet, counterintuitively, it is possible to be both egoist and altruist, a combo which arises in "certain epochs, when disaggregated society can no longer serve as an objective for individual activities" (SU, Bk 2, Ch 6; 289).[113] These epochs are rife with what Stepan Trofimovich calls "civil grief," the burgeoning *weltschmerz* in response to deplorable conditions in society and the world at large (D, Pt 1, Ch 1; 14). Durkheim states that the afflicted feel so disconnected that they "seek some durable object" to which they can "attach themselves permanently and which shall give meaning to their lives" (SU, Bk 2, Ch 6; 289). They thus "create[e] out of whole cloth some ideal reality" and to their fabricated demiurge "they assign all attachment to existence which they ascribe to themselves" (SU, Bk 2, Ch 6; 289). Essentially, what they do is concoct and attach themselves to a false god.

Kirillov takes that radically aberrant step of "create[ing] out of whole cloth" an "ideal reality," but his godhead *is* self-hood (SU, Bk 2, Ch 6; 289).[114] "[H]aving put an end to God" and instead "having developed a belief in self-will," Kirillov is set on being the "one man," the first, who "must kill himself without fail" (D, Pt 3, Ch 6; 685). Kirillov is self-chosen to "begin and prove . . . the attributes of [his own] godhood," and serve as sacrificial lamb to "begin and end and thus open the door" to "salvation" (D, Pt 3, Ch 6; 686). Kirillov's mindset approximates Durkheim's list of altruistic deaths. It includes the Bhils, who "cast themselves" from the top of a rock "to devote themselves to Shiva," and Japanese "fanatics," who "throw themselves into the water weighed with stones . . . while singing their idol's praises" (SU, Bk 2, Ch 4; 224). Unlike Durkheim's examples, Kirillov's sacrificial quest is not for authentic afflatus. Instead, he casts himself from life in devotion to Kirillov while "singing" praises to idol Kirillov.

Kirillov thus conforms to and deviates from Durkheim's definition. Durkheim states that the altruist "seeks to strip himself of his personal being in order to be engulfed in something which he regards as true essence" (SU, Bk 2, Ch4; 225). Through self-homicide, Kirillov "seeks to strip himself of his personal being in order to be engulfed in" the "true essence" of the Me-Me-Me that *is* his "personal being" (SU, Bk 2, Ch 4; 225). Durkheim could be analyzing Kirillov when he talks about situations "where the dignity of the person is the supreme end of conduct, where man is a God to mankind" (SU, Bk 3, Ch 3; 363). Durkheim says that in such situations, "the individual is readily inclined to consider the man in himself as a God and to regard himself as the object of his own cult" (SU, Bk 3, Ch 3; 363–64). Kirillov's bizarre anomic-egoistic-altruistic self-homicide whirls into a vicious tautological circle, one in which Kirillov makes himself into his cult and then sacrifices himself to the cult of self.

Durkheim's sociologically defined altruistic class has an affinity with two suicide types that Charles William Wahl defines psychologically. Wahl discusses the use of "suicide as an aid in coping with an overpowering thanatophobia" and "the phenomenon of infantile cosmic identification."[115] Wahl explains that those like Kirillov, who fear death, can seek to conquer it. They can do that by conceiving of death "not only as a surcease from pain . . . but also as an act whereby one acquires powers, qualities and advantages not possessed in the living state."[116] At times, the "expectant wish that death gives one immediate access to the Godhead" is also present.[117] Such an "expectant wish" becomes perspicuous when Kirillov egoistically, altruistically self-glorifies and equates his expiration with the acquisition of powers and "magical aspirations" of reigning as Godhead.[118] Such delusional ideation is evident when Kirillov divulges to Shatov those "seconds" in which he "suddenly feel[s] the presence of an eternal harmony" (D, Pt 3, Ch 5; 653), a description that recalls Prince Myshkin's fleeting pre-ictal vision.[119] For Kirillov, these rapturous seconds merge his being with "nature as a whole," and with "God, when he was creating the world" and shoot him "higher than love!" (D, Pt 3, Ch 5; 653). In these "five seconds" in which he "live[s] an entire lifetime," and for which he would "give [his] entire life," Kirillov divines a beatification of self that will overpower mortal fear, change his "earthly form," and engender a resurrection, a new life devoid of pain and childbirth, one in which "all will be like God's angels" (D, Pt 3, Ch 5; 653).[120]

Wahl explains that suicides stemming from an "infantile cosmic identification" tend to entail self-aggrandizement.[121] These individuals revert to a primitive stage of ego development, one in which they "cannot differentiate [themselves] from persons and objects in this world."[122] They believe that their "thoughts" and "body constitute all reality"; they thus buy into the bromide that "to kill oneself is to kill everything there is, the world and all other persons."[123] When this person self-kills, he or she "kills not one person but many," thereby committing "not only suicide but vicarious matricide, patricide, sororicide, fratricide, and even genocide."[124] While wedded to "solipsistic dereism," Kirillov believes that slaying fear, God, and himself will apotheosize the "I" into the man-God.[125] Not only will it authorize him to don the crown in lieu of Christ, but also gift him carte blanche to "bring about the end of the world" (D, Pt 2, Ch 1; 264). The irony here is that Kirillov's freaky mutation—that of anomic-egoistic-altruism—tends to invert poles, ablate the very free will that purports to propel it, and thus gestate the raw antithesis—that of unfree powerlessness.

The contradiction inherent in Kirillov's death could not be more graphic than at the time he is pressured to sign his confession. At that point, he enslaves free will and methodically abjures each of his own assertions. This scene is one that Yuri Corrigan aptly links to "a fully embodied depiction of demonic possession," where "the 'half person' latches onto the 'paper person' . . . and assumes control of his being" and this "two hollowed-out selves merge to form a collective personality."[126] Kirillov insists that he "didn't bind himself in any way," proclaims that he "won't write anything" and that "there will be no piece of paper" (D., Pt 2, Ch 6; 414: Pt 3, Ch 6; 678). Yet, Kirillov almost instantly does an about-face, submits to Pyotr, and tells him "dictate and I'll sign" (D, Pt 3, Ch 6; 686).[127] After Kirillov swears that he "won't say a word about Shatov" and refuses to "write that [he] killed Shatov," he nevertheless "signs that he killed Shatov" (D, Pt 3, Ch 6; 677–78, 686). Kirillov keeps touting "his own free will" in bold declarations to Pyotr: "[t]here was only my own free will, and now there's only my own free will" (D, Pt 2, Ch 6; 414). He triumphantly informs Pyotr that "all will has become mine . . . and having developed a belief in self-will, I will dare to proclaim self-will, in the fullest possible sense" (D, Pt 3, Ch 6; 683). But as it turns out, the only will that prevails is Pyotr's: Kirillov obsequiously obeys each of his tyrant's marching orders. Here we might borrow a snippet of John Keats's verse to tell this puny man-god that Pyotr "hath thee in thrall!"[128]

THE ANOMIC PERMISSIBILITY OF EVERYTHING IN *THE BROTHERS KARAMAZOV*

When the Dostoevskys returned to Russia in July 1871, there were positive events: part of *Demons* was published and their son, Fyodor, was born.[129] Their emergence from exile, however, was marred by the resurfacing of Dostoevsky's creditors. Seeing the threat to her family, Anna Grigorievna immediately took charge, secured the rights to publish her husband's works, and negotiated reasonable rates of repayment with creditors.[130]

Despite such financial struggles, Dostoevsky's reunions with friends, like Apollon Maikov and Nikolay Strakhov, revitalized him. He also forged a relationship with Vsevolod Solovyov, the son of the famous historian S. M. Solovyev. Vsevolod Solovyov encouraged Dostoevsky and became his staunch supporter. These later years also proved fruitful: *Demons* was published in 1871–1872, *The Adolescent* in 1875, and his successful mono-journal *A Writer's Diary* was launched in 1876. At the end of 1877, Dostoevsky, however, stopped writing the *Diary* to finish what would become his last novel. Shortly thereafter, the Dostoevskys' fourth child, Alexei, died before reaching the age of three.[131] Little wonder that Dostoevsky's "hero," whose name is Alyosha, and the tragic death of children figure into his final triumph, *The Brothers Karamazov* (1879–1880).[132] In the novel, not only does Ilyusha

Snegiryov succumb to consumption at a tender age, but a woman mourning the death of her three-year-old, Alexei, the last of her four children, seeks consolation from Elder Zosima.

The Brothers Karamazov, which began serializing in 1879, is his crowning achievement, in which he pursues the theme that he tackled in *Notes from Underground*: the conflict between reason and Christian faith. His preoccupation with the tension between reason and faith, however, germinated prior to *Notes from Underground*, but on a more subliminal level. While imprisoned in Omsk, Dostoevsky began to embrace the Christ of the Gospels and reject the ideology of the Petrashevsky Circle.[133] Other prison realizations and memories, recounted in *Notes from the House of the Dead*, also infiltrate his last novel. While in Omsk, Dostoevsky met D. I. Ilyinsky, who was convicted of parricide, "stripped of nobility and government service rank" and "sentenced to hard labor for twenty years."[134] This nobleman was adjudicated innocent after serving ten years. Dostoevsky's narrator, Goryanchikov, who "never notices any particular signs of cruelty" in Ilyinsky, suspects all along that he is not guilty and opines on the "full depth of tragedy . . . of a young life ruined by such a terrible accusation."[135] Ilyinsky's miscarried justice resurfaces in *The Brothers Karamazov* as the erroneous parricide conviction of Dmitri Fyodorovich Karamazov.[136]

Further, in his final novel, Dostoevsky delves into suicidal anomy more deeply than he had in any previous work. In Mitya's trial, the prosecutor Ippolit Kirillovich bemoans the rash of Russian suicides: "look at how our young men are shooting themselves—oh, without the least Hamletian question of 'what lies *beyond*,' . . . as if this matter of our spirit, and all that awaits us beyond the grave, had been scrapped long ago in them, buried and covered with dust" (BK, Bk. 12, Ch 6; 694).[137] Dostoevsky envisions the expulsion of faith and the supersessive installation of reason as cataclysmic because it goads people into self-annihilating, dilly-dallying with the devil, and doxogolizing "everything is permissible." Taking the permissibility of *everything* to its literal extreme can even condone cannibalism and as explored in this chapter's conclusion, *The Brothers Karamazov* hints at the possibility of pandemical anthropophagy.

Durkheim suggests that everything becomes permissible when individuals are stripped of the tempering "regulative force," which he denominates the "check-rein" (SU, Bk 2, Ch 5; 248, 258). Both Durkheim and Dostoevsky see the intact family unit as early on fostering the controls that repel the kind of execrable impulses churning within a character like Fyodor Pavlovich Karamazov. Familial bonds can even prevent vices from being generationally transmitted. In *The Brothers Karamazov*, the sons come from a ruptured family with an "evil buffoon" father and sadly, they evoke the infants that Rousseau discards in *Confessions* (BK, Bk 1, Ch

1; 8). In 1745, Rousseau met Therese Levasseur, a twenty-two or twenty three-year-old laundry maid, who became his lover and eventually, his wife. In his *Confessions*, Rousseau says that Therese bore him five children whom they instantly dumped in a foundling hospital. Rousseau rejoices in this by calling it "so good, so sensible, so legitimate."[138] Miller speaks of Dostoevsky's "life-long argument with Rousseau," and one such peeve was likely Rousseau's use of the foundling home as the depository for his unwanted offspring.[139]

In the early 1870s, Dostoevsky was stewing over the breakdown of the Russian family, and it is unremarkable that in sporadic invective aimed at Rousseau, Dostoevsky takes pokes at foundling homes. In *Demons*, for example, when the midwife Arina Prokhorovna comes to help Shatov's wife give birth to Stavrogin's baby, she offers to "send the baby to a foundling home" (D, Pt 3, Ch 5; 650). Shatov, soundly rejects this offer, and shouts, "[h]e *is* my son" and "will never leave me for any foundling home!" (D, Pt 3, Ch 5; 656).[140] In *The Brothers Karamazov*, Ivan's repulsive devil affiliates himself with the "foundling hospital," where he proudly goes for his smallpox inoculation (BK, Bk 11, Ch 9; 639).

When Dostoevsky returns to the topic of accidental families in *The Brothers Karamazov*, which he introduced earlier in *The Adolescent*, Fyodor's habit of forgetting about his offspring is comparable to Rousseau's and the devil's approach to child-rearing. In fact, Fyodor, who started his career as a "sponger," resembles the devil, who is also a "sponger," and as Ivan surmises, when men of this sort have children, "the children are always brought up somewhere far away, by some aunts" (BK, Bk. 11, Ch 9; 636). Fyodor, moreover, is not just a diabolical buffoon who demits his parental obligations. The narrator in *The Brothers Karamazov* calls him "worthless," "depraved," and "muddleheaded" and portrays him as impregnating his sphere with calamity (BK, Bk 1, Ch 1; 7).[141] Fyodor's children—Dmitry, Ivan, and Smerdyakov, who is rumored to be his illegitimate son, could in fact be Rousseau's discarded children all grown-up.[142] It should not astonish readers that Mitya plans suicide, Ivan considers suicide as a future option, and Smerdyakov goes through with it. Only one son, Alyosha, manages to secure the arterial nutrients that enable him to embrace life.

Mitya Plans It

In the novel, Mitya asks, "why should I go on living?" (BK, Bk 9, Ch 5; 478). He confesses that he "redeem[ed] the pawned pistols, to load them, and to put a bullet into my sconce at dawn" (BK, Bk 9, Ch 5; 478). As the forgotten child of Fyodor's tumultuous first marriage, Mitya has precise plans to dispose of himself. Joseph Sabbath's "concept of the expendable child,"

Howard Kushner's theory of "incomplete mourning" and Durkheim's anomic typology all shed light on the self-destructive impulses that bring Mitya to the brink of ruin.[143]

Expendability

Fyodor's first wife, Adelaida Ivanovna Miusov, belonged to a wealthy aristocratic family, and shortly after elopement, it became "clear that she felt only contempt for her husband and nothing more" (BK, Bk 1, Ch 1; 8). As a child, Mitya was deprived of any semblance of family, home life, or a robust collective, and thus lands in the situation that Durkheim sees as predisposing individuals to suicide. Early on, Mitya lived amidst "a very disorderly life, full of eternal scenes" (BK, Bk 1, Ch 1; 8). He possibly witnessed the "frequent fights" between his parents and knew that his mother, "endowed with remarkable physical strength," repeatedly beat his father (BK, Bk 1, Ch 1; 8–9). Internalizing this early turbulence, Mitya became volatile.

When Mitya reached the age of three, his mother ran off with a "destitute seminarian" and eventually perished in Petersburg (BK, Bk 1, Ch 1; 9). At that point, Mitya was left with a single parent, but as the narrator explains, Fyodor "totally and utterly abandoned his child . . . not out of malice towards him and out from any wounded matrimonial feelings, but simply because he totally forgot about him" (BK, Bk 1, Ch 2; 10). Because Fyodor set up "a regular harem in his house" and indulged in the "most unbridled drinking," Mitya was initially exposed to this "iniquitous den" (BK, Bk 1, Ch 1, 2; 9, 10). But the faithful family servant, Grigory, came to the rescue, took the toddler home, and cared for him. If this had not happened, Mitya might have been like a foundling with "no one to change [his] shirt" (BK, Bk 1, Ch 2; 10). After residing in the servants' cottage for nearly a year, Pyotr Alexandrovich Miusov, the cousin of Mitya's late mother, became Mitya's guardian. By then, Mitya was so forgotten that he is not even on his father's radar screen. The narrator hints at this while describing Fyodor's reaction to Miusov's arrival: he "looked for a while as if he had no idea what child it was all about, and was even surprised, as it were, to learn that he had a little son somewhere in the house" (BK, Bk 1, Ch 2; 11).[144]

As the narrator is quick to point out, Miusov is a problematic guardian: like Stepan Trofimovich, he is a "a liberal of the forties and fifties," and Miusov, estranged from Russia, is "a lifelong European" (BK, Bk 1, Ch 2; 10). Further, he name-drops social philosopher, Pierre-Joseph Proudhon, and anarchist, Bakunin, and is proud to have been in Paris during the February uprising of 1848. It should thus be instantly apparent to Dostoevsky's veteran readers that Mitya's accidental guardian embodies the trends and "isms" that Dostoevsky came to detest in later years and even blamed for the unraveling

Russian family. Moreover, right after being appointed guardian, Miusov did what readers might expect: he shirked his in *loco parentis* role, pawned Mitya off on one of his mother's cousins in Moscow, and then settled in Paris. Like Fyodor, "he, too, forgot about the child" (BK, Bk 1; Ch 2; 11).[145] When the Moscow lady died, Mitya was foisted on one of her daughters, and after that, was apparently re-homed a fourth time. His father's rejection and all the ensuing unsettling itinerance made him the self-destructive "expendable" child, susceptible to suicide.[146]

Sabbath explains that "[t]he expendable child refers to one who no longer can be tolerated or needed by his family."[147] He adds that "[o]nce this condition of becoming the expendable child in a family has developed, it is only a question of time until an episode of felt rejection sets off the suicide attempt."[148] In the novel, Mitya is inclined to be jealous, dreads rejection, and is "oppressed" by "all the ugliness and horror of his struggle with his own father" over Grushenka (BK, Bk 8, Ch 1; 365). Later, "the imminent return" of the "fatal man," who once abandoned Grushenka also, but only initially, pushes his rejection button (BK, Bk 8, Ch 1; 365).

On top of being a suicide-prone "expendable child," Mitya's youth resembles that of Nastasya Filippovna, who was similarly tossed from residence to residence. Like Nastasya Filippovna, Mitya illustrates Kushner's hypothesis about "incomplete mourning," which is caused by parental death or disappearance at a child's early age.[149] And like Nastasya Fillippovna's, Mitya's loss is redundant and aggravated. After all, he did not merely lose a parent, but he was essentially ejected like Rousseau's infants: his mother abandoned him almost *ab initio* and his father simply forgot about him. Subsequently, when Mitya was passed along, he reexperienced expendability and endured either death or abandonment by all parental figures. Drawing upon Durkheim and Freud, Kushner states that individuals with "unresolved grief" tend to harbor rage, crave revenge, lose control, and unleash destruction on others and themselves.[150] Mitya intermittently manifests these proclivities, which began with his "disorderly adolescence and youth" (BK, Bk 1, Ch 2; 11).

From the narrator, readers learn that young Mitya led a tempestuous life and squandered "a great deal of money" (BK, Bk 1, Ch 2; 11). When he confesses to Alyosha in the gazebo, Mitya calls himself "just a brute of an officer who drinks cognac and goes whoring," who can "sink into the deepest, the very deepest shame of depravity" (BK, Bk 3, Ch 3; 170). He talks about the "insects . . . to whom God gave sensuality" and equates himself with "that very insect" (BK, Bk 3, Ch 3; 108). He reminisces about his bacchanalian era of "throw[ing] fistfuls of money around" and savoring "music, noise, gypsy lanes, dark and remote little crannies, away from the main square" where "there lay the unexpected nuggets in the dirt" (BK, Bk 3, Ch 4; 108–9). Mitya thus confirms the narrator's account and provides specifics.

Due to unbridled spending, Mitya found himself in debt and for this, he blamed Fyodor. Mitya was the only one of Fyodor's sons who grew up believing that he would inherit property through his mother and would become financially independent. Before his coming of age, however, he received nothing and after that, Fyodor "fobbed him off with small sum, with short-term handouts" (BK, Bk 1, Ch 2; 12). When Mitya came to town to square his affairs with Fyodor, he realized that he had nothing and could not even get an accounting. He learned "that he had already received the whole value of his property in cash from Fyodor . . . and might even be in debt to him" (BK, Bk 1, Ch 2; 12). Mitya feels tricked, cheated, and loses "all reason" (BK, Bk 1, Ch 2; 12).

Mitya's relationship with Fyodor further deteriorates when his lascivious father plots to steal his paramour, Grushenka, by promising her 3,000 rubles if she comes to him in the night (BK, Bk 3, Ch 5; 120).[151] Durkheim says that a suicidal anomic will hurl frequently "threats and accusations against a particular person to whom the responsibility for the suicide's unhappiness is imputed" (SU, Bk 2, Ch 6; 284). In the throes of a toxic oedipal triangle, Mitya tells Alyosha that he wants to kill, and might not be able to resist killing, his father.[152] Without a "check-rein," Mitya jealously "seizes the old man by the two surviving wisps of hair on his temples . . . and smashes him against the floor" (BK, Bk 3, Ch 9; 139). After an encore of "kick[ing] the fallen man in the face two or three times with his heel," Mitya vows to return and in a letter, even scripts his plan to finish the job (BK, Bk 3, Ch 9; 139).[153]

Mitya's anomic fury is so acute that he does not just target Fyodor Pavlovich, but he also indiscriminately slugs anyone who is even remotely tied to his father. Mitya whacks Grigory, his once surrogate father, with a brass pestle. Similarly, Mitya seizes his father's agent, Nikolai Ilyich Snegiryov, by the beard in a tavern, drags him into the street, and beats him publicly—an act with fatal consequences for his humiliated victim's family.[154] Early on in the novel, Mitya is portrayed as volatile, callous toward others, and oblivious to the consequences of his impulsive actions.

Many suicide theorists build upon Freud's observation that "thoughts of suicide" are really "murderous impulses against other redirected upon [the self]."[155] For example, John T. Maltsberger equates "murderous rage" with "dangerous psychic pain."[156] He explains that "when murderous hate holds sway," individuals "are in danger of turning it against themselves, sometimes because their consciences will not tolerate such a feeling without passing a death sentence."[157] He adds that when such "individuals fear that they can no longer restrain themselves from murder, they commit suicide instead."[158] By the time Mitya enters the suicide zone, his "murderous rage" leaves him teetering on the precipice of rack and ruin. Shame, suicidal narcissism, and multitiered guilt congeal to intensify his self-annihilative state.

Shame, Suicidal Narcissism, and Guilt

Mitya's shame revolves around the 3,000 rubles that his fiancé, Katerina Ivanovna Verkhovtsev, entrusts to him to deliver to her half-sister, Agafya. Instead, Mitya uses the money to whisk Grushenka off to Mokroe, where they squander rubles in wild revelry, replete with partying gypsy women and champagne. Later, Mitya tells Katerina that he delivered the money and would bring her a receipt. Although Mitya fails to confess the whole truth to Alyosha, interrogators later squeeze out every grisly detail. Mitya finally confesses that when he first took Grushenka to Mokroe, he only "squandered half of that cursed three thousand" and hid the rest in a pouch on his breast "in place of an amulet" (BK, Bk 9, Ch 7; 490–1). For Mitya, the 1,500 rubles have dual import: they serve both as a premeditated stab at quasi-redemption and as a self-imposed hair shirt:

> All the while I carried that fifteen hundred sewn up on my chest, I kept saying to myself every day and every hour: "You are a thief, you are a thief!" And that's why I raged all month, that's why I fought in the tavern, that's why I beat my father; because I felt I was a thief! I could not bring myself, I did not dare to reveal anything about the fifteen hundred even to Alyosha, my brother: so much did I feel myself a scoundrel. (BK, Bk 9, Ch 7; 493)

In his last binge with Grushenka, matters go from bad to worse. Mitya tears open the amulet to use the remaining half and hurls the ragged sheath into the gutter. In doing so, Mitya forfeits both his mode of self-laceration and his last shred of potential relief from relentless throbs of shame. The prosecutor, however, hits a raw nerve when he asks Mitya why he did not just tell all to Katerina Ivanovna and then borrow more funds for his next romp with Grushenka. Here, Mitya divulges his deepest shame—namely that he had entertained that very option.[159] Wahl could be psychoanalyzing Mitya and his "amulet" when he explains that the "most painful" suicidal motive arises in individuals who seek to extinguish self-blame through "an act of self-punishment."[160] Mitya admits that he is intent on self-punishment, even if it spells his death. By "beating himself on the chest," precisely where the punitive purse dangles, he "concealed more than shame," he "concealed ruin and suicide" (BK, Bk 8, Ch 3; 388).

Contained in Mitya's "ruin" is what psychiatrist Elizabeth Kilpatrick diagnoses as suicidal narcissism.[161] She writes, "[w]hen we understand narcissism not as love of the self, but as love of the idealized image of self, we become aware of the quantity of self-hate and alienation which must be present."[162] For suicidally narcissistic individuals, "death is not the major purpose of the suicidal act."[163] Rather, the superego, which identifies itself with the good self, is convinced that it can purge the bad self only through self-homicide.

How do narcissistically suicidogenic people, like Mitya, manage to survive? Kilpatrick explains that because survival is so difficult, it can be ephemeral. Such individuals try to make do by "unconsciously erect[ing] an idealized image and its counterpart, a despised image," and the backbreaking task is to "ward off anxiety and self-contempt by keeping the two images separated."[164] This process hurts like hell, engenders quandaries, and as Mitya puts it, makes him feel that "all contradictions live together" inside his soul (BK, Bk 3, Ch 3; 108). He proclaims, "[i]t's even more fearful when someone who has the ideal of Sodom in his soul does not deny the ideal of Madonna either," and thus, his "heart burns with it, verily, verily burns" (BK, Bk 3, Ch 3; 108).

Throughout the novel, Mitya continually gyrates between his combatant selves, from Sodom to Madonna.[165] This comes across in his confession to Alyosha and in redundant oxymoronic self-portraits. The dilemma Mitya confesses to Alyosha reveals what Kilpatrick calls that internecine "battle between his loved self and his hated self."[166] While serving as a lieutenant in small town, Mitya learns that his colonel, Katerina's father, had appropriated government funds. He hints to his friend Agafya that he might be willing to rescue Katerina with money if she would come to him "secretly" (BK, Bk 3, Ch 4; 112). Mitya's conflict heightens when Katerina, "the beauty of beauties," appears in his room, prepared to sacrifice herself for her father (BK, Bk 3, Ch 4; 111).

In his idiosyncratic way, Mitya mentally tests his oppositional selves—first, the despised insect or merchant and later, the respectable nobleman. His first thought was a "Karamazov thought," that of a "bedbug and scoundrel" (BK, Bk 3, Ch 4; 113). Ablaze and "breathless" with an impulse to seduce her right then, he counters that with his idealized self's vow to propose marriage the next day (BK, Bk 3, Ch 4; 114). He then realizes, however, that if he were to offer Katerina his hand, she would refuse to see him. The thought infuriates him and his despised inner merchant rears his ugly face: he contemplates "pull[ing] some mean, piggish merchant's trick" and giving Katerina a "sneering look" (BK, Bk 3, Ch 4; 114). He envisions his cruel, sarcastic mouth spewing, "[b]ut four thousand is much too much! . . . it's too much money, miss to throw away on such trifles" (BK, Bk 3, Ch 4; 114). This fantasy so seduces him that he almost implements it. But his ideal asserts itself to keep him from "howling with remorse" (BK, Bk 3, Ch 4; 114).

After shoving aside his "bedbug" or "evil tarantula" self, his superego summons the paragon—that of the nobleman (BK, Bk 3, Ch 4; 113–14). Mitya has 6,000 rubles from his father as a final settlement. He "silently" extricates a 5,000 ruble bank note, "hand[s] it to [Katerina,] open[s] the door to the hall for her, and stepping back, bow[s] deeply to her, with a most respectful and heartfelt bow" (BK, Bk 3, Ch 4; 114). When Katerina reciprocates, bows with her "forehead to the ground" and exits, Mitya pulls his sword from its scabbard, kisses it, and replaces it (BK, Bk 3, Ch 4; 114).[167] This gesture has not only phallic implications, but also suggests that his better self has repressed and conquered its reviled libidinous nemesis.[168] Mitya's victory, however, is short-lived.

Even though the "respectful" bowing self prevails over the "tarantula" in that scuffle, Mitya's internal conflict perennates, becoming more acute after Mitya dissipates Katerina's rubles (BK, Bk 3, Ch 4; 114). Mitya expresses his lancinating conflict through a series of oxymoronic self-portraits: "I have base desires and love baseness" but "I'm not dishonorable," "I am a man of base desire, I am honest" (BK, Bk 3, Ch 4; 109). This paradoxical refrain chimes again when Mitya responds to interrogation: "It's a noble man you are speaking with, . . . a man who has done a world of mean things, but who always was and remained a most noble person" (BK, Bk 9, Ch 3; 462). He elaborates that he has thirsted for nobility all his life, while "doing only dirty things" (BK, Bk 9, Ch 3; 462).[169] Mitya's antipodal selves bear kinship with Ivan's inner contention between conscience and the devil. Mitya declares that "[h]ere the devil is struggling with God and the battlefield is the human heart" (BK, Bk 3, Ch 3; 108). He tells Alyosha that he is "base and vile," and yet beneficent because he yearns to "kiss the hem of that garden in which my God is clothed" (BK, Bk 3, Ch 3; 107). His despicable self "follow[s] the devil," while his beloved self reaches for God and prays "I am also your son, Lord, and I love you" (BK, Bk 3, Ch 3; 107).

On top of shame and suicidal narcissism, there are three prongs of guilt simultaneously stabbing Mitya's fragile psyche. In addition to reviling himself for appropriating Katya's rubles, he is guilty of wanting his father dead. Menninger states that such guilt is potentially lethal because "in the unconscious a wish to destroy is quite equivalent to the actual destruction with regard to exposing the ego to punishment."[170] Menninger provides two examples: the Catholic Church, which demands that even thoughts of evil be confessed, and Dostoevsky's Mitya, who did not kill his father, yet seems "to demand punishment for himself as if he had done so."[171] Unlike his half-brother Ivan, Mitya can distinguish between wishing and doing. Despite that, he craves genuine reprisal for parricidal desire. He tells his interrogators, "Yes, unfortunately I wanted to kill him, wanted to many times . . . unfortunately, unfortunately!" (BK, Bk 9, Ch 3; 460–61). By admitting that "inside, in the bottom of [his] heart, [he] is guilty," he pleads for castigation (BK, Bk 9, Ch 3; 460).[172]

Wahl discusses the effort "to expiate the fantasied act of murder (death wishes) by operation of talion law," which is the most painful suicidal motive.[173] Mitya not only suffers from his patricidal wish, he even augments his guilt by furiously beating Fyodor, threatening to murder him, and writing an inculpatory note. Mitya's vicious attack on Grigory, the servant who was like a father to him, can be seen as an attempted patricide, which sharpens his guilt and makes him shout "crush me, punish me, decide my fate" (BK, Bk 9, Ch 3; 458). Mitya's agglomerated guilt thus turns his psychic pouch into a virtual powder keg. As Kilpatrick might explain it, Mitya, with his guilt and suicidal narcissism, desperately longs to install the ideal. This, however, can only be effectuated through slaughtering the reviled counterpart, who keeps committing atrocities. Mitya is not merely wincing from what Wahl calls "the most painful suicidal motive," or what Menninger labels the "law of conscience."[174] He is battered by sheer pre-suicidal excruciation.

Ivan Considers It

While Mitya plans suicide, Ivan considers it as a future option. Like other Dostoevsky characters, Ivan conflates "smash[ing] the cup [of life] on the floor" with leaving for America (BK, Bk 5, Ch 5; 263). Ivan tells Alyosha that "by the age of thirty, I will probably drop the cup, even if I haven't emptied it, and walk away," but promises that before he kills himself, he will "come to talk things over . . . once more . . . even from America" (BK, Bk 5, Ch 3; 230: Ch 5; 264). Ivan foretokens Freud because in him, Eros and Thanatos are relentlessly sparring.[175] In conversation with Alyosha, Ivan celebrates the life force: "the sticky little leaves that come out in the spring are dear to me, the blue sky is dear to me, some people are dear to me . . . some human deeds are dear to me" (BK, Bk 5, Ch 3; 230). Ivan, who professes to put logic on a pedestal, thus praises life as a "thing you love not with your mind, not with logic, but with your insides, your guts, you love your first young strength" (BK, Bk 5, Ch 3; 230). Nonetheless, Ivan hears the call of Freud's death drive, "the task of which is to lead organic matter back into the inorganic state."[176]

It is not surprising that Ivan experiences suicidal ideation. With a childhood not so different from Mitya's, Ivan likewise suffers from "incomplete mourning," "expendable-child" syndrome, "suicidal narcissism" and anomy.[177] But because Ivan is blessed with the intervention of Yefim Petrovich Polenov, he is somewhat less volatile and impulsive than his half-brother.

The Hijacked Childhood Plus an Intervention

Ivan's possible knowledge of his mother's attempted suicide may have put him at greater risk of following in her footsteps.[178] His mother, Sofia Ivanovna, grew up as the ward of a rich but abusive widow. No longer able to endure her guardian's "willfulness and eternal nagging," she tried to hang herself (BK, Bk 1, Ch 3; 13).

Saved from the noose, she eloped with Fyodor Pavlovich because "she would rather drown herself than stay with her benefactress" (BK, Bk 1, Ch 3; 13). Because Sofia was meek and without resources and because Fyodor felt that he had rescued her, he treated her abominably. He "trampled with both feet on the ordinary decencies of marriage, let "[l]oose women . . . gather in the house right in front of his wife" and even held "orgies" (BK, Bk 1, Ch 3; 13). Later, miserable Sofia deteriorated into a *klikusha* with "terrible hysterical fits" (BK, Bk 1, Ch 3; 13).[179] Nonetheless, in her first year of marriage, she gave birth to Ivan, three years later to Alyosha, and four years after that, she died. Like Mitya, Ivan was "totally forgotten and forsaken" and ended up living in the servants' quarters with Grigory and Marfa, the virtual foundling home. Like Mitya, Ivan experienced a sense of expendability at an early age. As with his half-brother, Ivan's sense of expendability was signed, sealed, and delivered. Ivan was "totally forgotten and forsaken" and landed in the virtual foundling home, the Grigory cottage (BK, Bk 1, Ch 3; 14).

Like Mitya, Ivan did not have much time to adjust to Grigory and his wife, Marfa, because only three months later, his mother's benefactress showed up, uprooted him from reconstituted soil, and repotted him in her home. Shortly after that, the old woman died and in Mitya-like déjà vu, Ivan was passed along. But this time, Ivan got the windfall that delivered the little nutrient that Mitya never received. In her will, the old woman left Ivan a thousand rubles for his education and her heir, Yefim Petrovich, "a most generous and humane man," educated the boy at his own expense and wisely invested the legacy for Ivan's benefit (BK, Bk 1, Ch 3; 15).

By the time Yefim Petrovich interceded, however, Ivan's sense of expendability, "unresolved grief," and "suicidal narcissism," derived from his blighted earlier years, rankled him.[180] Shneidman discusses victims of a "vandalized childhood," who have been "psychologically mugged or sacked," and have had "psychological needs . . . trampled on and frustrated by malicious, preoccupied, or obtuse adults."[181] He states, "I tend to believe that, at rock bottom, the pains that drive suicide relate primarily not to the precipitous absence of equanimity or happiness in adulthood, but to the haunting losses of childhood's special joys."[182] This pertains not just to Mitya, but also to Ivan, who is "gloomy and withdrawn" (BK, Bk 1, Ch 3; 15). Feeling the effects of the "vandalized childhood," Ivan "already perceived by the age of ten that he was indeed living in someone else's family and on someone else's charity" and that his "father was such that it was a shame to speak of him" (BK, Bk 1, Ch 3; 15).

The Beast Within

Like Mitya, Ivan internalizes a "despised" self-image, "which contains all his undesirable qualities and . . . fills him with self-contempt when not repressed."[183] His stress, however, is accentuated by the fact that he recoils from his idealized self as well. His ugly component touts the permissibility of everything and urges the purgation of conscience. His better self's conscience, however, directs him to repudiate an existence in which everything is permissible. Ivan's diatribe on theodicy, in which he inveighs against Christianity and faith in a God who lets innocent children suffer, divulges not only the "beast" repressively caged in Ivan's core, but also his agonizing psychic melee.

In his lecture, Ivan verbally lacerates Alyosha by vividly describing inexplicable acts of torture that adults inflict on children.[184] During this, he nonetheless insists that the perpetrators are, in all other respects, normal, humane, and not infrequently exceptional, maintaining that "these same torturers look upon all other examples of humankind even mildly and benevolently, being educated and humane Europeans, but they have a great love of torturing children" (BK, Bk 5, Ch 4; 241). Ivan postulates that "this peculiar quality exists in much of mankind—this love of torturing children, but only children," and that "[t]here is, of course, a beast hidden in every man, a beast of rage, a beast of sensual inflammability at the cries of the tormented victim, an unrestrained beast let off the chain" (BK, Bk 5, Ch 4; 241–42). He thereby acknowledges that the "beast" is thrashing about not only "in every man," but inside himself.[185]

Significantly, Ivan's discourses on neighbors and humanity reflect his own self-hatred. Ivan admits that he "never could understand how it's possible to love one's neighbors" (BK, Bk 5, Ch 4; 236). He too is a neighbor and is thus presumptively included in the caste that he deems "disgusting" and unworthy of love (BK, Bk 5, Ch 4; 236–37). Believing that "man has . . . created [the devil] in his own image and likeness," Ivan projects his negative self-image outward and accuses humankind of doing the same (BK, Bk 5, Ch 4; 239). But this too abrades his better self. In the midst of the tirade, Alyosha interrupts to tell Ivan, "You have a strange look as you speak . . . as if you were in some kind of madness" (BK, Bk 5, Ch 4; 238). What is sickening Ivan is not that cruel, godless, world, in which children are forced to suffer, but rather his inkling that if God does not exist, then all is permissible, and that all sweeps him into faithless darkness.

Self-disdain tied to misanthropy belies not just Ivan's lectures, but also is evident in his conduct. For instance, his hidden "beast of rage" is "let off the chain" right before his last meeting with Smerdyakov (BK, Bk 5, Ch 4; 241–42). On the way, a drunken peasant lurches into Ivan. He shoves him away and feels "an intense hatred for him . . . an irresistible desire to bring his fist down on him"(BK, Bk 11, Ch 8; 621). When the "little peasant, staggering badly, suddenly lurche[s] full force into Ivan[, t]he latter furiously shove[s] him away" (BK, Bk 11, Ch 8; 621). Beholding the "motionless, unconscious" peasant on the "frozen ground," Ivan conjectures that "[h]e'll freeze" to death (BK, Bk 11, Ch 8; 621). Yet, Ivan leaves him lying there. Although later

Ivan's contrite self takes pains to make amends to the victim, "self-hate and hostility" nevertheless convolves in his soul.[186] This comes across when he affixes the Karamazovian adjective to "baseness," and "carnivorous" instincts and in doing so, proclaims truant restraint to be his clan's signature trait (BK, Bk 5, Ch 5; 263). Victor Terras notes that "[o]n the psychological level, Ivan will readily believe that his brother Dmitry is a scoundrel and murderer because deep inside he knows that he himself is."[187] Ivan recognizes his kinship not only with Mitya, but with his abhorred non-father-father.

Although Ivan and Mitya are both full of self-loathing, their coping mechanisms differ considerably. Mitya buries his hijacked childhood and sense of expendability in dissolute sensuality. Ivan, however, secures a different anesthetic for his "psychache."[188] Because Ivan has an "unusual and brilliant aptitude for learning," he finishes school, enters university, and publishes his writings, which highlight his "practical and intellectual superiority" (BK, Bk 1, Ch 3; 15). But both divergent routes—the sensuous and the intellectual—lead these Karamazovs to consider "America," as their destination.[189] After his conviction, Mitya plans to seek exile in America while Ivan contemplates checking out, which "perhaps" he will do from America.

Spiritual Crisis

The irresolute battle between immorality and conscience triggers a spiritual conflict, which culminates in Ivan's psychotic break. Terras explains that in *The Brothers Karamazov*, Dostoevsky's "novelistic strategy is to show some men who believe in God and in immortality; and who are willing to accept the teaching of Christ; and some other men who reject God's world, Christ, and immortality, and who would rather create a world based on human reason."[190] Ivan's problem, however, is not that he is one or the other, but that he embodies both believer and denier, which causes an agonizing cognitive dissonance. Part of Ivan wants to reason his way to a world without God, but he cannot. This brings pain and guilt. Part of Ivan yearns to take that leap into faith in God, but he cannot. This brings more pain, more guilt.

Bishop Tikhon from *Demons*, Durkheim, and Ivan's Grand Inquisitor, but each in his own way shed light on Ivan's "lukewarm," spiritual, and sociological besetment. In *Demons*, Tikhon tells Stavrogin, "[t]he complete atheist stands on the next-to-last highest rung leading to the fullest and most complete faith (he may take that step, or he may not), but the indifferent man has no faith at all, except an ugly fear" (D, At Tik 1; 758–59). Tikhon recites the passage from Revelation, "you are neither cold or hot! Would that you were cold or hot! So, because you are lukewarm, and neither cold nor hot, I will spue you out of my mouth" (D, At Tik 1; 759).[191] Ivan is neither atheist nor believer, and like the Laodicean water in Revelation, he is neither cold nor hot and thus is spiritually unpotable.[192] By being betwixt and between, he is like the secularly indifferent man, consumed by "ugly fear" (D, At Tik 1; 759).

Although Durkheim chose secularism for himself, he would nevertheless acquiesce in Tikhon's perspective, but do so in his sociological vernacular. Durkheim saw faith as a social institution which creates collective consciousness. Like Dostoevsky, Durkheim felt that over time, religion was losing its sway. Faith was being not only eclipsed by science and reason, but also replaced by a cult of individualism. Durkheim held that faith is salvific for the very reason that it is a "society . . . capable of supporting a sufficiently intense life," supplying a "collective credo," and offering a "shared moral and social code" (SU, Bk 2, Ch 2; 159, 170).

Ironically, the Grand Inquisitor also espouses this Durkheimian tenet while implicitly diagnosing Ivan's illness:

> For the care of these pitiful creatures is not just to find something before which I or some other man can bow down, but to find something that everyone else will also believe in and bow down to, for it must needs be *all together*. And this need for *communality* of worship is the chief torment of each man individually, and of mankind as a whole, from the beginning of the ages. (BK, Bk 5, Ch 5; 254) (emphasis in original)

Like religion, atheism has an "all together" of its own. It can supply an ideology that its members "will also believe in" and quench that thirst for "*communality*" (BK, Bk 5, Ch 5; 254). But "lukewarm" Ivan neither taps into the "moral and social code" of faith nor can he gulp the "collective credo" of atheism (SU, Bk 2, Ch 2, 159, 170). As such he has no "*all together*" with either the believers or the nonbelievers. When interpreting "lukewarm" in Revelation, Samuel Wills explains that "[t]he delusions of the devil are cherished in preference to the wholesome truths of Divine Revelation."[193] Tikhon, Durkheim, and Ivan's Grand Inquisitor might agree and hold that lukewarmth is a devilish temperature, which can scald or glaciate a soul more than fire and ice.

Ivan's article on the ecclesiastical courts, his Euclidean diatribe, his prose-poem about the Grand Inquisitor, and his rendezvous with the devil expose that sulfurous state, in which Ivan vacillates between reason and faith, ponders self-annihilation, and eventually implodes. Ivan's article addresses the debate over whether ecclesiastical courts should be subordinate to the state or whether state courts should be absorbed by ecclesiastical tribunals that would decide disputes according to Christ's law. Ivan, however, asserts both opposing positions and thus, each party claims him as its advocate. It might be tempting to dismiss his two-faced strategy as youthful cowardice or a stab at diplomatic appeasement of all. But really what belies the lukewarm equivocation is his self-polemic, which compels him to sway from one pole to another.

There is a connection between the Euclidean speech and Ivan's gait. Alyosha observes that "Ivan somehow sway[s] as he walks," which matches his ratiocination (BK, Bk 5, Ch 5; 264). While speaking to Alyosha in the tavern, Ivan sways between two equations: non-Euclidean geometry, which accounts for God's justice, and Euclidean geometry, which accounts for earthly justice. Insisting that his is a "Euclidean, an earthly mind, and . . . [that] it is not for us to resolve things that are not of this world," Ivan beseeches Alyosha to "never think about . . . whether God exists or not" (BK, Bk 5, Ch 3; 235). Rebutting himself, Ivan implicitly shifts in the opposite, non-Euclidean direction. As Miller points out, Ivan, by "both introduc[ing] and grant[ing] the existence of non-Euclidean geometry as well as of God's justice . . . creates the equation only to show that it cannot encompass his whole reality."[194] Furthermore, Ivan inveterately contemplates "things that are not of this world" and fixates on the very question he deems taboo—"whether God exists or not" (BK, Bk 5, Ch 3; 235). Consequently, Ivan swings back and forth from godless logic to a cogitable God.

In an often-quoted letter, Dostoevsky writes, "if someone proved to me that Christ were outside the truth and it *really* were that the truth lay outside Christ, I would prefer to remain with Christ rather than with the truth."[195] Ivan's supposed allegiance to his own stubborn free will alludes to Dostoevsky's vow of fidelity to Christ, but it is inside out and backwards. When Ivan proclaims "[l]et the parallel lines even meet before my own eyes . . . I shall look and say, yes, they meet and still I will not accept it" (BK, Bk 5, Ch 3; 236), he is adhering to the apothegm that nonacceptance of divine justice is his right, his choice. He boasts that through sheer resolve, he can refuse to "accept" a divine truth, even one that materializes before his very eyes. But while oscillating from his decision to his dissent, Ivan divulges nothing but mistrust of his own deities—free will, reason, and earthly justice.

Ivan's prose-poem about the Grand Inquisitor's encounter with Jesus in the sixteenth century likewise illuminates his inner discord. Dostoevsky, who despised Catholics (especially Jesuits), made Ivan's Inquisitor a Jesuit.[196] In doing so, Dostoevsky intended his readers to dissect the Inquisitor's rhetoric and see his project as baneful. In the prose-poem, Ivan's Inquisitor reproaches Jesus for returning to earth to unravel what Roman Catholics have built over the last millennium and a half. As the prose-poem progresses, Ivan and Inquisitor merge as do Alyosha and Jesus. Like the Inquisitor, Ivan does all the talking, while like the prose-poem's Jesus, Alyosha listens silently. More expansively, the Inquisitor vocalizes what is raging within Ivan's soul—his doubts, self-disgust, and spiritual anguish.

The Inquisitor offers his version of New Testament events from the gospels of Matthew and John, in which the devil approaches Jesus with three temptations. The Inquisitor informs Jesus that had he taken the devil's offerings, he "would have furnished all that man seeks on earth, this is: someone to bow down to, someone to take over his conscience, and a means for uniting everyone at last into a common, concordant, and incontestable anthill" (BK, Bk 5, Ch 5; 257). He explains that there is "nothing more seductive for man than the freedom of his conscience, but there is nothing more tormenting either" (BK, Bk. 5, Ch 5; 254). He berates Jesus: "[i]nstead of taking over men's freedom you increased it and forever burdened the kingdom" (BK, Bk 5, Ch 5; 255).

Seeking to correct Christ's work by extracting the source of human misery—the burden of free will—the Inquisitor unveils his venture. He brags that in his kingdom, the masses will be persuaded that "they will only become free when they resign their freedom to us, and submit to us" and thus, everyone will become chattel (BK, Bk 5, Ch 5; 258). In the process, some will "exterminate" themselves and each other, while others will "crawl" to his feet and "cling in fear, like chicks to a hen" (BK, Bk 5, Ch 5; 258–59). Everything will be permitted, or as the Inquisitor trumpets, "we will allow them to sin" and "they will love us like children for allowing them to sin" (BK, Bk 5, Ch 5; 259). The Inquisitor claims that "[w]e will tell them that every sin will be redeemed if it is committed with our permission . . . and as for punishment for these sins, very well, we take it upon ourselves" (BK, Bk 5, Ch 5; 259). What the Inquisitor offers is the placation of Ivan's inner combatants, the one extoling "anything goes" and the other lionizing conscience.

Alyosha recoils in horror at the Ivan-Inquisitor empire, in which Christ's burden of free will is vanquished: "[i]t's Rome, and not even the whole of Rome, that isn't true—they're the worst of Catholicism, the Inquisitors, the Jesuits!" (BK, Bk 5, Ch 5; 260). Alyosha clamors, it is "simply a Roman army, for a future universal earthly kingdom, with the emperor—the pontiff of Rome at their head" (BK, Bk 5, Ch 5; 260). He detects "the lust for power, for filthy earthly lucre, enslavement . . . a sort of future serfdom with them as the landowners" and fears the worst, that "[m]aybe they don't even believe in God" (BK, Bk 5, Ch 5; 260). But Alyosha realizes that the Inquisitor's rebarbative gospel effectually flip flops into an affirmation of Jesus and tells his brother, "[y]our poem praises Jesus, it doesn't revile him . . . as you meant to" (BK, Bk 5, Ch 5; 260). Here Alyosha implies that Ivan's godless field is potentially fertile, that it has a seed of faith planted on it. When earlier Ivan smiles "like a meek little boy" and tells Alyosha, "perhaps I want to be healed by you," he imparts that potentiality as well (BK, Bk 5, Ch 3; 236).

Faith as the potential also comes across in the parallel between the prose-poem's Christ and Alyosha. At the prose-poem's denouement, Ivan's Christ senses that the Inquisitor will "hold to his former idea," yet he "approaches the old man in silence and gently kisses him on his bloodless, ninety-year-old lips" (BK, Bk 5, Ch 5; 262). Significantly that "kiss burns in [the] Inquisitor's heart" (BK, Bk 5, Ch 5; 262). Before the brothers part, however, there is an ectype: Alyosha "st[ands] up, [goes] over to [Ivan] in silence to gently kiss him on the lips" (BK, Bk 5, Ch 5; 263). After Ivan delightedly accuses his brother of "literary theft," Dostoevsky leaves readers with the impression that Alyosha's kiss is "burning" in Ivan's heart as well.[197]

Although Jesus's gentle love for the Inquisitor might augur prospective redemption for Ivan, the dialogue between the fictive and real kiss suggests that nothing will sprout without going through a major storm. Alyosha sees "hell in [Ivan's] heart and in [his] head," and reminds his brother of the things he cherishes, and asks, "[h]ow will you live, what will you love them with?" (BK, Bk 5, Ch 5; 263). With a "cold smirk," one suggestive of Smerdyakov's countenance, Ivan hails "Karamazov baseness," "drown[ing] in depravity" and "stifl[ing] his soul with corruption" (BK, Bk 5, Ch 5; 263). Here immorality, self-homicide, and the devil syndicate. Ivan refuses to "renounce" his Inquisitor's mantra, "everything is permitted," broods over possible suicide, and leans to the left.

In *The Brothers Karamazov* and elsewhere, left is the direction linked to the devil and to the renunciation of life. In *Crime and Punishment*, Svidrigailov, commands Raskolnikov, "You go right and I'll go left."[198] Through this, Svidrigailov succinctly maps out the ineluctable itinerary that starts with godless amorality and ends in self-annihilation. In *The Brothers Karamazov*, Ivan also tells Alyosha, "you go right, I'll go left" (BK, Bk 5, Ch 5; 264). In doing so, Ivan puts himself on that leftish trajectory, which conjures up the devil and could potentially take him to Svidrigailov's "America," which equates with a bullet in the head. A "sad and sorrowful" Alyosha notices that Ivan's "right shoulder, seen from behind, appear[s] lower than his left" (BK, Bk 5, Ch 5; 264). With its effect of elevating his left side, Ivan's posture foreshadows his rendezvous with the devil and his alliance with Smerdyakov, who also favors the left.[199]

Devilish Paleologic

The suicide theorists Shneidman and Farberow state the obvious, that "not all suicides are psychotic," but they also hold that suicide, hallucinations, and psychosis can colligate.[200] When the devil visits, Ivan is on the "verge of brain fever," struggling to stave off the "madhouse" and exhibiting signs of schizophrenia (BK, Bk 11, Ch 9; 634).[201] In an ambiguous scene evocative of *The Double*, Ivan tackles the mind-boggler: does the devil objectively exist?[202] Is he a hallucination? Is he Ivan himself? While Dostoevsky does not furnish pat answers, the devil gives readers another glimpse at Ivan's battlefield. His real, but hallucinatory, devil exposes the rivalry between Ivan's conscience and the rational convictions that incite insurrections against God and Christ.

Suicide theorists, Maltsberger and Buie, discuss hallucinations in suicidal individuals and the "shift between externalization to internalization."[203] While fending off madness, the psychotic seeks to "move [the hallucination] inside the head" so that it "is experienced not so much as an alien at all, but as one part of the self addressing the other."[204] Ivan's encounter with the devil follows this pattern. Ivan strives to internalize the hallucination by persuading himself that the devil *is* himself: he tells himself, the devil is "the embodiment of myself, but of just one side of me . . . of my thoughts and feelings, but only the most loathsome and stupid of them" (BK, Bk 11, Ch 9; 637). In his psychosis, Ivan attempts to establish his synonymy with the devil by unmasking his visitor as a plagiarist, incapable of "telling [him] anything new" (BK, Bk 11, Ch 9; 638).

In straining to make that shift from external to internal, Ivan exhibits what Shneidman and Farberow call "the deductive logic implicit in schizophrenic thinking."[205] In their article, they borrow Silvano Arieti's concept of "paleologic," which is as follows: "*Whereas the normal person accepts identity only upon the basis of identical subjects, the paleologician accepts identity based upon identical predicates.*"[206] Arieti gives an example of a psychotic patient whose paleologic thinking leads her to believe that she is the Virgin Mary in the following manner: the "Virgin Mary was a virgin; I am a virgin; therefore, I am the Virgin Mary."[207] Arieti explains that because this paleologician so "needs to believe that she is the Virgin Mary," the need "will arouse additional anxiety if it is not satisfied."[208] Ivan's paleologic thinking is analogous: the devil is loathsome; Ivan is loathsome; therefore, Ivan is the devil.

Initially, the devil corroborates Ivan's paleologic by sating that desperate need to believe that he and the devil are one. The devil assists by iterating his host's "Euclidean geometry of earthy justice" and by assuring him that he is Ivan, "only with a different mug" (BK, Bk 11, Ch 9; 638). But the merciless devil does not stop there. Like the narrator in *The Double*, the devil repeatedly retracts what he puts out there, piques anxiety, and deflects Ivan's paleologic. For example, when the devil parodies a well-worn aphorism from Terence that Ivan had never considered, Ivan, for at least a nanosecond, sees the devil as an ontological reality. The devil's methodology, one of redundant giveth and taketh away, duplicates Ivan's idiosyncratic vacillations between belief and disbelief. In fact, Ivan accuses the devil of doing just that: "[y]our goal is precisely to convince me that you are in yourself and are not my nightmare, and so now you yourself assert that you're a dream" (BK, Bk 11, Ch 9; 639).

When Ivan hits his visitor with the ultimate question—"[i]s there a God or not"—the devil, as noncommittal as his host, replies, "I just don't know" (BK, Bk 11, Ch 9; 642). Hearing himself parroted, Ivan asks, "[y]ou don't know, yet you see God?" (BK, Bk 11, Ch 9; 642). These words, of course, allude to Ivan's earlier assertion that, through sheer will, he can disavow non-Euclidean justice, even when it is proven right before his very eyes. This hurls Ivan back to his paleologic: [n]o, you are not in yourself, you are *me*, *me* and nothing else" (BK, Bk 11, Ch 9; 642). Not surprisingly, the devil has another trick up his sleeve to nudge Ivan in the opposite direction, establish his own existence, defeat Euclidean logic, and agitate. The devil next mesmerizes Ivan with a non-Euclidean parable replete with miracles and paradise.

The story is one Ivan created when he was seventeen years old. It portrays a man, like adult Ivan, who is a doubting "thinker . . . here on earth, who 'rejected all—laws, conscience, faith' and above all, the future life" (BK, Bk 11, Ch 9; 643). Upon death, this rebel is "sentenced to walk in darkness a quadrillion kilometers . . . and once he finishe[s] that quadrillion, the doors of paradise [will] be opened to him and he [will] be forgiven everything" (BK, Bk 11, Ch 9; 643). The rebel initially refuses, but after lying on the road for nearly a thousand years, he rises and "start[s] walking" (BK, Bk 11, Ch 9; 644). The tale ends with the protagonist in paradise, but "before he had been there two seconds," he has the revelation: "for those two seconds it would be worth walking not just a quadrillion kilometers, but a quadrillion quadrillion, even raised to the quadrillionth power" (BK, Bk 11, Ch 9; 644).

The parable has a twofold impact: Ivan's sudden recollection that the story originates with him (and not the devil) substantiates his paleological deduction that the devil is Ivan himself. But it also rouses Ivan's dormant faith. Significantly, the devil gets right to the nitty gritty when he tells Ivan, "hesitation, anxiety, the struggle between belief and disbelief—all that is sometimes such a torment for a conscientious man like yourself" (BK, Bk 11, Ch 9; 645). Then the devil ballyhoos his *modus operandi*: "I'm leading you alternatively between belief and disbelief" so that "when you've completely lost faith in me, then you'll immediately start convincing me to my face that I am not a dream but a reality" (BK, Bk 11, Ch 9; 645). After noting his host's vertiginous waggle from belief to disbelief, the devil tells Ivan that "[h]e will sow just a tiny seed of faith in [him], and from it an oak will grow" (BK, Bk 11, Ch 9; 645). The devil predicts that Ivan, who "secretly . . . want[s salvation] very, ver-ry much . . . will drag [himself] to the desert to seek it" thereby alluding to the grand Inquisitor, another Ivan creation (BK, Bk 11, Ch 9; 645).

Before this visit, Ivan had a handle on reality. Even with his rebellion, scorn of God's justice, and atheistic protestations, Ivan had a better self and moral compass pushing back. Now, confounded by the dualistic devil, who claims to be "the only man in all of nature who loves the truth and sincerely desires good," who himself dreams of reconciliation with God and of walking the "quadrillion," Ivan experiences an "unbearable," "agonizing," "throbbing in [his] brain" (BK, Bk 11, Ch 9; 647–48). The devil relentlessly pushes Ivan toward a mental crisis by parroting his vacillations: the devil prays for reunification with good and God and then in words reminiscent of suicidal Kirillov, he confoundingly lauds the "man-god" (BK, Bk 11, Ch 9; 648). As his grand finale, the devil starts droning the Karamazovian theme song—"everything is permitted" (BK, Bk 11, Ch 9; 648). Like Luther with his "inkstand," fragmentized Ivan hurls (or might not hurl) a glass at his guest.[209]

When Alyosha knocks, things fracture further. Now apoplectically ill, Ivan feels as if his "legs and arms" are bound (BK, Bk 11, Ch 9; 650).[210] He is bewildered by the room "in which the glass he had just thrown at his visitor [stands] before him on the table" and in which there is an empty sofa without a visitor (BK, Bk 11, Ch 9; 650). The context conveys that what transpired (and what readers witnessed) was hallucination. But even though the evidence preponderates, Ivan rails against it: "That was no dream! No. I swear it was not dream, it all just happened" (BK, Bk 11, Ch 9; 650).[211] At this point, Ivan has lost the ability to discern a line between reality and fantasy, between external and internal domains. When Ivan tells Alyosha about his meeting with the devil, he reverts to his symptomatic waffling, insisting that "it was not a dream!" that "he was here, sitting here, on that sofa" (BK, Bk 11, Ch 9; 652). From there, he interjects his paleologic, "*he*—is me, Alyosha, me myself. All that's low, all that's mean and contemptible in me!" (BK, Bk 11, Ch 10; 652).

Although Alyosha had come to tell Ivan that Smerdyakov hanged himself, Ivan responds by saying he already knew it. Smerdyakov now sits in Ivan's hebephrenic psyche and embodies a self-destructive option. It is here that Smerdyakov becomes not just a topic of conversation, but also the cacodemon, who is figuratively knocking on the door. Will Ivan open that door? Smerdyakov's death blends with the sedative that the devil offered Ivan (BK, Bk 11, Ch 9; 650). The devil told Ivan that "it's better to hang oneself" than to suffer such "torment" (BK, Bk 11, Ch 9; 645).[212] Alyosha foresees that "with Smerdyakov dead, no one will believe Ivan's testimony, but he will go and testify" (BK, Bk. 11, Ch 10; 655). Alyosha also realizes that his brother is still locked in battle: "God, in whom [Ivan does] not want to believe, and his truth [are] overcoming his heart, which still [does] not want to submit" (BK, Bk 11, Ch 10; 655). While Alyosha hopes that "God will win" and that his brother "will rise into the light of truth," he nevertheless can fathom Ivan "perish[ing] in hatred" and "taking revenge on himself" (BK, Bk 11, Ch 10; 655).

When Ivan comes to testify at Mitya's trial, it is evident that Ivan has not rejected self-homicide as an option: the narrator observes that Ivan looks as though he is "gloomily pondering something" and that his face "produced a morbid impression, at least on me" as it had something in it "resembling the face of a dying man" (BK, Bk 12, Ch 5; 684). With respect to Ivan, the novel leaves readers with irresolution: will Ivan veer to the left? Will he grab the noose and paleologically change his name to Smerdyakov?

Smerdyakov Goes through with It

Mitya plans to end his life at "the first hot ray of 'golden-haired Phoebus' in the morning," and Ivan considers "smash[ing] the cup on the floor" (BK, Bk 8, Ch 6, 410: Bk 5, Ch 5; 264). Rumored to be Fyodor Pavlovich's illegitimate son, Smerdyakov is the one who goes through with it. Like other suicidal characters in Dostoevsky's works, Smerdyakov hates Russia and seeks to abandon her. His destination, however, is not America, but France. Before heading to France or renouncing life, he has a plan, one that "was all thought out beforehand" (BK, Bk 11, Ch 8; 631). Smerdyakov fits Durkheim's anomic typology in which individuals kill themselves, but only after destroying others whom they blame for their misery.[213]

Smerdyakov's revenge is methodical and premeditated. On the night of Fyodor Pavlovich's murder, Smerdyakov reclines at the bottom of the stairs and shams an epileptic fit. Then he is taken to a cot behind the partition in Marfa's room where he keeps "moaning . . . softly" (BK, Bk 11, Ch 8; 626). After hearing a ruckus, Smerdyakov rises, investigates, finds Grigory covered in blood, and "decide[s] to finish it all right then and there" (BK, Bk 11, Ch 8; 628). He goes to the window, informs Fyodor that Grushenka has arrived, and knocks the secret signals. When Fyodor opens the door, Smerdyakov manages to get inside, grabs the "cast iron paperweight," and thrice hits Fyodor on the head (BK, Bk 11, Ch 8; 629). Smerdyakov cleans the paperweight, puts it back where it belongs, and reaches behind the icons to extract "three packets of iridescent hundred-rouble bills" (BK, Bk 11, Ch 8; 624). After dropping the envelope, along with the pink ribbon on the floor, he hides the money in a hole in the garden's apple tree. When all is said and done, Fyodor is dead, Mitya is wrongfully convicted, Ivan has a mental breakdown, and speechless Stinking Lizaveta has spoken.

Ransacked Childhood

While Mitya's and Ivan's destructive urges derive from their expendable childhoods, Smerdyakov's malignancy gestates in his mother's womb.[214] Smerdyakov's mother is Stinking Lizaveta, the village idiot, who goes "begging all over town as a holy fool of God" (BK, Bk 3, Ch 2; 97). In keeping with Russian tradition, which holds that it is impious to mistreat a *yurodivy*, the townspeople give Lizaveta compassion and kindness, which she passes on to others: "[w]hen she [is] given a kopeck, she would accept it and at once take it and put it in some poor box in the church or prison" (BK, Bk 3, Ch 2; 98). After her father's death, when Lizaveta becomes "even dearer, as an orphan, to all the pious people in town," someone rapes her (BK, Bk 3, Ch 2; 97). More likely than not, that someone is Fyodor.

While Mitya's trial teaches readers that circumstantial evidence does not always lead to truth, multiple clues point to Fyodor Pavlovich as Lizaveta's assailant. One evening when a bunch of tipsy men are returning home, they stumble upon Lizaveta, who is sleeping. When one "young sir" asks if it is possible to "regard such an animal as a woman," Fyodor remarks: "yes, she can be regarded as a woman, even very much so," and "there [is] even some piquancy in it of a special sort" (BK, Bk 3, Ch 2; 98). This occurs shortly after Fyodor Pavlovich learns of his first wife's death and he is indulging in an "outrageous" frenzy of "drinking and carousing" (BK, Bk 3, Ch 2; 99). Fyodor is thus primed for a new outrage and for him, nothing—not even the holy fool—is off limits. One day while drunk on cognac, Fyodor tells Ivan and Alyosha that "there has never been an ugly woman, that's my rule," which implies that for him any woman will suffice (BK, Bk 3, Ch 8; 136). As Fyodor elaborates on his strategy for forcible seduction, his vignette seemingly features Lizaveta as prey: he brags that "barefoot or ugly ones have to be taken by surprise" and "they must be surprised so that they're enraptured, smitten, ashamed that such a gentleman should have fallen in love with such a grimy creature" (BK, Bk 3, Ch 8; 136). Through this, he intimates that Lizaveta is rape material.

When it becomes obvious that Lizaveta is pregnant, a "strange rumor spread[s] all over town that the perpetrator was none other than Fyodor" (BK, Bk 3, Ch 2; 99). Although Lizaveta "could not speak a word," her resolve to deliver her baby in Fyodor's garden speaks volumes (BK, Bk 3, Ch 2; 98). Despite the vigilance of a wealthy woman who brings Lizaveta into her home for the birth, the pregnant holy fool escapes and miraculously manages to climb and then jump down from Fyodor's "high and sturdy garden fence" (BK, Bk 3, Ch 2; 99). When Grigory hears groans coming from the garden bathhouse, he discovers the dying Lizaveta with her newborn. Once again Grigory and Marfa invite a "foundling" into their home. The baby is baptized and named Pavel, but later "as if by unspoken agreement everyone starts calling him Fyodorovich" (BK, Bk 3; 100). Although Fyodor denies responsibility, he effectually accepts paternity by not objecting to the patronymic.

Although Mitya and Ivan suffer from "expendable-child" syndrome, they still possess an identifiable lineage.[215] Smerdyakov, however, lacks a sure pedigree, and Fyodor, Grigory, Mitya, and Ivan see him as less than expendable and let him know it. Fyodor calls him by a variant of his mother's nickname "Smerdyashchaya" which means "stinking." This forces Smerdyakov to bear the stigma of ancestral stench every day of his life.[216] Unlike the other sons, who are pawned off on relatives, educated, and can expect a paternal inheritance, Fyodor puts Smerdyakov to use as his cook. Smerdyakov understands that unlike legitimate Mitya, Ivan, and Alyosha, he will not inherit so much as a kopeck. At trial, the defense counsel Fetukovich outlines the effect this must have had on Smerdyakov: He "detest[s] his position as compared with that of his master's legitimate children: everything goes to them . . . and nothing to him; to them all the rights, to them the inheritance, while he is just a cook" (BK, Bk 12, Ch 12; 738).[217] As such, Fetukovich puts his finger on the resentment that Smerdyakov harbors throughout his life.

Even though defense counsel calls Grigory one of Smerdyakov's "benefactors," Smerdyakov resents him as well, and for good reasons (BK, Bk 12, Ch 12; 738). This accidental father does not shower his foundling with love and even scorns him because he links him not only to his dead "dragon" child, but also to Smerdyakov's nidorous origin (BK, Bk 3; Ch 1, 95). Although the narrator praises Grigory's love of children, it appears that he only loves Fyodor's discards and not his own. The same Grigory who "fussed over" toddler Mitya, recoils in "grief and horror" when his own baby is born with six fingers (BK, Bk 3, Ch 1; 95). He attributes the malformation to "unclean spirits," refers to the infant as an "it" unworthy of baptism, calls the "it" a "dragon," and basically shuns the "it" until "it" dies (BK, Bk 3, Ch 1; 95). While willingly carrying baby Smerdyakov into his home and "put[ting] him in [his wife's] lap," Grigory views the bastard as the "it's" successor because "he appeared on the very day . . . they buried their six-fingered [dragon]" and conjectures that the "dead one" sent him as a replacement (BK, Bk 3, Ch 2; 100; Ch 1; 96). As such, for Grigory, the "dragon" and the new baby are one and the same.

When Grigory tells his wife that Smerdyakov "was born of the devil's son and a righteous woman," he does not reveal his true impression of Lizaveta (BK, Bk 3, Ch 2; 100). He does, however, blurt out his real feelings to the community and to Smerdyakov himself. When the town blames Fyodor for the pregnancy, Grigory defends his master "energetically" and informs the people that Lizaveta is a "low creature" and that "[s]he herself is to blame" (BK, Bk 3, Ch 2; 99). Grigory scalds his accidental son with a samovar of words, ones that Smerdyakov "never could forgive": he tells Smerdyakov, "You are not a human being, you were begotten of bathhouse slime, that's who you are" (BK, Bk 3, Ch 6; 124). In doing so, Grigory inflicts an injury worse than the one Zosima limns when he implores adults to refrain from even "pass[ing] by a small child . . . in anger with a foul word" because "you may thereby have planted a bad seed in him and it may grow" (BK, Bk 6, Ch 3; 319). Grigory does not merely dispense "foul" words, but also resorts to physical abuse. Both words and deeds land on fertile ground, plant a seed, and indeed it grows. Smerdyakov exhibits the "diagnostic criteria" of "antisocial personality disorder," which is also "referred to as *psychopathy, sociopathy, or dyssocial personality disorder*."[218] Smerdyakov vents aggression on animals, which is not an uncommon sociopathic "feature."[219] As a child, he is "fond of hanging cats and then burying them with ceremony" (BK, Bk 3, Ch 6; 126). As an adult, Smerdyakov teaches children to stick pins in a piece of bread, feed that to dogs, and then revel in the creatures' suffering.

Durkheim stresses that family ties nourish the restraining force that fends off suicidal anomy. In the novel, Smerdyakov is essentially ejected from what little there is or ever was of a brotherhood, and Mitya and Ivan reinforce the detrusion. They effectually abrade Smerdyakov's wounds by interacting with one another while Smerdyakov is consigned to lurk like a virus around the periphery. Ivan and Mitya, along with Grigory and Fyodor, even periodically lacerate Smerdyakov with sarcasm and call him names, like "stinking lackey," "stinking Jesuit," and "boor" (BK, Bk 3, Ch 6; 123: Ch 7; 130: Ch 8;132).[220] Grigory slaps Smerdyakov and Ivan finds him so repulsive that he also gives him a whack.[221] When Smerdyakov becomes embroiled in the father-son contest over Grushenka, Mitya threatens to kill him while Fyodor "starts tormenting [him] with his torments" (BK, Bk,5, Ch 6; 269). Complaining of mistreatment, Smerdyakov tells Ivan that he is "thinking of taking [his] own life" (BK, Bk, 5, Ch 6; 269).

Like Durkheim, Shneidman analyzes the ramifications of family dysfunction. He attributes suicidal urges to ransacked childhoods in which psychological needs have been "trampled on" by "obtuse adults."[222] Although Mitya and Ivan are themselves haunted by the "losses of childhood's special joys," Fetukovich hits the nail on the head when he suggests that Smerdyakov has fared far worse: he "hated his origin, was ashamed of it, and gnashed his teeth when he recalled that he was 'descended from Stinking Lizaveta' " (BK, Bk 12, Ch 12; 738).[223] It turns out, however, that this "Balaam's ass" calculatedly conceals his powers, which are diabolical and anomic.

The Calculated Mask

Like other Dostoevsky characters, Smerdyakov not only fits Durkheim's anomic, but also his egoistic typology. Smerdyakov is "unsociable" and without "the slightest need for anyone's company" (BK, Bk 3, Ch 6; 125). Durkheim states that people who separate themselves radically from others "create nothingness within" and can resort to self-obliteration (SU, Bk 2, Ch 6; 279). Echoing these sentiments, Zosima says that those who "withdraw from others," "push people away," and "fall into complete isolation," effect "not the fullness of life, but full suicide" (BK, Bk 6; Ch 2; 303). Significantly, Smerdyakov implicitly pays homage to the suicidogenic state of self-imposed solitude when he praises "two desert hermits" (BK, Bk 3, Ch 7; 130).

Misanthropic Smerdyakov, who "seem[s] to despise the female sex as much as the male," is intermittently designated a "eunuch" (BK, Bk 3, Ch 6;

125–26).[224] The implied inability to engage in intimacy underscores his isolation, but the eunuch-like identity connotes more than that. It cordons him to the Castrates, the sect that Kondraty Selivanov founded in the latter half of the eighteenth century, which might explain a detail ostensibly inconsistent with Smerdyakov's antisociability: namely, his peculiar romance with Maria Kondratievna. Richard Peace suggests that her patronymic "(daughter of Kondratiy) seems to imply that Kondratiy is her spiritual father" and that she is the "Castrate madonna."[225] Peace also contends that when Smerdyakov moves into Maria's house, he lives apart in an annex, the "white hut," which again alludes to the Castrates, "who referred to themselves as 'The White Doves,' dressed in white, and called the process of castration itself 'whitening' [*ubeleniye*]."[226] Moreover, in his childhood home, Grigory takes interest in another sect, the Flagellants, who purify themselves through mortification of the flesh.

Beyond legating Smerdyakov to anchoritism and fanaticism, the image of the castrated eunuch ties into Menninger's analysis of "focal suicide."[227] Menninger discusses the *Skoptsy*, who believe that "Adam and Eve, our first parents, sinned by entering into a sexual relationship" and that the only way to purge the world of evil is to destroy the offending "organ of procreation."[228] Menninger aligns the religious mutilation rite with focally suicidal individuals, who condemn what they perceive as "sexual sins" and in "very direct and undisguised logic, . . . do the obvious thing of ridding themselves of the guilty part of their body."[229] Smerdyakov loathes Fyodor, the Adam, whom he sees as the sperm of evil and source of his misery. Thus, the eunuch references encapsulate Smerdyakov's revolt against the guilty "organ of procreation" and his psychic castration of both self and sire.[230]

The novel sets up a contrast between Zosima's Job and eunuch-like Smerdyakov, who anathematizes his birth and craves nonexistence.[231] By paraphrasing Job, Zosima illuminates Job's resilience, love of life, and unshakeable faith. Despite his ruin, Zosima's Job cries out, "naked came I out of my mother's womb and naked shall I return into the earth . . . the Lord gave and the Lord has taken away" before he "bless[es] . . . the name of the Lord henceforth and forevermore" (BK, Bk 6, Ch 6; 291). Antithetically, when Smerdyakov confesses to Maria Kondratievna, "I'd have let them kill me in the womb, so as not to come into the world at all," he impersonates a despairing Job, pining for self-aborticide (BK, Bk 5, Ch 2; 224).[232]

In his anomic revolt, Smerdyakov has cobbled together an operable survival mechanism, which, like Mitya's modality, entails juggling dual personae. But unlike Mitya's, Smerdyakov's schism is not an ideal seeking to quell the abhorrent self. Instead, his ideal *is* his abhorrent self, which Smerdyakov adroitly masks behind a pseudo persona, one with a Frenchified garb and guitar-prop. Upon returning from Moscow, Smerdyakov was "very well dressed, in a clean frock coat and linen" and spent "almost the whole of his salary on clothes, pomade, [and] perfume" (BK, Bk 3, Ch 6; 126). He "scrupulously brushed his clothes twice a day without fail and was terribly fond of waxing his smart calfskin boots with a special English polish" (BK, Bk 3, Ch 6; 126). These items are important accoutrements in Smerdyakov's campaign to varnish over his malodorous nascence and servile station.

Shakespeare's Iago, a villain who proclaims, "I am not what I am," could be Smerdyakov's precursor.[233] Ironically, the prosecutor, Ippolit Kirillovich, who touts his own psychological prowess, sounds like a "trustful" Othello duped by the deceiver's counterfeit façade.[234] He presents the lackey as "weak," "feeble minded," and "cowardly as a chicken" (BK, Bk 12, Ch 8; 707–8). In Ippolit Kirillovich's words, this toady is "a highly honest young man," who would "fall at [Mitya's] feet and kiss them" (BK, Bk 12, Ch 8; 707). He argues that Smerdyakov is "bullie[d] into serving as [Mitya's] spy and informer" and is "terribly tormented by remorse at his betrayal of his master" (BK, Bk 12, Ch 8; 707). When defense counsel Fetyukovich addresses the jury, he rebuts Ippolit Kirillovich with precision. In Fetyukovich's rendering, Smerdyakov is not the "timid," "guileless," "feebleminded," and "weak man [that] the prosecution has made him out to be" (BK, Bk 12, Ch 12; 738). Rather, once stripped bare, Smerdyakov "is a decidedly spiteful being, enormously ambitious, vengeful, and burning with envy," and these traits have been linked to suicidality (BK, Bk 12, Ch 12; 738).

Fetukovich spotlights Smerdyakov's "terrible mistrustfulness," which connects both with paleologic and the meticulous inspection of food (BK, Bk 12, Ch 12; 738). Multiple commentators have noted the doubling of Smerdyakov and Ivan, and here it appears that a facet of their shared consciousness is "paleologic," which can manifest in suicidal people.[235] Arieti holds that "paleologic" issues when a "vague menace is transformed into a specific threat."[236] Instead of the whole world being against the individual, there emerges a " 'they' in particular" and this "they" is gunning for the paleologician.[237] Consequently, what was once an individual's "mild sense of suspiciousness," turns into "the particular conviction that 'they' [are] follow[ing] him or [her]."[238] Arieti cites a patient who "used to feel that his wife 'poisoned' his life," which morphs into his delusional certainty that his wife is "putting poison in his food."[239] For the patient, the "abstract poisoning [becomes] a concrete and specific one."[240] Smerdyakov is analogous to Arieti's patient. Before eating, he "would hold a piece [of food] up to the light on his fork, and study it as if through a microscope, sometimes taking a long time to decide, and, finally would decide to send it into his mouth" (BK, Bk 12, Ch 12; 738: Bk 3, Ch 6; 125). And like Arieti's patient, Smerdyakov's conversion of the abstract to the concrete is a mealtime event. Although Marfa and Grigory ascribe Smerdyakov's preprandial due diligence to "squeamishness" and Fyodor to an innate flair for cooking, it is symptomatic of paleological mistrust (BK, Bk 3, Ch 6; 125). Like Arieti's patient, Smerdyakov adheres to the conviction that thorough indagations are necessary, not because "they" are abstractly poisoning his life, but because "they" are specifically poisoning his food.

Fetyukovich adduces that Smerdyakov's mistrust is hidden "behind a mask of naivety, and a mind capable of contemplating quite a lot" (BK, Bk 12, Ch 12; 738). What Fetyukovich postulates here is Smerdyakov's feigned identity, and part of that is his secret ability to wield his epilepsy as a weapon. The narrator's account of Smerdyakov's first seizure furnishes a clue to the machinations that unfold. While Grigory is tutoring Smerdyakov in the scriptures, his pupil "derisively" interjects, if the "Lord God created light on the first day, . . . [w]here did the light shine from on the first day?" (BK, Bk 3, Ch 6; 124). A "dumbfounded" Grigory reacts by giving Smerdyakov "a violent blow on the cheek" (BK, Bk 3, Ch 6; 124). Smerdyakov appears to endure the slap silently, hides in a corner for a few days, and postures as the meek lamb. Inwardly, however, Smerdyakov is contemplating revenge.

What happens next foretells what will become a calculated component of the murder plot. Shortly after the slap, Grigory, Marfa, and Fyodor discover that Smerdyakov has "the falling sickness," which will plague him for the rest of his life.[241] But there is something they do not discover: namely, that in lieu of learning the scriptures, Smerdyakov has learned about epilepsy's serviceability. Like a specimen in Skinner's lab, Smerdyakov got plentiful positive reinforcement: he saw that his inaugural fit effectuated a change in Fyodor, who suddenly started to "worry" about the lackey and even let him come upstairs (BK, Bk 3, Ch 6; 124). Smerdyakov saw that Fyodor bestowed a major benefit by "strictly" barring Grigory from further infliction of corporal punishment (BK, Bk 3, Ch 6; 124–25). Before the murder, Ivan asks Smerdyakov whether he is "going to pretend to have a three-day attack of the falling sickness," and he responds: "for an experienced man, it would be easy enough to do . . . [and] I would have every right to use such a means" (BK, Bk 5, Ch 6; 269–70).[242] Thus, early on, Smerdyakov gleaned that his falling sickness can serve as both shield and sword.

Symbiotic Dismantling

Although Bakhtin speaks of Smerdyakov's "gradual dialogic dismantling of Ivan's consciousness," this process is not just an Ivan thing.[243] Ivan and his alter-ego, Smerdyakov, symbiotically dismantle each other.[244] Ivan injects Smerdyakov with toxin and then in calculated moves, Smerdyakov returns the favor by injecting Ivan with his reconstituted toxin. After mephitic symbiosis, the doppelgangers triumph in unison: Smerdyakov self-destructs while Ivan mentally breaks down.

Readers get more insight into Ivan's indoctrination of Smerdyakov when the narrator recounts the theological dinner discussion at Fyodor Pavlovich's. It is here that readers see that Grigory is a poor pedagogue, that Smerdyakov is predisposed to blaspheme, and that two plus two adds up to a "broth maker" easily sucked into Ivan's twisted logic. Smerdyakov, who is permitted to stand beside the table while the master eats, starts showing up regularly once Ivan arrives. In fact, Smerdyakov seems to idolize this sultan of Euclidian reason, the one who proclaims that "there is no God" and "no immortality either" (BK, Bk 3, Ch 7; 134. By calling Smerdyakov "Balaam's ass," Fyodor sardonically alludes to the donkey of the false prophet, which serves as the forward to Smerdyakov's sermon, one which truckles to mentor Ivan (BK, Bk 3, Ch 6; 123).[245]

When the conversation turns to Foma Danilov, the Russian soldier who had been tortured and put to death by Muslims for refusing to relinquish his Christian faith, "Balaam's ass" enters the fray.[246] The biblical ass appears in "Numbers," when an "angel of the Lord" blocks his path while carrying master, Balaam.[247] When the ass sees the angel, it refuses to advance and furious Balaam "beat[s] it with his staff" and threatens to "kill [it] right now."[248] Once the Lord grants the ass the power of speech, he reproaches his master. Moreover, Balaam suddenly sees "the angel of the Lord standing in the road with his sword drawn" and confesses, "I have sinned."[249] In Numbers, the ass speaks sanctified truth and in *The Idiot*, it is an ass that awakens Prince Myshkin to life. But by calling his cook "Balaam's ass," Fyodor Pavlovich reveals his ignorance of the biblical text, plus he gets it ass-backwards because Smerdyakov brays the kind of sacrilege that can only rouse death.

While Grigory and others appear to respect the martyred Foma Danilov, Smerdyakov calls him a dimwit. In sophistic apery of Ivan's dogma, Smerdyakov explains that if this soldier had "renounced Christ's name and his own baptism," there would have been no sin because he would be instantly "excommunicated from the Holy Church like a heathen," and thus, rendered incapable of committing a Christian sin (BK, Bk 3, Ch 7; 128). His circular reasoning is a pastiche of what the devil deems "Jesuit casuistry" when he tells Ivan about the plight of the noseless man.[250] Smerdyakov embellishes this sermon by indicating that faith is nothing but a bargaining tool to be utilized for personal gain. In his circular fashion, Smerdyakov proselytizes that faith can be manipulated to absolve people of responsibility for anything, including the repudiation of faith itself. Smerdyakov begins by claiming, "if you have faith even as little as the smallest seed," you can work miracles (BK, Bk 3, Ch 7; 130). From there, he hypothesizes a two-horned dilemma. If he were the one forced to choose between Christianity or conversion to "the unclean Mohammedan faith," he might try to order the mountain to "move and crush [his] tormentor" (BK, Bk 3, Ch 7; 131). If the miracle happens, he can go on "praising and glorifying God" (BK, Bk 3, Ch 7; 131). But if the mountain does not oblige, he would have license to doubt in "such a terrible hour of mortal fear" (BK, Bk 3, Ch 7; 131). Without the miracle, he could surmise that he is not destined for "the fullness of the Kingdom of heaven," so it is reasonable to renounce faith, "keep his skin on," and hope that one day "merciful God" might forgive him (BK, Bk 3, Ch 7; 131). Smerdyakov has thus reconfigured Ivan's pragmatic godlessness into Smerdyakovianism, which literally permits any and every alternative. If you can use it, why not?

Fyodor Pavlovich sees that Smerdyakov is pandering to his mentor and tells Ivan that "[Smerdyakov] arranged all this for you, he wants you to praise him" (BK, Bk 3, Ch 7; 128). But Smerdyakov is not just infected with Ivan's ideology, he has also assimilated Ivan's suicidogenic vacillation between belief and nonbelief. After being identified as "Balaam's ass," who spoke and performed a miracle, Smerdyakov impugns himself by sneering at miracles and declaring that "no one in our time . . . can shove a mountain into the sea" (BK, Bk 3, Ch 7; 130). Yet, he somehow retains his peasant-like belief in the sacred powers of two desert hermits. Fyodor Pavlovich deems this "Russian faith," and Alyosha concedes that it is "quite Russian" (Bk, Bk 3, Ch 7; 131). This indicates that within Smerdyakov, there remains at least a sliver of faith that chafingly coexists with Ivan's rational atheism.

The discussion that follows Smerdyakov's sermon identifies the role of the peasantry in Ivan's atheistic agenda. After the "Balaam-ass" preachment, Fyodor asks Ivan what he has done to endear himself to Smerdyakov and Ivan answers, "he's a lackey and a boor. Prime cannon fodder . . . when the time comes" (BK, Bk 3, Ch 8; 132). In saying this, Ivan reminds his audience that this post-emancipation house serf is part peasant after all. It threads back to the narrator's comparison of Smerdyakov to the "stray little peasant in a ragged caftan" in Kramskoy's painting, *The Contemplator* (BK, Bk 3, Ch 6; 126). It is here that Smerdyakov takes shape as the synecdoche, the representative of the new breed of peasantry, who will "give a start" and wake up. Uprooted from communal soil, resentful of their social niche, convinced of their superiority over other peasants, Smerdyakov stands for a class primed for enlisting in Ivan's regimen. Ivan admits that "[t]here will be others and better ones, but . . . [f]irst [Smerdyakov's] kind and then the better ones" (BK, Bk 3, Ch 8; 132).[251] Smerdyakov is thus the gudgeon in Dostoevsky's dreadful premonition that peasants will serve as the initial hatchery for the crusade, led by the young Ivans, to rid Russia of Christian faith. In fact, Smerdyakov's plummet says it all: he ingests Ivan's caustic dogma, destroys others, and ultimately eradicates himself. His fate inflates into the broader paradigm whereby the purgation of faith and Christ from the womb of the motherland is pre-doomed to extirpate souls and cause Russia's demise.

As mentioned, anomic people must incinerate others first and Ivan empowers Smerdyakov to do just that. By inoculating Smerdyakov with his canon, "everything is permissible," Ivan smooths the way for Smerdyakov to do his everything—to wreak havoc and even make mincemeat of the inoculator. The poison Smerdyakov delivers is composed of insights he has extracted from his "contemplation" of Ivan's psyche. Smerdyakov has gleaned that Ivan's Achilles heel is his tendency to efface the demarcation between thought and deed.[252] Smerdyakov recognizes that when desire conflates with conduct, it releases copious guilt; and he is cognizant of Ivan's inner torment, that rivalry between an overactive conscience and conscienceless rationality. Such prehensions facilitate Smerdyakov's ability to stealthily groom Ivan to serve first as his accomplice, then as his toady. But after the murder, Smerdyakov deploys the most potent psychological musketry to pulverize his scullion.

Before the murder, there is a conversation at the gate, one in which Smerdyakov partially sketches the plan and purports to recruit Ivan as partner. But as things unravel, Ivan sinks from master to colleague, and then, to subordinate. Smerdyakov supplies Ivan with details while hinting at the possibility of his shamming an epileptic seizure. He also intromits a monetary stimulant: "[b]ut if your father was to die now . . . then each one of you would get a sure forty thousand all at once" (BK, Bk 5, Ch 6; 273). Although Ivan finds this talk "suspicious" and it "perplexe[s]" him, he, in quest of willful ignorance, tries to shove it all back into the recesses of his unconscious (BK, Bk 11, Ch 6; 604).

Over time, Smerdyakov unsettles Ivan by becoming increasingly familiar. That is, Smerdyakov "treat[s] Ivan as if they are "somehow in league and as if there is "something agreed to and kept secret" (BK, Bk 5, Ch 6; 267). But when Ivan starts to obey Smerdyakov's directives and leave for Chermashnya, Ivan castigates himself: "[w]hy did I report to him that I was going to Chermashnya?" (BK, Bk 5, Ch 7; 280). At that juncture, Ivan, who prides himself on free will and on his superiority over the "broth maker," joltingly realizes that he is now slavishly taking orders. To remedy that, Ivan boards the train for Moscow in lieu of the commanded destination, but this is nothing but self-trickery. Ivan neither liberates himself nor reinstates his mastery because whether it be Chermashnya or Moscow, he is still effectuating his boss's objective by getting out of the way.[253] Prior to departure, Smerdyakov positively reinforces Ivan's compliance with praise: "[i]t's always interesting to talk with an intelligent man" (BK, Bk 5, Ch 7; 279). These words linger in Ivan's brain. But later Smerdyakov incisively retracts the "praise" and recasts his phrase as a "reproach" for Ivan's disgraceful abandonment of his family on the eve of calamity (BK, Bk 11, Ch 6; 608). By turning his praise to blame, Smerdyakov ratchets up Ivan's latent sense of guilt.

After the murder, but in gradations, Smerdyakov comes clean to Ivan. In doing this, he does not seek to atone, appease his conscience, or accept responsibility. Non-repentant Smerdyakov aims to insert the toxin that will aggravate Ivan's preexisting guilt, charge him with murder, and abrade his already imperiled mental state. At the first of their three meetings, Smerdyakov acts as if the two are still in cahoots and gets Ivan to strike a deal: Ivan promises that he will not mention Smerdyakov's ability to fake seizures and in return, Smerdyakov agrees not to testify to that or "report the whole of [their] conversation by the gate" (BK, Bk 11, Ch 6; 609).

Although Ivan leaves that initial meeting "completely convinced of Mitya's guilt," it is evident that the Smerdyakovian serum is surging through his bloodstream (BK, Bk 11, Ch 6; 610). It incites Ivan to do what he habitually does—mentally erase the line between wishing and doing—and it is then that he starts to corrosively self-indict. This becomes evident when Ivan asks Alyosha for his opinion: "tell me, did you think . . . that I wished for father's death" and "didn't you also think . . . that I was precisely wishing for 'viper to eat viper'—that is, precisely for Dmitri to kill father" (BK, Bk 11, Ch 6; 611). From there, he cautiously recedes from intimating that he merely wanted the parricide and ebbs toward implicating himself in the deed itself: "didn't you also think . . . that I myself would not even mind helping him along" (BK, Bk 11, Ch 6; 611). Alyosha's affirmative retort prompts Ivan to return to Smerdyakov for the second toxic dose that will further fuse the death wish with homicide and quicken insanity.

At the second meeting, Smerdyakov has changed. Like Balaam's ass, who stands up to his master, Smerdyakov no longer seems frail, has cast aside the timid veneer, and speaks with a bold tone. No longer groveling at Ivan's feet and with a "decidedly malicious, unfriendly and even haughty" look, Smerdyakov rolls up his sleeves and starts pricking psychic nerve endings (BK, Bk 11, Ch 7; 615). He accuses Ivan of knowingly abandoning his father to be murdered. Then, in an implicit acknowledgement that this barb had its intended effect, Smerdyakov "insolently" insinuates that Ivan appears to be "out of [his] mind" (BK, Bk 11, Ch 7; 614). Smerdyakov, however, does not stop there, but instead calculatedly plunges his needle deeper: "I meant that maybe you yourself were even wishing very much for your parent's death then" (BK, Bk 11, Ch 7; 614). This time, he hits the raw ganglion, which causes Ivan to jump up and wallop Smerdyakov before nursing his own wound. Ivan asks, "you thought I was at one with Dmitri in wanting to kill father?" (BK, Bk 11, Ch 7; 614). Smerdyakov takes another poke: "as for wanting someone else to kill—that you did want" (BK, Bk 11, Ch 7; 615). The next jab sinks even deeper: Smerdyakov adds, "it was just as if you told me . . . you can kill my parent, I won't prevent you" (BK, Bk 11, Ch 7; 616).[254] Having hit the bull's eye, Smerdaykov "look[s] at Ivan almost with delight"; Ivan is now Smerdyakov's work in progress (BK, Bk 11, Ch 7; 616).

When Ivan leaves Smerdyakov, he is afflicted with psychic pyemia and on the verge of a mental break. He is "trembling" and murmuring to himself, "Yes . . . I wanted the murder. I precisely wanted it!" (BK, Bk 11, Ch 7; 617). When he reaches Katerina, he seems not only "insane," but on the brink of taking that mental leap from guilty death wish to guilty murder: he confesses to Katerina, "if it was [Smerdyakov who killed [father,] and not Dmitri, then, of course, I am a murderer too" (BK, Bk 11, Ch 7; 617). Even after Katerina produces the document that "mathematically" proves that Mitya is the killer, Ivan feels as if Smerdyakov has cut a "certain unhealing scratch . . . on his heart" by infusing him with the monetary motive for what is rapidly becoming Ivan's crime (BK, Bk 11, Ch 7; 619).[255] Smerdyakov had intimated that Mitya's conviction is in Ivan's best interest because it would enlarge Ivan's share of the inheritance. Ivan perceives those words as an accusation of his complicity, gives it credence, and then decides to atone for it by "sacrific[ing] thirty thousand from his own portion to arrange for Mitya's escape" (BK, Bk 11, Ch 7; 620). Swaying in another direction to examine his motives for the sacrifice, Ivan asks, "[i]s it because in my soul I'm just as much a murderer?" (BK, Bk 11, Ch 7; 620). No longer the ass, Smerdyakov is now master, and he alone can speak to Ivan's question. It is then that Ivan returns for the third dose that will transmute psychic murder into de facto parricide and finalize his mental collapse.

At the third meeting, the former lackey is now head honcho, and he addresses Ivan with "unheard-of-arrogance" (BK, Bk 11, Ch 8; 622). Significantly, this final meeting jolts forth in increments that Ivan will internalize and later relive when he testifies at Mitya's trial. The meeting starts with disclosure of Ivan's desire for his father's death, which is initially tempered with a partial not-guilty plea. From there, it modulates into a proffer of proof and ends with Ivan's condemnation. It is, of course, Smerdyakov who orchestrates this self-damning overture from start to finish. Initially, Smerdyakov pushes Ivan to believe that knowledge of the parricide plot plus not staying to stop it equals liability. Smerdyakov expands the equation to cast Ivan as not a mere accomplice, but as the person calling the shots: "[y]ou killed him, you are the main killer, and I was just your minion. . . and I performed the deed according to your word" (BK, Bk 11, Ch 8; 623). But treatment is not over. By transforming Ivan into the master conniver, Smerdyakov is just prepping him for the most potent infusion of devastating guilt.

The added adrenalin in Smerdyakov's syringe is concocted from sludge extracted from Ivan's psyche: it is a composite of Ivan's diabolophobia, his Euclidean proof, and his credo that "everything is permissible."

Ivan's diabolophobia comes into play when he is "convulsively" rattled by Smerdyakov "pull[ing] his left leg from under the table" and "roll[ing] up his trouser" to remove the stolen rubles (BK, Bk 11, Ch 8; 624). As Terras has pointed out, Ivan fears that Smerdyakov might expose a cloven hoof, which is associated with the devil.[256] But there is more to Ivan's terror than this and it is linked to Ivan's allegiance to Euclidean proof. As much as Ivan fears the devil, he fears that mathematical proof that will unequivocally establish that he is not just a vicarious coconspirator, but instead the direct sole perpetrator. Smerdyakov displays the proof, the "three packets of iridescent hundred-rouble bills," and then, by reciting Ivan's ideology, "everything is permitted," he rubs raw the injection site (BK, Bk 11, Ch 8; 624–25). This, of course, debilitates Ivan and primes him for the terminal tactic: Smerdyakov goads Ivan away from taking refuge in mere guilty nonfeasance toward owning criminal malfeasance: "You knew about the murder and you told me to kill him" and therefore "I want to prove it to your face . . . that in all of this the chief murderer is you alone. . . It's you who are the most lawful murderer" (BK, Bk 11, Ch 8; 627). At first, Ivan feebly resists and says, "I swear to you that I was not as guilty as you think, and perhaps I did not put you up to it all" (BK, Bk 11, Ch 8; 631). But then, Ivan brings in his own guilty verdict: "I shall give evidence against myself tomorrow in court, I've decided! I shall tell everything, everything" (BK, Bk 11, Ch 8; 631).

When Ivan takes the stand, he is, as Dostoevsky once said about Raskolnikov, trapped and "*compelled* to denounce himself."[257] He hands the stolen lucre to the bailiff and gives testimony, which adheres to the pattern of his earlier utterances to Smerdyakov. That is, Ivan discloses his guilty desire for his father's death, but initially tempers it by identifying Smerdyakov as the perpetrator. He states, "I got it from Smerdyakov, the murderer, yesterday. I visited him before he hanged himself. It was he who killed father, not my brother" (BK, Bk 12, Ch 5; 686). From there, Smerdyakov becomes the invisible prosecutor leading the witness: Ivan reiterates his responses to the strategic maneuvers that earlier converted him from wisher to coconspirator: "He killed him on my instructions . . . Who doesn't wish for his father's death?" (BK, Bk 12, Ch 5; 686). From there, Ivan takes the fatal plunge from coconspirator into the abyss of self-damnation: "I'm simply a murderer" (BK, Bk 12, Ch 5; 686).

At this point, the membrane between wishing and doing is gone. When Ivan asks "[w]ho doesn't wish for his father's death" and answers, "[e] veryone wants his father dead," he welds his personal guilt onto collective guilt and in doing so, effaces yet another boundary, the one between his own psyche and the collective unconscious (BK, Bk 12, Ch 5; 686). In response to the judge's demand for evidence, Ivan scours the courtroom for witnesses, but sees two empty-occupied chairs: first, there is Smerdyakov, but he "won't send evidence from the other world" and second, there is the devil, whose testimony will be deemed "inadmissible" (BK, Bk 12, Ch 5; 686–87). Ivan next regresses to the paleologic that presided over his chat with his "wretched, paltry devil" (BK, Bk 12, Ch 5; 687). In Arieti's words, Ivan "grasps the re-emerging paleologic level in order to reach the conclusion that he desires" and urgently needs.[258] But this time, Ivan's paleologic has triplicated. He no longer strives to eradicate the partition between self and devil, but now he must amalgamate three—self, devil, and Smerdyakov. Shadowy Smerdyakov had to have been cheering in the stands because his dismantling project is done to a frazzle. Seemingly possessed, Ivan emits a "frenzied cry" as the "fateful" Ivan-Smerdyakov-Devil troika gallops "headlong, perhaps to its destruction" (BK, Bk 12, Ch 5; 687: Ch 9; 722).[259]

While suicide is still a possibility on Ivan's horizon, for Smerdyakov it is a *fait accompli.* Suicide theorist Paul Quinnett holds that "despair," or "hopelessness is the one common thread among the majority of those who elect the suicide option" and that "[d]espairing of any future solution to their problems, the utterly hopeless frequently find themselves thinking, 'What's the use? I might as well be dead.' "[260] Leonard M. Moss and Donald M. Hamilton call the condition "frustration" or the "relinquishing of any prospect of gaining necessary satisfactions from the present."[261] Herbert Hendin opines that the affective suicide state is "closer to desperation than hopelessness or despair" because it "implies not only a sense of hopelessness about change but a sense that life is impossible without such change."[262] Shneidman's name for this is "impotent ennui," or the "despondent feeling that everything is hopeless, and I am helpless."[263] All such modifiers fit Dostoevsky's Iago.

While comparing Smerdyakov to the "contemplator," the narrator projects alternate destinies: "perhaps suddenly . . . he will drop everything and wander off to Jerusalem to save his soul, or perhaps he will suddenly burn down his native village, or perhaps he will do both" (BK, Bk 3, Ch 6; 127). In that string of "perhapses," there is an omitted terminus: namely, outright suicide as sequitur to despair, hopelessness, frustration, desperation, and "impotent ennui."[264]

In their final meeting, Ivan observes that Smerdyakov is no longer studying French, but is immersed in *The Homilies of Our Father Among the Saints, Isaac the Syrian.*[265] This detail resonates with import. Having figuratively incinerated his Karamazovian village, perhaps Smerdyakov instinctively clamors for Jerusalem, for soul cleansing, or for Saint Isaac's seventh-century spiritual tutelage. Perhaps he craves a reunion with his peasant roots, return to Russian faith, and revival of those desert hermits, who conceivably once inhabited the cockles of his heart. But going backwards is impossible. Perhaps he likewise despairs of his hopeless present—stagnation in Russia—and is frustrated after forsaking his dream-future in France. As desperate for the change that he needs yet knows is unattainable, this desiccated eunuch embodies "impotent ennui."[266] What happens next when going back is impossible, when the present is unbearable, and the future is blocked? When nothing exists but the gridlock of despair, hopelessness, frustration, and desperation, the only remaining "perhaps" is that noose of quietus.

CONCLUSION: ANOMY, NIHILISM, AND ANTHROPOPHAGY

Finding "three sub-genres" in *Demons*, Robert L. Belknap sees it as not just a society and anti-nihilistic novel, but also a psychological one.[267] If we acquiesce in Durkheim's proposition that "suicide is a social fact," then *Demons* is also sociological fiction. Believing that "[w]hoever dares to kill himself is God," Kirillov fits Durkheim's anomic class, which, mixed with egoism and altruism, seeks to self-deify through death (D, Pt1, Ch 3; 128).[268]

Speaking of suicide in "infantile cosmic identification," Wahl alerts us to a tragic irony, one that applies to Kirillov.[269] Wahl states that "perhaps the saddest thought of all is to see the suicide as he really is" and explains: "[i] nstead of leaving the world as he fantasies it, desolated and sere, stricken and laid waste by the magnitude of his act, he gains only a personal surcease from pain and a small footnote on the inside pages of a newspaper."[270] That "small footnote" is Kirillov, who, after having fantasized about the "magnitude" of an act that would inflate him into omnipotence, ends up as a mere carcass, shattered skull, and "splashes of blood and brains" (D, Pt 3, Ch6; 692). After promising to acquit Stavrogin and Pyotr's gang of all atrocities by pinning blame on himself, Kirillov signs that supposedly impactful suicide note. But the cooked-up confession dwindles into half-assed knavery when the investigators discover that "Kirillov could not have failed to have accomplices" (D, Pt 3, Ch 8; 738).[271]

As the agent of destruction, Pyotr illustrates Durkheim's conviction that suicide and homicide can be bedfellows. Durkheim explains that "[w]here average morality has a ruder character and human life is less respected, [individuals] will revolt, declare war on society and kill, instead of killing himself" (SU, Bk 3, Ch 2; 341). This, of course, fits Pyotr like a glove. He says that "if [he] were in [Kirillov's] place, to show self-will [he] would kill someone else, and not [himself]" (D, Pt 3, Ch 6; 684).

On the other hand, Stavrogin is "the defeated person," who "resign[s] himself, confess[es] his impotence . . . and withdraw[s] from the fight by withdrawing from life" (SU, Bk 3, Ch 2; 341). Bereft of faith in God, Stavrogin is torn from the Russia that is Dostoevsky's "*living stream of life*."[272] What Tikhon calls "secular indifference" started with the 1940s idealist, Stepan Trofimovich, who evoked in Stavrogin the "vague sense of that eternal sacred anguish," tore him from the Durkheimian "regulative force," and introduced what becomes his restless, suicidogenic reach for that "strong silk cord" (D, At Tik 1; 76; Pt 1, Ch 2; 45; Pt 3, Ch 8; 748: SU, Bk 2, Ch 5; 248).

Stepan Trofimovich also tutored and had an impact on Shatov, Dasha, and Liza: Liza attests that she can "remember all of [his] lectures by heart" and it is feasible that Stepan's "stories of how Columbus was on his way to discovering America" and how "poor emigrants were being transported from Europe to America," inspired Shatov's ill-fated voyage to the United States (D, Pt 1, Ch 3; 118–19). The implication here is that the forbears, the Belinskys, Granovskys, and Herzens, who are the "liberals, socialists, free thinkers," and members of the Westernized Russian intelligentsia, share blame not just for Stavrogin, but for a whole generation, including Pyotr and the herd of 1960s nihilists.[273]

Stepan's influence is most pronounced in Stavrogin, who becomes the embodiment of superfluity, Durkheimian anomy. Stavrogin's self-sabotage after boarding school, his pokes at the societal nose, ears, lips and eyes, and his effort to smite faith by delivering his damning manifesto to Bishop Tikhon evince the absence of that crucial restraint or "check-rein." Moreover, the common thread in Stravogin's antics is self-destruction, seen in his potentially fatal duel with Gaganov—an attempted suicide. The voices of third parties—a Shatov, Marie, Mary, Liza, and Darya—who indict Stavrogin as a fraudulent, impotent nothing, prefigure his last letter in which he complains that "everything is always shallow and flaccid" and sentences himself to death (D, Pt 3, Ch 8; 746).

Durkheim states that having no goals or having "goals of infinity" are equivalent because both lead to "exasperated weariness" and the disquiet that Shneidman calls "psychache" (SU, Bk 2, Ch 6; 284). Durkheim and Shneidman's theories are pertinent to Stavrogin's dream of "The Golden Age," based on Claude Lorrain's painting "Acis and Galatea," which is likely the sincerest part of the manifesto shared with Tikhon (D, At Tik 2; 775). Stavrogin's dreamscape pictorializes "psychache" and the unattainable "goals of infinity."[274] Within it, colors, sounds, and aromas synthesize into a prelapsarian realm, which is inaccessible to the anomic "*degenerate out of ennui*."[275] Lorrain's "magical panorama" is an "earthly paradise" where lived "beautiful people" who "got up and went to sleep happy and innocent," where "groves were filled with their joyous songs," where all is confluent with "love and artless joy," and where the sun "rejoic[es] in its beautiful children" (D, At Tik 2; 775). Stavrogin, who "seems to have lived through all of these sensations in his dream," arises "for the first time in [his] life" with his eyes "literally wet with tears," and experiences a fleeting "feeling of happiness, as yet unknown [to him], [which] passe[s] through [his] heart until it hurt" (D, At Tik 2; 775).

Durkheim believes that "goals of infinity" and "needs require[ing] more than can be granted" lead to "continual friction," pain, and self-homicide (SU, Bk 2, Ch 5; 246–48). The evanescing of Stavrogin's "panorama" captures the unrealizability. Needy and "desperate to bring back the now vanished dream," Stavrogin closes his eyes and strains to retrieve the irretrievable, paradisiacal Golden Age (D, At Tik 2; 776). But in lieu thereof, his Last Summoner arrives as a "tiny red spider," identical to the one that intruded before Matryosha hung herself (D, At Tik 2; 776).[276] After the spider, the apparition of "emaciated" Matryosha herself materializes to enjoin Stavrogin to copy her death (D, At Tik 2; 776). For Stavrogin, Matryosha is the hallucination he "can't help but summon" and because he "simply can't live with it," he is driven to placate dissonance by duplicating her hanging (D, At Tik 2; 776).

But there is more to this vision of Matryosha, who "shak[es] her head and brandish[es] her tiny little fist at" Stavrogin (D, At Tik 2; 776).[277] Her gestures deliver a pithy message to *Demons*' readers about malignity's inherently expanding scope. Kirillov, who trumpets his "free will . . . in the fullest possible sense," conversely relinquishes free will, obeys Pyotr, and thus assumes vicarious liability for his tyrant's deeds (D, Pt 3, Ch 6; 683). Stavrogin is similarly situated. Although he technically rebuffs Pyotr's efforts to recruit him as the revolution's figurehead, he finds himself nevertheless conscripted. Like Matryosha, readers "shak[e]" their heads and "brandish their fists" at this "idol, footloose, son of a landowner," and realize that Stavrogin is complicit in the spate of corpses that are directly or indirectly linked to Pyotr's villainy (D, Pt 2, Ch 1; 282). Shatov identifies Kirillov as one victim when he informs Stavrogin that the self-professed man-God, with his suicide obsession, is "your creation" because you "poisoned" his heart (D, Pt 2, Ch 1; 275).

In addition to Kirillov's suicide, Stavrogin had a hand in many other deaths—Shatov's, the Lebyadkins's, Marie's, Liza's and Fedka's. After Shatov's slap, the narrator observes that Stavrogin's rage is "a cold, calm, and . . . *rational* rage," which is "the most repellent and most dreadful kind there can be" (D, Pt 1, Ch 5; 227). It is this "*rational* rage" that kicks in when Stavrogin refrains from immediate, hot retaliation and instead calculates cold revenge. Stavrogin hatches the plot to kill Shatov by informing Pyotr, "you need Shatov's blood," and advising him to "put four members of a circle up to bumping off a fifth, on the pretext that he's going to inform, and the blood that's been spilled will immediately bind them together in a single knot" (D, Pt 2, Ch 6; 428; Ch 8; 460).[278] This tragedy, moreover, does not end with a shot to Shatov's forehead. As Lyamshin's reverberating "animal-like" shriek portends, the iniquity gyres outward to claim other lives (D, Pt 3, Ch 6; 670).

Marie is drained from giving birth to Stavrogin's baby, but when her husband, Shatov, fails to come home, she runs to Kirillov, sees the suicide, grabs her newborn baby, and rushes out into the brutal cold to seek help. After that, both Marie and her newborn sicken and die.

The authorities find the bodies of the Lebyadkins, along with their serving maid, in a partially burned down house on the edge of town. Fedka, along with his cohort, the Shpigulin worker, Fomka, stabbed them to death, set a fire, and stole their money. While Stavrogin did not literally wield the knife, he is nevertheless culpable. He tells Liza, "I didn't kill them and I was against it, but I knew they would be killed, and I didn't stop the killers" (D, Pt 3, Ch 3; 589).[279] Stavrogin is also implicated in Liza's death. He fails to prevent her from visiting the murder scene, where the unruly crowd ends up striking her on the head and sentencing her to death for being "Stavrogin's woman" (D, Pt 3, Ch 3; 597). Because Stavrogin is a link in the chain of causation that leads to the Lebyadkins's murder, he is effectually complicit in all that ensues. This includes the death of Fedka, whose head Fomka "bashe[s] in" in their spat over the stolen loot (D, Pt 3, Ch 4; 624).

If they could speak, the corpses of Kirillov, Shatov, the Lebyadkins, Marie, Liza, and Fedka, along with Matryosha's "brandishing" fist, would attest to the fact that anomy, neither self-contained nor confined to self-homicide, inevitably litters the landscape with graves. Governor von Lembke and the chronicler make this point as well when they suggest that nihilistic demons that microcosmically possess psyches and souls invariably break loose to wreak macrocosmic conflagrations. In the throes of the raging fire in Zarechye, von Lembke conflates enflamed brains with the torched landscape, exclaims that "[t]he fire is in people's minds, and not on the roofs of houses," and shouts "It's all arson! This is Nihilism!" (D, Pt 3, Ch 2; 570–71). The chronicler similarly admonishes that nihilistic notions "in people's minds" are the embers that start fires, like the ones that "raged all summer long in towns and villages" and can be heard in the "stupid murmurings about arson [that] were taking firmer hold among the common people" (D, Pt 2, Ch 6; 381). The chronicler does not mince words when he lets *Demons* readers know that the province is going to hell in a handbasket: "cholera was on the rise" while "serious outbreaks of cattle plague had appeared" and "[r]obberies were twice as frequent as before" (D, Pt 2, Ch 6; 381).[280]

After the suicides, the murders, the deaths, the riotous literary matinee and ball, along with the pyrolytic "sparks and embers [flying] in all directions," one may well wonder what remains in this "panic-stricken society?" (D, Pt 3, Ch 2; 569; Ch 8; 738). What is left behind is a wasteland populated by savagery, self-interest, and unspeakable loss. Utopian Shigalyov is the only one who defies Pyotr before Shatov's murder. He alone leaves, protesting that the plan "represents the sort of pernicious deviation from the normal path that has always done the utmost harm to the cause" (D, Pt 3, Ch 6; 666).[281] But even Shigalyov, who reputedly "doesn't fit into any of the categories of those who've been accused" and is "scheduled to be set free" is not squeaky clean (D, Pt. 3, Ch 8; 741). He was best positioned to save or warn Shatov and yet did nothing (D, Pt 3, Ch 8; 741). There are, however, those, like Tolkachenko, Liputin, and Ensign Erkel, who are blatantly unrepentant.[282] Others, like Virginsky and Lyamshin, are motivated wholly or partially by self-interest and squeal to mitigate their fates.[283]

Those who are neither dead nor arrested survive as mere shards of what their former selves. Von Lembke's career is destroyed, and he retreats into madness. His wife Yuliya's ambitions and reputation are shredded after Pyotr manipulated and "made a fool of her" (D, Pt3, Ch 8; 740). Devastated Mavriky Nikolayevich has lost his fiancé, Liza, and drifts off "somewhere for good" (D, Pt 3, Ch 8; 743). Old Madame Drozdova grows senile, while Varvara and Dasha end up losing anyone and everything that ever mattered to them. The missing pieces of the cataclysmic puzzle, however, are Pyotr and Stepan Trofimovich. Both are integral to this chapter's inaugural promise to elaborate on *Demons*' temporal transcendence, which, like mythological Janus, has two faces—one looking back at the past and the other forth to the future.

Although diabolical Pyotr has absconded, he is not past and gone. The futuristic face of *Demons* knows that Pyotr is still alive and in hiding, likely awaiting an opportune time to return and strike again. It is not surprising that multiple commentators have described *Demons*, with its metastatic Nechaev, as prophetic fiction. Kjetsaa points out that the novel predicts what is imminent, declaring that "[i]n Dostoevsky's eyes Nechaev's evil deed was a fresh sign that Russia had entered the apocalyptic age of socialism."[284]

In a similar vein, Andre Gide wrote that *Demons* "prophesies the revolution of which Russia is presently in the throes."[285] Others, like Igor Shafarevich, Boris Pasternak, and Alexander Solzhenitsyn, posit that Dostoevsky not only predicts the Soviet police state, which resembles Shigalyov's plan, but also foresees the politicide that follows the October Revolution.[286] Richard Pevear goes further to propose that Dostoevsky oracularly envisions Lenin, who "precocious[ly appears] as the unnamed final speaker at the disastrous fete—a man of about forty, bald front and back, with a grayish little beard, who while delivering his incomprehensible harangue, keeps raising his fist over his head and bringing it down as if crushing some adversary to dust."[287] In essence, Dostoevsky's masterpiece invites readers to see it as the soothsayer for any and all eras in which a power-crazed sociopath takes the helm and seeks to "demoralize everyone and throw everything into chaos" (D, Pt. 3, Ch 8; 740).[288]

The contentions that *Demons* auspicates actual historical-political eras are surely persuasive, but the gnome that *Demons* delivers is even more timeless and transcendent. The novel alerts readers to demonic anomy's propensity to trigger not just suicides, but also holocausts, cataclysms, and bloodbaths. Moreover, as further developed in this book's concluding chapter, it is Dostoevsky's cognizance of suicide's link to amorality, atheism, nihilism, and even anthropophagy that compelled him to create counteractant forces. In fact, this polemic nucleates in both *Demons* and *The Brothers Karamazov*.

While the futuristic ken in *Demons* beholds pernicious Pyotr, its other Janus-face stares both back and forth at Stepan Trofimovich. Becoming both yesteryear and the morrow, this 1840s' man evolves into the novel's glimmer of light. Near novel's end, Stepan Trofimovich leaves town on foot and meets Sofya Matveyevna, the travelling gospel seller. When she reads him the passage from Luke, the one in the novel's epigraph, which describes "demons [coming out] of the man and enter[ing] the swine," Stepan Trofimovich recognizes them as "the sores, all the contagions, all the uncleanness, all the demons, large and small, who have accumulated in our great and beloved sick man, our Russia" (D, Pt 3, Ch 7; 723–4). Now evolved and evolving, Stepan Trofimovich accepts responsibility. He admits that the possessed are "us and them, and my son Petrusha . . . and I perhaps am the first standing at the very head . . . and we shall all drown, and that's no more than we deserve, because that's precisely what we're fit for" (D, Pt 3, Ch 7; 724). Significantly, after that leap "from a rock into the sea," what bobs up is hope that mother Russia "will be protected by a great idea and a great will from on high" and that "the sick man will be healed and 'will sit at the feet of Jesus' "(D, Pt 3, Ch 7; 724).

Stepan Trofimovich builds upon that "great idea" when Varvara Petrovna arrives and summons a priest. He "seems to gain a new lease on life," forgives everyone, and ecstatically rekindles his love of God, declaring "God is necessary to me because he is the only being who is capable of eternal love" (D, Pt 3, Ch 7; 732). He also asks, "what is more precious than love?" and answers, "[l]ove is higher than existence, love is the crown of being" (D, Pt 3, Ch 7; 732–33). In contrast to Kirillov, who shakes in his boots right up until his final second, Stepan Trofimovich does not have "the slightest fear of death" (D, Pt 3, Ch 7; 731). Stepan Trofimovich realizes that "immortality is necessary . . . because God would not want to commit an injustice and utterly quench the flame of love for him once it has been kindled" (D, Pt 3, Ch 7; 731–32). Satanic Pyotr, suicidal Stavrogin, and man-god Kirillov are "deprived of what is immeasurably great" and "die in despair" (D, Pt 3, Ch 7; 734). But Stepan's fate is antithetical. He alone retrieves Stavrogin's irretrievable "vanished dream," "bow[s] down before the Great idea," and enters the "eternal, immeasurable" Golden Age (D, Pt 3, Ch 7; 734).

While Stepan Trofimovich's epiphany refutes the amoral, atheistic, and nihilistic demons that provoke suicides and rampant destruction in *Demons*, *The Brothers Karamazov* too has its contrapositives. Mitya's heart and conscience are "purified under the storm of misfortune"; Alyosha's soul counters "the darkness of worldly wickedness" with "the light of love"; and Zosima endorses a life of "active love" (BK, Bk 1, Ch 4; 18: Bk 2, Ch 4; 56).[289] They triadically offset the menacing tenebrous backdrop, which is the godlessness that permits everything.[290] Overarching the entire novel is Dostoevsky's prayerful hope that Mitya's renewal, Alyosha's deeds, and Zosima's teachings will inhabit readers' hearts to ignite or reignite faith in Christ and the soul's immortality.

Mitya's inchoate regeneration projects "beckoning light" into the novel (BK, Bk 9, Ch 8; 508). Mitya diagnoses his own malaise as arising from the battle between the ideals of Sodom and the Madonna in his soul (BK, Bk 3, Ch 3; 108) and thus fits the diagnosis of "suicidal narcissist," who "unconsciously erects an idealized image and its counterpart, a despised image."[291] Although Mitya "thirsts" for the ideal and "for his resurrection and renewal," through most of the novel Mitya gets his marching orders from Sodom (BK, Bk 8, Ch 1; 366). And for Sodom, everything is permissible. Sodom permits Mitya to sink into depravity, go "whoring," plan his father's murder, brutalize his father, publicly beat Snegiryov, squander his fiancée's rubles on another woman, and smash Grigory's skull with a pestle.

But Mitya incrementally begins to change and inch toward a spiritual regeneration. In a letter to Nikolay Lyubimov, Dostoevsky suggests that the "Preliminary Investigation" at which Mitya "experiences a purification of his heart and conscience under the storm of misfortune and false accusation," is Mitya's veritable point of conversion.[292] While Mitya may be Dostoevsky's creation, he has free will, takes on a life of his own, and starts transforming earlier than his author's letter implies. It is likely that his renewal invisibly and silently began with Grigory washing him in a tub, and with Dr. Herzenstube's gift, the pound of nuts, a kindness Mitya remembers his entire life.

Before the "Preliminary Investigation," a touch of empathic awakening *is* visible. We see Mitya rescue the forester and drunk Lyagavy from a fire in their hut and persistently nurse the "fume poisoned drunkard" despite his exhaustion (BK, Bk 8, Ch 2; 377). Later we see him stop in his tracks to put his "new white handkerchief" to Grigory's head and "senselessly try to wipe the blood from his forehead and face" (BK, Bk 8, Ch 4; 394). After that, Mitya believes that he has killed his surrogate father and thus feels unworthy of Grushenka. It is then that readers hear Mitya vocalize heartfelt altruism. Although Grushenka appears to be running back to her old paramour, Mitya puts her interests first and says, "I won't interfere, I'll remove myself, I'll know how to remove myself. Live, my joy" (BK, Bk 8, Ch 5; 397). At this point, Mitya is shifting from a desire to possess an object of sensuous infatuation toward what will mature into devotional love. These scintillas of change precede and thus add credibility to the renewal unfolding during and after the "Preliminary Investigation."

In the "Preliminary Investigation," as Mitya confesses, readers detect change (albeit still rudimentary) in him. In stages, Mitya emerges from the "vile bog he had gotten stuck in" and ebbs toward the light, his dream "of the other, [the] renewed and . . . 'virtuous' life" (BK, Bk 8, Ch 1; 366).[293] When Mitya tells his interrogators that he has "found out more in this one cursed night than [he has] learned in twenty years of living," it rings true (BK, Bk 9, Ch 6; 486). Before this, even with preludial breakthroughs, Mitya was still myopically fixated on Mitya and mostly callous to the pain he had inflicted on others. Only after unbosoming his guilty shame to his interrogators do the feelings of others begin to tingle his heart. That is, for a flash, Mitya can feel what Katerina might have felt had he asked her to finance his next fling with Grushenka. But his treatment of Katerina is not the only offense that dawns on him.

The investigation takes him from his shame over Katerina's rubles into the deeper recesses of his conscience. This happens when the interrogator reminds Mitya that he has been out and about, planting evidence against himself, "spreading" rumors and "even shout[ing] everywhere about the three thousand [he] had spent . . . and not fifteen hundred" and that there were "dozens" available to attest to this (BK, Bk 9, Ch 7; 496). Here Mitya begins to grapple with his most heinous crime, one that both Menninger and Dostoevsky spell out. Menninger explains that the reason Mitya self-incriminates by "display[ing] all sorts of circumstantial evidence" is because he now understands "that to have wished for his father's death . . . carrie[s] with it a burden of guilt almost as great as if he had indeed perpetrated the act."[294] In a letter, Dostoevsky says precisely that Mitya "accepts with his soul punishment not for what he did, but for the fact that he was so hideous that he could and did want to commit the crime."[295] It is no wonder that Mitya ends up thanking his interrogators for taking a "burden from [his] soul" (BK, Bk 9, Ch 7; 499).

Mitya's dream of "the wee one," which follows close on the heels of his interrogation, figures prominently in Mitya's rebirth. In his dream, there is a "bony" woman with her breasts "all dried up, not a drop of milk in them" and a baby in her arms "crying, crying, reaching out its bare little arms, its little fists somehow all blue from the cold" (BK, Bk 9, Ch 8; 507). When Mitya repeatedly asks, "[w]hy are they crying," a peasant replies, "[t]he wee one's cold, its clothes are frozen, they don't keep it warm" (BK, Bk 9, Ch 8; 507). Like Raskolnikov in the epilogue to *Crime and Punishment*, Mitya's heart jumpstarts, and he feels a "tenderness such as he has never known before surging up," which, in turn, makes him crave "do[ing] something for them all, so that the wee one will no longer cry, so that the blackened, dried up mother of the wee one will not cry either, so that there will be no more tears in anyone from that moment on, and it must be done at once, at once without delay" (BK, Bk 9, Ch 8; 508).

The dream of the "wee one" helps to extricate Mitya from Sodom and bring him closer not only to the ideal of the Madonna, but also to Zosima's "active love." Moreover, Mitya has an epiphany, like the one Zosima's dying brother Markel articulates, which assigns all individuals responsibility "for everyone and everything" (BK, Bk 6, Ch 2; 289).[296] Kilpatrick explains that with suicidal narcissists, the superego identifies with the ideal self so much that it is compelled to quash the despicable self through self-slaughter.[297] But by novel's end, Mitya has walked his "quadrillion kilometers," discards suicide as an option, and intends "to live and live, to go on and on along some path, toward the new beckoning light" (BK, Bk 9, Ch 8; 508). Although Mitya's decision to dodge his Siberian sentence and seek exile in America has generated controversy, it make sense as his punishment.[298] As Shatov and Kirillov would attest, life in America is grueling hell; for Svidrigailov, it equates with a self-imposed death sentence. Mitya's chosen fate, however, seems to be a middle ground for someone who is wrongfully convicted, but nevertheless seeks penance for his sorted vile deeds and thoughts. In a sense, Alyosha's imprimatur on the decision is a nod to readers: "you're innocent," Alyosha tells Mitya, and your escape will instill a "greater duty in yourself" and "do more for your regeneration" than bearing that Siberian cross (BK, Ep., Ch 2; 763).

Alyosha, who anomalously evades the Karamazovian affliction, is another beacon of light. Unlike Mitya, Ivan, and Smerdyakov, Alyosha does not plan, consider, or commit suicide. Rather, he celebrates life. What makes Dostoevsky's "hero" so different from his brothers? Using an epithet for Christ, the narrator tells us that Alyosha is "simply an early lover of mankind" (BK, Bk 1, Ch 4; 18). Unlike his siblings, who are haunted by their "vandalized" childhoods, Alyosha bonds with his mother. Even though she dies when Alyosha is only four years old, he remembers her "all his life" along with "her face, her caresses" and these memories "emerge . . . as specks of light . . . against the darkness" (BK, Bk 1, Ch 4; 18).[299] Alyosha also maintains a decent rapport with his father by staying nonjudgmental toward him, even when Fyodor is submerged in his "den of dirty iniquity" (BK, Bk 1, Ch 4; 19). In his childhood, Fyodor came to love Alyosha "sincerely and deeply," and "more than such a man had . . . ever managed to love anyone else" (BK, Bk 1, Ch 4; 19). Thus, Alyosha is neither branded "expendable" nor entirely stripped of the familial ties that suicidologists believe repel thanatotic impulses.[300]

Durkheim's antidote to suicide is "a cohesive and animated society," in which there is "a constant exchange of ideas and feelings from all to each and each to all" (SU, Bk 2, Ch 3; 210). Securing that Durkheimian life raft of cohesion is Alyosha's innate gift. As the narrator imparts, Alyosha "possesse[s] in himself, in his very nature, . . . artlessly and directly, the gift of awakening a special love for himself" (BK, Bk 1, Ch 4; 19). Wherever he goes, Alyosha attracts love and fosters robust collectivity. This occurs in Yefim Petrovich Polenov's household, at school, with Snegiryov's family, amongst young Kolya's coterie, and with the elder Zosima, "to whom he became attracted with all the ardent first love his unquenchable heart" (BK, Bk 1, Ch 4; 18).[301] What might throw some readers for a loop are the indications that Alyosha would join a group of revolutionaries in Dostoevsky's plotted sequel to *The Brothers Karamazov*.[302] But having Dostoevsky's hero secure a new alliance, even one radically different from the monastery, conforms to Alyosha's tropistic leaning toward the light of collectivity.

Significantly, Dostoevsky's cherubic Alyosha always remains a flesh and blood individual with doubts and frailties. As a novice monk, he confesses to Lise that he might not "even believe in God" (BK, Bk 5, Ch 1; 220). He endures a spiritual crisis after Zosima's death, when the corpse emits an "odor of corruption" that evokes a cacophony of posthumous criticism (BK, Bk 7, Ch 1; 330). Alyosha even fleetingly imbibes a little Ivan-poison, which he admits to Ratikin: "I do not rebel against my God, I simply 'do not accept his world' " (BK, Bk 7, Ch 2; 341). Alyosha also has a touch of that Karamazovian sensuality and is thus not impervious to temptation, which becomes apparent when Grushenka seductively sits on his lap. Yet, throughout the novel, Alyosha's role is steadfastly salutary. As Richard Pevear points out, Alyosha "has the function of an *angelos*, a messenger in the most literal sense . . . and he is almost the only one in the novel who *can* hear."[303]And Alyosha does get an earful.[304] Practically every character in his milieu confesses to him, and, in variegated ways, Alyosha fosters healing. By making him celestial yet believable, Dostoevsky creates a paragon, but a human one, whom readers can hear, emulate, and use as a template for virtuous living.[305]

In Skotoprigonevsk, Zosima is the quintessential facula, radiating "the experience of active love" and personifying the best of *starchestvo* (BK, Bk 2, Ch 4; 56). He urges us to "try to love [our] neighbors actively and tirelessly" (BK, Bk 2, Ch 4; 56). He promises that "the more [we] succeed in loving, the more [we will] be convinced of the existence of God and the immortality of [y]our soul" (BK, Bk 2, Ch 4; 56). He prescribes embrocation for what ails Ivan: when "you reach complete selflessness in the love of your neighbor, then undoubtedly you will believe, and no doubt will be able to enter your soul" (BK, Bk 2, Ch 4; 56). But as with Alyosha, this spiritual father is also made of flesh and blood and in his life story, his *zhitie*, he reveals his struggles and missteps.[306]

In his youth, Zosima (then named Zinovy) was a member of the Cadet Corps, in which colleagues were "proud of [their] drunkenness, debauchery, and bravado" (BK, Bk 6, Ch 2; 296). There Zinovy was "transformed into an almost wild, cruel, and absurd creature" and after acquiring money, he led a "depraved and free bachelor's life" (BK, Bk 6, Ch 2; 295–96). When he became attached to a young woman, "selfishness" prevented him from proposing marriage (BK, Bk 6, Ch 2; 296). Later, when he discovered that all along this young lady had a fiancé whom she eventually married, Zinovy is furious and full of "loathsome . . . revenge and wrath" (BK, Bk 6, Ch 2; 297). Even though duels were "strictly forbidden," Zinovy challenged his rival (BK, Bk 6, Ch 2; 297).

The night before the duel, Zinovy returned home, "ferocious and ugly," and smacked his orderly Afanasy, bloodying his face (BK, Bk 6, Ch 2; 297). The next morning, nature hymned in Zinovy's ear as he beheld the garden, watched the rising sun, and heard birds singing. At that second, Zinovy recalled the blows he delivered the night before and "it was as if a sharp needle went through" his soul, making him sob (BK, Bk 6, Ch 2; 298). As he recounts this, Zosima declares: "heart of my heart, truly each of us is guilty before everyone and for everyone, only people do not know it, and if they knew it, the world would at once become paradise" (BK, Bk 6, Ch 2; 298). Zinovy's meditation engendered action: he threw himself at Afansy's feet to beg his forgiveness. At the duel, after a "shot just graze[s] his cheek," Zinovy hurled his own pistol into the trees and begged his adversary's forgiveness (BK, Bk 6, Ch 2; 299). In a pantheistic vision, Zinovy saw God everywhere and cried, "look at the divine gifts around us: the clear sky, the fresh air, the tender grass, the birds, nature is beautiful and sinless, and we, we alone, are godless and foolish, and do not understand that life is paradise" (BK, Bk 6, Ch 2; 299). Zinovy resigned his commission, entered the monastery, and was reborn as Zosima.

Zosima's past, riddled with hominal flaws, offenses, and blunders, along with the "odor of corruption," that "issues from [his]coffin" dispatches an audible message to readers: namely, Zosima is mortal and everyone—all of us—can regenerate, rekindle reverence, and access the elder's "paradise" (BK, Bk 7, Ch 1; 330). Significantly, those in the elder's life, like Markel and the mysterious visitor Mikhail, reinforce the conviction that such an ascent from Zinovy's pit to Zosima's paradise is humanly possible. Zosima's older brother, Markel, was originally a "hot-tempered and irritable" child, who did not believe in God (BK, Bk 6, Ch 2; 287). But before death, Markel knew that "each [individual] is guilty before everyone, for everyone and everything," and told the servants that "if God were to have mercy on [him] and let him live, [he] would begin serving [them]," and thus, he found himself "in paradise" (BK, Bk 6, Ch 2; 289–90). Mikhail's pilgrimage, which begins with darkness and ends with light, parallels that of Markel. Mikhail murdered a woman for rejecting his marriage proposal, but after years of guilty anguish, he confessed to Zosima. When Mikhail informed the authorities and furnished them with plentiful, tangible evidence, they decided that "the unfortunate man had gone mad," and declined to prosecute (BK, Bk 6, Ch 2; 311).[307] In the end, on his death bed, Mikhail told Zosima that his heartfelt repentance had paid off because he "felt joy and peace for the first time after so many years," saw brilliant God as merciful, and "rejoice[d] as in paradise" (BK, Bk 6, Ch 2; 311–12).

The Brothers Karamazov, with its realm of light and the "active love" that pushes back against the dark antipodal orb where "everything is permitted," atavistically resuscitates Manichaeistic duality. Miusov expounds upon the contents of darkness: when "everything is permitted," and "every separate person, who believes neither in God nor . . . immortality, the moral law of nature . . . change[s] immediately into the exact opposite of the former religious law, and that egoism, even to the point of evil doing," is not only "permitted . . . but should be acknowledged as . . . necessary [and] . . . most reasonable" (BK, Bk 2, Ch 6; 69). Mitya sums it up more succinctly: "without God and the future life . . . one can do anything" (BK, Bk 11, Ch 4; 589). But what does darkness permit? What falls under the rubric of "anything?" Zosima replies that it permits "cruel pleasures," along with "gluttony, fornication, ostentation, boasting and envious rivalry with one another" (BK. Bk, 6, Ch 3; 317). Alyosha says that "anything" entails "drown[ing] in depravity" and "stifl[ing] the soul in corruption" (BK, Bk 5, Ch 5; 263).

Other characters and events either enact or reveal what lightlessness permits. According to Fyodor Pavlovich, it permits installing a "regular harem in his house," holding "orgies," indulging in unbridled "drinking and carousing so outrageously," raping a *yurodivy*, aspiring to steal his son's paramour, and forgetting his children (BK, Bk 1, Ch 3; 13; Bk 3, Ch 2; 99). In Mitya's trial, it permits a miscarriage of justice in which legal players seek not truth, but their self-interested goals of awing an audience with their own "deific talents."[308] It permits Ivan to inject Smerdyakov, the "broth-maker," with godless gospel and sign on as silent partner in his villainy. It permits Smerdyakov to harm animals, teach boys to torture dogs, murder Fyodor Pavlovich, frame Mitya, dismantle Ivan, and take his own life.

Miusov and the Grand Inquisitor both concur that darkness permits anthropophagy.[309] As a gestalt, *The Brothers Karamazov* solemnly declares that the dark sphere, infected with ruptured families, atheism, and disbelief in immortality, does not merely permit, but actually breeds polymorphic, anomic, and egoistic pathologies. Where does it all end? It ends when it is not just permissible, but even "necessary" and "most reasonable" for individuals to self-annihilate and for the species to self-annul by consuming human flesh (BK, Bk 2, Ch 6; 69).

NOTES

1. Emile Durkheim, *Suicide: A Study in Sociology*, trans. John A. Spaulding and George Simpson (NY: The Free Press, 1951), 287 (hereinafter "SU"). All further citations are from this translation. Hereinafter, I will include the book and chapter number, as well as the page number from the Spalding translation, in parentheses in the text.

2. Fyodor Dostoyevsky, *Demons*, trans. Robert A Maguire (NY: Penguin Books, 2008), 128 (hereinafter "D" in the text). All citations are from this translation. Hereinafter, I will include the part and chapter number, as well as the page number from the Maguire translation, in parentheses, in the text.

3. Fyodor Dostoevsky, *The Brothers Karamazov*, trans. Richard Pevear and Larissa Volokhonsky (NY: Farrar, Straus and Giroux, 1990) 410 (Mitya) 264 (Ivan). (hereinafter "BK"). All citations are from this translation, unless otherwise indicated. Hereinafter, I will include the part and chapter number, as well as the page number from the Pevear and Volokhonsky translation, in parenthesis in the text.

4. For more discussion of "everything is permitted," see Amy D. Ronner, *Dostoevsky and the Law* (NC: Carolina Academic Press, 2015), 206–7 n.484. See also Durkheim, Ibid., 285 (Durkheim points out that anomic suicide "may be preceded by homicide or by some other violent outburst.").

5. See also, Ronner, *Dostoevsky and the Law*, Ibid., 207–8 n. 485 (discussing "active love" in *The Brothers Karamazov*).

6. See Richard Peace, *Dostoyevsky: An Examination of the Major Novels* (UK: Bristol Classical Press, 1992), 141 (discussing how "The Life of a Great Sinner" furnished material for other novels).

7. Ibid.

8. See Letter from Fyodor Dostoevsky to Nikolay Strakhov (March 24, 1870) in *Fyodor Dostoevsky Complete Letters*, trans. David A. Lowe (MI: Ardis Publishers, 1990), Vol. 3 [hereinafter *Letters* Vol. 3], 241.

9. Letter from Fyodor Dostoevsky to Apollon Maykov (March 25, 1870) in *Letters* Vol. 3, Ibid., 245.

10. See *The Notebooks for The Possessed*, ed. Edward Wasiolek and trans. Victor Terras (IL: The University of Chicago Press, 1968) [hereinafter *The Notebooks for The Possessed*], 27 ("I noticed a spot [on my chest] . . . which was extremely painful . . . my lungs again are full of phlegm . . . I keep wheezing and finding breathing difficult . . .I am also having right now, an attack of hemorrhoids, . . . [p]ain in my stomach"); Ibid., 28 ("Very soon after the fit, . . . a painful, literally unbearable pressure in my chest . . . [a] feeling that I might die of it").

11. Ibid., 28 (There is an "unprecedented increase in the frequency of these fits, as compared to anything I have experienced since I have had the disease" and it

"seems that the disease is entering a new, malignant phase."); Ibid., 29 ("[A]woke . . . with a feeling that I had had a fit" and "I had a headache and my body was aching all over."); Ibid. (I had a "most violent fit" and "I fell down and hurt my forehead.").

12. Edward Wasiolek, "Introduction," in *The Notebooks for The Possessed*, Ibid., 2–3.

13. Letter from Fyodor Dostoevsky to Apollon Maykov (March 25, 1870) in *Letters* Vol. 3, Ibid., 245. See also Letter from Fyodor Dostoevsky to Vera and Sofya Ivanova (May 1870), Ibid., 253 ("[M]eanwhile, returning to Russia is extremely essential, so much so that staying here any longer is becoming an absolute impossibility."); Letter from Fyodor Dostoevsky to Nikolay Strakhov (May 28, 1870), Ibid., 258 ("Oh. . . its so unbearable for me to live abroad that I can't even tell you!"); Letter from Fyodor Dostoevsky to Sofya Ivanova (July 1870), Ibid., 262 ("It's most distressing of all here for me to see Anna Grigorievna's homesickness. She very much wants to go to Russia" and "[t]hat's what most upsets me here."); Letter from Fyodor Dostoevsky to Sofya Ivanova (August 1870), Ibid., 267 ("The main thing is that I need to return to Russia . . . But I can't tell you in detail the torments and disadvantages that I suffer from life abroad," and "I'll omit all the psychological ones (homesickness, the necessity of Russian reality for me as a writer, and so forth)."); Letter from Fyodor Dostoevsky to Nikolay Strakhov (March 1871), Ibid., 325 ("I can't stand it, I am having such a hard time writing. I need to go to Russia . . . no matter what happens, I need to come back.").

14. Geir Kjetsaa, *Fyodor Dostoevsky: A Writer's Life*, trans. Siri Hustvedt and David McDuff (NY: Fawcett Columbine, 1987), 262.

15. Ibid.

16. See generally Joseph Frank, *Dostoevsky: The Mantle of the Prophet, 1871–1881* (NJ: Princeton University Press, 2002), 424 ("Dostoevsky had been almost hysterical on hearing of the failed assassination in 1866."); Kjetsaa, Ibid., 180 ("A young nihilist, Dmitri Karakozov, had attempted to assassinate the Tsar," and "[w]hen the writer heard the news, he was so agitated that his entire body shook.").

17. Ibid. ("The murder had been carried out by five men, two of whom had lured the victim into a grotto, where the rest of the gang was waiting" and "[s]hortly thereafter, his corpse was discovered in a transparent block of ice.") According to Wasiolek, "Dostoevsky first learned of Nechaev in December of 1869, probably in the reading room of the Dresden library, hunched over one of those Russian newspapers which he pursued and read all over Europe." *The Notebooks for The Possessed*, Ibid., 6. Wasiolek points out that "Nechaev insisted on total obedience" and Ivanov "opposed him, refused to obey an order of Nechaev's, and threatened to start a rival group." Ibid., 9. In *Demons*, the narrator explains that "it was . . . well known that [Pyotr] hated Shatov personally," that "there had been a quarrel between them at one time," and that "Pyotr Stepanovich never forgave an insult." *Demons*, Ibid., 611. Later when Kirillov learns of the murder, he shouts at Pyotr, "[y]ou did this because he spat in our face in Geneva!" and Pyotr replies, "[f]or that and for something else as well." Ibid., 678.

18. Wasiolek, *The Notebooks for The Possessed*, Ibid., 6.

19. See Wasiolek, *The Notebooks for The Possessed*, Ibid., 9 ("Dostoevsky had very little to add to the real-like Nechaev. He was as fantastic as anything the imagination could invent, or discover.").

20. See Kjetsaa, Ibid., 146 (claiming that Dostoevsky met Bakunin, "the man who had been sentenced to death several times for his revolutionary activity in Europe" and "had just escaped from Siberia and was now ready for new assignments."). See also Joseph Frank, *Dostoevsky: A Writer in His Time* (NJ: Princeton University Press, 2010), 554. Frank states that although the Dostoevskys were not present, Bakunin spoke at the second session of Congress and "made a stirring impromptu speech in French calling for the breakup of the Russian Empire and expressing the hope that its armies would be defeated in the future." Ibid. He "also called for the destruction of all 'centralized states' to make way for the formation of a United States of Europe organized freely on the basis of new groupings once the old state frameworks had been demolished." Ibid.

21. After the murder, Nechaev escaped and hid abroad, but in 1872 he was arrested in Zurich and turned over to the Russian authorities. Wasiolek explains that "[m]ost European countries did not permit the extradition of political refugees but did permit the extradition of common criminals, and it was as a common criminal that the tsarist government persuaded the European powers to help in the search for Nechaev." *The Notebooks for the Possessed*, Ibid., 10. Although he was "sentenced to twenty years of hard labor in Siberia," he was instead sent to the Alexei-Ravelin in St. Petersburg" where it was less likely he could exert influence over other political prisoners, yet while there "he continued to invoke fantasmal worlds, convincing his guards and his keepers that invisible threads tied him to every tremor that touched the empire." Ibid. Wasiolek adds that "[s]hortly before his unrepentant death in 1882, he had extensive and intimate contacts with members of 'The People's Will' and their successful attempt on the Tsar's life in 1881." Ibid.

22. Letter from Fyodor Dostoevsky to Apollon Maykov (March 25 1870), *Letters* Vol. 3, Ibid., 246.

23. Ibid. See also Letter from Fyodor Dostoevsky to Nikolay Strakhov (May 28, 1870), *Letters* Vol. 3, Ibid., 258 ("I am writing with great ardor for *The Russian Herald* and cannot at all guess what will come of this. Never before have I taken on a similar theme and in such a manner."); Letter from Fyodor Dostoevsky to Sofya Ivanova (October 9 1870), *Letters* Vol. 3, Ibid., 277 ("The idea is bold and big" and the "whole problem is just that I keep taking topics that are beyond me. The poet in me always outweighs the artist.").

24. Letter from Fyodor Dostoevsky' to Mikhail Katkov (October 8 1870), *Letters* Vol. 3, Ibid., 275. Dostoevsky states that "[w]ithout doubt, it is useful to portray such a person; but he alone wouldn't have enticed me." Ibid. He adds, "I don't think that those pathetic monstrosities are worthy of literature," but "[t]o my own surprise, that character is turning out in my hands to be a half-comic character." Ibid.

25. See generally Wasiolek, *The Notebooks for the Possessed*, Ibid., 7.

26. Ibid. See also Frank, *Dostoevsky: A Writer in His Time* (NJ: Princeton University Press, 2010), 604 ("Once he had fixed on Granovsky as the prototype of the generation of the 1840s (though many others will be amalgamated into the type,

particularly Herzen), Dostoevsky's imagination began to work rapidly."); Ibid., 610 ("In addition to Strakhov's article on Granovsky, another of his contributions to *Dawn*, a major series on Herzen published soon after the great man's death in Paris in January 1870, can also be linked to Dostoevsky's presentation of the character of Stepan Trofimovich").

27. Ibid. See also Wasiolek, *The Notebooks for the Possessed*, Ibid., 7; In *Demons*, Survey Vasilyevich Liputin, the putative socialist follower of Charles Fourier's ideas, also partially resembles Miliukov, Ibid., 7 n 9.

28. See Frank, *Dostoevsky: A Writer in His Time*, Ibid., 642–45. Frank explains that "Dostoevsky's target is unmistakable" and that "Turgenev's aristocratic airs and manner, his preference for residence in Europe, his demolition of Russian culture in *Smoke*, the philosophical pessimism revealed most overtly in his prose poems, the squeamish, self-protective egoism that Dostoevsky saw most blatantly manifested in the article about the execution of Troppman—nothing is spared!" Ibid., 643. See also Dostoevsky, *Demons*, Ibid., 408 ([E]ven though Karmazinov was the one who sauntered up to exchange kisses, he merely offered his own cheek."); Letter from Fyodor Dostoevsky to Apollon Maykov (August 1867) in *Fyodor Dostoevsky Complete Letters*, ed. and trans. David A. Lowe (MI: Ardis Publishers, 1989), Vol. 2 [hereinafter *Letters* Vol. 2], 257 (Speaking of Turgenev, Dostoevsky writes, "I also dislike the aristocratically farcical embrace of his with which he starts to kiss you but offers you his cheek.").

29. In a letter, Dostoevsky writes, "[t]hen there was a change again in the summer: yet another character [Stavrogin] appeared with claims to being the real *hero of the novel*, so that the former hero [Pyotr] (an interesting character, but one really not worthy of the title of hero) receded into the background." Letter from Fyodor Dostoevsky to Nikolay Strakhov (October 9, 1870), *Letters* Vol. 3, Ibid., 283.

30. See generally Ronner, *Dostoevsky and the Law*, Ibid., 13 (discussing Dostoevsky's involvement in the Petrashevsky circle).

31. Frank describes "the famous session of the Petrashevsky Circle at which Dostoevsky read Belinsky's *Letter to Gogol* [,] . . . the most powerful indictment against serfdom ever penned in Russia, and Dostoevsky used it to effectively reinforce the argument that serfdom was too morally intolerable to be endured a moment longer." Joseph Frank, *Dostoevsky: The Seeds of Revolt, 1821–1849* (NJ: Princeton University Press, 1976), 287.

32. Kjetsaa, Ibid., 64 ("The goal of Spechnev's Russian Society was to lay the groundwork for political revolution."). See also Harriet Murav, *Russia's Legal Fictions* (Ann Arbor: The University of Michigan Press, 1998) ("The primary activity . . . consisted in discussions—of the conditions of the peasantry, of Fourier's utopian socialism, of Belinsky's broad-ranging critique of Russian society . . . [and] some possible involvement with the printing of revolutionary pamphlets.").

33. Kjetsaa, Ibid., 64.

34. Letter from Fyodor Dostoevsky to Mikhail Katkov (October 8, 1870), *Letters* Vol. 3, Ibid., 275. Dostoevsky adds, "[b]ut I think that this character is a tragic one" and "[i]n my opinion he is both a Russian and a tragic character." Ibid. He explains, "I will be very sad if he is not a success" and "I'll be even sadder if I

hear the judgment that it's a stilted character" because "I took it from my heart . . . [and] it's a character that rarely turns up in all his typicality, but it's a Russian character (of a certain level of society))." Ibid. See Richard Pevear, "Forward" in Fyodor Dostoevsky, *Demons*, trans. Richard Pevear and Larissa Volokhonsky (NY: Vintage Classics, 1995), vii–xxiii (discussing Speshnev and his influence on Dostoevsky and on the character, Stavrogin). See also Amy D. Ronner, "Is Stavrogin Leading Us by the Nose? The Nihilistic Confession," *Dostoevsky Studies*, XX (2016), 71–101 (discussing the sources for *Demons* and Stavrogin). Frank states that "[n]o clues to any prototype for his character can be found in Dostoevsky's notes, and a debate has raged for years over whether he may not have been inspired by Bakunin." Frank, *Dostoevsky: A Writer in His Time*, Ibid., 645. He, however, believes that "if we are to link Stavrogin with any actual person, the likeliest candidate would be the enigmatic figure of Nikolay Speshnev, whom Dostoevsky called his Mephistopheles during the days of his involvement in the Petrashevsky Circle." Ibid.

35. In the excluded chapter, "At Tikons," Stavrogin claims that his faith is "imperfect," and Tikhon tells him that "complete atheism is more respectable than secular indifference." Dostoevsky, *Demons*, Ibid., 758. Tikhon elaborates: "the complete atheist stands on the next-to-last highest rung leading to the fullest and most complete faith (he may take that step, or he may not), but the indifferent man has no faith at all, except an ugly fear." Ibid., 758–59.

36. Letter from Fyodor Dostoevsky to Nikolai Lyubimov (March-April 1872) in *Dostoevsky Complete Letters*, ed. and trans. David A Lowe (MI: Ardis Publishers, 1991), Vol. 4 [hereinafter *Letters* Vol 4], 23. The "superfluous man" has been defined as one "genuinely committed to ideas but genuinely incapable of implementing them, who is confronted by the still more devastating truth that the divide between his head and his heart makes him ineffectual in love, inept in relationships, and superfluous in his own time." Richard Freeborn, "The Nineteenth Century: The Age of Realism, 1855–89," in *The Cambridge History of Russian Literature*, ed. Charles A. Moser (UK: Cambridge University Press, 1992), 281. Victor Terras explains that "[t]he notion that Evgenii Onegin was the first 'superfluous man' in Russian literature was read into the text by Belinskii and soon became standard" and that Pechorin of Lermontov's *A Hero of Our Time*, who is "meant to be a successor to Onegin . . . is set up as a member of a lost generation, a strong and capable man with no purpose in life—another version of Russian 'superfluous man,' as Belinskii was quick to point out." Victor Terras, "The Realist Tradition," in *The Cambridge Companion to the Classical Russian Novel*, eds. Malcolm V. Jones and Robin Feuer Miller (UK: Cambridge University Press, 1998), 196, 197.

37. Fyodor Dostoevsky, *Crime and Punishment*, trans. Richard Pevear and Larissa Volokhonsky (NY: Vintage Books, 1993), 262. Stavrogin, a Speshnev-like superfluous man, is a self-flagellator but the kind that flogs the organs of society before resorting to the consummate self-flog - -namely, self-murder as the release from relentless throbs of anomy.

38. Robert L. Belknap points out that "some narrators are omniscient and can see into everybody's mind, while others, including most first-person narrators, usually present one character's thoughts and dreams at first hand, but learn about

all others from their looks, actions, or words" and adds that "Dostoevsky's narrator in *Demons* shifts among these identities." Robert L. Belknap, "Introduction" in Dostoevsky, *Demons*, Ibid., xxiv–xxv. See also Deborah A. Martinsen, *Surprised by Shame* (OH: The Ohio State University Press, 2003), 104 ("By creating a subjective, ambivalent narrator, Dostoevsky forces the authorial audience to be wary" and in *Demons*, Dostoevsky "creates a narrator grappling with his own gullibility."); David Stromberg, "The Enigmatic G__v: A Defense of the Narrator-chronicler in Dostoevsky's *Demons*, *The Russian Review*, 71 (July 2012), 463 (defending "G___v by looking closely at how he functions both as a character and a narrator, isolating his actions and words in order to see what kind of G___v emerges against the background of his own diegetic world—and how his narrative idiosyncrasy may be related to his character's moral position.").

39. There are numerous references to Stavrogin's anger throughout the novel. See Dostoevsky, *Demons*, Ibid., 309 ("'A knife, a knife!' [Stavrogin] kept repeating in overwhelming anger"); Ibid. ("He grabbed the tramp by the scruff of the neck, and with all the anger that had built up inside him, flung him against the bridge as hard as he could."); Ibid., 320 (Stavrogin's "face expressed anger."); Ibid., 787 ("At Tikhon's Stavrogin says, "perhaps I can't hold out and in my rage I'll commit a new crime.").

40. Fyodor Dostoevsky, *A Writers Diary* I (1873–1876), trans. Kenneth Lantz (IL: Northwestern University Press, 1994), 550 (discussing his character, Stepan Trofimovich). See also Fyodor Dostoevsky, *A Writers Diary* II (1877–1881), trans. Kenneth Lantz (IL: Northwestern University Press, 1994), 1041–42 (discussing accidental families). Dostoevsky explains that "the accidental nature of today's Russian family consists in the loss among contemporary fathers of any common idea about their families—an idea common to all fathers that binds them together, an idea in which they could believe and could teach their children to believe, passing on to them this faith for the rest of their lives." Ibid. See also Carol Apollonio, *Dostoevsky's Secrets: Reading Against the Grain* (IL: Northwestern University Press, 2009), 117–18 (pointing out that the "new radical socialisms embraced the concept of *fraternite*, of solidarity among radicalized members of the younger generation as they worked to replace the patriarchal structures of the past with a new social order [, that] Dostoevsky depicts broken families with irresponsible or missing fathers as a microcosm of these larger social breakdowns [and that] his exploration of a morally and politically loaded concept of 'brotherhood' begins with *Demons*"); Vladimir Golstein, "Accidental Families and Surrogate Fathers: Richard Grigory and Smerdyakov," in Fyodor Dostoevsky, *The Brothers Karamazov*, trans. Susan McReynolds Oddo (NY: W.W. Norton & Co., Inc. 2011), 761 (pointing out that "in the case of Stepan Verkhovensky . . ., his liberalism is by far less important in the making of his son than his absenteeism"). The accidental family also appears in Dostoevsky's *The Adolescent* where Arkady Makarovich Dolgorunky, who is raised by foster parents and a tutor and has seen his putative father, Andrei Petrovich Versilov only once, has never met his legal father, the peasant Makar Dolgoruky. Later, the dysfunctional Karamazovs form the fulcrum of *The Brothers Karamazov*, where Dmitry, who is literally forgotten by his non-father-father, spends his youth "running about without

boots on his feet, and his little breeches hanging by one button." Dostoevsky, *The Brothers Karamazov*, Ibid., 674.

41. Anna Schur in *Wages of Evil: Dostoevsky and Punishment* (IL: Northwestern University Press, 2012), 15 aptly suggests that "while Dostoevsky rejects the malleable self of materialist psychology—that is, the self that is passively molded and remolded by the changing conditions of its environment—he does not fully deny the morally shaping significance of the empirical circumstances of one's life, and especially of one's childhood."

42. Edwin S. Shneidman, *The Suicidal Mind* (NY: Oxford University Press, 1996), 4 (italics in original).

43. Ibid.

44. Ibid.

45. Ibid. See also Andrew F. Henry and James F. Short, Jr., "The Sociology of Suicide," in *Clues to Suicide*, eds. Edwin S. Shneidman and Norman L. Farberow (NY: McGraw-Hill Book Company, Inc., 1957), 68 ("The sociologic evidence suggests that suicide is a form of aggression against the self aroused by some frustration, the cause of which is perceived by the person as lying within the self."); Leonard M. Moss and Donald M. Hamilton, "Psychotherapy of the Suicidal Patient," in *Clues to Suicide*, Ibid., 100 (discussing one of the "coexisting unconscious or partially conscious determinants of . . . suicide" as the "expression of hopelessness and frustration - -a relinquishing of any prospect of gaining necessary satisfactions from the present environment or reality situation").

46. Shneidman, *The Suicidal Mind*, Ibid., 4.

47. Louis Breger, *Dostoevsky: The Author as Psychoanalyst* (NY: New York University Press, 1975), 134. Breger points out that Stavrogin's "immoral and antisocial acts may be grouped into three categories, attacks on authority and conventional society" as well as "attacks of various kinds on women." Ibid.

48. Stepan Trofimovich is referring to characters in Shakespeare's plays *Henry IV, Parts 1 and 2* (1597). See notes in Dostoevsky's *Demons*, Ibid., 802 n. 3.

49. Edwin S. Shneidman, *The Suicidal Mind* (NY: Oxford University Press, 1996), 4. With respect to *belaya goryachka*, it "signifies *delirium tremens*, an episode of delirium usually brought on by a withdrawal from alcohol, although it may be induced as the result of heavy alcohol consumption." Notes in Dostoevsky in *Demons*, Ibid., 802 n. 8.

50. Dostoevsky, *Demons*, Ibid., 240 (Stavrogin "was suffering from an abscessed tooth," that "had merely come loose" and "[t]he abscess . . . had persisted for a whole week only because the sickman had refused to receive the doctor and have the swelling lanced in time.").

51. Plato, *The Last Days of Socrates*, trans. Hugh Tredennick and Harold Tarrant (NY: Penguin Books, 2003), 121 (*Phaedo).*

52. Sigmund Freud, *The Psychopathology of Everyday Life*, trans. A. Brill (SC: Columbia, 1901) (Chapter 8, Erroneously Carried-Out Actions).

53. Karl A. Menninger, *Man against Himself* (NY: Harcourt, Brace & World, Inc., 1966), 317.

54. Edwin S. Shneidman, *The Suicidal Mind*, Ibid., 62–63.

55. Michael A. Church and Charles I. Brooks, *Subtle Suicide: Our Silent Epidemic of Ambivalence about Living* (CA: Praeger, 2009), xi.

56. Shneidman, *The Suicidal Mind*, Ibid., 62; Plato, Ibid., 121 (*Phaedo*); Menninger, Ibid., 317; Church and Brooks, Ibid., xi. See also Steve Taylor, *Durkheim and the Study of Suicide* (UK: MacMillan Press, Ltd., 1982), 152–54. Taylor discusses "thanatation," in which "the gamble with death is the very essence of the act." Ibid., 152. He discusses Graham Greene, who in his youth, . . . dispelled . . . feelings of suffocating boredom and inertial" by "playing Russian roulette" and Sylvia Plath, who "had driven off the road knowing full well that it *might* kill her." Ibid., 153.

57. See Irina Reyfman, *Ritualized Violence Russian Style: The Duel in Russian Culture and Literature* (CA: Stanford University Press, 1999), 78 (explaining that Mikhail Lunin (1787–1845) reputedly engaged in reckless dueling and at one time even initiated a duel so that his opponent had the "opportunity to experience the sensation of standing in front of a gun").

58. The chronicler distinguishes Stavrogin from the Decembrist and states that he would defy death "without any sense of enjoyment, and only out of unpleasant necessity, and unenthusiastically, lackadaisically, even with a feeling of boredom." Dostoevsky, *Demons*, Ibid., 227.

59. *The Notebooks for the Possessed*, Ibid., 303.

60. With respect to the excluded chapter, Katkov, editor of *Russkii Vestnik*, refused to publish Stavrogin's confession, "At Tikhon's" due to its prurience. After Dostoevsky failed to persuade Katkov to change his mind, he had to accommodate the absence of that chapter. Frank, *Dostoevsky: A Writer in His Time*, Ibid., 622–23. In his letter to Katkov's assistant, Dostoevsky wrote: "[e]verything very obscene has been thrown out; the main thing has been shortened; and this whole half-insane escapade has been sufficiently indicated, but will be indicated even more strongly subsequently. I swear to you that I could not omit the essence of the matter." Letter from Fyodor Dostoevsky to Nikolai Lyubimov (March–April 1872) in *Letters* Vol. 4, Ibid., 23. When the novel appeared in book form, Dostoevsky did not reinstate the chapter, but thankfully it resurfaced amongst Dostoevsky's papers in 1921 and was published the following year.

61. See Dostoevsky, *Demons*, Ibid., 816 n. 28 (explaining that the Don Cossack Stenka Razin (1630–71) "is a popular hero in Russian folklore, and the subject of numerous folksongs and tales").

62. Stavrogin talks to Kirillov about suicide in the wake of an "evil deed or, more important, a shameful act, that is, something disgraceful, but very base indeed . . . so that people would remember it for a thousand years and hold it in contempt for a thousand years." Dostoevsky, *Demons*, Ibid., 261. Here too Stavrogin is planning his assault on Tikhon, Russia, the rest of the world, and most significantly himself, by disseminating his manifesto.

63. Frank, *Dostoevsky: A Writer in His Time*, Ibid., 625.

64. Dostoevsky researched this and addressed it in *The Brothers Karamazov*, when the narrator, elaborating on the elder's role in confession, explains that he is the one "who takes your soul, your will into his soul and into his will," and that all disciples accept an eternal confession to the elder, and in indissoluble bond between

the one who binds and the one who is bound." Dostoevsky, *The Brothers Karamazov*, Ibid., 27–28. Readers learn in *The Brothers Karamazov* that the elders, feared as gaining inordinate power, met with criticism that specifically targeted confession. Ibid. The opponents "shouted that the sacrament of confession was being arbitrarily and frivolously degraded." Ibid.

65. See Ronner, *Dostoevsky and the Law*, Ibid., 142–43 (discussing confession). See also Robin Feuer Miller, *The Brothers Karamazov: Worlds of the Novel* (CT: Yale University Press, 2008), 31 (explaining that Dostoevsky was one of the founders of the *pochvennichestvo* movement [and thus] when characters express the desire to kiss the earth and water it with tears, they are echoing a fundamental belief of their creator").

66. Ronner, *Dostoevsky and the Law*, Ibid., 142–43. See also Roger B. Anderson "Mythical Implications of Father Zosima's Religious Teachings," in Dostoevsky, *The Brothers Karamazov*, Susan McReynolds Oddo, trans. Ibid., 733 (explaining how Zosima "expresses a disturbing tendency, by Christian standards, to worship the earth and all forms of creation as being endowed with holy meaning" and that Russian critic R. Pletnev aligns the monk with "anthropomorphism and pantheism" and "considers Dostoevsky to be close to the *Strigol'niki* heresy, the old Russian practice of confessing to the soil rather than to Christian priests").

67. Apollonio, Ibid., 137.

68. Dostoevsky, *The Brothers Karamazov*, Ibid., 27–28 (discussing the "indissoluble bond" in confession). See also Miller, *Dostoevsky: Worlds of the Novel*, Ibid., 30 (explaining that Dostoevsky "was both attracted and repelled by the act of confession—attracted by its moments of rare and precious authenticity, repelled by the many self-justificatory and arrogant uses to which it could be put"); Amy D. Ronner, *Dostoevsky and the Law*, Ibid., 123–210. The chapter called, "The Confessant Gene: *Crime and Punishment* and *The Brothers Karamazov*," explores confessions in some of Dostoevsky's novels. Many scholars have analyzed and questioned the confessions in Dostoevsky's fiction. What follows are just some noteworthy examples: Mikhail Bakhtin, *Problems of Dostoevsky's Poetics* (MN: University of Minnesota Press, 2009), 227 (discussing Dostoevsky's *Notes From Underground* as a "confessional *Ich-Erzahlung*" in which there is "extreme and acute dialogization" and literally not a single monologically firm, undissociated word"); Peter Brooks, *Troubling Confessions* (IL: University of Chicago Press, 2001), 32 (describing the "self-abasing and self-aggrandizing confessional speeches of Dostoevsky's Karamazov, or Raskolnikov, or his Underground Man"); Deborah A. Martinsen, Ibid., 92 (explaining that "Dostoevsky's experiments in confession not only manifest his lifelong polemic with Rousseau, they also express his lifelong interest in narrative form" and that "[b]oth lying and confession are rhetorics of identity" or vehicles for self-presentation"); Robin Feuer Miller, "Dostoevsky and Rousseau: The Morality of Confession Reconsidered," in *Dostoevsky: New Perpsectives*, ed. Robert L. Jackson (NJ: Prentice Hall, 1984), 82 (stating that in Dostoevsky's works, "[c]onfessions may seek to provoke, titillate or lie; the narrator may expose, disguise, justify, or lacerate himself, . . . [b]ut rarely does the confession consist of a simple repentant declaration of wrongdoing or moral weakness").

69. Shneidman, *The Suicidal Mind*, Ibid., 4.

70. Apollonio, Ibid., 137.

71. Shneidman, *The Suicidal Mind*, Ibid., 4.

72. Jean-Jacques Rousseau, *Confessions*, trans. Angela Scholar (UK: Oxford University Press, 2000). In *Confessions*, Rousseau steals a ribbon from his employer, intending it as a gift for the young servant, Marion, who was a "good girl virtuous and totally loyal." Ibid., 82. He then blames the theft on Marion, and this "victim of [his] false witness" is fired, bereft of the likelihood of ever securing a decent position, and thus, sentenced to a life of "wretchedness and destitution." Ibid., 83. Echoing his precursor Rousseau, Stavrogin contends that he falsely accused his landlord's daughter, Matryosha, of stealing his pen knife. The mother responds by thrashing the child, an outcome that Stavrogin could have blocked because he knew that the knife was sitting on his own bed. See Robin Feuer Miller, "Dostoevsky and Rousseau: The Morality of Confession Reconsidered," in Jackson, Ibid., 82 (explaining that "Dostoevsky's scrutiny and critique of the literary confession frequently assumed the form of a veiled polemic with Rousseau and with his *Confessions* (1781)").

73. Erwin Stengel, *Suicide and Attempted Suicide* (NY: Jason Aronson, Inc., 1974), 44. See also Edwin S. Shneidman and Norman L. Farberow, "The Logic of Suicide," in *Clues to Suicide*, Ibid., 35 (After a study of over 700 suicide notes, they find that there tends to be "concern with the direct or indirect reaction of others, specifically what explicit thoughts are being entertained toward the individual.").

74. Viggo W. Jensen and Thomas A. Petty, "The Fantasy of Being Rescued in Suicide," in *Essential Papers on Suicide*, eds. John T. Maltsberger and Mark J. Goldblatt (NY: New York University Press, 1996) [hereinafter *Essential Papers*], 133. They point out that "[t]he fantasy of being rescued may, however, be expressed only through slips of the tongue and inadvertent behavior" and "[i]n such cases, the subject frequently is not aware of or will not acknowledge thoughts of suicide, death, or destruction." Ibid., 135.

75. Mikhail Bakhtin, Ibid., 6–7. See also Victor Terras in *Reading Dostoevsky* (WI: University of Wisconsin Press, 1998), 10 (pointing out that "Bakhtin showed that Dostoevsky's text creates a polyphonic concert of living voices, one of which is the narrator's (which itself may well be dialogic!), rather than a homophonic narrative dominated by the narrator's voice.")

76. Bakhtin, Ibid., 6.

77. See Nina Pelikan Straus, "Every Woman Loves a Nihilist: Stavrogin and Women in Dostoevsky's *The Possessed, Novel* (Spring 1994), 271–86. Straus explores the question, [w]hat the author mean[s] by surrounding his nihilist hero Stavrogin with several women with whom he is sexually intimate and who successively expose his weakness." Ibid., 276. She points out that "Stavrogin is unmasked by several women he harms" and that "[w]omen are the clues to the secret's discovery and to the difference between Stavrogin's levels of being (his appearance and his reality) as replicated by the novel's structure." Ibid.

78. Frank, *Dostoevsky: A Writer in His Time*, Ibid., 657.

79. Ibid., 658 ("Whatever confusion may exist in her mind, her demented second sight, like that traditionally possessed by a 'holy fool' (*yurodivy*) has now pierced through to his ultimate incapacity for true selflessness.").

80. Marya asks, "have you read about Grishka Otrepyev, that was cursed in seven Cathedrals?" Dostoevsky, *Demons*, Ibid., 306. Otrepyev was the first of three pretenders to the throne during the Time of Troubles (1598–1613), who claimed to be Prince Dmitry, Ivan the Terrible's son, who had died in 1591. Frank states that Stavrogin "is not the 'prince,' nor the genuine Lord and Rule of Russia, but only Grishka Otrepeyev, 'cursed in seven cathedrals,' the impious and sacrilegious 'impostor' and 'false pretender'—Ivan the Tsarevich - -that Peter Verkhovensky wishes to use to betray and mislead the hapless Russian people." Frank, *Dostoevsky: A Writer in His Time*, Ibid., 658.

81. See Apollonio, Ibid., 122 (explaining how [i]n depicting the relationship between Stavrogin and the characters in his circle, Dostoevsky draws upon a potent and recurring theme in Russian history—the tale of the tsar-pretender of the seventeenth-century 'time of troubles' (*smutnoe vremia*)").

82. After leaving Marya, Stavrogin repeats "in overwhelming anger . . . "[a] knife, a knife!'" and upon meeting Fedka takes out his wallet and "toss[es] him one bill from the wad, then a second, a third and a fourth." Dostoevsky, *Demons*, Ibid., 309, 312. The knife also appears in the missing chapter, "At Tikhons," when Matryosha's mother comes to tell Stavrogin about her daughter's suicide and parrots Marya by making a phallic reference to Stavrogin's knife: Matryosha's mother blames herself (and implicitly Stavrogin's instrument of seduction) when she utters, "[i]t was all because of your knife that I made her feel bad." Ibid., 773. See also Straus, Ibid., 281 ("[W]ith her words in his mind about the 'knife' [Stavrogin] carries both as a phallus and murder weapon, he runs into the street shouting 'a knife, a knife!'—only to meet the low-life criminal Fedka, who is his true mirror.")

83. In conversation with Stavrogin, Pyotr claims that he could guess that Stavrogin and Liza "spent the whole night in the room sitting side by side on chairs." Dostoevsky, *Demons*, Ibid., 587. See Apollonio, Ibid., 135 (explaining that "the clear association between Stavrogin and the castrate sect (*Skoptsy*) begs the blunt question of sexual impotence or celibacy" and noting "the close resemblance between Stavrogin and Mikhail Bakunin, who by all accounts, and despite his considerable charisma was himself reputed to be impotent").

84. Stavrogin tells Darya, "[y]ou seem to be interested in me, just as some superannuated sick-nurses for some reason take an interest in one particular patient in preference to others." Dostoevsky, *Demons*, Ibid., 325. Later, he says, "'A nurse! Hmm! . . . But maybe I do need something like that after all.'" Ibid., 326.

85. Henry A. Murray, "Dead to the World: The Passions of Herman Melville," in *Essays in Self-Destruction*, ed. Edwin S. Shneidman (NY: Jason Aronson, Inc., 1967), 9.

86. Lawrence S. Kubie, "Multiple Determinants of Suicide," in *Essays in Self-Destruction*, Ibid., 459.

87. Ibid. See also Dostoevsky, *Demons*, Ibid., 201 ("[H]his face really did 'look like a mask.'"); Ibid., 254 ("His face was pale and stern, but looked utterly frozen and immovable; . . . he certainly looked like a lifeless wax figure.").

88. Letter from Fyodor Dostoevsky to Apollon Maykov (March 25, 1870) in *Letters* Vol. 3, Ibid., 245.

89. Shneidman, *The Suicidal Mind*, Ibid., 4–7.

90. Ibid., 4.

91. Imitation or contagion is also called "the Werther effect," named after Johann Wolfgang von Goethe's novel, *The Sorrows of Young Werther*, in which the protagonist, inflicted with *weltschmerz*, kills himself. In its wake, the popular novel spawned copycats. See David P. Phillips, "The Influence of Suggestion on Suicide: Substantive and Theoretical Implications of the Werther Effect," in *Essential Papers*, Ibid., 290–313; Kay Redfield Jamison, *Night Falls Fast: Understanding Suicide* (NY: Vintage Books, 1999), 278 (describing how "young men were found dead by gunshot dressed in blue frock coats and yellow waistcoats, with a copy of Goethe's novel nearby"); Andrew Solomon, *The Noonday Demon: An Atlas of Depression* (NY: Scribner, 2015), 250–51 ("The contagion of Suicide is incontrovertible" and "[w]hen Goethe's *The Sorrows of Young Werther* was published . . . copycat suicides in the mode of Goethe's protagonist were committed across Europe."). See also Fyodor Dostoevsky, *A Writer's Diary*, Vol. (1873–1876), trans. Kenneth Lantz (IL: Northwestern University Press, 1994), 300 (While mentioning suicide accounts in the newspapers, Dostoevsky discusses how "[w]hen young Werther ends his life, he regrets, in the last lines he left, that he will never again see 'the beautiful constellation, the Great Bear,' and bids it farewell.")

92. Phillips, "The Influence of Suggestion on Suicide," in *Essential Papers*, Ibid., 290–313. Although Durkheim is one of his "sociological gods," Phillips seeks to refute Durkheim's claim that "the effects of suggestion on suicide are only local" and that "suggestion serves merely to precipitate a suicide a little sooner than it would otherwise have occurred." Ibid., 290, 305.

93. Durkheim, calling this phenomenon "imitation" or "contagion" relates the "well-known story of the fifteen patients who hung themselves in swift succession in 1772 from the same hook in a dark passage of the hospital." Durkheim, Ibid., 97. He also discusses how in "1813, in a little village of Saint-Pierre-Monjay, a woman hanged herself from a tree and several others did likewise at a little distance away," and "[w]hen Lord Castelreagh threw himself into Versuvius, several of his companions followed his example." Ibid., 131. See also Solomon, Ibid., 250–51 ("If one person commits suicide, a group of friends or peers will frequently follow" and "[l]ocations for suicide are used over and over again, carrying the curse of those who have died: the Golden Gate Bridge in San Francisco, Mount Mihara in Japan, particular stretches of railway lines, the Empire State Building.").

94. Eric Marcus, *Why Suicide* (NY: Harper One, 1996), 36.

95. "One observed that this was the very best way out, and that the young man couldn't have come up with anything more intelligent than that; another concluded that though it was only for an instant, he'd had a good life." Dostoevsky, *Demons*, Ibid., 364.

96. See Dostoevsky, *Demons*, Ibid., 419 (With respect to Shatov, Kirillov explains, "we just avoid each other. We spent too long a time lying side by side in America.").

97. According to the notes in *Demons*, this line is "taken almost verbatim from P.I. Ogorodnikov's travel essay 'From New York to San Francisco and Back to Russia.'" *Demons*, Ibid., 809 n. 7.

98. Letter from Fyodor Dostoevsky to Apollon Maykov (March 25, 1870) in *Letters* Vol. 3, Ibid., 245 (speaking of his longing for Russia).

99. See *Dostoevsky: The Notebooks for Crime and Punishment*, ed. and trans. Edward Wasiolek (IL: University of Chicago Press, 1967) [hereinafter *The Notebooks for Crime and Punishment*], 239 ("Nihilism is base servility of thought. A Nihilist is a lackey of thought.").

100. See also *Demons*, Ibid., 101 (The chronicler describes Kirillov as a man who "seemed rather pensive and distracted, spoke haltingly and somehow ungrammatically, somehow transposing his words and getting all mixed up if he had to create a longer sentence.").

101. Dostoevsky, *Demons*, Ibid., 684 (Kirillov states, "[f]or me there is no higher idea than the non-existence of God" and that "[m]an has done nothing but invent God in order to live without killing himself.").

102. Fyodor Dostoevsky, *Crime and Punishment*, Ibid., 511. See also Ronner, *Dostoevsky and the Law*, Ibid., 202–3 (discussing "Mitya's decision (in *The Brothers Karamazov*) to dodge his Siberian sentence and instead seek exile in America" and how "[b]oth Mitya and Dostoevsky, who himself experienced self-imposed exile, knows that being uprooted from Russian soil is not a cakewalk").

103. At one point, Pyotr, noticing that "somethings not quite right here," sees that Kirillov has "boiled chicken and rice" but hasn't "started in on it," and he ultimately takes the food for himself. *Demons*, Ibid., 676.

104. Menninger, Ibid., 88–89.

105. Edwin S. Shneidman "Orientations Toward Death," in *The Psychology of Suicide: A Clinician's Guide to Evaluation and Treatment*, eds. Edwin S. Shneidman, Norman L. Farberow, and Robert E. Litman (NJ: Jason Aronson Inc., 1994), 10. Psychology professors Church and Brooks, similarly point to "people who are living 'on the edge' and at the same time, [are] wasting their lives" with "risky behaviors, self-neglect, carelessness, and negative mood states," which they call "subtle suicide." Church and Brooks, Ibid., xi. Kirillov is subtly suicidal before his overt suicidal act.

106. Menninger, Ibid., 142. Edwin S. Shneidman, *The Suicidal Mind*, Ibid., 63.

107. See Derek Offord, "Nihilism and Terrorism," in *Dostoevsky in Context*, eds. Deborah A. Martinsen and Olga Maiorova (UK: Cambridge University Press, 2015), 49 (explaining the significance of the word "prejudices"). Offord discusses the ideology of Chernyshevsky, Dobrolyubov, Pisarev, and others, who denied "that human beings had a spiritual dimension or altruistic impulses" and challenged "established religious moral and aesthetic beliefs" as so-called "prejudices." Ibid.

108. This is a paraphrase of Revelation 10:6. See also Fyodor Dostoevsky, *The Idiot*, trans. David McDuff (NY: Penguin Books, 2004), 265 (Prince Myshkin, in pondering his epileptic fits, recalls what he told Rogozhin that "in that moment I somehow begin to understand the extraordinary phrase '*there should be time no longer.*' ").

109. Kirillov's concept of the Man-God has roots in the discussions of the 1840s among the members of the Petrashevsky Circle, many of whom were proteges of German philosopher, Ludwig Feurbach, who authored *The Essence of Christianity*, which "was even more radical in its secularization of the divine, and argued that, instead of God having created Man in His own image, exactly the opposite was true." Joseph Frank, *Dostoevsky: The Seeds of Revolt, 1821–1849* (NJ: Princeton University Press, 1976), 186. It is also connected to the theories of Nikolay Mombelli, whose article was read at a Petrashevsky Circle meeting, which envisioned people "becom[ing] moral divinities—absolute gods, only in a human body." *Demons*, Ibid., 814–15 n. 20 (explaining the origins of Man-God).

110. As translated, the French phrases are "[l]ong live the republic . . .[l]ong live the democratic, social and universal republic or death . . .[l]iberty, equality, fraternity or death!" *Demons*, Ibid., 837 n. 4.

111. See Donald A. Nielsen, "Dostoevsky in the Mirror of Durkheim," in *Durkheim, The Durkheimians and the Arts*, eds. Alexander Riley, W.S.F. Pickering and William Watts Miller (NY: Durkheim Press/Berghahn Books, 2013), 95–118. Nielsen calls Durkheim the "heir to a long tradition of French social thought, much of it utopian, socialist, and positivist in inspiration, which emerged in the wake of the French Revolution and included names such as Montesquieu, Rousseau, Fourier, Saint-Simon, and Comte." Ibid., 95. Although concluding that this "renovated socialist," who freed himself "from the taint of Marxist historical materialism," had "evidently never read Dostoevsky," Nielsen nevertheless foists Kirillov, as egoist, under the Durkheim-lens. Ibid.

112. Ibid., 100.

113. Durkheim explains that "we call the suicide caused by intense altruism *altruistic suicide*[,] . . .]b]ut since it is also characteristically performed as a duty, the terminology adopted should express this fact." *Durkheim*, Ibid., 221. He concludes that we should "call such a type *obligatory altruistic suicide*." Ibid.

114. While Kirillov "in a fever of ecstasy . . . point[s] to an icon of the Savior before which a lamp was burning," he purports to reject Christ, "who live[d] amidst a lie and . . . die[d] for a lie," and thus "the salvation for all" depends entirely on him—Kirillov—to prove his truth that "God does not exist." Dostoevsky, *Demons*, Ibid., 684–85.

115. Charles William Wahl, "Suicide as a Magical Act," in *Clues to Suicide*, Ibid., 26–28.

116. Ibid., 27–28.

117. Ibid., 28.

118. Ibid., 26 (Such "magical aspirations may constitute largely overlooked motives for suicide.").

119. Fyodor Dostoevsky, *The Idiot*, Ibid., 265.

120. Matthew 22:30 ("For in the resurrection they neither marry nor are given in marriage, but are like angels in heaven.").

121. Wahl, Ibid., 28.

122. Ibid., 29.

123. Ibid.

124. Ibid., 30.

125. Ibid., 28 ("The use of magical defenses is obvious to us when it adopts the form of the solipsistic dereism of the hebephrenic or catatonic schizophrenic, but is not so obvious when the conscious rational superstructure is left largely intact, as is the case in the average suicide candidate.").

126. Yuri Corrigan, *Dostoevsky and the Riddle of the Self* (IL: Northwestern University Press, 2017), 95.

127. See Ibid. ("Though Kirillov . . . regards Pyotr with contempt, Dostoevsky depicts his subsequent possession by Pyotr, a process dramatized in the latter's act of dictation.").

128. John Keats, "La Belle Dame Sans Merci" (revised version) in *Keats: Poems & Selected Letters*, ed. Carlos Baker (NY: Charles Scribner's Sons, 1962), 250–51.

129. Letter from Fyodor Dostoevsky to Sofya Ivanova (July 18, 1871) in *Letters* Vol. 3, 365 ("God gave me a son Fyodor (who at this moment is being swaddled and he is yelling with a strong healthy cry).").

130. Kjetsaa, Ibid., 266.

131. In a letter to Pasha, Dostoevsky writes: "Our Alyosha died yesterday, from a sudden fit of epilepsy, which he had never had before." Letter from Fyodor Dostoevsky to Pavel Isaev (May 16, 1878) in *Fyodor Dostoevsky Complete Letters*, trans. David A. Lowe (MI: Ardis Publishers, 1991), Vol. 5 [hereinafter *Letters* Vol. 5], 241.

132. See Dostoevsky's preface, "From the Author," in *The Brothers Karamazov*, Ibid., 3 (I "start[] out on the biography of my hero, Alexei Fyodorovich Karamazov").

133. See Marcel Proust, "Dostoievski," in *Marcel Proust on Art and Literature: 1896–1919*, trans. Sylvia Townsend Warner (NY: Carroll & Graf Publishers, Inc., 1997), 380 ("For Dostoievski, forced labour was probably the stroke of good fortune which set free his inner life").

134. Fyodor Dostoevsky, *Notes from the House of the Dead*, trans. Boris Jakim (MI: William B. Eerdman's Publishing Co., 2013), 17. See also Ronner, *Dostoevsky and The Law*, Ibid., 260 (discussing Ilynsky).

135. Ibid., 260.

136. Freud traces parts of the plot in *The Brothers Karamazov* to Dr. Dostoevsky's mysterious death. See generally Sigmund Freud, "Dostoevsky and Parricide," in F.M. Dostoevsky, *Stavrogin's Confession: Suppressed Chapters from The Possessed*, trans. Virginia Woolf and S.S. Koteliansky (CT: Martino Publishing, 2014), 87 (theorizing that Dostoevsky's father's violent demise filled him with conflicted emotions that the novelist later visits in the Karamazov murder). But see Kjetsaa, Ibid., 29–36 (explaining why "the facts contradict Freud's theory" and "[t]he absolute parallels . . . drawn been Mikhail Andreyevich and Fyodor Karamazov are also dubious"); Frank, *Dostoevsky: A Writer in his Time*, Ibid., 45 ("The 'facts' that Freud adduces can be shown to be extremely dubious at best, and at worst simply mistakes.").

137. There are numerous commentaries on suicide in Dostoevsky's, *A Writer's Diary*. See, e.g., Fyodor Dostoevsky, *A Writer's Diary*, Vol. 1, Ibid., 299 (Speaking of people who commit suicide, he states that although the newspapers say that this "happens because such people think too much," his "conviction is quite contrary:

he doesn't think at all; he simply isn't capable of formulating an idea" and "[i]t's the behavior of utter swine."); Ibid., 496–97 (explaining that "[s]ome people accept living crushed, while others do not and they kill themselves," and discussing a girl who committed suicide because she "got *tired*, very tired, so tired that she wanted to rest"); Ibid., 650–56 (After discussing the suicide of Elizaveta Aleksandrovna Herzen, daughter of Alexander Herzen, and of the girl who served as a prototype of the heroine of "The Meek One," he pens "the thoughts of one person - -a materialist . . .who committed suicide *out of boredom.*"); Ibid., 733 ("Underlying this confession of a man who is going to die 'by logical suicide' is the necessity of the immediate conclusion, here and now, that without faith in one's soul and its immortality, human existence is unnatural, unthinkable, and unbearable."); Ibid., 737 ("[I]n our age people who have never concerned themselves with any higher questions also kill themselves" and they do it "mysteriously, for no apparent reason."); Ibid., 742 ("Destroying one's self is a serious thing, despite any *chic* that may be involved, and an epidemic of self-destruction spreading among the educated classes is an extremely serious thing which warrants constant observation and examination.") *A Writer's Diary*, Vol. 2, Ibid., 844–46 ("The Boy Celebrating His Saint's Day" in which he discusses a child who hung himself and that "powerful sense of some oppressive injustice, an anguished, precocious and tormenting sense of one's own insignificance, a morbidly intensified question: 'Why do they *all* dislike me so?'"); Ibid., 1156–1158 (discussing "the suicide of General Hartung in Moscow during the session of the Circuit Court . . . after he heard the jurors pronounce him guilty" and stating that "this is . . . a tragedy (a very deep one)—the destiny of Russian life").

138. Rousseau, Ibid., 348. At one point in *Confessions*, Rousseau seeks to justify himself by saying that he "trembled at the thought of handing [his children over to [some] badly brought-up family so that they might be even more badly brought up." Ibid., 406. He supposedly "decided that the risks of having them educated by the foundlings were considerably fewer." Ibid.

139. Robin Feuer Miller, "Dostoevsky and Rousseau: The Morality of Confession Reconsidered," in Jackson, *Dostoevsky New Perspectives*, Ibid., 83. Miller explains that he "condemned Rousseau's philanthropy (*chelovekoliubie*) as well as his habit of confession," Ibid.

140. *The Notebooks for The Brothers Karamazov*, ed. and trans. Edward Wasiolek (IL: The University of Chicago Press, 1971) [hereinafter *The Notebooks for The Brothers Karamazov*], 23 (Dostoevsky writes, "At Mikhail Nikolaevich's (foundling home)").

141. Fyodor is a sensuous version of Foma Fomich Opiskin, a character, in Dostoevsky's *The Village of Stepanchikovo*, who starts out as a sickening sycophant and after attaining wealth and power, dominates and inflicts misery on his household.

142. See Martinsen, *Surprised by Shame*, Ibid., 61 (explaining that Dostoevsky "has a sociopolitical as well as a metaphysical agenda in his novel," and "[w]ith his portrayal of narcissistic paternity," he "obliquely criticizes all bad fathers, including negligent landowners and tsars, parasites on the constituencies they are obligated to protect").

143. Joseph C. Sabbath, "The Suicidal Adolescent—The Expendable Child," in *Essential Papers on Suicide*, Ibid., 185–99; Howard I. Kushner, *Self-Destruction in the Promised Land: A Psychocultural Biology of American Suicide* (NJ: Rutgers University Press, 1989); Durkheim, *Suicide*, Ibid., 241–76.

144. The narrator points out that even "[t]hough Pyotr Alexandrovich may have exaggerated, still there must have been some semblance of truth in his story." Dostoevsky, *The Brothers Karamazov*, Ibid., 11. He also suggests that Fyodor could have been "play-acting" because he liked to "suddenly take[e] up some unexpected role" even "when there was no need for it, and even to his own disadvantage." Ibid.

145. The narrator further embellishes Pyotr's character by pointing out that while he had no problem forgetting about Mitya, "the outbreak of the February revolution so struck his imagination that he was unable to forget it for the rest of his life." Dostoevsky, *The Brothers Karamazov*, Ibid., 11.

146. Sabbath, Ibid., 185–99.

147. Ibid., 195.

148. Ibid., 196.

149. Kushner, Ibid., 119 (describing "incomplete mourning" as a "profound sense of unresolved loss").

150. Ibid. Kushner explains that "[f]or Durkheim, the loss resulted from an individual's social and cultural alienation," and "for Freud, the loss resulted from disconnection from one's self." Ibid. See also William Styron, *Darkness Visible: A Memoir of Madness* (NY: Vintage Books, 1992) (applying Kushner's theory to his own suicidal state).

151. Anna A. Berman discusses how "triplicity plays out differently between brothers vs. father-son." *Siblings in Tolstoy and Dostoevsky: The Path to Universal Brotherhood* (IL: Northwestern University Press, 2015), 59. She points out that while "Ivan and Dmitri are not rent asunder by their overlapping interests in Katerina Ivanovna, but instead are brought together," for "Dmitri and Fyodor . . . there is no longer even the attempt at coexistence." Ibid. She explains that father and son "use [Grushenka] as a 'conduit' for their virulent hatred of each other." Ibid.

152. See Susanne Fusso, *Discovering Sexuality in Dostoevsky* (IL: Northwestern University Press, 2006), 113–14 (explaining how "Dmitri and Fyodor are locked in a fierce struggle over Grushenka," a "relationship . . . often called 'Oedipal' with the Freudian sense of the term in mind"). Fusso points out that "Dostoevsky's version of the father-son rivalry is closer to the original myth of Oedipus (and its treatment in the tragedy of Sophocles) than to Freud's version." Ibid., 114. She adds: "[i]t is Laius's abandonment of Oedipus that makes psychologically possible the realization of the prophecy he fears [and] Oedipus kills a father who is not really a father (and marries a mother who is not really a mother) in Fetiukovich's sense." Ibid.

153. In the novel, Mitya even scripted his plans to kill Fyodor in a letter to Katya, stating: "I give you my word of honor, I will go to my father and smash his head in." Dostoevsky, *The Brothers Karamazov*, Ibid., 618. After Ivan incriminates himself in Mitya's trial, Katya, who is in "hysterics," dashes forth with that letter. Ibid., 687.

154. Katerina describes Mitya's "rash and unjust act of seizing Snegiryov's beard." Dostoevsky, *The Brothers Karamazov*, Ibid., 193. She explains that when

Mitya "seized [the captain] by the beard in front of everyone, led him outside in that humiliating position, and led him a long way down the street, . . . the captain's son, who goes to the local school, just a child, saw it and went running along beside them, crying loudly and begging for his father, and rushing up to everyone asking them to defend him, but everyone laughed." Ibid. She adds that Snegiryov is "very poor" and "he and his family, a wretched family of sick children and a wife—who it seems, is insane—have fallen into abject poverty." Ibid., 193–94. The incident—"one of those acts that [Mitya] alone could bring himself to do"—damages Snegiryov's family and causes his son to be bullied and teased. Ibid., 193.

155. Sigmund Freud, *Totem and Taboo*, trans. and ed. James Strachey (NY: W.W. Norton & Co., 1989), 191 n. 63. See also Freud, "Mourning and Melancholia" in *A General Section from the Works of Sigmund Freud*, ed. John Rickman, M.D. (NY: Anchor Books, 1989), 133 ("We have long known that no neurotic harbors thoughts of suicide which are not murderous impulses against others redirected upon himself, but we have never been able to explain what interplay of forces could carry such a purpose through to execution.").

156. John T. Maltsberger, "Suicide Danger: Clinical Estimation and Decision," in *Essential Papers on Suicide*, Ibid., 574–83.

157. Ibid., 578.

158. Ibid.

159. Mitya states: "I will now confess all my infernality to you . . . and you yourselves will be surprised at what baseness a combination of human feelings can sink to. Know then, that I already had the solution in mind . . . to announce my betrayal to her, and for that betrayal, to carry through that betrayal, . . . and immediately run off with another woman." Dostoevsky, *The Brothers Karamazov*, Ibid., 495.

160. Wahl, Ibid., 25–26. He states that "[i]t appears that expiation of personal guilt and achievement of a hostile wish by guilt induction are almost invariably present in every suicidal attempt or act." Ibid., 26.

161. Elizabeth Kilpatrick, "A Psychoanalytic Understanding of Suicide," *American Journal of Psychoanalysis* 8, no. 1 (1948), 13–23.

162. Ibid., 19.

163. Ibid., 18.

164. Ibid.

165. See Miller, *The Brothers Karamazov: Worlds of the Novel*, Ibid., 32–33 (Readers "witness firsthand the struggle between God and the devil in Mitya's heart. Mitya crisply presents that amorphous conflict in terms of three potential scenarios that occur to him during his moment of crisis").

166. Ibid.

167. Mitya explains that her bow to the ground was "not like an institute girl but like a Russian woman." Dostoevsky, *The Brothers Karamazov*, Ibid., 114. Her bow is suggestive of the *pochvennichestvo* movement. See Miller, *The Brothers Karamazov: Worlds of the Novel*, Ibid., 31 ("Dostoevsky was one of the founders of the *pochvennichestvo* movement [, and thus,]when his characters express the desire to kiss the earth and water it with their tears, they are echoing a fundamental belief of their creator.").

168. See Miller, *The Brothers Karamazov: Worlds of the Novel*, Ibid., 90 ("Mitya had, in a gesture loaded with phallic significance, pulled his sword from its scabbard, kissed it, and replaced it," which embodied both his lust and honorable repression of it.").

169. See also Dostoevsky, *The Brothers Karamazov*, Ibid., 119 ("I can be a mean man, with passions mean and ruinous, but a thief, a pickpocket, a pilferer, that Dmitri Karamazov can never be!"), 492 ("I'm a beast, a man with no more self-restraint than a beast, right am I right? But still not a thief! Not an outright thief, not outright . . . I squandered it, but I did not steal it!").

170. Menninger, Ibid., 54.

171. Ibid.

172. Menninger explains that Mitya, "accumulated and displayed all sorts of circumstantially incriminating evidence." Ibid. Also, he "put himself through the horrible torture of trial and permitted himself to be sentenced to life imprisonment, when he could easily have escaped it by the proper maneuvers in the court room." Ibid. Menninger points out that "Dmitri knew that to have wished for his father's death as he had (he even went so far as to plan it) carried with it a burden of guilt almost as great as if he had indeed perpetrated the act." Ibid., 55

173. Wahl, Ibid., 26.

174. Wahl, Ibid; Menninger, Ibid., 54.

175. See Sigmund Freud, "The Ego and the Id," in *A General Selection from the Works of Sigmund Freud*, Ibid., 224. Freud conceived of two instincts, one of which is Eros, "compris[ing] not merely the uninhibited sexual instinct proper and the impulses of a sublimated or aim-inhibited nature derived from it, but also the self-preservative instinct . . . assigned to the ego," and the other, Thanatos, the death drive, the task of which is to lead organic matter back into the inorganic state." Ibid.

176. Ibid. See also Sigmund Freud, *Civilization and Its Discontents*, ed. James Strachey (NY: W.W. Norton & Company, Inc., 1962), 66 ("I drew the conclusion that besides the instinct to preserve living substance[,] . . . there must exist another, contrary instinct seeking to dissolve those units and to bring them back to their primaeval inorganic state.").

177. See Kushner, Ibid. ("incomplete mourning"); Sabbath, Ibid ("expendable child'); Kilpatrick ("suicidal narcissism"); Durkheim, *Suicide*, Ibid. (anomy).

178. See Eric Marcus, Ibid., 19. He states that a person is more likely to resort to suicide if a family member has done so but admits that there "is no clear agreement on why this is the case." Ibid. He opines that "[b]iology and genetics . . . come into play, since depression and schizophrenia, which are leading factors associated with suicide, can be passed on from one general to the next." Ibid. He adds that "personality traits may be inherited, including self-destructive tendencies, as well as a greater or lesser ability to cope with life's challenges." Ibid. Menninger states that "there is no convincing scientific evidence that the suicidal impulse is hereditary and there is much psychoanalytic evidence to show that these cases of numerous suicides in one family may be explained on a psychological basis." Ibid., 59. He says that "the element of suggestion" can "point the way for the actual self-infliction of the death sentence." Ibid., 60.

179. See Apollonio, Ibid., 152 (explaining that "in Russian folk culture, 'shrieking' (*Klikushestvo*) was a mental illness resembling hysteria that afflicted peasant women and was often perceived as a form of demonic possession").

180. See Sabbath, Ibid. (expendability); Kushner, Ibid. ("unresolved grief"); and Kilpatrick, Ibid. ("suicidal narcissism").

181. Shneidman, *The Suicidal Mind*, Ibid., 163–64.

182. Ibid., 164.

183. Kilpatrick, Ibid., 18.

184. Ivan also chronicles the life of an abused-child, Richard, who is discarded by his parents and grows up among Swiss mountain shepherds, who beat him, "[teach] him nothing," and send "him out to tend the flocks in the cold and wet, with almost nothing to eat." Dostoevsky, *The Brothers Karamazov*, Ibid., 239. See generally Letter from Fyodor Dostoevsky to Nikolay Lyubimov (May 10, 1879) in *Letters* Vol. 5, 82–83 (describing Book 5 of *The Brothers Karamazov* for the upcoming issue of *The Russian Herald*). Dostoevsky elaborates on Ivan, who "takes up a theme that *I think* irrefutable—the senselessness of the suffering of children—and derives from it the absurdity of all historical reality." Ibid., 83. He adds, "[e]verything that my protagonist says in the text . . . is based on reality." Ibid. See also Ronner, *Dostoevsky and the Law*, Ibid., 177–80 (discussing Ivan's diatribe on theodicy); and Amy D. Ronner "Dostoevsky as Juvenile Justice Advocate and Progenitor of Therapeutic Jurisprudence," in *St. Thomas Law Review* 30 (2017), 5–41 (discussing the physical and psychological abuse of children as a recurrent theme in Dostoevsky's writings).

185. See Deborah A. Martinsen, "Ingratitude and the Underground," in *Dostoevsky Studies* 17 (2013), 20 (pointing out that the "underground man sees humans as ungrateful in part because he projects his self-image onto others").

186. Kilpatrick, Ibid., 17.

187. Victor Terras, *A Karamazov Companion: Commentary on the Genesis, Language, and Style of Dostoevsky's Novel* (WI: University of Wisconsin Press), 52.

188. Shneidman, *The Suicidal Mind*, Ibid., 4 (defining "psychache").

189. Terras, *Reading Dostoevsky,* Ibid., 128 (speaking of the "subtext, intertext, and ambiguity" in *The Brothers Karamazov* and pointing out that "Fiodor Pavlovich, old Adam, carries in his lustfulness, the seed of the personalities of his three sons: Ivan whose passion is intellectual, Dmitry, whose passion is sensual and Aliosha, whose passion is spiritual"). But see Miller, who has a more robust perspective: she says that it "is common place to discover in the three Karamazov brothers an allegory about spirit (Alyosha), mind (Ivan), and body or heart (Mitya) [, b]ut this classification becomes woefully inadequate and thin once one takes more than a cursory glance at them." *The Brothers Karamazov: The Worlds of the Novel*, Ibid., 29.

190. Terras, *A Karamazov Companion*, Ibid., 48.

191. Revelation 3:15–16. See notes in Dostoevsky, *Demons*, Ibid., 841 n. 7 (explaining that Tikhon recites the passage from the Apocalypse in the Russian translation," but "since he is reciting by heart, there are minor inconsistences—he incorporates a few words from the more archaic Church Slavonic translation").

192. Stob points out that "Laodicea was a financially successful and well-fortified city, but it had compromised its position and future by overlooking the important

consideration of an adequate water supply." William S. Stob, *The Church of the Laodiceans: Then and Now* (William S. Stob: 2017), 9. Laodicea received hot water from miles away, which came through pipes, but when it arrived the water was not cold and thus it was lukewarm and useless. Jesus makes his point to the Laodiceans by referring to something familiar—their daily reality. Stob states that "[f]or being lukewarm toward the Son of God, and for their compromise of the Word of God, the Lord has rejected this Church" and thus "Christ told them, '*I will spue thee out of my mouth.*'" Ibid., 15. Speaking of these verses from Revelation, Sequeira similarly opines that Christ is using the water metaphor to "evaluat[e] Laodicea's spiritual condition." Jack Sequeira, *Laodicea: Christ's Urgent Counsel to the Lukewarm Church in the Last Days* (ID: Pacific Press Publishing Assoc., 1995), 29. Sequeira states that Christ is speaking of self-righteousness and gives "four reasons" this is so "nauseating to Christ" that "He will have to spit [them] out if [they] remain lukewarm": "hypocrisy," "unbelief," "selfishness" and "denying Christ." Ibid., 44–49.

193. Samuel Wills, *The Seven Churches of Asia: An Exposition* (NY: M.W. Dodd, 1854), 334.

194. Miller, *The Brothers Karamazov: The Worlds of the Novel*, Ibid., 59–60. When Ivan chronicles the life of Richard, he sways and professes to have no faith earthly justice either. After the earthly justice system condemns Richard to death, he finds truth in God and Christian faith. Although the "pious" citizens rejoice in his transformation and "his brothers" smother him with kisses, the earthly justice system turns its back on him. Dostoevsky, *The Brothers Karamazov*, Ibid., 240. Richard ends up on the scaffold where the guillotine whacks off his head.

195. Letter from Fyodor Dostoevsky to Natalya Dmitrievna Fonvizina (end of January, third week of February, 1854) in *Fyodor Dostoevsky Complete Letters,1832–1859*, ed. and trans. David Lowe and Ronald Meyer (MI: Ardis Publishers, 1988), Vol. 1 [hereinafter *Letters* Vol. 1], 195.

196. See Letter from Fyodor Dostoevsky to Apollon Maykov (December 23, 1868) in *Letters* Vol. 3, Ibid., 113 (speaking of plans to write an "enormous novel called *Atheism*" about a character who "loses his faith in God[,] . . . checks out the new generations, atheists, Slavs and Europeans, Russian fanatics and anchorites, priests[, and] gets hooked strongly, by the way, by a Jesuit, a propagator, a Pole[, who] sinks him into the depths of flagellantism—and at the end finds both Christ and the Russian land"). See also Denis Dirscherl, *Dostoevsky and the Catholic Church* (IL: Loyola University Press, 1986), 121 (explaining how Dostoevsky has been called the enemy of the Jesuits).

197. See Miller, *The Brothers Karamazov: The Worlds of the Novel*, Ibid., 65 (discussing the "complex interplay . . . between Alyosha as listener (audience) and sometimes critic and Ivan as author and sometimes critic[,] which "becomes more complex as the reader begins to discern the similarities between Ivan and his Grand Inquisitor and between Alyosha and Jesus").

198. Fyodor Dostoevsky, *Crime and Punishment*, Ibid., 483.

199. See e.g., Dostoevsky, *The Brothers Karamazov*, Ibid., 267 ("[h]is squinting left eye winked); Ibid., 268 ([h]is squinting left eye seemed to say"); Ibid., 269 (he "put his left foot forward"); Ibid., 605 ("his left eye . . . seemed to be hinting

at something"); Ibid., 613 ("his left eye began winking"); Ibid., 624 (he "suddenly pulled his left leg from under the table").

200. Edwin S. Shneidman and Norman L. Farberow, "The Logic of Suicide," in *Clues to Suicide*, Ibid., 36. See also Shneidman, *The Suicidal Mind*, Ibid., 58 ("[T] here is at least a touch of schizophrenia or insanity in every suicide in the sense that, in suicide, there is *some* disconnection between thoughts and feelings.").

201. See Letter from Fyodor Dostoevsky to Nikolay Lyubimov (August 10, 1880) in *Letters* Vol. 5, 262 ("My hero [Ivan], of course sees hallucinations too, but confuses them with his nightmares. It is not just a physical (diseased) trait here, when a person begins at times to lose the distinction between the real and the unreal (which has happened to almost every person at least once in his life) but as a spiritual trait as well, which coincides with the hero's character . . ."); Letter from Fyodor Dostoevsky to Alexander Blagonravov (a doctor) (December 19, 1880) in *Letters*, Vol. 5, Ibid., 303 (thanking the doctor "for . . . informing [him] of the accuracy of [Ivan's mental illness [as depicted" and saying that "[a]n expert's opinion will support me, and you have to agree that under the circumstances . . . Ivan . . . could not have had any hallucination other than that one.").

202. See Ronner, *Dostoevsky and the Law*, Ibid., 57–121 ("The Impenetrable Mental Capacity Doctrine: *The Double*") The section of the book analyzes *The Double*, in which readers cannot distinguish between what is real and what is hallucination." Ibid., 62. That is, "Dostoevsky intentionally keeps readers in limbo, leaving them to wonder if anything at all really happens to his Golyadkin." Ibid.

203. John T. Maltsberger and Dan H. Buie, Jr., "The Devices of Suicide: Revenge, Riddance and Rebirth," in *Essential Papers*, Ibid., 406.

204. Ibid.

205. Edwin S. Shneidman and Norman L. Farberow, "The Logic of Suicide," Ibid., 31.

206. Silvano Arieti, "Schizophrenia: The Psychodynamic Mechanisms and the Psychostructural Forms" in *American Handbook of Psychiatry*, Vol. 3 (e-Book: International Psychotherapy Institute, 2016), 70–71. See also Silvano Arieti, *Interpretation of Schizophrenia* (NY: Basic Books, Inc. 1974). He explains that "because in a developmental theoretical framework this logic seemed to be a precursor of our normal secondary process logic, it was called *paleologic* (from the Greek *palaios*, "ancient and old". Ibid., 229. In contrast, "the usual logic of the normal human being, who uses secondary process cognition, is generally called Aristotelian, because Aristotle was the first to enunciate its laws." Ibid.

207. Arieti, "Schizophrenia: The Psychodynamic Mechanisms and the Psychostructural Forms," Ibid., 71. See also *Interpretation of Schizophrenia*, Ibid., 231. Speaking of a patient who "thought he was Switzerland," Arieti explains that "at the time . . . Switzerland was one of the few free countries in the world" and he needed to identify himself with the concept of freedom. Ibid. Consequently, the paleologic was as follows: "'Switzerland loves freedom, I love freedom. I am Switzerland.'" Ibid.

208. Arieti, "Schizophrenia: The Psychodynamic Mechanisms and the Psychostructural Forms," Ibid.

209. See Dostoevsky, *The Brothers Karamazov*, Ibid., 794 n. 25 ("[I]t is said that Martin Luther (1483–1546) was tempted by the devil while translating the Bible and threw his inkstand at him.").

210. See generally Deborah A. Martinsen, "The Devil Incarnate," in *Dostoevsky's Brothers Karmazov: Art, Creativity and Spirituality*, eds. Predrag Cicovacki and Maria Granik (Heidelberg: Universitatsverlag Winter, 2010), 55 ("Dostoevsky uses the devil's disappearance to signal the profoundly private nature of Ivan's hallucination: he dissipates as soon as the external world, in this case Alyosha's knock on the window, obtrudes on his interiority.").

211. See Letter from Fyodor Dostoevsky to Nikolay Lyubimov (August 10, 1880), in *Letters* Vol. 5, Ibid., 262 ("[I]n denying the reality of the phantom, [Ivan] defends its reality when the phantom disappears. *Tormented by lack of faith, he (unconsciously) wishes at the same time that the phantom were not imaginary, but something real.*).

212. The devil also talks about suicide when he relates an incident involving an "afflicted marquis, who confesses to his "Jesuit spiritual director and says, "'Give me back my nose." Fyodor Dostoevsky, *The Brothers Karamazov*, Ibid., 646. When the Jesuit gives no consolation, "[t]he unfortunate young man [goes] home and [shoots] himself." Ibid. The devil refers to "real Jesuit casuistry," and the implication here is that it can drive one to renounce life.

213. See Durkheim, *Suicide*, 284–85.

214. See Marcel Proust, *A la Recherce Du Temps Perdu*, Vol. 3, ed. Pierre Clarac and Andre Ferre (Paris, 1954), 380 (suggesting that *The Brothers Karamazov* is an ancient myth of crime, vengeance and expiation that begins with the rape of Stinking Lizaveta). See also Terras, *A Karamazov Companion*, Ibid., 119–20 (discussing Proust's perspective). Smerdyakov tells Maria Kondratievna, "I could have done better . . . and I'd know a lot more, if it wasn't for my destiny ever since childhood." Dostoevsky, *The Brothers Karamazov*, Ibid., 224.

215. Sabbath, Ibid., 185.

216. Smerdyakov tells Maria Kondratievna that "I'd have killed a man in a duel with a pistol for calling me low-born, because I came from Stinking Lizaveta without a father, and they were shoving that in my face in Moscow, it spread there thanks to Grigory." Dostoevsky, *The Brothers Karamazov*, Ibid., 224.

217. Ibid., 225 (Smerdyakov calls Fyodor "a madman" and says that Mitya "is worse than any lackey, in his behavior, and in his intelligence, and in his poverty . . . and he's not fit for anything, but . . . he gets honor from everybody.").

218. *Diagnostic and Statistical Manual of Mental Disorders: Fifth Edition* (DC: American Psychiatric Publishing, 2013), 659.

219. Ibid.

220. In the chapter, "Disputation," Grigory calls Smerdyakov a "scoundrel," "broth-maker," and after telling him "[y]ou're anathema and cursed even now," he hisses "[y]ou're lying, curssse, you!" Fyodor Dostoevsky, *The Brothers Karamazov*, Ibid., 128–30.

221. See e.g., Dostoevsky, *The Brothers Karamazov*, Ibid., 614 (Ivan "jumped up and hit [Smerdyakov] as hard as he could on the shoulder with his fist, so that he rocked back towards the wall.").

222. Shneidman, *The Suicidal Mind*, Ibid., 164.
223. Ibid. (stating that what drives suicide is "the haunting losses of childhood's special joys").
224. See also Dostoevsky, *The Brothers Karamazov*, Ibid., 605 (Smerdyakov's "dry eunuch's face seemed to have become very small.").
225. Peace, Ibid., 262.
226. Ibid.
227. Menninger, Ibid., 231–85 (Self-Mutilations).
228. Ibid., 252.
229. Ibid., 270.
230. Ibid., 252.
231. See Golstein, Ibid., 768 ("In one of his rare monologues, Smerdyakov expresses the Job-like wish to have never been born," which "alerts us to the harsh reality of his life.). See also Vladimir Kantor, "Pavel Smerdyakov and Ivan Karamazov: The Problem of Temptation," in Fyodor Dostoevsky, *The Brothers Karamazov*, ed. Susan McReynolds Oddo, Ibid., 696, 701 (Connecting Job to Ivan, he states that "the utterances of Ivan and those of the Biblical hero coincide to a striking extent.").
232. Job 10: 18–20 ("Why then have You brought me out of the womb? Oh, that I had perished and no eye had seen me! I would have been as though I had not been. I would have been carried from the womb to the grave.").
233. Fyodor Dostoevsky, *The Notebooks for The Idiot*, ed. Edward Wasiolek and trans. Katharine Strelsky (NY: Dover Publications, Inc., 1967), 66 ("Plan for Iago . . . The Idiot's character -- - an Iago. But he ends up divinely. He renounces, and so forth."). In William Shakespeare's play, *Othello*, Iago (addressing Roderigo) promises that he will never "wear [his] heart upon [his] sleeve for daws to peck at" and states, "I am not what I am" (1.1.64–65).
234. Referring to Pushkin's *Table-Talk*, the narrator imports Shakespeare's Othello to differentiate between betrayal of trust and Mitya's "seething" jealousy and points out that "'Othello is not jealous, he is trustful." Dostoevsky, *The Brothers Karamazov*, Ibid., 380–81. See also *Notebooks for the Brothers Karamazov*, Ibid., 130 ("True, Othello is not jealous as Pushkin said: he is much too calm in searching for details . . . Jealousy is not like that.").
235. See e.g., Frank, *Dostoevsky: The Mantle of the Prophet*, Ibid., 593 (Smerdyakov's "function . . . is to serve as Ivan's alter-ego."); Apollonio, Ibid., 200–1 n.33 ("Ivan and Smerdiakov are, based on a great deal of figurative, and some scraps of literal, evidence, doubles."). For discussion of "paleologic," see Arieti, "Schizophrenia: The Psychodynamic Mechanisms and the Psychostructural Forms," Ibid., 70–71; Shneidman and Farberow, "The Logic of Suicide," in *Clues to Suicide*, Ibid., 31–40.
236. Silvano Arieti, *Creativity: The Magic Synthesis* (US: BasicBooks, 1976), 82.
237. Ibid.
238. Ibid.
239. Ibid.
240. Ibid.

241. See Harriet Murav, *Russia's Legal Fictions* (MI: University of Michigan Press, 2001), 208 (Smerdyakov "suffers from epilepsy, which is "a disease associated with demonic possession.").

242. See Udaya Seneviratne, "Fyodor Dostoevsky and His *Falling Sickness*: A Critical Analysis of Seizure Semiology," *Epilepsy & Behavior* 18 (2010), 424, 427 (While diagnosing Dostoevsky with "a partial epilepsy syndrome most probably arising from the dominant temporal lobe," the medical doctor discusses Smerdyakov's "simulation" of a prolonged seizure).

243. Bakhtin, Ibid., 222.

244. Dostoevsky, *The Brothers Karamazov*, Ibid., 266 ("Ivan . . . realized at the first sight of him that the lackey Smerdyakov was also sitting in his soul, and that it was precisely this man that his soul could not bear.").

245. Numbers 22: 21–34.

246. See Fyodor Dostoevsky, *A Writers Diary*, Vol. 2, Ibid., 820–23 ("Foma Danilov, a Russian Hero, Tortured to Death").

247. Numbers 22: 23–24.

248. Ibid., 27–29. Gifted with the power of speech, the ass asks "[w] hat have I done to you to make you beat me these three times?" Ibid., 28.

249. Ibid., 31–34.

250. Ivan's devil chatters about the "Jesuit spiritual director" who tried to console the Gogolesque man deprived of his nose. Dostoevsky, *The Brothers Karamazov*, Ibid., 646. When this man tells the priest that he would rather have his nose put out of joint for the rest of his life than to have no nose at all, the priest pontificates: "your desire has already been fulfilled indirectly for having lost your nose, you have thereby, as it were, had your nose put out of joint all the same." Ibid. See Nikolai V. Gogol, "The Nose" in *The Overcoat and Other Tales of Good and Evil* (NY: W.W. Norton & Co., 1957), 203 (the story of a barber who finds his severed nose in his morning bread). Loss of the nose was associated with the saddle nose of syphilis, a hideous deformity that occurs when the bridge of the nose caves into the face and the flesh rots away, and in literature, it imparts depravity.

251. Fyodor Dostoevsky, *The Brothers Karamazov*, Ibid., 132 (Ivan adds, "[t]he rocket will go off, but it may fizzle out. So far, the people do not much like listening to these broth-makers.").

252. See Peter Brooks, *Troubling Confessions* (IL: University of Chicago Press, 201), 59 (""[W]hereas Mitya is forever making distinctions between thoughts and deeds, Ivan's confession thoroughly blurs them, offering Smerdyakov's deed as a version of his own thoughts, and indeed of everyone's thoughts.").

253. Ivan asks Smerdyakov, "why were you sending me to Chermashnya then?" and he answers it himself, "[y]ou were asking me to leave . . . go, you said, get out of harm's way." Fyodor Dostoevsky, *The Brothers Karamazov*, Ibid., 607.

254. See Letter from Fyodor Dostoevsky to Ye. N. Lebedeva (November 8, 1879) in *Letters* Vol. 5, 164 (discussing how "the old man was killed by the servant Smerdyakov"). Dostoevsky elaborates: "Ivan . . . participated in the murder only obliquely and remotely, only by (intentionally) keeping from bringing Smerdyakov to his senses during the conversation with him before his departure for Moscow and

stating to him clearly and categorically his repugnance for the crime conceived by him." Ibid. He adds that "Ivan clearly saw and had a premonition of [the crime] . . . and thus *seemed to permit* Smerdyakov to commit the crime" and that this "*permission* was essential for Smerdyakov." Ibid.

255. Katerina presents Ivan with a letter Mitya wrote in a drunken state where he gives his "word of honor" that he "go to [his] father and smash his head in and take [the money] from under his pillow" Fyodor Dostoevsky, *The Brothers Karamazov*, Ibid., 618.

256. Terras, *A Karamazov Companion*, Ibid., 382 ("Did Ivan expect the devil's cloven hoof to emerge from it?").

257. Fyodor Dostoevsky to Mikhail Katkov (September 1865) in *Letters* Vol. 2, Ibid., 185 (Speaking of Raskolnikov, Dostoevsky writes that "God's justice, earthly law comes into its own, and he finishes by being *compelled* to denounce himself.").

258. Arieti, "Schizophrenia: The Psychodynamic Mechanisms and the Psychostructural Forms," Ibid., 71.

259. At Mitya's trial, the prosecutor describes a "galloping" troika as the finale of his speech. Fyodor Dostoevsky, *The Brothers Karamazov*, Ibid., 722.

260. Paul G. Quinnett, *Suicide: The Forever Decision* (NY: Crossroad Publishing Co., 2016), 75.

261. Moss and Hamilton, Ibid., 100.

262. Herbert Hendin, "Psychodynamics of Suicide, with Particular Reference to the Young," in *Essential Papers on Suicide*, Ibid., 616.

263. Shneidman, *The Suicidal Mind*, Ibid., 132.

264. Ibid.

265. Fyodor Dostoevsky, *The Brothers Karamazov*, Ibid., 625 (*The Homilies of Our Father among the Saints, Isaac the Syrian* was a "thick yellow book, the only one lying" on the table). See Terras, *A Karamazov Companion*, Ibid., 22. He explains that "Saint Isaac . . .anchorite and bishop towards the end of the sixth century, seems to have had more than casual influence on the religious doctrine expressed in Father Zosima's exhortations." Ibid. He explains that "[a] new Slavonic translation of Isaac's sermons and wisdoms had been prepared by Paissy Velichkovsky in 1787 . . . and Dostoevsky owned an 1858 edition of this book." Ibid., 22–23.

266. Shneidman, *The Suicidal Mind*, Ibid., 132.

267. Belknap, "Introduction," Dostoevsky, *Demons*, Ibid., xviii–xix.

268. Emile Durkheim, *The Rules of Sociological Method*, trans. W.D. Halls and ed. Steven Lukes (NY: Free Press, 2013), 78–100 (explaining social facts). See also Diane Harriford and Becky Thompson, *When the Center Is on Fire* (TX: University of Texas Press, 2008) (discussing Durkheim's "famous concept" of "social facts" and how "[m]yths, suicide, patriarchy, languages, the division of labor, and racism are all examples of social facts").

269. Wahl, Ibid., 28.

270. Ibid., 30.

271. Before signing the suicide note, Kirillov says "everything that's hidden will become manifest," and to some extent that prediction came to fruition. Dostoevsky, *Demons*, Ibid., 686.

272. Letter from Fyodor Dostoevsky to Apollon Maykov (March 25, 1870) in *Letters* Vol. 3, Ibid., 245.

273. See George G. Weickhardt, "Book I of Dostoevsky's *Demons*: A Slow Start?" *Dostoevsky Studies* 12 (2008), 61–65. He explains that "Dostoevsky obviously wanted to show how liberals, socialists, and free thinkers not only paved the way for but actually gave birth to the revolutionaries and 'monsters' of the sixties, such as Nechaev, Chernyshevskii and Dimitri Karakozov." Ibid., 61. See also Ronner, "Is Stavrogin Leading us by the Nose? The Nihilistic Confession," Ibid., 100 ("[T] hese forbear[s] . . . inseminated the nation's womb with and even built the cradle for the future annihilators—the swinish nihilists of the Sixties."). In *Demons*, Ivan Turgenev should be added to the list of those who are to blame.

274. See Frank, *Dostoevsky: A Writer in His Time*, Ibid., 661 ("No matter what he may think, Stavrogin cannot entirely eliminate his *feeling* for the difference between good and evil" and "[t]his irrepressible sentiment breaks forth from his subconscious . . . in Stavrogin's famous dream of 'the Golden Age.'"). See also Shneidman, *The Suicidal Mind*, Ibid., 4 (defining "psychache").

275. Letter from Fyodor Dostoevsky to Nikolai Lyubimov (March–April 1872) in *Letters* Vol. 4, Ibid., 23.

276. See Richard Peace, Ibid., 177 (explaining that when the dream "is blotted out by the tiny red spider, . . . perhaps the message which may be drawn from the dream and its obliteration is that complete freedom for man to do exactly as he pleases cannot be reconciled with earthly paradise").

277. In *Confessions*, Rousseau steals a ribbon and blames the theft on the young servant, Marion, and confides: "I am so troubled by this cruel memory, and so distressed, that I lie sleepless in my bed, imagining the poor girl advancing towards me to reproach me for my crime as though I had committed it only yesterday." Rousseau, Ibid., 83–84. In Stavrogin's manifesto, the image of Matryosha resembles Marion's reproach.

278. After Shatov's murder, although Lyamshin initially "exonerated . . . Stavrogin from any participation in the secret society, and from any agreement with Pyotr," he later admitted that he had deliberately shielded Stavrogin." Dostoevsky, *Demons*, Ibid., 741.

279. When Stavrogin encounters Fedka, he tosses an "entire wad" of banknotes at him, which could be construed as a payment to an assassin. Dostoevsky, *Demons*, Ibid., at 312. When Stavrogin meets Darya, he tells her, "I gave [Fedka] all the money in my wallet, and he's now utterly convinced that I gave him an advance!" Ibid., 325. Darya replies, "Can you really not see that they've completely entangled you in their net!" Ibid.

280. At the governor's ball, more than half the public in attendance, who own or live in the town of Zarechye, learn that it is "burning in three separate places." Dostoevsky, *Demons*, Ibid., 566 The literary fete plus the ball are chaotic failures and the chronicler describes how the whole fiasco ended: "[t]oward morning they pulled down Prokhorych's stall, drank themselves senseless, danced the Komarinsky unexpurgated, made a filthy mess of the rooms, and only at dawn did part of this gang, completely drunk, arrive at the scene of the fire, which was already dying down, to create new disorders." Ibid., 567.

281. Peace points out that "Shigalev, the doctrinaire theorist, first figured in the notebooks under the name Zaytsev, an extreme nihilistic journalist of the sixties, who had fled abroad and at the time of the novel's conception was associated with Bakunin in the First International." Peace, Ibid., 160. He also points out that Shigalev's "view of the society of the future seems to have much in common with the crystal palace described in *Notes from Underground*: in both, man's happiness can only be achieved through the restriction of his freedom of action and choice." Ibid., 174.

282. Tolkachenko, who is arrested after he runs away, is devoid of guilt and even seemingly proud of his role in the mayhem: he "blames himself with all modesty," makes "eloquent-sounding speeches," and "strikes poses . . . to make an effect." Dostoevsky, *Demons*, Ibid., 743. Liputin, armed with a doctored passport, had "every chance of slipping across the border." Ibid., 742, Instead Liputin does himself in by staying in Petersburg, where he devotes himself to a "life of debauchery." Ibid. After authorities find him drunk in a brothel, he perjures himself while preparing for trial with a delusional "certain sense of triumph and hope." Ibid. Similarly, Erkel, from whom "not one word of repentance has been extracted, . . .either maintain[s] silence or [does] his best to pervert the truth." Ibid. This uncontrite "fanatical victim of political circumstances," who has "little possibility of getting a lighter sentence," has inadvertently spawned another victim—his own mother, who needed his "paltry salary" for support. Ibid. Weak, sick and "old before her time," Erkel's mother is left "weeping and grovel[ing] as she begs [for her son's release]." Ibid.

283. Virginsky, who is arrested along with his entire household, takes a different approach to the fallout, one aimed at improving his own situation. While he tells all and starts "giving evidence without constraint," he behaves with a "certain dignity," refuses to "retreat[] from a single one of his 'bright hopes," and presents himself as "naively enticed 'by the whirlwind of concurrent circumstances.'" Ibid. As such, absolving himself of responsibility, he is working for and "count[ing] on" a mitigated sentence. Ibid. Lyamshin, the author of that "inhuman" shriek at Shatov's murder scene, is albeit somewhat ambiguously looking out for number one. Initially Lyamshin tries to escape, but returns home, hunkers down, and after an unsuccessful suicide attempt, turns himself in to the authorities to divulge almost everything. When interrogators asked "why so many murders, scandals and vile acts [have] been committed," Lyamshin provides unabated truth—that it was all about destruction for the sake of destruction, that everything was "for the purpose of 'systematically shaking the foundations, systematically undermining society and all principles'" and "for demoralizing everyone and throwing everything into chaos." Ibid., 740. He, however, initially pollutes his confession by "deliberately shield[ing] Stavrogin" in hopes that the absconded aristocrat will not only get him a reduced sentence, but also supply him with money and recommendation letters in exile. Ibid., 741. Thus, his confession, possibly the most heartfelt in the bunch, is not entirely free of self-interest.

284. Kjetsaa, Ibid., 253. Aligning the novel with Swedenborg's "doctrine of correspondences," which imbibes the concept of the physical mirroring the spiritual, Kjetsaa explains that "[f]or Dostoevsky, *Revelation*, far from being merely a consolatory epistle to first-century Christians during the persecution they suffered, was

first and foremost an eschatological prophecy that was being fulfilled in his own time." Ibid.

285. Andre Gide, *Dostoevsky* (NY: New Directions Books, 1961), 162. Gide also asks, "[w]hither does Dostoevsky lead us?" and adds that "[s]ome will say that he leads us straight to Bolshevism, although they know the horror Dostoevsky professed for anarchy." Ibid.

286. See Igor Shafarevich, "Socialism in Our Past and Future," in Alexander Solzhenitsyn, Mikhail Agursky, A. B., Evgeny Barabanov, Vadim Borisov, F. Korsakov, and Igor Shafarevich, *From Under the Rubble*, trans. A. M. Brock, Milada Haigh, Marita Sapiets, Hilary Sternberg, and Harry Willetts under the direction of Michael Scammell (MA: Little Brown & Company, 1974), 53 ("The classic description of the socialist concept of equality is 'Shigalyovism'—the socialist utopia quoted by Dostoevsky in *The Possessed.*"); Alexander Gladkov, *Meetings with Pasternak*, trans. Max Hayward (NY: Harcourt Brace Jovanovich, 1973), 34 (Pasternak "was very worked up and kept referring to Dostoyevski—I remember a phrase about Shigalyov."); Boris Pasternak, *I Remember: Sketch for an Autobiography*, trans. Manya Harari (NY: Pantheon Books, Inc. 1959), 90 ("I can't help feeling that Paolo Yashvili was no longer capable of comprehending anything at all when, bewitched by the ideas first enunciated by Shigalyov . . . which were so prevalent in 1937, he gazed at his sleeping daughter . . . and imagined that he was no longer worthy of looking at her . . . and blew out his brains."). See also Belknap, "Introduction" in Dostoevsky, *Demons*, Ibid., xxviii (suggesting that it oracularly "belongs best to the twentieth century when a few Stavrogins empowered thousands of Pyotr Stepanovichs to drive herds of 'capital', to use Nechaev's term, to slaughter about a hundred million people, the very number Shigalyov and Pyotr hit on").

287. Richard Pevear, "Forward" in Dostoevsky, *Demons*, trans. Richard Pevear and Larissa Volokhonsky, Ibid., 10.

288. See Peace, Ibid., 175 (speaking of "Shigalev's system" where "nine-tenths of humanity is to be turned into a herd, whilst the remaining tenth enjoys absolute freedom and unrestricted powers over the rest," states that "Shigalev would even be prepared for a 'final solution' in the manner of Hitler" and that "the herd-like nine-tenths of humanity could be blown up, if he thought this were possible").

289. Dostoevsky speaks of Mitya's "purification" in his letter to Nikolay Lyubimov (November 16, 1879), in *Letters*, Vol. 5, Ibid., 165.

290. See Deborah A. Martinsen, "Introduction," in *Notes from Underground, The Double and Other Stories*, trans. Constance Garnett (NY: Barnes & Noble Classics, 2003), xxxvi (Speaking of *Notes From Underground*, she points out that "[t]o debunk contemporary theories of rational or enlightened egoism, Dostoevsky proposes acts of love and compassion.")

291. Kilpatrick, Ibid., 18.

292. Dostoevsky, Letter to Nikolay Lyubimov (November 16, 1879), in *Letters*, Vol. 5, Ibid., 165.

293. In the chapter, "Kuzma Samsonov," Mitya dreams of this "renewed and now 'virtuous' life" and "like a great many men in such cases . . . believe[s] most of all

in a change of place." Dostoevsky, *The Brothers Karamazov*, Ibid., 366. Later Mitya comes to see that the change must happen within his own heart and soul.

294. Menninger, Ibid., 54–55.

295. Dostoevsky, Letter to Nikolay Lyubimov (November 16, 1879), in *Letters*, Vol. 5, Ibid., 165.

296. See generally Ralph E. Matlaw, "On Translating *The Brothers Karamazov*" in Dostoevsky, *The Brothers Karamazov*, ed. Susan McReynolds Oddo, Ibid., 672 ("Since the leading idea of the novel is that we are all responsible for everyone and everything, it would not have done to translate the word 'responsible' as 'guilty,' for that would both limit the meaning and introduce an unwarranted legal note, perhaps also a more specifically psychiatric connotation that Dostoevsky may have intended.").

297. Kilpatrick, Ibid.

298. See generally Paul J. Contino, "Incarnational Realism and the Case for Casuistry: Dmitry Karamazov's Escape," in *Dostoevsky's Brothers Karamazov: Art, Creativity, and Spirituality*, Ibid., 131 (discussing the debate over whether Mitya "[s]hould accept his sentence in Siberia or escape to America with Grushenka" and concluding that Mitya's ultimate decision is "a good one"); Ronner, *Dostoevsky and the Law*, Ibid., at 203 (explaining that "[b]oth Mitya and Dostoevsky, who himself experienced self-imposed exile, knows that being uprooted from Russian soil is not a cakewalk" and that for "Russia-loving Mitya," toiling away in some foreign land is a form of flogging) But see Gary Rosenshield, *Western Law, Russian Justice: Dostoevsky, The Jury Trial, and the Law* (WI: University of Wisconsin Press, 2005), 211 ("Dostoevsky presents the escape to America, especially to his contemporary readers, as not only completely inappropriate for Dmitry but, literally speaking, patently ridiculous."); Carol Flath, "The Passion of Dmitry Karamazov," in *Slavic Review* 58 (1999), 595 ("[I]t is inconceivable that Dmitry should accede to the pressure to flee to America; instead he must go into Siberian exile, go below the earth (in an analogy to Christ's time spent in the tomb, or perhaps to his entire life spent 'below,' here on earth.")).

299. See Dostoevsky, *The Brothers Karamazov*, Ibid., 21 (suggesting that Alyosha's loves his mother even when remembering her "sobbing as if in hysterics, with shrieks and cries, seizing him in her arms, [and] hugging him so tightly that it hurt"). When Mitya does not complete his studies and instead goes to see his father, it becomes "clear that he [is] looking for his mother's grave." Ibid.

300. Sabbath, Ibid. (expendable child syndrome).

301. When he comes to live with Yefim Petrovich Polenov, Alyosha "attache[s] everyone in the family to himself so much that they decidedly considered him, as it were, their own child." Dostoevsky, *The Brothers Karamazov*, Ibid., 19. Alyosha's special knack accompanies him to school where his schoolmates "love him so much that he could decidedly be called everyone's favorite." Ibid., 20. Pyotr Alexandrovich Miusov, states that Alyosha is "'perhaps . . . the only man in the world who, were you to leave him alone and without money on the square of some unknown city, [he] would not perish . . . for he would immediately be fed and immediately be taken care of." Ibid., 21.

302. See *Dostoevsky Portrayed by His Wife: The Diary and Reminiscences of MME. Dostoevsky*, Ibid., 181 (discussing Dostoevsky's plan to write the second part of *The Brothers Karamasov*, in which nearly all the characters would reappear twenty years later"); Frank, *Dostoevsky: The Mantle of the Prophet*, Ibid., 727 (describing a conversation that Aleksei Suvorin had with Dostoevsky, one in which he said that in his sequel, Alyosha would become a Russian Socialist and the Grand Duke Alexander Mikhailovich's recollection that Suvorin said that Dostoevsky planned for Alyosha to become "an anarchist" and "kill the Tsar."); Kjetsaa, Ibid., 355 (Drawing upon Suvorin's account, he states that Dostoevsky "had the idea of writing a sequel to *The Brothers Karamazov* in which Alyosha would appear as a revolutionary and be executed for a political crime," but adds that "Suvorin's account . . . is . . . far from being authenticated.").

303. Richard Pevear, "Introduction" in Dostoevsky, *The Brothers Karamazov*, Ibid., xviii.

304. On top of Mitya's and Ivan's confessions, Katerina tells Alyosha that she knew all along that Mitya had failed to deliver the rubles, and that she would endure anything from, or for her faithless fiancé. Confessing to being as "wicked as can be," Grushenka admits to Alyosha that she wanted to ruin him and had promised Rakitin twenty-five rubles if he would deliver the prey to her door. Dostoevsky, *The Brothers Karamazov*, Ibid., 353. Snegiryov divulges his life story. Kolya relates the details of his friendship with Ilyusha, which ruptured when, upon Smerdyakov's urging, his friend performed a "beastly trick" of feeding the dog Zhuchka bread with a pin in it. Ibid., 535. Kolya discloses even more—his "egoistic vanity and base despotism," which have plagued him his whole short life. Ibid., 556.

305. See Contino, Ibid., at 132 (stating that *The Brothers Karamazov* can help readers "become better people" through its persuasion "that a saintly Christian life [is] both real and possible for them").

306. See Frank, *Dostoevsky; The Mantle of the Prophet*, Ibid., 623 (defining *zhitie* as a story "narrated . . . in a style intended to awaken pious and reverential responses, and to communicate a sense of serenity opposed to the agitations and passions depicted elsewhere").

307. Mikhail's fate starkly contrasts with that of Richard, whose life Ivan chronicles. After Richard is "caught, tried, and condemned to death," he finds truth in God, "repent[s]" and turns to Christian faith. Dostoevsky, *The Brothers Karamazov*, Ibid., 240. But after the "pious and philanthropic" citizenry rejoice in his transformation and "his brothers" smother him with kisses, Richard is "dragged up onto the scaffold, laid down on the guillotine, and his head is whacked off in brotherly fashion." Ibid.

308. See Ronner, *Dostoevsky and the Law*, Ibid., 283–84 (stating that "[b]oth prosecutor and defense counsel finesse psychological theories and impressive narratives to elicit jury sympathies for or against Mitya, but none of these are motivated by concerns with truth, justice, or responsibility toward the accused, the victim or society"). Rather, "[t]hese legal players manipulate empathy, rhetoric, and storytelling solely for self-aggrandizement and to persuade attentive attendees of their own deific talents." Ibid., 284. Even the judge "is 'rather vain' and "chiefly concerned with his own image as the 'progressive man.'" Ibid. (quoting Dostoevsky, *The Brothers Karamazov*, Ibid.,

658). See also Rosenshield, Ibid., 17 (explaining how "the [lawyers] use of narrative is done less in the interest of the state or the defendant than in the interest of the lawyers themselves, who wish to display their talents in the courtroom to a national audience" and how "[i]n the end, empathy, storytelling, orality, and emotion becomes tools for person and professional self-aggrandizement").

309. See Dostoevsky, *The Brothers Karamazov*, Ibid., 69 (Pyotr Alexandrovich says that when nothing is "immoral any longer, everything would be permitted, even anthropophagy."); Ibid., 258 (The Grand Inquisitor explains that "there will be centuries more of the lawlessness of free reason, of their science and anthropophagy—for having begun to build their Tower of Babel without us, they will end in anthropophagy.").

Chapter 5

The Conclusion

The Antonymous Creative Process

Chapter 1 introduces certain strands of psychoanalytic thought, which tie into Dostoevsky's fictional suicides and Durkheim's etiology. The chapter opens with a passage from *A Writer's Diary* in which Dostoevsky puzzles over the epidemic of suicides that "occur with no evident reason."[1] Yet, in his fiction, Dostoevsky does offer reasons, ones upheld by suicide theorists, like Durkheim, who also identify the major precipitating cause of suicide as an individual's rupture with salutary collectives, like family, community, and faith. Dostoevsky's imprisonment in Omsk Fortress planted the seed for this understanding. While serving his sentence, he began to intuit that human beings at their apex live collectively cohered, and that homicide equals self-homicide.

Chapter 2 focuses on Dostoevsky's autobiographical novel, *Notes from the House of the Dead*, which predates Durkheim's *Suicide* by more than three decades. Here, Dostoevsky illustrates Durkheim's typology of fatalistic suicide, which emerges in contexts characterized by excessive regulation where a populace forced to adhere to the same routine day after day feels irremediably stuck with no egress or amelioration in sight. In the novel's prison, Dostoevsky demonstrates that excessive regulation, coercion, and sense of futility aggravate the preexisting propensities of some men and goad them to re-offend through fatalistic self-destructive acts.

Chapter 2 thus poses a larger question: how do some inmates manage to plod along and survive? Dostoevsky answers, and Durkheim would likely agree, that the prisoners' saving grace is their quest for *sobornost'*. Although most commentators concede that *sobornost'* is virtually untranslatable, Konstantin Mochulsky succinctly names it "organic collectivity."[2] The early Slavophil, Aleksey Khomyakov amply describes it as "*the combination of freedom and unity of many persons on the basis of their common love for the same absolute values*"; in his writings, *sobornost'* embraces a "unanimous love for Christ and Divine righteousness."[3] In defining religion as "eminently collective," Durkheim outlines his sociological analogue to *sobornost'* as "*a unified system of beliefs and practices relative to sacred things . . . that unite in a single moral community called a church.*"[4]

Sobornost' also coheres with what Goryanchikov, Dostoevsky's narrator, sees as the vaccine immunizing the *Dead House* inmates against the suicidogenic impellent within prison walls. The prisoners attempt to construct what Durkheim calls "a cohesive and animated society" by building a collective subculture, sharing hopes of returning to collective origins, or engorging collective nutrients through labor (SU, Bk 2, Ch 3; 210). Goryanchikov's diagnosis shows that he not only grasps the essence of *sobornost'*, but also Durkheim's conviction that it is crucial for people to enlist in a society with an "intense collective life," one which yields "preservative value," and reinforces the will to live (SU, Bk 2 Ch 2; 170). Specifically, prison bestows a sustaining, parting gift on Goryanchikov, which upon release he can integrate into his daily life. This is not just his vocation as a tutor, but also the attendant realization that the practice of pedagogy can give him some role, even if minimal, in his new community.

By contrast, Dostoevsky left Siberia with surplus creative energy and plenty of raw material. In prison, Dostoevsky not only experienced the rigors of incarceration, but he also observed, memorized, and most poignantly listened to and really heard the discordant, surrounding voices. This primed him to become what Bakhtin calls "the creator of the polyphonic novel" and fostered what became his evolving dialectical artistry.[5] Upon release what also simmered was Dostoevsky's Russian messianism, along with a resolve to inculcate an, empathic collective unity in his writing. Later he pictorialized these ideals as the Golden Age or vocalized them through Zosima's "experience of active love" (BK, Bk 2, Ch 4; 56). Moreover, his years in Siberia propelled him toward another crowning achievement—the Pushkin Memorial speech in Moscow, delivered six months before his death.

Tolstoy had declined to attend the event—leaving Dostoevsky and Turgenev—long-standing rivals—as the stars.[6] Initially, it appeared that Turgenev, the aristocrat, presented with an honorary doctorate for his "talented mastery of Pushkin's language," and described as "first among the delegates," would be the favorite.[7] The tides turned, however, when Turgenev's speech failed to mesmerize the audience. Although Turgenev praised Pushkin, he neither condemned the radicals' criticism of the poet nor gave him his due as a national world poet, equal to William Shakespeare, Moliere, and Johan Wolfgang von Goethe.[8] In a letter to his wife, Anna, Dostoevsky shared his disapproval and declared that Turgenev had actually "denigrated Pushkin by refusing him the title of national poet."[9]

The next day, by contrast, Dostoevsky gave one of the most famous and electrifying speeches in Russian history. While lauding Pushkin as "prophetic," Dostoevsky projects his own ideas about salvific fellowship onto the "national writer" who "revealed the universality and brotherhood of peoples" (WD, 1880, Ch 2; 1281, 1293). The speech not only showcases Dostoevsky's mature ideology, it also reveals the contrapuntal energy driving his fiction. While Dostoevsky acknowledges the European influence in Pushkin's development, he takes a poke at Turgenev by stressing that even the poems from his earliest work disclose the "extraordinary independence of his genius" as seen in the personal suffering and depth of self-consciousness displayed (WD, 1282). Here and throughout the speech, Dostoevsky essentially limns his own work as he discusses that of his "prophetic" precursor.

Dostoevsky initially focuses on Pushkin's "The Gypsies," the poem in which the Russian nobleman Aleko leaves civilization to join his gypsy mistress and her wandering tribe. Aleko is the seeker who has lost his way because he has lost connection with the Russian people and through him, Dostoevsky crystalizes arguments he has been making since the 1860s. He even pauses to contemporize Aleko by speaking to the faces before him: "if in our day they no longer frequent the camps of the gypsies to look for universal ideals in their wild and distinctive way of life and to seek in the bosom of nature some respite from our confused and ridiculous Russian life—the life of educated society—then, still, they go running off to socialism" (WD, 1282).

Bounding off Aleko, Dostoevsky expansively defines the Russian type who "came into being in . . . educated society" and became "detached from the People," which he dates back to the early second century after the "great Petrine reforms" (WD, 1282). He points out that most Russians "even then" were not aware of detachment and simply went about their business "in a regular, leisurely, peaceful fashion" (WD, 1282–83). But even if it occurred to "the chosen few," or to "a tenth of those who began to be troubled," then "through them the remaining vast majority [would] be deprived of their peace of mind" (WD, 1283). But instantly after this backward glance, Dostoevsky taps into the future to prognosticate looming woe: "the same thing awaits them all in due time if they do not take the road to salvation through humble communion with the People" (WD, 1283).

After this excursus, Dostoevsky paints a picture of alienation mingled with desperation to fit in and blend. Dostoevsky conjectures that Aleko "perhaps belongs to the hereditary nobility and very likely owns serfs," yet "[takes] advantage of the freedoms of the nobility and indulge[s] in a little fantasy to fall in love with people who live 'outside the law' and lead a trained bear in a gypsy camp" (WD, 1283). Then when Dostoevsky speaks of Aleko's isolation, he takes on allusive, autobiographical tones. He says, that Aleko feels like a "stranger in his own land," and this estrangement is reminiscent of what

Dostoevsky himself endured in prison (WD, 1283).[10] His Goryanchikov feels like a "stranger" and due to his nobleman status, knows that the other inmates will never see him as "*one of them*" (DH, Pt 2, Ch 7; 263). Like the *Dead House* convict, who is a "chunk severed from [his old] life, a piece of bread cut off from the loaf, "Aleko suffers like "a blade of grass, torn from its stem and carried off by the wind" (DH, Pt 2, Ch 3; 217: WD, 1283).

Next Dostoevsky discusses the gypsies' parting words to Aleko, which he folds into his own warning to those who have detached themselves from native soil. The gypsies drive Aleko away when he commits murder, and Dostoevsky glosses the paradox. Although Aleko strives to fit in with the gypsies, who "have no laws or civilization," the moment he is offended, he goes on the attack, and then girds his loins with his nobleman rank: he reminds himself that "he belongs to one of the fourteen classes" and can "appeal . . . to the law of attack and punish"(WD, 1284). Dostoevsky concedes that this is "rather farfetched," but he pounces on the gypsy's parting words, which are authentic: "[d]epart from us, O haughty man" (WD, 1284). From there, Pushkin's poem becomes a loom whereby Dostoevsky weaves in his own thematic threads about the "People's truth and the People's wisdom" (WD, 1284). Dostoevsky turns to scold not just Aleko but others of his vintage: "[h]umble thyself, O haughty man; first curb thy pride. Humble thyself, O idle man; first labor on thy native soil" (WD, 1284).

Dostoevsky points out Aleko's flaw—that he looks outside of himself for salvation—which connects him to both his Dmitri Karamazov and members of the audience, who also exhibit this tendency. In *The Brothers Karamazov*, when Mitya yearns for a new life of "resurrection and renewal," the narrator remarks, "like a great many men in such cases, he believe[s] most of all in a change of place: if only it weren't for these people, if only it weren't for these circumstances, if only one could fly away from this cursed place—then everything would be reborn!" (BK, Bk 8; Ch 1; 366). This change-of-place syndrome has been Aleko's impasse all along. Dostoevsky critiques "bizarre and impatient" Aleko for "seek[ing] salvation from external things first of all" and for imagining that truth might exist in Europe (WD, 1283). In touting humility, Dostoevsky seeks to disillusion Pushkin's Aleko, his own Mitya, and the superfluous specimens in the audience: "The truth is not outside you but within" and is to be "found first in your own work to better yourself" (WD, 1284). Dostoevsky finishes with Aleko by delivering the redemptive potion: "[c]onquer yourself, humble yourself, and you shall be freer than you even you imagined; you will embark on a great task and make others free, and you will find happiness, for your life will be made complete and you will at last understand your People and sacred truth" (WD, 1284).

When Dostoevsky nimbly pivots into Pushkin's second era to share his interpretation of *Eugene Onegin*, he again imports facets of his own fiction, articulates his own concept of "universal harmony," and employs contrast. Dostoevsky sees Pushkin's Onegin as another Aleko, a nobleman alienated from the people. Yet, in his reading, Onegin exhibits early signs of the "noble demon of secret ennui" that haunts his own Stavrogin (WD, 1285).[11] He is the sort who "loves his native land, but he has no faith in it" (WD, 1285). When he kills Lensky, he does it "simply out of spleen," and Dostoevsky conjectures that it is the same spleen that spawns Onegin's unrequited "longing for a universal ideal" and sacred truth (WD, 1285). Then Dostoevsky turns to flesh out the central contrast.

In setting up the disparity between Onegin, who has "heard of the ideals of his native land, but doesn't believe in them," and Tatiana, who is the "strong character who stands solidly on her native soil," Dostoevsky portrays them as the expression of his own doctrine of *pochvennichestvo* (WD, 1285). Onegin is an educated Russian alienated from the Russian soil, while Tatiana, the "apotheosis of Russian womanhood," is deeply connected to it. Dostoevsky contends that Pushkin should have named his poem after her because she is "unquestionably its protagonist" (WD, 1285).[12] When Onegin first meets Tatiana in the provincial countryside, he looks down on her, disregards her, and spurns her because he is incapable of appreciating her or even beginning to understand her. Yet, over time she solves the Onegin "riddle," comes to "understand him completely," and whispers, "Is he a parody perchance" (WD, 1286).

Significantly, Dostoevsky believes that Tatiana not only sees Onegin for what he is, but that she alone grasps "the higher harmony of the spirit" (WD, 1287). When the two meet again in Petersburg, Tatiana is now a celebrated society lady, married to an old general whom she cannot love because she still loves Onegin. When the "eternal wanderer" spies Tatiana in this "new, dazzling, unattainable setting," he is awed, dumbstruck by her charms, falls at her feet, professes his undying love and devotion, and begs her to run off with him (WD, 1288). But Tatiana firmly refuses. Dostoevsky takes pains to clarify that despite her change in circumstances, Tatiana retains her humble, moral core.

Dostoevsky broaches what is perhaps one of the peskiest questions in Russian literature: namely, "[w]hy did [Tatiana] refuse to follow [Onegin] even though she admitted she loved him?" (WD, 1287). In answering, Dostoevsky spells out his own belief that one cannot "found happiness on the unhappiness of another" (WD, 1287). In concluding his interpretation, Dostoevsky once again directly addresses his audience: "[h]appiness is found not only in the pleasures of love, but also in higher harmony of the spirit" (WD, 1287). This Tatiana becomes not Pushkin's but Dostoevsky's protagonist. Dostoevsky even scripts a speech for her: "[l]et it be that I alone have no happiness; let my unhappiness be immeasurably greater than the unhappiness of this old man; finally, let no one, not even this old man, ever learn of my sacrifice and appreciate it; but I do not want to be happy after having destroyed another!" (WD, 1288).

Dostoevsky's Tatiana also serves to refute the position held by Vissarion Belinsky and self-proclaimed protégée, Kolya Krasotkin (*The Brothers Karamazov*).[13] Belinsky believed that Tatiana's mother had all but forced her to marry the old general, and thus, her marriage, founded on neither love nor free will, was simply immoral. In rebutting Belinsky (and adolescent Kolya who parrots him while trying to impress Alyosha), Dostoevsky restores Tatiana's majestic free will. He asserts that while Tatiana's mother may have "implored her" to marry the general, "but still it was she and no one else who gave her consent; it was she, after all, who swore to be a faithful wife to him" (WD, 1287). But Dostoevsky does not stop there.

Dostoevsky proceeds to gild the lily by casting Tatiana's rejection of Onegin as a decision freer than free. He explains that if Tatiana's husband had died and she was now released from her marital vows, she still would not have joined that shallow "eternal wanderer." For Tatiana knows full well that Onegin "loves only his new fantasy and not her, the Tatiana who is as humble as before!" (WD, 1289). In fact, she suspects what is likely the case—that Onegin (like Dostoevsky's Svidrigailov) is "incapable of loving anyone" (WD, 1289).[14] Unlike Onegin, who has "no soil under his feet," Tatiana possesses that "unshakeable and indestructible" essence that flows from "contact with her native land, her native People and their sacred values" (WD, 1289).

Dostoevsky asserts that as a character, Tatiana is not *sui generis* because she belongs among a "whole series of positively beautiful Russian types" that Pushkin "found among the Russian people" (WD, 1290). These include the "Russian chronicler monk" in *Boris Godunov* and the peasant in "Tale of the Bear." (WD, 1290–91). Although Dostoevsky asserts that there are "many experts on the People among our writers," and while they have talent and write "lovingly about the People," they intermittently, haughtily show "a wish to raise the People to their own level and make them happy by doing so" (WD, 1290). But in Pushkin, there is "precisely something that *truly* makes him akin to the People, something that reaches almost to the level of simple-hearted tenderness" (WD, 1290–91). Dostoevsky envisions that extant "unshakeable force" as faith in "Russian individuality," the "strength of [the] People," and the "future independent mission in the family of European peoples" (WD, 1291). He proclaims that none of this would exist without Pushkin. Dostoevsky, however, does not halt, but instead proffers additional evidence, which he plucks from Pushkin's last works.

Dostoevsky asserts that in Pushkin's third, unfinished period, "universal ideas shine forth most brightly," and it is here that the "poet stands forth as an almost miraculous and unprecedented phenomenon" (WD, 1291).

Dostoevsky places Pushkin on a pedestal above the "creative geniuses of immense magnitude," like "the Shakespeares, Cervanteses, and Schillers," because he alone had "the capacity to respond to the whole world" (WD, 1291). Dostoevsky substantiates this claim by again relying on contrast, but this time between the European poets and the supreme Pushkin: European poets tend to interpret other nationalities from their own national vantage point, whereas Pushkin alone can embody "himself fully within another nationality" (WD, 1292). After providing examples from Pushkin's poems, Dostoevsky goes where Turgenev had declined to go. He states "that there has not been a poet so able to respond to the whole world as Pushkin," who, with his "astounding depth" had the "ability to infuse his spirit into the spirit of other nations" (WD, 1293). Dostoevsky proclaims that "nowhere in any other poet anywhere in the world has such a phenomenon been repeated" (WD, 1293).

From there, Dostoevsky elaborates on his ideal of collective unity. He starts by likening Pushkin's achievements to Peter the Great's reform, but not before asking, "[w]hat [is] the significance of this reform for us?" (WD, 1293). He replies that the reform entailed the adoption of "European clothing, customs, inventions, and European science," but while Peter initially had utilitarian objectives, he let his "secret instinct" lead him toward something "immensely broader" and the Russian people followed suit (WD, 1293). They began to strive toward the "universal brotherhood" of all people. (WD, 1294). Here Dostoevsky sprinkles in Zosima-like axioms about "friendship and complete love," the hope of "eliminat[ing] contradictions," and "excus[ing] and reconc[iling] differences" (WD, 1294). Dostoevsky then attributes Slavophilism and Westernizing to a "great misunderstanding" because the true Russian mission is "unquestionably pan-European and universal," and the goal is to "become a brother to all people, a *panhuman*, if you like" (WD, 1294). These words inadvertently rhyme with tenets of Ivan Kireyevsky, one of the early ideologists of the Slavophile movement in Russia.[15] Dostoevsky recommends the balm for "Europe's anguish," as the "panhuman and all-unifying Russian soul" which will embrace "harmony" and the "law of Christ's gospel" (WD, 1294).[16]

Dostoevsky fortifies his vision by pulling Pushkin back into his messianic discourse and by painting him as the progenitor of collective unity, which resided in the very "universality and panhumanness of his genius" (WD, 1295). Dostoevsky then exhorts his audience to settle their conflicts without weapons or violence, unify, and embrace that power of brotherly love. To say that Dostoevsky's audience went wild is a litotes. In a letter to his wife, Dostoevsky describes the ensuing euphoria: "When I spoke at the end, however, of the *universal unity* of people, the hall was as though in hysteria. When I concluded—I won't tell you about the roar, the outcry of rapture:

strangers among the audience wept, sobbed, embraced each other, and *swore to one another to be better, not to hate one another from now on, but instead to love one another*."[17]

In *A Writer's Diary*, Dostoevsky penned an "Explanatory Note" in which he uses the techniques employed in the speech and identifies in Pushkin's work the dualism of darkness and light, which became the recurrent texture in his own writing. Dostoevsky's points to Pushkin's disclosure of darkness: he was "the first to uncover and indicate the essential, pathological actuality of our educated society, historically detached from its native soil and elevating itself above the People" (WD, 1880, Ch 1; 1271). And Dostoevsky even suggests that Pushkin foresaw that such paths of superfluity lead to suicide, which is the ultimate rejection of self.[18] Yet, in that same *Diary* entry, Dostoevsky projects the salvational glow that simultaneously emanates from Pushkin: "the idea of the universal fellowship of humans, of brotherly love, the sober view that forgives enmity, distinguishes and excuses that which is dissimilar, eliminates contradictions" (WD, 1274).

In apotheosizing Pushkin in the speech proper, Dostoevsky yokes together the oppositions he sketches in his "Explanatory note," which also surface in his own and his predecessor's work. He notes that Pushkin "identified the type of the Russian wanderer," yet "placed beside him the type of positive, indisputable beauty of the Russian woman" (WD, 1880, Ch 2; 1289–90). Dostoevsky not only exalts Pushkin's "positively beautiful Russian types," but explores the nether regions in his work (WD, 1290). This happens when Dostoevsky shifts to the antithesis to diagnose the evils that arise from egoism and alienation in Pushkin's "The Egyptian Nights":

> [H]ere we see these earthly gods, who have been enthroned as divinities over their people, who despise the very spirit of their people and its aspirations, who no longer believe in it, who have become solidary gods in truth and who have gone mad in their isolation, who in their anguish and weariness while waiting to die seek diversion in outrageous brutalities, in insectlike voluptuousness, the voluptuousness of a female spider devouring her mate. (WD, 1293)

This exegesis, thus, draws on Dostoevsky's signature modalities. The quoted passage links to the base egoism depicted in multiple Dostoevsky novels, to the vile infection in Rodion Raskolnikov's Siberian nightmare, to the infectious plague in the Ridiculous Man's dream, to facets of cannibalistic brutality in *Demons*, and to certain Grand Inquisitorial edicts.

While chapter 2 examines the combatant suicidal and life-affirming forces in the *Dead House* prison, chapters 3 and 4, especially in their conclusions, underscore other conjoined antipodes in Dostoevsky's novels. But initially, chapter 3 first employs the Durkheimian lens to explore egoistic self-annihilation in *Crime and Punishment* and *The Idiot*. After analyzing Svidrigailov's blast to the brain, Nastasya Filippovna's self-imposed death penalty, and Ippolit Terentyev's botched suicide, the chapter ends by outlining the glimmers of light amidst the all-enveloping blackness. In *Crime and Punishment*, the hope beams as a "might be"—the possibility of Raskolnikov's "gradual renewal, . . .gradual regeneration, . . . gradual transition from one world to another" (CP, Ep., Ch 2; 551). The narrator offers this possibility after Raskolnikov embraces Sonia, thereby ousting Svidrigailov, the specter of egoistic suicide, and discovers that "instead of dialectics, there is life" (CP, Ep., Ch 2; 550).

Despite its bleaker ending, *The Idiot* too offers moments of light. There is the silent prayer of the condemned man on the scaffold who vows that if he can "get his life back," he "would make each minute into a lifetime" and "waste nothing in vain" (Id, Pt. 1, Ch 5; 72). There is the moment when Ippolit gets to do just that—make each minute count through active loving. Ippolit rises from his sickbed of solipsistic contemplation to rescue an impoverished medic and his family, an act that permits him to taste the spiritual vitality that comes from "giv[ing] away part of his personality and absorb[ing] part of another" (Id, Pt 3, Ch 6; 472). As Durkheim might say, Ippolit unshackled himself from the egoistic gallows to "disperse existence beyond its own limitation" (SU, Bk 2, Ch 6; 279). Finally, *The Idiot* gives us the luminous Prince Myshkin whose voice suggests things that "might have been." As the product of Dostoevsky's endeavor to portray "a positively beautiful person," the prince is the one who might have derailed Nastasya Filippovna's egoistic-anomic quest for death by proxy, might have alleviated Ippolit's suicidal thanatophobia, might have persuaded Parfyon Rogozhin to trade his blade for the cross, and might have effectuated salutary change in others, like Lukian, Lebedev, Ganya Ivolgin, Ivan Ptitsyn, and the boxer, Keller.[19] None of them, however, accept what the prince has to offer. Sadly, his gifts could have transformed the possibilities—those might have beens—into done deals.

Chapter 4 turns to anomy, which drifts through the sombrous godlessness of *Demons* and *The Brothers Karamazov*. In *Demons*, anomy collaborates with nihilism as the town plummets into chaotic ruin after Pyotr Verkhovensky orchestrates upheaval. In *The Brothers Karamazov*, anomy conspires with atheism, the devil, and perfidy, all of which haunt Skotoprigonevsk and spawn ruptured families, fratricide and miscarried justice. In both novels, those who jolt the societal equilibrium, like Stavrogin, Kirillov, and Smerdyakov, either hang or shoot themselves. But as in *Notes from the House of the Dead*, *Crime and Punishment*, and *The Idiot*, the later novels juxtapose the itineraries leading to self-annihilation with the alternatives, the lighted routes heading toward universal fellowship and faith.

In *Demons*, Stepan Verkhovensky's final wanderings supply that alternative, the one embracing the promise that mother Russia "will be protected by a great idea and a great will from on high" and that "the sick man will be healed and 'will sit at the feet of Jesus' " (D, Pt 3, Ch 7; 724). Stepan comes to know that "God is necessary . . . because he is the only being who is capable of eternal love" and that immortality is "necessary" because "God would not want to . . . utterly quench the flame of love for him once it has been kindled" (D, Pt 3, Ch 7; 731–32). While his satanic son Pyotr flees and anomic Stavrogin and man-God Kirillov "die in despair," Stepan dies without "the slightest fear" holding that "eternal, immeasurable" Golden Age in his pocket (D, Pt 3, Ch 7; 734).[20]

In *The Brothers Karamazov*, the dark and light are so at odds that they atavistically simulate Manichaeistic dualism. There is the dark realm, where everything, including atheism, disbelief in immortality, egoism, fratricide, miscarried justice, and even cannibalism, is permitted. But there is an equal but opposite orb of light repelling the negativism. It shines in Mitya Karamazov's heart and conscience as he is "purified . . . under the storm of misfortune."[21] After his dream of "the wee one," Mitya feels a "tenderness . . . surging up," reaches for his Madonna ideal, aspires to alleviate suffering and converge with that "new beckoning light" (BK, Bk 9, Ch 8; 508). It also emanates from Alyosha Karamazov's soul, which infiltrates "the darkness of worldly wickedness" with "the light of love" (BK, Bk 1, Ch 4; 18). Wherever Alyosha goes, he listens, hears, fosters bonds, and helps catalyze healing. But in Skotoprigonevsk, Zosima is the quintessential bright light, radiating "active love" and proclaiming that "the more [we] succeed in loving, the more [we will] be convinced of the existence of God and the immortality of [our] soul" (BK, Bk 2, Ch 4; 56).

What might readers glean from Dostoevsky's amalgamated polarities? Could this be a ploy to counteract the Werther effect? Afterall, Dostoevsky gets to the source to repel the prototype—Werther himself. As discussed earlier, the publication of Goethe's *Werther* bred copycats: men dressed like Werther shot themselves in the head and left copies of Goethe's novel nearby. In early pages of his 1876 *Writer's Diary*, Dostoevsky invokes Werther and antidotally prescribes what the prayer for Goethe and his Werther should be—"O Great Spirit, I thank Thee for the human image that Thou hast given me" (WD, 1876, Ch 1; 300).

Durkheim calls the Werther effect "imitation" or "contagion," which he sees not as an individual phenomenon but one derived from group dynamics. He claims that contagion arises in spheres devoid of collectivity, community, and shared beliefs. In such situations, people fill the void by constructing fellowship on and bonding over the renunciation of existence itself. Tautologically, they treat their pathological emptiness with the emptiness of self-inflicted death. As such, suicidal contagion stems from dismal communion, whereby the rabble, "desperate for all, collectively decide upon death" (SU, Bk 1, Ch 4; 132). While Dostoevsky's fiction presents multiple suicides, it seeks to fend off contagion. Dostoevsky strives to deter wannabe Werthers by emboldening the voices of those characters who inveigh against lethality, extol "collective unity," and commend synergy predicated on shared faith.

Dostoevsky was not the first or last to grapple with suicidogenic forces. If we momentarily step back, we may recognize what Freud got right—that the drive to eviscerate our own existence is universal. Moreover, if we are willing to be courageously, ruthlessly honest, we might detect this menacing presence in normative daily life. It can sporadically sneak up as ideation or chronically slither in to instigate that slow march toward self-destruction. The ghoul of ideation visits in quick blips: while perching on a high ledge, individuals might suddenly feel the urge to drop into oblivion; while wielding an ordinary kitchen knife, they might momentarily envision slicing their wrists; while waiting for the train, they might experience a little tug to jump onto track; while lighting a campfire, they might fleetingly consider self-immolation; while driving on a dark, skiddy road, they might feel the pull to plunge into the deep, Grim Reaper's ditch; while crossing a bridge, they might impulsively crave descent into a watery grave; while extracting a pill from a bottle, they might suddenly imagine swallowing a fistful; while pulling into the garage, they might visualize the doors sealing and poisonous fumes lulling them into a forever slumber; while handling a rope, they might picture themselves limply dangling by the neck; while storing a gun, they might feel impelled to press the cold barrel to their skulls and blast consciousness to smithereens. Such ideation happens to be widespread and can be so acute that some individuals find relief by surrendering to such morbific urges. Sometimes, and what is more likely the norm, folks just get on with their business, coexist with that ideational ghoul, and resist such euthanasic entreaties.

What Karl Menninger expansively classifies as the "chronic" and "focal" self-annihilative trajectories are different from the ideational detours.[22] People on the path to indirect suicide are simply those who cannot walk through life without putting an irksome pebble in their own shoe. Their weapons are not risky heights, knives, trains, fires, slippery roads, bridges, sleeping pills, carbon monoxide, ropes, or guns. Instead, they resort to things like hyperbolic ascetism, eating disorders, or self-mutilation to obtain the sought result—skeletal emaciation, morbid obesity, or hideous deformity. At times, they conscript a proxy, a popular veiled substitute for the overt act of self-murder. These bane-seekers enlist others, like spouses, partners, or friends, to kill them or abuse them, or to effectively impede their attempts to attain happiness or their full potential. Hordes of others court self-destruction through addiction to drugs, alcohol, or gambling.

Dostoevsky was no stranger to the hobbling effects of irresistible addiction. His compulsive gambling intensified while he was filling his notebooks for *The Idiot* with executions, deaths, arson, rape, murder, and suicide. During this time, Dostoevsky's gambling flared up with such raw intensity that he was catapulting into what Michael A. Church and Charles I. Brooks call "the subtle suicide zone."[23] He was even taking his wife down with him. Dostoevsky's letters and his wife's memoir portray the couple's desperation as the gambling fiend, like Marmeladov's dipsomania, threatened to haul away life's essentials. But while self-condemned to the roulette gallows and in the throes of this self-expunging binge, Dostoevsky's creative process intensified, and he birthed a novel full of self-destruction. Dostoevsky's perilous gambling-Siren thus compelled him to tether himself to the mast of creative energy. Essentially, the writer replaced seductive, destructive roulette with a figurative, creative game of Russian roulette.

As discussed earlier, Steve Taylor discusses Russian roulette and links it to "thanatation" whereby individuals, who crave relief from suicidal impulses, engage in "ludenic" ordeals.[24] For example, thanationist Graham Greene played Russian roulette, which let him "exorcise death" and at least "in the short run" made him feel as if he had "defeated" it.[25] Yet, it is equally important to emphasize that while Dostoevsky was cranking out his major works, Russia was in the midst of a suicide epidemic.[26] During this time, Dostoevsky's writing table became a Russian roulette table of sorts, but his "thanatation" was evolving into something different from Greene's risky shot to the head. Over time, Dostoevsky sought neither to vanquish *memento mori* nor to exorcise his self-destructive propensities. Instead, he was bewailing the suicides strewn over his beloved Russian earth and contemplating her invasion by those devils who nag, goad, and prod humanity to eradicate itself. With that dismal vista before him, Dostoevsky minted his own form of thanatation roulette and mobilized polarized combatants to deliver the magic bullet.

Moreover, if we dig deeper into the juxtaposed polarities that dynamize Dostoevsky's fiction, we might find yet another telos, one that exceeds the aim of sending a message to his readers and importuning them to resist the Werther effect, reject darkness, and passionately leap into the "beckoning light." His plentiful collocated contradictions—like mind versus heart, egoism versus collectivity, atheism versus faith, indifference versus empathy, *ad infinitum*—tie into Samuel Taylor Coleridge's formula for creativity—the "juxta-position and *apparent* reconciliation of widely different or incompatible things."[27] For Dostoevsky, the battlefield for his incompatible warriors is that of artistry itself. There in its trenches, the cognizance of the universal human drive to self-destruct is engaged in an indefatigable tussle with the voracious hunger to create. Dostoevsky even built into his fiction dioramas of his creative roulette workshop where contrarious erotic and suicidogenic impulses whirl frenetically. Stavrogin's dream of "The Golden Age" and "The Dream of a Ridiculous Man: A Fantastic Story," are two prime examples. In both, there is a narrator who not only tells the story but also guides readers on a virtual tour of the deepest recesses of their author's antonymous creative process.

In Stavrogin's Golden Age dream, readers momentarily dwell in the prelapsarian sphere, with its "earthly paradise," exquisite colors, jubilant people, and groves "filled with joyous songs" (D, At Tik 2; 775). In a flash, all such vibrant fecundity evanesces, and readers descend into the underworld of suicide where the "emaciated" vision of Matryosha is "shaking her head and brandishing her fist" (D, At Tik 2; 776). Stavrogin confesses that he "can't help but summon up" Matryosha, yet because he "simply can't live with" her apparition, he joins her in death (D, At Tik 2; 776).

Dostoevsky's creative process and facets of Stavrogin's dream fit into Taylor's explication of Russian roulette and thanatation. Taylor suggests that in Russian roulette, death is not death. Rather, the thanationist is convinced "that a 'death' has in fact taken place and that 'someone different' has arisen from the ashes."[28] In Stavrogin's dream (and in Dostoevsky's creative process), the "brandishing" fist of suicide is always present, always summoning. But for Dostoevsky, it was also always impelling its nemesis—the artist—to reactively neologize. For Stavrogin, the "brandishing fist" entices him to take his own life. But for Dostoevsky, the apparition of suicide activates artistic thanatation that resolves with a bang, which in a blink effectuates pseudo-death. Then instanter, new life arises in the form of literature in which life-affirmation is poised to vanquish self-annihilation.

The contrastive opposites in Stavrogin's dream reappear in "The Dream of Ridiculous Man: A Fantastic Story." Dostoevsky included this story in his *A Writers Diary*, in which other entries, like "The Sentence," focus on the suicide epidemic (WD, October 1876, Ch 4; 653–56: 1877, Ch 2; 953).[29] The Ridiculous Man's narrative shifts rapidly, pulsating from darkness to light to darkness, and ultimately dispatches a dazzling, new light. In the inaugural darkness, the narrator, a putative "madman," is determined to end his own life (Ch 1; 365). In fact, Durkheim could be diagnosing Dostoevsky's narrator when he points out that as consciousness "separates itself too radically from other beings," it conjures up nothingness both within and without, and thus leaves the egoist with "nothing to reflect upon but its own wretched misery" (SU, Bk 2, Ch 6; 279). The Ridiculous Man complains of a very Durkheimian "terrible misery growing in [his] soul," which he attributes to his "conviction" that "*nothing in the world mattered*" and that "*nothing*," including other people, exists for him (Ch 1; 365–66). In fact, he is more ridiculous than Dostoevsky's "Underground Man" or Chernyshevsky's Lopukhov, both of whom engage in robust sidewalk collisions with pedestrians.[30] The Ridiculous Man, however, is so detached, so numb, that he is oblivious to those he bumps in the street.

In the story, Dostoevsky employs a technique that Victorian art critic John Ruskin dubbed the "pathetic fallacy," whereby the artist projects an inner state onto the external world.[31] Here fallacy manifests as a bleak evening with "cold, gloomy almost menacing rain" and a sky of "fathomless black patches," which mirrors the Ridiculous Man's *schmerz* (Ch 1; 366–67). In the dark sky, the narrator sees and hears a star telling him to kill himself forthwith. But while staring, he has a chance encounter with a "shivering and shuddering" little girl, who begs him to help her dying mother (Ch 1; 367). He responds by gruffly stamping his foot, yelling at her, and shooing her away.

After that, the Ridiculous Man returns home and here Dostoevsky uses a poetic device that T. S. Eliot named "objective correlative."[32] Like Raskolnikov's claustrophobic abode, the narrator's room equals his impoverished soul and psyche. It "is small and poor," and through the meager partition, postlapsarian noises filter in because a "perfect Sodom [is] going on" within and around him (Ch 1; 368). Significantly, he calls his sofa "Voltairean," which suggests his Frenchified erudition and links him to atheistic "up-to-date Russian progressive[s], who pander to science and reason" (Ch 1; 368: Ch 4; 376). But despite himself, the recollection of the little girl derails his plan to shoot himself in the head, activates his insensate heart, and makes him feel pain and pity. He finds this to be so "incongruous" with his egoistic detachment that he reflexively strains to reclaim darkness and reassert despotic me-ness (Ch 2; 369).

Charles William Wahl analyzes "the phenomenon of infantile cosmic identification," whereby suicidal people enter a locus of "hypostatization" and "dereism," equate the whole world with the self, and thus believe that through their death, they can commit "matricide, patricide, sororicide, fratricide, and even genocide."[33] The Ridiculous Man restates Wahl's theory: he says, "it is likely that nothing will exist for any one when I am gone, and that as soon as my consciousness is extinguished the whole world will vanish too and become void like a phantom, as a mere appurtenance of my consciousness, for possibly all this world and all these people are only me myself" (Ch 2; 370). Despite that delusion, he postpones his self-deifying death, falls asleep in his chair, and has a dream. The dream, however, is not "spurred on by reason but by desire, not by the head but by the heart" (Ch 2; 370).

In his dream, the Ridiculous Man shoots himself in his newly awakened heart. He then descends into darkness where "it gr[ows] horribly black around" him (Ch 3; 371). After that, he finds himself in a coffin and realizes that he is "utterly dead," a state that correlates with the *rigor mortis* of his nonlife life (Ch 3; 372). From there, he starts spiraling through spatial darkness where "never, never had there been such darkness," where he suddenly beholds a star, realizes that there "is life beyond the grave," and catches sight of the sun "that gave life to *our* earth" (Ch 3; 372–73). The "*our*" is crucial here because in his dark pre-suicidal psyche, the "our" is his own death, which will extinguish everything and all. But in blatant contradiction, the antipodal orb of light affirms life and has "kindred power" (Ch 3; 374). It bestows life not just on the "I" but on the kindred "our," on everything and all. It is here that the Ridiculous Man's thoughts concur with Dostoevsky's chastisement of Goethe's Werther: "I love and can love only that earth which I have left, stained with my blood, when, in my ingratitude, I extinguished my life with a bullet in my heart" (Ch 3; 374). But this Ridiculous Man is still unenlightened and knows only the fallen world in which beings "can only love with suffering and through suffering" (Ch 3; 374).

After contemplating the earth he has left, the Ridiculous Man abruptly finds himself in a duplicate earth, a prelapsarian kingdom of "bright light," where live "the children of the sun" who are "untarnished by the fall" (Ch 3; 375). This utopia with its "festive radiance" is a near clone of Stavrogin's Golden Age (Ch 3; 375). Its citizens have no need for science because "their knowledge [is] higher and deeper" (Ch 4; 376). They live in peace with animals and interact without quarrels or jealously. The "old people die peacefully" and like Stepan Verkhovensky, are "convinced" of their immortality (Ch 4; 377). Their lives conform to what Khomyakov lauds in his religious, philosophical tracts—that "indissoluble union between love and freedom."[34] With neither discord nor cacophony, they freely sing in a loving, "musical and harmonious chorus" (Ch 4; 377). While reflecting on the divisive home he has left behind, the Ridiculous Man revisits his old "presentiments" where his "hatred for [the] earth" was always mixed with a "yearning anguish" (Ch 4; 378). Like Mitya Karamazov, who self-defines in oxymorons, the narrator's glance at his old self leads him to meld love and hate: "why could I not hate them without loving them? . . . why could I not love them without hating them?" (Ch 4; 378).

Just as the "fullness of life" crescendos into painlessly painful blissful light, it joltingly inverts into its anthesis—abysmal darkness (Ch 4; 378). That is, "something happen[s] so awful, something so horribly true" and that something is *him* (Ch 4; 379). Like "a vile trichina," the narrator has infected the kingdom with his fallen pathogenic self, which effectuates a peripeteia of mammoth proportion (Ch 5; 379). As in Raskolnikov's epiphanic nightmare, the Ridiculous Man sees the plague of egoism spreading and ravaging everything. The populous begins "to struggle for separation, for isolation, for individuality, for mine and thine" (Ch 5; 380). They extol suffering, kowtow to science, discover the "beauty of lying," begin torturing animals, commit crimes, invent twisted earthy justice, construct guillotines, and wage cruel wars (Ch 5; 379).

This blighted world ineluctably turns into the very fiefdom of suicide, one in which "the instinct of self-preservation [grows] rapidly weaker," where Werthers replicate and Matryoshas "brandish" their fists (Ch 5; 381). There are whole "religions with a cult of non-existence and self-destruction for the sake of the everlasting peace in annihilation" (Ch 5; 381). As the Ridiculous Man "[weeps] over them, [pitying] them," he stretches his hands out to them "in despair, blaming, cursing and despising" himself, readers get a glimpse of the author's creative process and stare into the barrel of that gun primed to fire in esemplastic roulette (Ch 5; 381). Like the thanationist, the Ridiculous Man suddenly feels as "though [he] is dying," but conversely awakens to a "a different life," one "renewed, grand and full of power!" (Ch 5; 382: Ch 2; 371).

The Ridiculous Man's plunge into that dark kingdom with its self-annihilative forces propels him to claw skyward toward renewal, toward "immeasurable ecstasy" (Ch 5; 382). Significantly, it is then that he starts preaching. Or rather, he starts *creating*. While he is trying to "find out what words to say," he seeks to convey "the living image" of truth (Ch 5; 382). Even after he has "lost command of words," he vows to "keep talking," and rises to the pinnacular task of transmitting the sacred message that "the main thing is to love others as oneself" for "nothing else is needed" (Ch 5; 383). After his roulette-like rebirth, the Ridiculous Man's life's blood no longer pumps from the head, but instead flows freely from his heart. He seeks out the little girl, who catalyzed his renewal and urges organic collectivity, love of Christ and faith in an immortality that "shall go on and on" (Ch 5; 383).

Like Dostoevsky's Ridiculous Man, the poet A. Alvarez was reborn "as a different person," after his flirtation with self-homicide.[35] When Alvarez woke up after swallowing forty-five sleeping pills, he birthed a book about "the power the [suicidal] act has exerted over the creative imagination."[36] In it, Alvarez acknowledges that each death "has its own inner logic and unrepeatable despair," and that many people are predisposed to suicide, but he finds it uncanny that the "casualty-rate among the gifted seems out of proportion."[37] He attributes this in part to the artist's "continuous, restless urge to experiment" and the "constant need to change, to innovate, to destroy the accepted styles."[38] He adds that the fact that artists are never "absolved from the labor of art" exacerbates their plight.[39] What also compounds lethality is the artistic compulsion to tackle the perilous "perennial question, 'What am I?' " and do it without the "benefit of moral, cultural or even technical securities."[40]

Dostoevsky too was never "absolved from the labor of art" and his writings, letters, his wife's memoirs, and biographies by others even reveal a propensity to foist suffering upon himself. As an artist, Dostoevsky also felt compelled to wrestle the Alvarez-bogeyman, the question—"What am I?" Alvarez's point that suicide rate amongst the gifted is disproportionately high is convincing, and Dostoevsky was possibly one of the most gifted writers in the world. Yet, he did not take his own life. Why? It might be tempting to simply dodge this snag by pointing to Dostoevsky's near-death experience before the firing squad and surmise that like the pardoned man in *The Idiot*, he vowed to treasure that unforeseen gift and, thus, savor each waking moment. It is also conceivable that his epilepsy imbued him with élan vital. Dostoevsky himself suggests this in *The Idiot* when he describes the nanoseconds before the ictal howl: there is an "undreamed-of sense of completeness, proportion, reconciliation and an ecstatic, prayerful fusion with the highest synthesis of life" (Id., Pt 2, Ch 5; 264). Perhaps the aborted execution, which left him with mortality whispering in his ear, and his falling sickness, with its ineffable afflatus, in league quickened him to do what Victorian art critic *Walter Pater*, so passionately adjures—namely, to "burn always with this hard gem-like flame" and strive to "maintain the ecstasy."[41]

But what underlies Dostoevsky's triumph goes beyond the windfalls of Nicholas I's pardon or epilepsy's ecstatic jolts. Dostoevsky was partly empowered by his conviction that through his artistry he could channel surrounding lethality into creative energy. Nonetheless, an even more armipotent pursuit was afoot. While disclosing suicide after suicide in his fiction and in *A Writer's Diary*, Dostoevsky was synchronously building an indestructible oppositional fortress. His fortress, however, had the safe framework that Alvarez feels other artists lack, which are rafters of "moral, cultural or . . . technical securities."[42] In the end, Dostoevsky's fortress was essentially Durkheimian, decidedly collective, and intrinsically musical.

In discussing Dostoevsky's creative process, Jacque Catteau names multiple critics, who "compare Dostoevsky's novels to music" and use words like "counterpoint, fugue, symphony, oratorio, the mode of Beethoven, the orchestration of Mahler," to make their point and *his* point that "the novelist seized time and reconstructed it according to his own laws."[43] We might take the liberty of adding an unexpected voice—that of Walter Pater, who knights music as the "ideally consummate art" due to the inseparability of import and medium and says that "*[a]ll art constantly aspires toward the condition of music.*"[44] Pater saw that in other art forms, it is possible to distinguish matter from form, yet art's overarching goal is to obliterate that distinction.

Dostoevsky's compositions, perhaps more uniquely than those of most narrative artists, attain that aspirational fusion of message and form. Over time, the crux of Dostoevsky's message was becoming more about *sobornost*' and "the panhuman" Russian soul, which can placate discord by merging all into a collective to share love of Christ and faith in the soul's immortality. But for Dostoevsky, collective unity transcends import and becomes an indivisible message-form-process. The process—that of artistry—is one in which the toiler stirs in disparate ingredients, blends incompatibles, and combines impugning couplets, which coalesce into and emerge as an elixir of universality. Through such alchemy, Dostoevsky converted his cognizance of suicide's pluripresence into something contrapositive, something life-affirming, something organic, and something which extols-*is* simultaneously both the "all-unifying Russian soul" and "all-unifying" musical artistry.

NOTES

1. Fyodor Dostoevsky, *A Writer's Diary*, trans. Kenneth Lantz, Vol. 1 (1873–1878) (IL: Northwestern University Press, 1994), 734 (hereinafter in the text, it is "WD"). All citations of *A Writer's Diary*, Volumes 1 and 2, are from this translation. Hereinafter, I will include the references to the Lantz translation, in parenthesis in the text.

2. Konstantin Mochulsky, *Dostoevsky: His Life and Work*, trans. Michael A. Minihan (NJ: Princeton University Press, 1967), 506 n. 8 (explaining that the term "organically collective" (*soborny*) . . . is associated with Slavophile theorist Aleksey Stepanovich Khomyakov (1804–1860)" and "can readily be felt upon Dostoevsky's thought and . . . ideas of personality, freedom love of Christ and the 'complete universality of mankind' "). See also Semyon L. Frank, *The Spiritual Foundations of Society*, trans. Boris Jakim (OH: Ohio University Press, 1987), vii (Translator's Preface). Boris Jakim writes that "*Sobornost'*—an untranslatable word which is related to the words *sobirat'* (to gather) and *sobranie* (meeting)—is defined by Frank as the living, inner, organic unity of society." Ibid.

3. N. O. Lossky, *History of Russian Philosophy* (UK: George Allen and Unwin Ltd.), 35, 41. See also Frank, Ibid., 61 (explaining that the "religious feeling is the feeling of belonging to that absolute principle which lies at the base of the universal *sobornost'* of being" and that "human *sobornost'*" is "the feeling of belonging to the whole" and "is essentially the mystical religious feeling of rootedness in the mysterious depths of being which embrace the individual").

4. Emile Durkheim, *The Elementary Forms of Religious Life*, trans. Carol Cosman (UK: Oxford University Press, 2001), 46.

5. Mikhail Bakhtin, *Problems of Dostoevsky's Poetics*, ed. and trans., Caryl Emerson (MN: University of Minnesota Press, 2009), 7.

6. See Geir Kjetsaa, *Fyodor Dostoevsky: A Writer's Life*, trans. Siri Hustvedt and David McDuff (NY: Fawcett Columbine Books, 1987), 356 ("Tolstoy was one of the few who refused to attend: a celebration of this type was in his view a great sin, the more so because he believed the people were completely indifferent to this

aristocratic poet."). At the celebration, writer Dmitri Grigorovich was assigned the task of keeping the "two rivals" (Dostoevsky and Turgenev) apart. Ibid., 358.

7. Ibid., 358, 359. In a letter, Dostoevsky writes: "The professors . . . are paying court to Turgenev, who is absolutely turning into a personal enemy of mine." Letter from Fyodor Dostoevsky to Konstantin Pobedonostev (May 19, 1880), in *Complete Letters*, trans. David Lowe, Vol. 5 (MI: Ardis Publishers 1991) [hereinafter *Letters* Vol. 5], 200. See also Letter from Fyodor Dostoevsky to Anna Dostoevskaya (June 2–3, 1880), Ibid., at 224 ("[T]here was a gathering at Turgenev's of almost all the participants (I was excluded!) . . . [T]hey simply left me out . . . [T]his is Turgenev and Kovalevsky's doing.").

8. See Joseph Frank, *Dostoevsky: The Mantle of the Prophet, 1871–1881* (NJ: Princeton University Press, 2002), 516 (explaining that "Turgenev tried to unite a eulogy of Pushkin with an apologia for his rejection by the radical critics of the 1860s; and he had also expressed his own opposition, as a liberal Westernizer, to the Slavophil and Populist idolization of 'the people' "). Frank states that Turgenev called Goethe, Moliere, and Shakespeare "*narodnoi* poets," which for him "means imparting to the values of one's own culture a national (*natsionalnie*) significance, thus attaining a level of universality that transcends mere class or regional boundaries." Ibid., 515.

9. Letter from Fyodor Dostoevsky to Anna Dostoevskaya (June 7, 1880), in *Letters* Vol. 5, Ibid., 233. See also Frank, Ibid., 515 ("Turgenev was completely at odds with the reigning mood of the vast majority of the audience."); Ibid., 516 ("The exhilaration of the ceremony was badly deflated by [Turgenev's] embarrassing denial, which seemed to indicate the continued inferiority of Russian culture, supposedly being celebrated, vis-à-vis Europe.").

10. See letter from Fyodor Dostoevsky to Mikhail Dostoevsky (January–February 1854), in *Dostoevsky's Letters*, Vol. 1, ed. and trans. David Lowe and Ronald Meyer (MI: Ardis Publishers, 1988), 186–87 (describing Omsk as a place with "coarse people, irritable and spiteful," who "greeted us nobles with hostility and . . . would have eaten us up if they had been allowed to").

11. See Letter from Dostoevsky to Nikolai Lyubimov (March–April 1872) in *Dostoevsky Complete Letters*, Vol. 4, ed. and trans. David A. Lowe (MI: Ardis Publishers, 1991), 23 (Speaking of Stavrogin, Dostoevsky writes that he is a "whole type . . . *our* type, a Russian, a person idle not out of a desire to be idle, but who has lost touch with everything native and most important, faith: a degenerate *out of ennui*, but a conscientious person who makes every convulsive, martyr-like effort to be renewed and to start believing again.").

12. In his speech, Dostoevsky unexpectedly compliments Turgenev by praising his character, Liza, from *A Nest of Gentlefolk*. Fyodor Dostoevsky, *A Writers Diary*, Vol. 2, Ibid., 1285.

13. See Dostoevsky, *The Brothers Karamazov*, trans. Richard Pevear and Larissa Volokhonsky (NY: Farrar, Straus and Giroux, 1990), 555 (Kolya admits that he hasn't actually read Belinsky, but he did read "the part about Tatiana, why she didn't go with Onegin."). Kolya is referring to Vissarion Belinsky's "Ninth Essay on Pushkin" (1844–1845). Incidentally, most in the audience likely understood Dostoevsky's inuendo.

14. See Fyodor Dostoevsky, *Crime and Punishment*, trans. Richard Pevear and Larissa Volokhonsky (NY: Vintage Books, 1993), 473 (Svidrigailov's wife, Marfa, suspects all along that he is "incapable of serious love.").

15. See Lossky, Ibid., 25 (Stating that Kireyevsky did not tell "Russians to turn their backs on Western-European civilization," but said that "the task . . . consists in . . . the Orthodox Church, transcending European civilization without supplanting it but on the contrary embracing it in their fullness" and thus giving it "the highest meaning and the final development").

16. In his speech, Dostoevsky trumpets the "general reunification of all people of all the tribes of the great Aryan race." Fyodor Dostoevsky, *A Writer's Diary*, Vol. 2, Ibid., 1294. See generally Frank, Ibid., 526 ("This was the first time he had employed the word 'Aryan,' which reveals the influence of the anti-Semitic literature of the period, and it provoked a great deal of criticism."). See also Amy D. Ronner, *Dostoevsky and the Law* (NC: Carolina Academic Press, 2015), 29 n. 98, 41–42 n. 160, 281 n. 24 (discussing Dostoevsky's anti-Semitism).

17. Letter from Fyodor Dostoevsky to Anna Dostoevskaya (June 8, 1880), in *Letters* Vol. 5, Ibid., 236. See also Frank, Ibid., 527 ("The effect of this speech on the audience was absolutely overwhelming, and the emotions it unleashed may be compared with the hysterical effusions typical of religious revival meetings.").

18. See Fyodor Dostoevsky, *A Writers Diary*, Vol. 2, Ibid., 1271 (The "negative type" is "a restless and alienated man, lacking faith in his native soil and its native strength, rejecting Russia and ultimately, himself.").

19. See Letter from Sofya Ivanova (January 13, 1868) in *Fyodor Dostoevsky's Complete Letters*, trans. David A. Lowe (MI: Ardis Publishers, 1990), Vol. 3, 17 (speaking of his effort to perfect Prince Myshkin).

20. See Fyodor Dostoevsky, *A Writer's Diary*, Vol. 1, Ibid., 307 ("The Golden Age in Your Pocket").

21. Letter from Fyodor Dostoevsky to Nikolay Lyubimov (November 16, 1879) in *Letters*, Vol. 5, Ibid., 165 (speaking of the purification of Mitya's "heart and conscience").

22. Karl Menninger, *Man Against Himself* (NY: Harcourt, Brace & World, Inc, 1966).

23. Michael A. Church and Charles I. Brooks, *Subtle Suicide: Our Silent Epidemic of Ambivalence about Living* (CA: Praeger, 2009).

24. Steve Taylor, *Durkheim and the Study of Suicide* (UK: MacMillan Press, Ltd., 1982), 152.

25. Ibid., 153. He also discusses Sylvia Plath, who "had driven off the road knowing full well that it *might* kill her," but "having survived, she was then able to write freely about the act because it was behind her." Ibid. The "car crash . . . became 'another death' that she had 'come through.' " Ibid.

26. See Irina Paperno, *Suicide as a Cultural Institution in Dostoevsky's Russia* (NY: Cornell University Press, 1997), 3 (pointing out that "[b]etween the 1860s and the 1880s, Russia was believed to have experienced an 'epidemic of suicides' ").

27. Samuel Taylor Coleridge, *Biographia Literaria*, Chapter XVIII in *English Romantic Writers*, ed. David Perkins (NY: Harcourt, Brace & World, Inc., 1967), 474.

28. Taylor, Ibid., 150.

29. Although "The Dream of a Ridiculous Man," is contained in *A Writer's Diary*, all citations are from Fyodor Dostoevsky *Notes from Underground, the Double, and Other Stories*, trans. Constance Garnett (NY: Barnes & Noble Classics, 2003). Hereinafter, I will include the chapter and page number from the Garnett translation in parenthesis in the text.

30. In *Notes from Underground*, the underground man is obsessed with avenging himself on an officer who expects him to be the one to step aside on the street and he thus plans to assert equal footing by refusing to budge. In Chernyshevsky's novel, *What Is to Be Done?*, the hero shoves a well-dressed officer into a ditch for expecting the poorly dressed Lopukhov to make way for him on the pavement.

31. John Ruskin, *Modern Painters*, Vol. III (UK: George Allen, 1906), 161–77 ("Of the Pathetic Fallacy"). According to Ruskin, it is "eminently characteristic of the modern mind," whether in literature or art, to endeavor "to express something which he, as a living creature, imagines in the lifeless object," while the classical and medieval artists "were content with expressing the unimaginary and actual qualities of the object." Ibid., 178.

32. See T. S. Eliot, "Hamlet," (1919), reprinted in *Selected Prose of T.S. Eliot*, ed. Frank Kermode (NY: Harcourt Brace Jovanovich, 1975), 48 ("The only way of expressing emotion in the form of art is by finding an 'objective correlative'; in other words, a set of objects, a situation, a chain of events which shall be the formula of that *particular* emotion; such that when the external facts, which must terminate in sensory experience, are given, the emotion is immediately evoked."). See also Ronner, Ibid., 98 (discussing the use of "objective correlatives" in Dostoevsky's "The Double").

33. Charles William Wahl, "Suicide as a Magical Act," in *Clues to Suicide*, eds. Edwin S. Shneidman and Norman L. Farberow (NY: McGraw-Hill Book Co., Inc., 1957), 28–30.

34. Lossky, Ibid., 38.

35. Taylor, Ibid., 151 (discussing A. Alvarez's suicide attempt).

36. A. Alvarez, *The Savage God: A Study of Suicide* (NY: W.W. Norton & Company, 1990), 166.

37. Ibid., 259.

38. Ibid.

39. Ibid., 277.

40. Ibid., 260.

41. Walter Pater, *Studies in the History of the Renaissance* (UK: Oxford University Press, 2010), 120. Pater points to Rousseau's sixth book of the *Confessions* in which he "describes the awakening in him of the literary sense" and explains that "[a]n undefinable taint of death had always clung about him." Ibid. Pater also references Victor Hugo's precept that "we are all under sentence of death but with a sort of indefinite reprieve." Ibid. See also Ibid., 178–79 (explanatory notes).

42. Alvarez, Ibid., 260.

43. Jacques Catteau, *Dostoevsky and the Process of Literary Creation* (UK: Cambridge University Press, 2005), 445. He lists E. M. de Vogue, Vyacheslav

Ivanov, Leonid Grossman, V. L. Komarovich, M. Bakhtin, Paul Claudel and A. A. Gozenpud. Since his book was originally published in 1978, many more names could be added to the list.

44. Pater, Ibid., 124. For solid reasons, the editor, Matthew Beaumont, chose to reproduce the text of Pater's book as it appeared in 1873, but that edition had excluded an important chapter, "The School of Giorgione." Consequently, Beaumont included it as an appendix. The citation here is to that appendix.

Selected Bibliography

Aldridge, David. *Suicide: The Tragedy of Hopelessness*. PA: Jessica Kingsley Publishers, 1998.

Alvarez, A. *The Savage God: A Study of Suicide*. NY: W.W. Norton & Co., 1990.

Apollonio, Carol. *Dostoevsky's Secrets: Reading Against the Grain.* IL: Northwestern University Press, 2009.

Apollonio, Carol, editor and translator. *The New Russian Dostoevsky: Readings for the Twenty-First Century*. OH: Slavica, 2010.

Apollonio, Carol. "The Passion of Dmitrii Karamazov." *Slavic Review* 58, no. 3 (Fall 1999): 584–99.

Arieti, Silvano. *Creativity: The Magic Synthesis*. NY: Basic Books, 1976.

Arieti, Silvano. *Interpretation of Schizophrenia*. NY: Basic Books, Inc., 1974.

Bakhtin, M. M. "Forms of Time and of the Chronotope in the Novel." In *The Dialogic Imagination: Four Essays*. Edited by Michael Holquist and translated by Caryl Emerson and Michael Holquist. TX: University of Texas Press, 1981.

Bakhtin, M.M. *Problems of Dostoevsky's Poetics*. Edited by Caryl Emerson. MN: University of Minnesota Press, 1984.

Belknap, Robert L. *The Genesis of "The Brothers Karamazov": The Aesthetics, Ideology, and Psychology of Making a Text*. IL: Northwestern University Press, 1980.

Belknap, Robert L. *Plots*. NY: Columbia University Press, 2016.

Belknap, Robert L. *The Structure of "The Brothers Karamazov*." IL: Northwestern University Press, 1989.

Berman, Anna A. *Siblings in Tolstoy and Dostoevsky: The Path to Universal Brotherhood.* IL: Northwestern University Press, 2015.

Blake, Elizabeth A. *Dostoevsky and the Catholic Underground*. IL: Northwestern University Press, 2014.

Bowers, Katherine. "Ol'ga Umetskaia and "*The Idiot*." In *A Dostoevskii Companion: Texts and Contexts*. Edited by Katherine Bowers, Connor Doak, and Kate Holland. MA: Academic Studies Press, 2018.

Breger, Louis. *Dostoevsky: The Author as Psychoanalyst.* NY: New York University Press, 1990.

Brooks, Peter. *Reading for the Plot: Design and Intention in Narrative.* MA: Harvard University Press, 1984.

Brooks, Peter. *Troubling Confessions.* IL: University of Chicago Press, 2001.

Camus, Albert. *The Myth of Sisyphus and Other Essays.* Translated by Justin O'Brien. NY: Vintage, 1983.

Catteau, Jacques, *Dostoyevsky and the Process of Literary Creation.* Translated by Audrey Littlewood. Cambridge: Cambridge University Press, 1989.

Cherkasova, Evgenia. *Dostoevsky and Kant: Dialogues on Ethics.* Amsterdam: Rodopi, 2009.

Church, Michael A. and Brooks, Charles I. *Subtle Suicide: Our Silent Epidemic of Ambivalence about Living.* CA: Praeger, 2009.

Coetzee J.M. "Confession and Double Thoughts: Tolstoy, Rousseau, Dostoevsky." In *Comparative Literature* 37, no. 3 (1985): 193–232.

Colt, George Howe. *November of the Soul: The Enigma of Suicide.* NY: Scribner, 2006.

Contino, Paul. "'Descend That You May Ascend': Augustine, Dostoevsky, and the Confessions of Ivan Karamazov." In *Augustine and Literature.* Edited by Robert P. Kennedy, Kim Puffenroth, and John Doody. NY: Lexington Books, 2006: 179–214.

Contino, Paul. "Incarnational Realism and the Case for Casuistry: Dmitry Karamazov's Escape." In *Dostoevsky's Brothers Karamazov: Art, Creativity and Spirituality.* Edited by Predrag Cicovacki and Maria Granik, Heidelberg: Universitatsverlag Winter, 2010.

Corrigan, Yuri. *Dostoevsky and the Riddle of the Self.* IL: Northwestern University Press, 2017.

Doak, Connor: "Masculine Degeneration in Dostoevskii's *Demons.*" In *Russian Writers at the Fin de Siecle: The Twilight of Realism.* Edited by Katherine Bowers and Ani Kokobobo. Cambridge: Cambridge University Press, 2015: 105–25.

Dostoevsky, Anna. *Dostoevsky: Reminiscences.* Edited and translated by Beatrice Stillman. NY: Liveright, 1975.

Dostoevsky, Fyodor. *A Writer's Diary.* Translated by Kenneth Lantz. IL: Northwestern University Press, 1994.

Dostoevsky Fyodor. *The Adolescent.* Translated by Richard Pevear and Larissa Volokhonsky. NY: Vintage Classics, 2003.

Fyodor Dostoevsky. *The Brothers Karamazov.* Translated by Richard Pevear and Larissa Volokhonsky, New York: Farrar, Straus, and Giroux, 1990.

Fyodor Dostoevsky. *Complete Letters.* Vol. 1. Translated by David Lowe and Ronald Meyer. Vol. 2–5. Translated by David Lowe. MI: Ardis Publishers, 1988–1991.

Dostoevsky, Fyodor. *Crime and Punishment.* Translated by Richard Pevear and Larissa Volokhonsky. NY: Vintage Books, 1993.

Dostoevsky, Fyodor. *Demons.* Translated by Robert A Maguire. NY: Penguin Books, 2008.

Dostoevsky, Fyodor, *The Idiot*. Translated by David McDuff. UK: Penguin Books, Ltd., 2004.

Dostoevsky, Fyodor. *The Notebooks for The Brothers Karamazov*. Edited and translated by Edward Wasiolek. IL: University of Chicago Press, 1971.

Dostoevsky, Fyodor. *The Notebooks for Crime and Punishment*. Translated by Edward Wasiolek, IL: University of Chicago Press, 1967.

Dostoevsky, Fyodor. *The Notebooks for the Idiot*. Edited by Edward Wasiolek and translated by Katharine Strelsky. NY: Dover Publications, Inc., 1967.

Dostoevsky, Fyodor. *The Notebooks for the Possessed*. Edited by Edward Wasiolek and translated by Victor Terras. IL: University of Chicago Press, 1968.

Dostoevsky, Fyodor. *Notes from the House of the Dead*. Translated by Boris Jakim. MI: William B. Eerdmans Publishing Co., 2013.

Dostoevsky, Fyodor. *Notes from Underground, the Double and Other Stories*. Translated by Constance Garnett. NY: Barnes & Noble Classics, 2003.

Dostoevsky, Fyodor. *Poor Folk and Other Stories*. Translated by David McDuff. NY: Penguin Books, 1988.

Durkheim, Emile. *The Division of Labor in Society*. Translated by W.D. Halls. NY: Free Press, 2014.

Durkheim, Emile. *The Rules of Sociological Method*. Translated by W.D. Halls and edited by Steven Lukes. NY: Free Press, 2013.

Durkheim, Emile. *Suicide: A Study in Sociology*. Translated by John A. Spaulding and George Simpson. NY: The Free Press, 1951.

Eliot, T.S. "Hamlet." In *Selected Prose of T.S. Eliot*. Edited by Frank Kermode. NY: Harcourt Brace Jovanovich, 1975.

Emerson, Caryl. *The First Hundred Years of Mikhail Bakhtin*. NJ.: Princeton University Press, 1997.

Fedotov, George P. *The Russian Religious Mind: Kievan Christianity, the Tenth to the Thirteenth Centuries*. NY: Harper & Brothers, 1960.

Fenichel, Otto. *The Psychoanalytic Theory of Neurosis*. NY: W.W. Norton & Co., 1945.

Ferracuti, Franco. "Suicide in a Catholic Country." In *Clues to Suicide*. Edited by Edwin S. Shneidman and Norman L. Farberow. NY: McGraw-Hill, 1957.

Feuer, Kathryn. "Stiva." In *Russian Literature and American Critics*. Edited by Kenneth N. Brostrom. MI: University of Michigan Press, 1984: 347–56.

Frank, Joseph. *Dostoevsky: The Mantle of the Prophet, 1871-1881*. NJ: Princeton University Press, 2002.

Frank, Joseph. *Dostoevsky: The Miraculous Years, 1865-1871*. NJ: Princeton University Press, 1995.

Frank, Joseph. *The Seeds of Revolt, 1821-1849*. NJ: Princeton University Press, 1979.

Frank, Joseph. *The Stir of Liberation, 1860-1865*. NJ: Princeton University Press, 1986.

Frank, Semyon L. *The Spiritual Foundations of Society*. Translated by Boris Jakim, OH: Ohio University Press, 1987.

Freud, Sigmund. *Beyond the Pleasure Principle*, CT: Martino Publishing, 2009.

Freud, Sigmund. *Civilization and Its Discontents.* Edited and translated by James Strachey. NY: Norton, 1961.

Freud, Sigmund, "Mourning and Melancholia." In *A General Selection from the Works of Sigmund Freud.* Edited by John Rickman. NY: Anchor books, 1989.

Freud, Sigmund. *The Psychopathology of Everyday Life*. Translated by A Brill. SC: Columbia, 1901.

Freud, Sigmund. *Totem and Taboo*. Translated and edited by James Strachey. NY: W.W. Norton & Co., 1989.

Fusso, Susanne, *Discovering Sexuality in Dostoevsky.* IL: Northwestern University Press, 2006.

Fusso, Susanne, *Editing Turgenev, Dostoevsky, and Tolstoy: Mikhail Katkov and the Great Russian Novel.* IL: Northern University Press, 2017.

Golstein, Vladimir. "Accidental Families and Surrogate Fathers: Richard Grigory and Smerdyakov." In *The Brothers Karamazov.* Translated by Susan McReynolds Oddo and edited by Fyodor Dostoevsky. NY: W.W. Norton & Co., Inc., 2011.

Harriford, Diane and Thompson, Becky. *When the Center Is on Fire: Passionate Theory for Our Times.* TX: University of Texas Press, 2008.

Holland, Kate. "The Legend of the Ladonka and the Trial of the Novel." In *A New Word on "The Brothers Karamazov."* Edited by Robert L. Jackson. IL: Northwestern University Press, 2004: 192–99.

Holland, Kate. *The Novel in the Age of Disintegration: Dostoevsky and the Problem of Genre in the 1870s.* IL: Northwestern University Press, 2013.

Holquist, Michael. *Dostoevsky and the Novel.* NJ: Princeton University Press, 1977.

Ivanits, Linda. *Dostoevsky and the Russian People*. Cambridge: Cambridge University Press, 2008.

Jackson, Robert Louis. *The Art of Dostoevsky: Deliriums and Nocturnes.* NJ: Princeton University Press, 1981.

Jackson, Robert Louis. *Dostoevsky's Quest for Form: A Study of His Philosophy of Art.* CT: Yale University Press, 1966.

Jamison, Kay Redfield. *Night Falls Fast: Understanding Suicide*. NY: Vintage Books, 1999.

Jensen, Viggo W. and Petty, Thomas A. "The Fantasy of Being Rescued in Suicide." In *Essential Papers on Suicide.* Edited by John T. Maltsberger, M.D, and Mark J. Goldblatt, M.D. NY: New York University Press, 1996.

Jones, Malcolm V.: *Dostoyevsky: The Novel of Discord.* NY: Barnes and Noble Books, 1976.

Kantor, V.K. "Pavel Smerdyakov and Ivan Karamazov: The Problem of Temptation." In *Dostoevsky and the Christian Tradition.* Edited by George Pattison and Diane Oenning Thompson. Cambridge: Cambridge University Press, 2001.

Kilpatrick, Elizabeth. "A Psychoanalytic Understanding of Suicide." In *American Journal of Psychoanalysis* 8, no. 1 (1948): 13–23.

Kitzinger, Chloe. "Illusion and Instrument: Problems of Mimetic Characterization in Dostoevsky and Tolstoy." PhD. Dissertation. University of California, Berkeley, 2016. ProQuest (10150919).

Kjetsaa, Gier. *Fyodor Dostoevsky: A Writers Life*. Translated by Siri Hustvedt and David McDuff. NY: Ballantine Books, 1989.
Knapp, Liza. *The Annihilation of Inertia: Dostoevsky and Metaphysics.* IL: Northwestern University Press, 1996.
Knapp, Liza. *Anna Karenina and Others: Tolstoy's Labyrinth of Plots*. WI: University of Wisconsin Press, 2016.
Kokobobo, Ani. *Russian Grotesque Realism: The Great Reforms and the Gentry Decline*. OH: Ohio State University Press, 2018.
Kushner, Howard. *Self-Destruction in the Promised Land: A Psychocultural Biology of American Suicide*. NJ: Rutgers University Press, 1989.
Lacan, Jacques. *The Four Fundamental Concepts of Psychoanalysis*. Translated by Alan Sherman. NY: W.W. Norton & Co., 1998.
Litman, Robert E. "Sigmund Freud on Suicide." In *Essays in Self-Destruction.* Edited by Edwin S. Shneidman. NY: Jason Aronson, Inc., 1967.
Lukes, Steven. *Emile Durkheim, His Life and Work: A Historical and Critical Study.* CA: Stanford University Press, 1973.
Maltsberger, John T. "Suicide Danger: Clinical Estimation and Decision." In *Essential Papers on Suicide*. Edited by John T. Maltsberger, M.D, and Mark J. Goldblatt, M.D. NY: New York University Press, 1996.
Maltsberger, John T. and Buie, J., Dan H. "The Devices of Suicide: Revenge, Riddance, and Rebirth." In *Essential Papers on Suicide*. Edited by John T. Maltsberger, M.D., and Mark J. Goldblatt, M.D. NY: New York University Press, 1996.
Marcus, Eric. *Why Suicide?* NY: Harper One, 2010.
Martinsen, Deborah A. "The Devil Incarnate." In *Dostoevsky's Brothers Karamazov: Art, Creativity and Spirituality.* Edited by Predrag Cicovacki and Maria Granik. Heidelberg: Universitatsverlag Winter, 2010.
Martinsen, Deborah A. "Ingratitude and the Underground." In *Dostoevsky Studies* 17 (2013): 7–21.
Martinsen, Deborah. "Introduction." In *Notes from Underground, The Double and Other Stories.* Translated by Constance Garnett. NY: Barnes & Noble Classics, 2003.
Martinsen, Deborah A. "Shame's Rhetoric, or Ivan's Devil, Karamazov Soul." In *A New Word on "The Brothers Karamazov*." Edited by Robert L. Jackson. IL: Northwestern University Press, 2004.
Martinsen, Deborah A. *Surprised by Shame: Dostoevsky's Liars and Narrative Exposure*. OH: Ohio State University Press, 2003.
Matzner-Gore, Greta. *Dostoevsky and the Ethics of Narrative Form: Suspense, Closure, Minor Characters*. IL: Northwestern University Press, 2020.
McReynolds, Louise. *Murder Most Russian: True Crime and Punishment in Late Imperial Russia*. NY: Cornell University Press, 2013.
McReynolds, Susan. *Redemption and the Merchant God: Dostoevsky's Economy of Salvation and Antisemitism*. IL: Northwestern University Press, 2018.
Meerson, Olga. *Dostoevsky's Taboos*. Dresden: Dresden University Press, 1998.
Menninger, Karl A. *Man against Himself*. NY: Harcourt Brace & World, Inc., 1966.

Miller, Robin Feuer. *"The Brothers Karamazov": Worlds of the Novel.* CT: Yale University Press, 2008.

Miller, Robin Feuer. "Dostoevsky and Rousseau: The Morality of Confession Reconsidered." In *Dostoevsky: New Perspectives.* Edited by Robert L. Jackson. NJ: Prentice-Hall, 1984: 82–98.

Miller, Robin Feuer. *Dostoevsky and "The Idiot": Author, Narrator, and Reader.* MA: Harvard University Press, 1981.

Miller, Robin Feuer. *Dostoevsky's Unfinished Journey.* CT: Yale University Press, 2007.

Mochulsky, Konstantin. *Dostoevsky: His Life and Work.* Translated by Michael A. Minihan. NJ: Princeton University Press, 1967.

Morris, Marcia A. "Expedient Sanctity: The Making of a Russian Passion-Sufferer." In *Sanctity as a Story: Narrative (In) Variants of the Saint in Literature and Culture across the Centuries.* Edited by Halszka Lelen. Berlin: Peter Lang, 2020.

Morris, Marcia A. *The Literature of Roguery in Seventeenth-and Eighteenth-Century Russia.* IL: Northwestern University Press, 2000.

Morris, Marcia A. *Russian Tales of Demonic Possession: Translations of Savva Grudtsyn and Solomonia.* MD: Lexington Books, 2014.

Morris, Marcia A. *Saints and Revolutionaries: The Ascetic Hero in Russian Literature*, NY: State University of New York Press, 1993.

Morris, Marcia A. *Writing the Time of Troubles: False Dmitry in Russian Literature.* MA: Academic Studies Press, 2018.

Morrissey, Susan K. *Suicide and the Body Politic in Imperial Russia.* Cambridge: Cambridge University Press, 2006.

Morson, Gary Saul. *The Boundaries of Genre: Dostoevsky's "Diary of a Writer" and the Traditions of Literary Utopia.* TX: University of Texas Press, 1981.

Morson, Gary Saul. *Narrative and Freedom: The Shadows of Time.* CT: Yale University Press, 1994.

Morson, Gary Saul. "Verbal Pollution in '*The Brothers Karamazov*.'" In *Critical Essays on Dostoevsky*. Edited by Robin Feuer Miller. MA: Hall, 1986.

Murav, Harriet. *Holy Foolishness: Dostoevsky's Novels and the Poetic of Cultural Critique.* CA: Stanford University Press, 1992.

Murav, Harriet. *Russia's Legal Fictions.* MI: University of Michigan Press, 2001.

Naiman, Eric. "Gospel Rape." In *Dostoevsky Studies* 22 (2018): 11–40.

Naiman, Eric. "Kalganov." In *Slavic and East European Journal* 58, no. 3 (Fall 2014): 394–418.

Nielsen, Donald A. "Dostoevsky in the Mirror of Durkheim." In *Durkheim: The Durkheimians and the Arts.* Edited by Alexander Riley, W.S.F. Pickering, and William Watts Miller. NY: Berghahn Books, 2013.

Offord, Derek. "Nihilism and Terrorism." In *Dostoevsky in Context.* Edited by Deborah A. Martinsen and Olga Maiorova. Cambridge: Cambridge University Press, 2015.

Orwin, Donna Tussing. *Consequences of Consciousness: Turgenev, Dostoevsky, and Tolstoy.* CA: Stanford University Press, 2007.

Paperno, Irina. *Suicide as a Cultural Institution in Dostoevsky's Russia.* NY: Cornell University Press, 1997.

Pater, Walter. *Studies in the History of the Renaissance*. UK: Oxford University Press, 2010.

Peace, Richard. *Dostoevsky: An Examination of the Major Novels*. Cambridge: Cambridge University Press, 1971.

Perlina, Nina. *Varieties of Poetic Utterance: Quotation in "The Brothers Karamazov."* MD: University Press of America, 1985.

Pevear, Richard. "Foreword." In Fyodor Dostoevsky, *Demons*. Translated by Richard Pevear and Larissa Volokhonsky. NY: Vintage, 1994: vii–xxiii.

Phillips, David. "The Influence of Suggestion on Suicide: Substantive and Theoretical Implications of the Werther Effect." In *Essential Papers on Suicide*. Edited by John T. Maltsberger, M.D., and Mark J. Goldblatt, M.D. NY: New York University Press, 1996.

Plato. *The Last Days of Socrates*. Translated by Hugh Tredennick and Harold Tarrant. NY: Penguin Books, 2003.

Quinnett, Paul. *Suicide: The Forever Decision*. NY: Crossroad Publishing Co., 2016.

Ray, Isaac, *A Treatise on the Medical Jurisprudence of Insanity*. Edited by Winfred Overholster. MA: The Belknap Press of Harvard University Press, 1962.

Reyfman, Irina. *Ritualized Violence Russian Style: The Duel in Russian Culture and Literature*. CA: Stanford University Press, 1999.

Rice, James. *Dostoevsky and the Healing Art: An Essay in Literary and Medical History*. MI: Ardis Publishers, 1985.

Ronner, Amy D. *Dostoevsky and the Law*. NC: Carolina Academic Press, 2015.

Ronner, Amy D. "Is Stavrogin Leading Us by the Nose? The Nihilistic Confession." In *Dostoevsky Studies* 20 (2016): 71–101.

Ronner Amy D. *Law, Literature, and Therapeutic Jurisprudence*. NC: Carolina Academic Press, 2010.

Rosenshield, Gary. *Western Law, Russian Justice: Dostoevsky, the Jury Trial, and the Law*. WI: University of Wisconsin Press, 2005.

Rousseau, Jean-Jacques. *Confessions*. Translated by Angela Scholar. UK: Oxford University Press, 2000.

Ruskin, John. *Modern Painters*. UK: George Allen, 1906.

Ruttenberg, Nancy. *Dostoevsky's Democracy*. NJ: Princeton University Press, 2008.

Sabbath, Joseph C. "The Suicidal Adolescent - - The Expendable Child." In *Essential Papers on Suicide*. Edited by John T. Maltsberger, M.D., and Mark J. Goldblatt, M.D. NY: New York University Press, 1996.

Scanlan, James P. *Dostoevsky the Thinker*. NY: Cornell University Press, 2002.

Schopenhauer, Arthur. "On Suicide." In *Suffering, Suicide, and Immortality*. Translated by T. Bailey Saunders. NY: Dover Publications, Inc., 2006.

Schur, Anna. *Wages of Evil: Dostoevsky and Punishment*. IL: Northwestern University Press, 2012.

Shneidman, Edwin S. "Orientations Toward Death." In *The Psychology of Suicide: A Clinician's Guide to Evaluation and Treatment*. Edited by Edwin S. Shneidman, Norman L. Farberow, and Robert E. Litman. NJ: Jason Aronson Inc., 1994.

Shneidman, Edwin S. *The Suicidal Mind*. NY: Oxford University Press, 1996.

Solomon, Andrew. *The Noonday Demon: An Atlas of Depression.* NY: Scribner, 2015.

Spektor, Sasha. "From Violence to Silence: Vicissitudes of Reading in "*The Idiot.*" In *Slavic Review* 72, no. 3 (Fall 2013): 552–72.

Stengel, Erwin. *Suicide and attempted Suicide.* NY: Jason Aronson, Inc., 1974.

Stone, I.F. *The Trial of Socrates.* NY: Anchor Books, 1989.

Straus, Nina Pelikan. "Every Woman Loves a Nihilist: Stavrogin and Women in Dostoevsky's "*The Possessed.*" In *Novel* (Spring 1994): 271–86.

Styron, William. *Darkness Visible: A Memoir of Madness.* NY: Vintage Books, 1992.

Taylor, Steve. *Durkheim and the Study of Suicide.* UK: The MacMillan Press, Ltd., 1982.

Terras, Victor. *A Karamazov Companion: Commentary on the Genesis, Language, and Style of Dostoevsky's Novel.* WI: University of Wisconsin Press, 1981.

Terras, Victor. *Reading Dostoevsky.* WI: University of Wisconsin Press, 1981.

Thompson, Diane Oenning. "'*The Brothers Karamazov'" and the Poetics of Memory.*" Cambridge: Cambridge University Press, 1991.

Todd, William Mills, III. "Introduction." In *The Idiot.* Translated by David McDuff and edited by Fyodor Dostoevsky. UK: Penguin Books, Ltd., 2004.

Todd, William Mills, III. "To Be Continued: Dostoevsky's Evolving Poetics of Serialized Publication." In *Dostoevsky Studies* 18 (2014): 23–33.

Wahl, Charles William, "Suicide as a Magical Act." In *Clues to Suicide.* Edited by Edwin S. Shneidman and Norman L. Farberow. NY: McGraw-Hill, 1957.

Wasiolek, Edward. *Dostoevsky: The Major Fiction.* MA: MIT Press, 1964.

Young, Sarah. *Dostoevsky's "The Idiot" and the Ethical Foundations of Narrative: Reading, Narrating, Scripting*. UK: Anthem, 2004.

Author Index

Subject Index

About the Author

Amy D. Ronner, PhD, JD, professor of law (emeritus), lives in Miami, Florida, and Aspen, Colorado. In addition to her law degree from the University of Miami School of Law, she has a PhD and an MA in English Language and Literature from the University of Michigan. Her BA degree is from Beloit College, where she majored in English Composition and Creative Writing. Before becoming a lawyer and law professor, Dr. Ronner enjoyed her first career as a teaching fellow and lecturer in the literature departments at the University of Michigan and University of Miami, where she taught Creative Writing and Literature. She is the author of five books covering topics like law, literature, therapeutic jurisprudence, appellate practice, LGBT rights, and civil rights. Her previous book *Dostoevsky and the Law* (2015) is a multidisciplinary exploration of Dostoevsky's transcendent insights into contemporary legal doctrines, offenders, crimes, investigations, and trials. In addition to publishing many articles dealing with Russian and world literature, human rights, psychology, therapeutic jurisprudence, and constitutional law, Ronner has been a keynote speaker, presenter, and discussant at various conferences all over the world.

www.ingramcontent.com/pod-product-compliance
Ingram Content Group UK Ltd.
Pitfield, Milton Keynes, MK11 3LW, UK
UKHW041841031026
15587UKWH00002B/924

9 781793 607812